A PEAK HISTORY HANDBOOK

by

Denys Hill

Denys Hill has an honours degree in history from London University and a doctorate from the University of Warwick. His early education was in Clowne and Staveley, places not in the scenic Peak District.

MOORLEYS Print & Publishing

First published in Great Britain 2010

Copyright © 2010 Denys Hill Ltd

914.25'11'04857   DA670 D43

British Library Cataloguing in Publication Data
All rights reserved. No part of this publication may be
reproduced, stored in a retrieval system, or
transmitted, in any form or by any means,
electronic, mechanical, photocopying, recording
or otherwise, without the prior
written permission of the Publishers.

British Library Cataloguing in Publication Data.
A catalogue record for this book is available
from the British Library.

ISBN 978 0 86071 648 8

Printed in Great Britain by the MPG Books Group,
Bodmin and King's Lynn

A Commissioned Publication of

MOORLEYS
Print & Publishing

23 Park Road, Ilkeston, Derbyshire DE7 5DA
Tel/Fax: 0115 932 0643 email: info@moorleys.co.uk
www.moorleys.co.uk

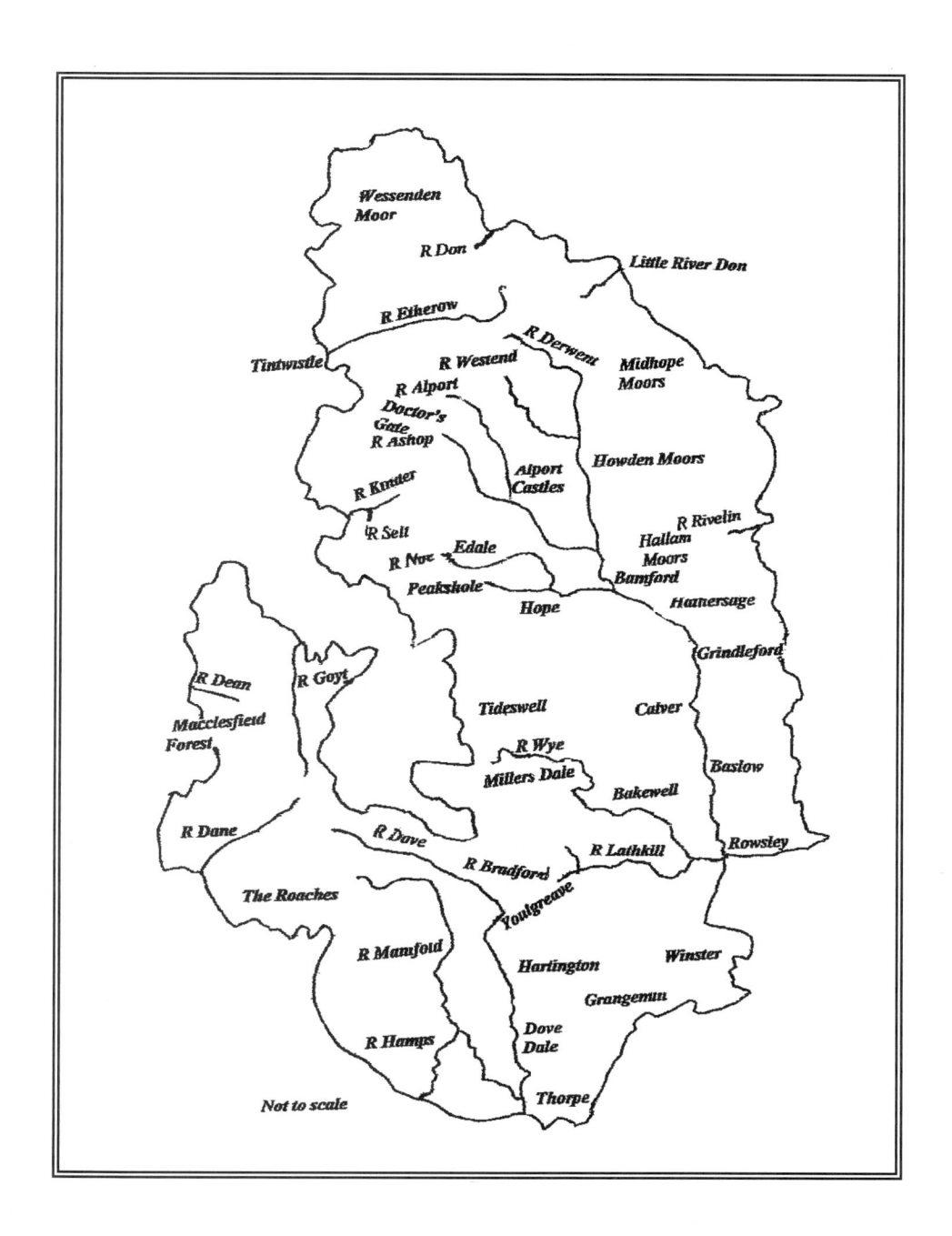

*In memory of S. K. Gregory, an outstanding teacher of
history at Staveley-Netherthorpe Grammar School*

Peak Rivers Map

Contents

	page
Preface	7
Acknowledgments	7
Key	8
Abbreviations	8
Peak Peoples	9
Peak Places	35
Church and Chapel	57
Working and Earning	68
Wars and Battles	93
The Natural World	96
Incomers	102
Home and Family Life	110
Glossary of Peak Terms	123
Additional Information	153

Charts and Diagrams

		page
1.	People Profiles	9
2.	Individual Identity Factors	9
3.	Overseas Connections	33
4.	Languages and Peak Place Names	56
5.	Church History Web	57
6.	Granges	62
7a.	Church Graphics	63
7b.	Church Architecture Styles	64
8.	Economic History Web	67
9.	Ubiquitous Farming	77
10.	Animal Raw Material Products	78
11a.	Metal Ore Extraction Sites	79
11b.	Economic Aspects	79
12.	Rock Extraction Sites	80
13.	Water and Wind Mills	81
14.	Railways	83
15.	Transport Route Planning	84
16.	Saltways	86
17.	Live Cattle Supply Chain	88
18.	Cattle Carcasses Supply Chain	89
19a.	Military History Web	92
19b.	Battles	92
20.	The Natural World Web	96
21.	Incomer Network	102
22.	Bronze Age Sites	106

23. Roman Occupation	107
24. Saxon Settlement	108
25. Domesday Survey	109
26. Social History Web	110
27. Tumuli on named Lows	119
28. Fire and Light	120
29. Spread of Manors	121
30. Schools and Colleges	122

Drawings

Peak Rivers Map	3
Tideswell Church and Its Surroundings	6
Creative Contributors	32
Eyre Family Halls	33
Robert Pursglove	34
Stanton Moor Shooting Lodge	56
Religious Order Landowners	63
Contrasting Places of Worship	64
Stone Crosses	65
Baptismal Fonts	66
Place Name Influences	67
Useful Trees	76
Water Mill	78
Large Bay Window Halls with Small Panes	80
Three Storey Halls	82
Two Storey Halls	83
Manor Houses	85
Imposing Frontage Halls	87
Symmetrical Gabled Bays	89
Sough Mine Drainage	90
Ore Deposit Positions	90
Fighting Men with Their Armour	94
Peak Men in Conflicts Map	95
Stone Sepulchral Slabs	95
Wildlife	101
Foods	105
Economic, Military and Religious Incomers Map	106
Viking Ship	108
One Gable End Bay Halls	121
Derwent Valley Residences	152

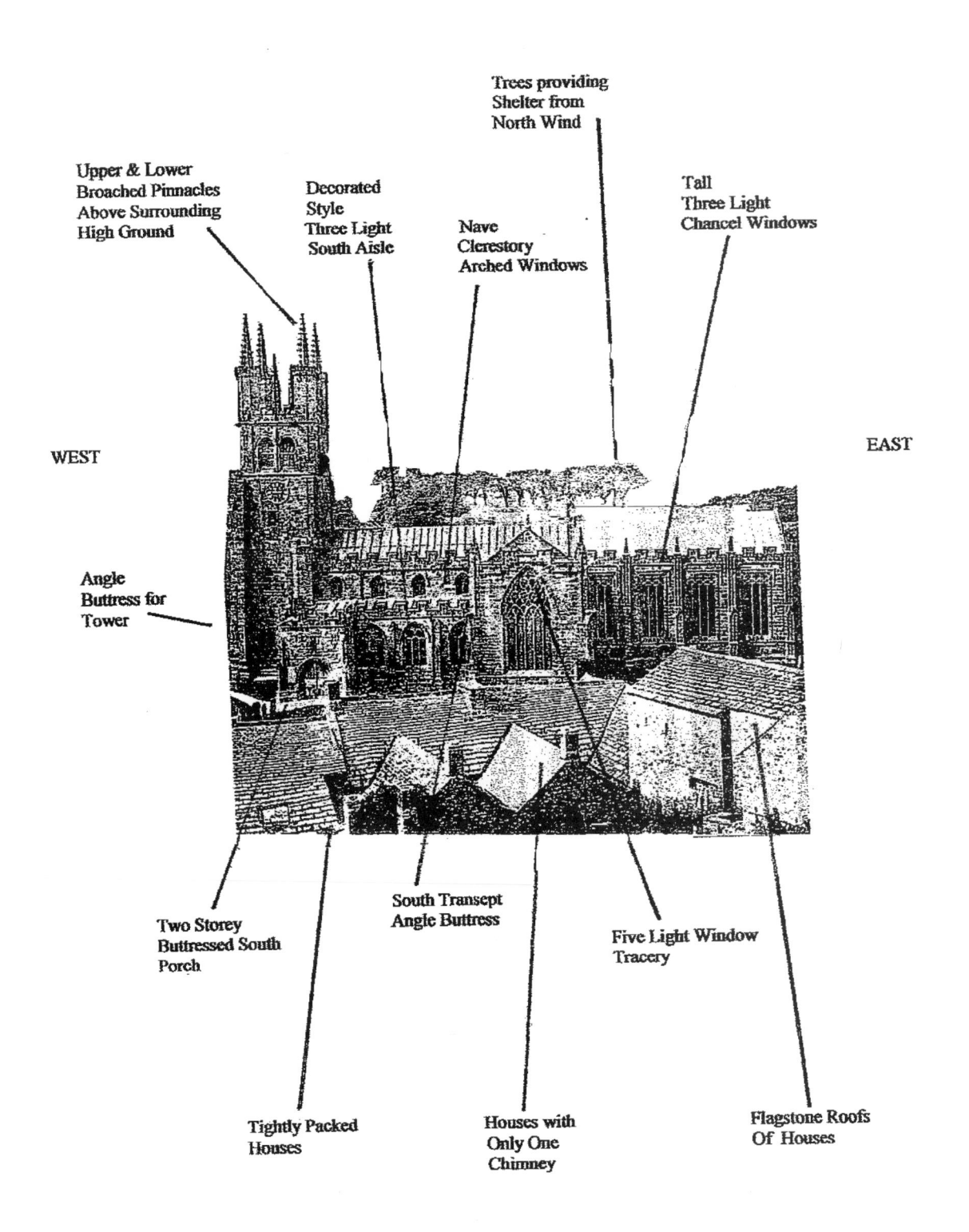

Tideswell Church and Its Surroundings

PREFACE

This handbook fits together the people, and places, in the intricate, historical fabric of the Peak National Park areas of Cheshire, Derbyshire, Staffordshire and Yorkshire. People living and working in these areas not only had local links, with other people and places in the Peak, but also elsewhere in the British Isles and Europe. The contemporary natural environment affected their lives; they were part of church, economic, military, settlement and social history from early times.

Stone Ages	Ancient History	Dark Ages	Medieval History	Modern History
Palaeolithic Mesolithic Neolithic	Celts Bronze Age Iron Age Romans	Saxons Danes	Normans Plantagenets	Church, economic, military, political, settlement and social developments.

Many current site, place, street and personal names, which originated in the past, remind residents, visitors and students of the Peak's long, intricate, interesting history.

Information Presentation
Avoiding the time-consuming chore of poring over maps and reference books, to find places in this wide rural area, is necessary whatever one's interests. For that reason Ordnance Survey four figure grid references, together with, latitude and longitude references, for linked places overseas, are routinely shown in *italics*. Grid references also help distinguish places with identical names, in different locations, such as Hurdlow *0260* and *1166*. Names of people are in *italics*. Dates are in [...]. Single inverted commas '...' indicate cross references to other entries. A combination of alphabetic arrangement, underlining, **bold** and *italic* type highlight key words and network links. Diagrams illustrate clusters, scatter and relationships. A glossary of terms, with many Peak examples, underpins the themes and topics. Additional information, at the end of the book, lists museums, books and journal articles, including some early ones, as well as those in wider historical contexts.

Dialect, common and scientific names are given wherever possible in the interests of accuracy and cross-curricular study. Unfortunately precise dates, and meanings, are not available for all categories. Dates of monarch's reigns, centuries and estimates are used for approximation when precise dates are unavailable. Extracts from the entry for Elton illustrate the presentation.

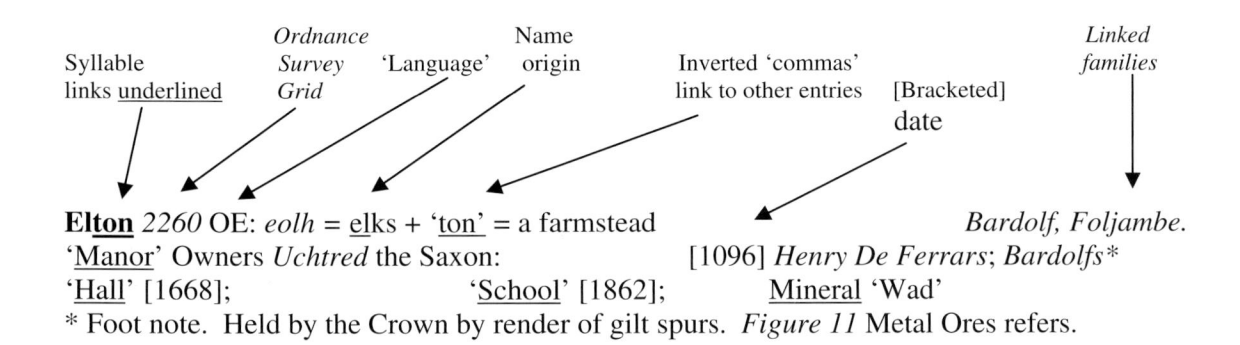

Syllable links underlined / *Ordnance Survey* Grid / Name 'Language' origin / Inverted 'commas' link to other entries / [Bracketed] date / *Linked families*

Elton *2260* OE: *eolh* = elks + 'ton' = a farmstead   *Bardolf, Foljambe.*
'Manor' Owners *Uchtred* the Saxon: [1096] *Henry De Ferrars*; *Bardolfs**
'Hall' [1668];   'School' [1862];   Mineral 'Wad'
* Foot note. Held by the Crown by render of gilt spurs. *Figure 11* Metal Ores refers.

Acknowledgements
Invaluable assistance received from staff at record offices, and libraries, in Chester, Matlock, Sheffield and Stafford, and at Oxford University Press, together with that of Betty Cocking, Chris Eddy, Shirley Ellins, Geoffrey Farthing, Jennifer Fox, John Moorley, Alan Rose, Barbara Smith, Trevor Staniforth and A J Williams is much appreciated.

David & Charles, publishers of English Field Names [1972] by J Field and The Industrial Archaeology of Derbyshire [1969] by F Nixon. The English Place Names Society, publishers of Place Names of

Derbyshire [1959] by K Cameron, and Routledge, publishers of A Dictionary of English Surnames by P H Reaney & R M Wilson and M C Rintoul, A Dictionary of People and Places in Fiction, kindly allowed me to quote from these books. HarperCollins, publishers of Collins English Dictionary 5th edition [2000] granted permission to use relevant entries.

Key: Normal type for Places and Sites, *italics* for names of people, Ordnance Survey grid and latitude and longitude references, Single inverted commas '…..' refer to links with other parts of the handbook. Square brackets [ ] enclose dates.

Abbreviations

Domesday Book	DB	Italian	It
Breton	Obr	Latin, Classical	CL
Celtic Welsh	CW	Latin, Medieval	ML
Cornish	Co	Norse, Old	ON
Dutch, Middle	MD	Saxon	S
English, Middle	ME	Scandinavian, Old	OS
English, Old	OE	Danish, Old	OD
French, Anglo Norman	ANF	Norwegian, Old	Ono
French, Old	OF	Swedish, Old	Osw
German, Middle High	MHG	Scottish	Sc
German, Middle Low	MLG	Welsh	W
German, Old High	OHG	Township in a lead field	Pb
German, Old Low	OLG		

Peak Peoples

Figure 1	People Profiles
Occupations	Resources
PRIMARY	
Farmers	Fauna
Foresters	
Miners	Flora
Quarry workers	
SECONDARY	Fuel
Builders & constructors	
Manufacturers	Land
Processors	
TERTIARY	Minerals
Administrators and	
lawyers	Rocks
Clergy and pastors	
Inventors and Investors	Water
Medical practitioners	
Nobility and Gentry	Wind
Servants	
Soldiers	Wood
Teachers	
Traders	

Activities	Languages	Religions
Building	European	Anglican
Constructing	-Northern	
Consuming	-Southern	Celtic
Educating	-Western	
Extracting		Non-
Fighting	Peak	conformist
Manufacturing	Dialects	
Relaxing		
Trading	British	Roman
Travelling	Regional	Catholic
Worshipping	dialects	

Figure 1, People Profiles, and *Figure 2*, Individual Identity Elements, show a multiplicity of factors relevant to Peak people's profiles. *Figures 3, 5, 19, 21 & 26* complement these.

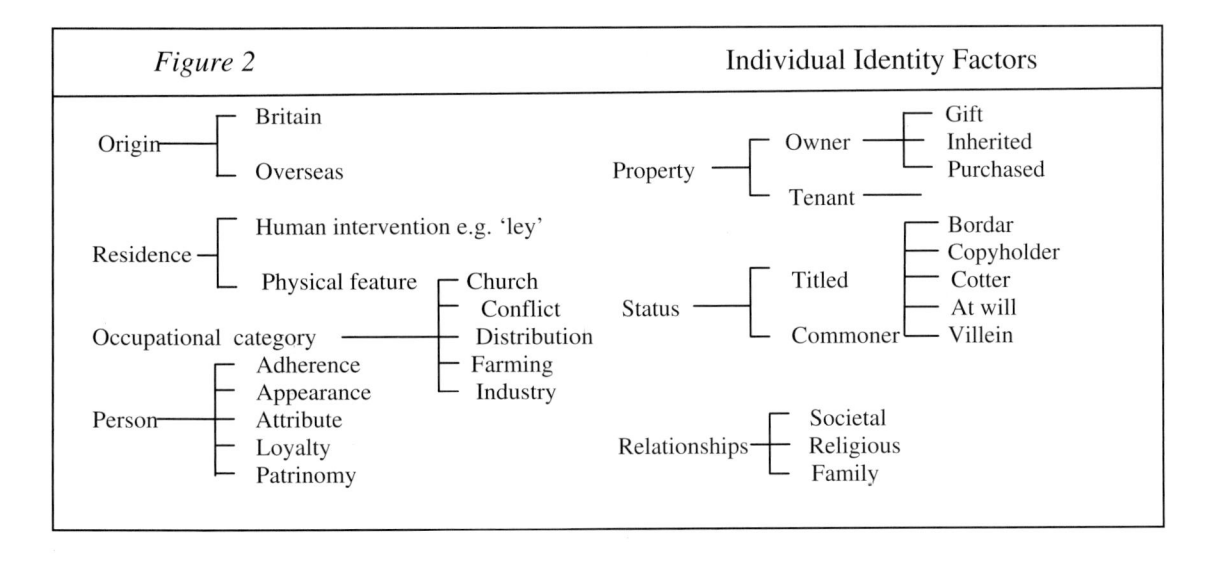

Figure 2 — Individual Identity Factors

- Origin
  - Britain
  - Overseas
- Residence
  - Human intervention e.g. 'ley'
  - Physical feature
- Occupational category
  - Church
  - Conflict
  - Distribution
  - Farming
  - Industry
- Person
  - Adherence
  - Appearance
  - Attribute
  - Loyalty
  - Patrinomy
- Property
  - Owner
    - Gift
    - Inherited
    - Purchased
  - Tenant
- Status
  - Titled
  - Commoner
    - Bordar
    - Copyholder
    - Cotter
    - At will
    - Villein
- Relationships
  - Societal
  - Religious
  - Family

Abney: *A residence name: Abney 1979.* 'Sheriffs' of Derbyshire: *James* [1656], *Charles* [1825].

Adderley: *A personal + residence name combination: Ealdred's + 'ley'* = a clearing. 'Moiety manor': ½ Snitterton *2760 Charles* about [1670] by heiress *Felicia Milward.* Sold to *Henry Ferne.* 'Knight': Of Derbyshire returned to Parliament *William* [1383], [1385] and [1390].

Agard: *A residence name:* OD: *alger* = a river + *gard* = an enclosure. 'Manor': Chatsworth *1670* purchased [1550]. 'Sheriffs': Of Derbyshire: *Henry* [1625], *John* [1639], *Charles* [1661].

Allen/Alen: *An origin name: a* Celtic *personal name or A residence name: old land i.e. grassland that has recently been cultivated.* 'Moiety': *John* died [1574] Stanton Ley and Hall *2564.* Marriage: *Constance* from Wheston *1376* to *George Meverell* [1509-47]. Arable farmer: *George* about [1588]. Last of line: *John* died [1700]. Estates descended to his infant nephew *John Bo(w)den* (aged 4 years) but were filched by the *Freemans.*

Allyn: *An allegiance name:* OBr: *Alain* = a popular saint. Marriage: *Elizabeth* to *Henry Balguy* on the death of his first wife [17th century].

Alsop: *A residence name:* Alsop en le Dale *1655 Gamel de Halesoppe* [1175], 'Baron' Hindlip of Hindlip and Alsopp [1886]. 'Manor': Litton *1675 John,* purchased from the *Lytton* family [1597].

Archer: *An occupation name: Bowman.* OF: *archier.* ME: *archere.* 'Manors': Abney* *1979* [1307-27]; Highlow* *2180* [1307-27]; Little Hucklow* *1678* [1272-1307]; *William,* senior *Eyre* of Holme *2169* and Highlow *2180,* changed his name to *Archer* about [1700]. When *Joan Archer (nee Eyre)* died, Holme Hall *2169* and Highlow Manor *2188* were sold by order of Chancery to *Robert Birch* and the *Duke of Devonshire* respectively, * after *Peverell* forfeited these manors.

Ardglass: Earl See *Cromwell.*

Arkwright: *An occupation name:* ME: *maker of chests. Sir Richard* [1732-92] inventor of the spinning frame for cotton thread [1779]. 'Moiety manor': ½ Snitterton *2760* purchased from the *Thackers*; Wensley *2261.* Both in the [18th century]. Buildings: Lumford Cottages and Mill, Bakewell *2168,* Cressbrook Mill *1772* about [1785]. 'Investor'.

Armiger: or Lameley *An occupation name: Armour bearer.* Latin: *armae* = arms + *gerere* = to bear. 'Manor': Tideswell *1575 Thomas* given by *King John* [1199-1216].

Armine: *An allegiance name: Ermin,* an ancient Germanic god. 'Manor': Brushfield *1672 Sir William* purchased [1628].

Arundel and Surrey: 'Earl' *Roger de Montgomery* [1067]. Related to *Fitz-Alan,* Duke of Norfolk, *John Fitz-Alan* [1433]. 'Moiety manor': ⅓rd Monyash *1566* by co-heiress [1616].

Ashton: *A residence name:* OE: *aesc* = ash + *'ton'* = a farmstead *or an origin name:* Ashton *5069,* Cheshire. 'Manor': Padley *2579* uncertain date of purchase. Hall: *Robert* of Stoney Middleton *2375* purchased Ford *0882* from the *Cresswell* heiress [1648]. Possibly sold to *William Bagshawe* of Litton *1675* and Hucklow *1678* also about [1648]. 'Sheriff': Of Derbyshire: *Robert* [1664-65].

Avenell: *An OG common name: Avo.* 'Manors': Possibly Baslow 2572 [12th century]; Bubnell *2472 William* [1086]; Nether Haddon *2266* [1154-89] by 'knight' service; One Ash *1665* [1154-89]; Over Haddon *2066* [12th century]. Marriages: *Avicia* daughter of *William* to *William de Vernon* [1195]; her dowry comprised part of Haddon Manor *2266.* Gifts: By *Sir William* [1189-99] One Ash *1665* to Roche Abbey ('Cistercian') *5498,* Conkesbury *2065* to Leicester Abbey ('Augustinian'), possibly Ashopton *1986* to Dunstable Priory ('Augustinian') *0221.*

Bache: *A residence name: Near a stream.* OE: *baece* = a stream. 'Manor': Stanton *2563* by purchase [16th century]. On the death of *William* it was transferred to his heiress, and her husband, *John Thornhill* [1698]. Hall: Stanton *2563* rebuilt [1779].

Badaly: *Margery* of Alstonefield *1355* died [1731] aged **107.**

Bagshawe: *A residence name: 2168* OE: *bacgq* = a badger + *scaega* = a copse or thicket. Before [1066] they lived near Ford *0653.* Branches of the family descended from *Edward I* [1239-1307], *Edward III* [1312-77], *John of Gaunt* [1340-99] Scottish kings – *James I* [1394-1437], *James II* [1430-60], *James IV* [1473-1513]; *Thomas,* lawyer resident of Bakewell Hall [1686].

'Sheriffs': Of Derbyshire: *John* [1696]* of Hucklow *1777* * Litton *1675*, Richard [1721], *William* [1805], *Francis* [1868] * 'Currency'.

Apostle of the Peak: *William* born Litton Hall *1675* [17/01/1628-1702]. Buried in Chapel en le Frith *0580*. First sermon preached at Wormhill *1274*. Disinherited by his father. Ejected from his living at Glossop *0393* and retired to Ford *0882* [1662]. He preached regularly at Ashford in the Water *1969*, Bradwell *1781*, Chelmorton *1169*, Ford *0882*, Hucklow *1777*, Malcoffe *0782*, Middleton *1963* after [1672]. Wrote **50** volumes of sermons and Christian treatises.

Cricketer *Harry* on whose grave headstone, in Eyam churchyard *2176*, is engraved an umpire's raised finger signifying Out! Lawyer: *Thomas* took up residence at Bakewell Hall *2168* [1636]. He succeeded to the estates on death of his brother, *Henry,* also a lawyer, and his five nephews, heirs of *Henry.*

Marriages: *Henry* to daughter and heiress of *Thomas Cokayne* [16th century]; *Rachel*, daughter and heiress of The Ridge *0062* Bagshawe estates baptised [18/08/1685]; Daughter of Thomas to *William Fitzherbert* of Tissington *1752*. A daughter to *William Barber* of Malcoff/Malcalf *0782*, cousin of Derwent Hall *2383* Barbers.

Battles: *Colonel B.* orphaned at 6, lived with his uncle at Ford Hall *0882*, fought for *Robert Clive* in India about [1738].

Halls: Bakewell *2168* built [1684] by *Thomas* ('Squire' Bagshaw) died [April 1721] then inhabited by *Barkers* of Darley, Ford *0882*, The Ridge *0062* [1135-54], Wormhill *1274*.

'Manors': Abney *1979* [1377-99]; because they were hereditary 'foresters in fee', sold to *Francis Bradshawe* about [1597]; Grindlow *1877* [18th century]; Litton *1675 Nicholas* [1606] then possibly *Francis* [1620] purchased later sold to *Bradshawes*; Wormhill *1274 William* [1625-49] and *Adam* [1646-1724] purchased.

Balguy/Bauegay: *An origin name:* Possibilities Beaugency *47°47'N 1°38'E* or Bernay *49°05'N 0°36'E* or Bernay *48°05'N 0°40'E*. Descended from *Edward I* [1239-1307]. Large estates: Hope *1783*. 'Sheriff': Of Derbyshire *Henry* [1681]. Residence: Derwent Hall *2383* sometimes. Built by *Henry*, attorney and founder of a private bank, using the wealth of *Grace Barber* [1672]. Site bought from the *Wilsons*. Cattle market [1715] Hope *1683* founded by *John*. Marriage: *Henry* to *Elizabeth Allyn* of Tideswell *1575* on the death of first wife, *Grace Barber* of Rowlee *1599*.

Author and translator: Medical works, Inferno by Dante from Italian: *Charles* born [1708] at Derwent Hall *2383*. 'Literary connections'. Memorial: *Henry* Church of St Peter, Hope [1685]. *Figure 3*, Overseas Connections, refers.

Banks: *A residence name:* OD: *banke* = bank of a river. 'Moiety manor': ½ Snitterton *2760* [17th century] possibly purchased from *Hodgkinsons*.

Barber: Of Rowsley *2566* and Malcoff(e) *0782*. *An occupation name:* OF: *barbier* = barber (hair cutting, surgery, teeth extraction. Property: *Edward* of Rowlee *1589* [1570]. Marriages: *Grace* to *Henry Balguy* [17th century]. *William* of Malcoff *0782* to daughter of *William Bagshawe*, "Apostle of the Peak" [17th century].

Bardolf: *An origin name:* OG: *Bardolfus de Fotipoi* [12th century]. 'Manors': Elton *2260* [12th century] and possibly Stanton *2563* [12th century].

Barker: *An occupation name:* tanner of leather using bark. ON: *borkr* = bark. Darley branch. Residents of Bakewell Hall *2168* after *Thomas Bagshawe* died [1721].

Barlow: *A residence name:* OE: *bere* = barley + *hlaw* = a hill *or an origin name:* Barlow *3474*, Northeast Derbyshire. Marriages: *Dorothy Meverell* to *John* [1509-47].

'Manor': Stoke *Thomas 2376* purchased from *Lord Grey* of Codnor *4149*, the alchemist [1473].

Barnesley: *A residence name:* OE: *bere* = barley + *ley* = a clearing. 'Manor': Youlgreave *2064* by heiress [? 16th century].

Basset: *An appearance name:* OF: *basset* = low stature. 'Sheriffs': Of Derbyshire: *William* [1476], *Richard* [1512], *William* [1540], [1578 &1589] Battle: *Ralph* fought for *Simon de Montfort* at Evesham [1265] against *Henry III* [1216 -72] yet *Henry III* [1216-72] allowed *Ralph's* widow to stay at Bubnell *2472*. Memorials: Church of St Bartholomew, Blore *William and Joan* [1463].

'Manors': possibly Baslow *2573*, [1195] probably by *Elizabeth Avenell* of Haddon and heiress; [1195] Bubnell *2472 Simon*, died [1205] Justice Itinerant (Eyre) of Derbyshire by heiress, *Elizabeth Avenell*; [1205] *Elizabeth* paid 80 marks (£53) to *King John* to be allowed to remain a widow and retain her lands,

[1378] passed to Blore *1349* branch of Bassett family; Nether Haddon *2266* by heiress [1195]; Hartington estates *1360* of *Thomas* of Middleton *1963* sold to *Hugh* of Hartington *1360* [1823]. Hall: Blore *1349* [15th century] (now demolished).

Bateman: *A loyalty name:* servant of <u>Bartholomew</u>, one of *Jesus'* disciples or a reference to the Massacre of St Bartholomew's Day [24/08/1572]. Originated from Hartington *1360* but later there were two branches of the family. 'Sheriffs': Of Derbyshire: *Hugh* [1792], *Robert* [1812], *Thomas* [1823]. Hall: Hartington *Hugh* died [1616] Buried at Youlgreave *2064*. Philanthropist: *Thomas* gave money for Hartington *1360* poor to buy clothes. Antiquarian: *Thomas* born [8/11/1821] in Rowsley *2566* died [1861]. Grandson of Sheriff *Thomas*. Lived at 'Lomberdale' Hall *1963*. Memorial: *Thomas* Church of St Giles, Hartington *1360*. Tomb: *Thomas* Congregational Church, Middleton by Youlgreave *1963*. Marriages: *Robert* or *Richard* to *Ellen Topleyes* of Tissington *1752*. *Robert*, a Junior member of the Worshipful Company of Grocers. *William* (not the Hartington Hall *Batemans*) to someone named *Helen* from Youlgreave *1963*. *Thomas* to *Rebekah Clegg*. Builder: Hartington Hall: *Thomas*, 'yeoman' farmer [1611]. Author: Vestiges of the Antiquities of Derbyshire by *Thomas Bateman*. 'Manor': Middleton by Youlgreave *1963* with *Curzon* purchased [1719]. 'Moiety manor': *Elizabeth* about [1700].

Beelegh: *A residence name:* <u>Beage's</u> + OE: <u>ley</u> = clearing. 'Manor': Beeley *2667 Warren de* [1189-99].

Bennett: *An allegiance name:* follower of St <u>Benedict</u> [?480-?550] of Bakewell *2168*. His house was used for the Derbyshire heraldic visitation [1662]. 'Benedictines'.

Beorn/Beornwulf/Burnwulf: Nephew of King *Swein/Sweyn Estrithson, Forkbeard,* of Denmark (nephew of Earl *Godwines'* wife and *Cnut*), cousin of *Swein* son of Earl *Godwine*, a supporter of *Edward the Confessor* [1042-1066], earl of the Middle Angles/Mercia (Peak region). He was murdered by his cousin *Swein's* men on board a ship at Bosham *8004* [1049].

Beresford/Bafford: *A residence or origin name: 1258* OE: <u>bera</u> = a bear or <u>beofor</u> = a beaver + <u>ford</u> 'Viscount' [1823] Extinct [1854]. Memorials: Fenny Bentley *1750*, Church of St Edward. *Thomas* and wife, *Agnes*. Battles: *Sir Thomas* at Agincourt [1415] and in the Wars of the Roses [1455-85] 'Alabaster'; *Marshal Beresford* Albuera [1811] against Napoleon in Spain *38°41'N 6°47'W*. Family size: *Thomas* fathered 16 sons and 5 daughters. Last of original family: Died early [17th century]. The hall passed to *Stanshopes* of Elvaston *4132* but was bought by Marshal *Beresford* [1825] then bequeathed to Mr *Beresford-Hope* restorer of Sheen Church *1161*. Canon residentiary of Lichfield, bachelor of law, 'Manor': [1220-41].

Bernak(e)/Padley: Bailiff of Peak Forest [1255-6] *Gervase* reported colt strangled by a wolf in Edale *1285*. 'Manors': Padley *2579* [12th century]; Stoney Middleton *2375* [12th century] sold by *Richard de* to *William Furnival* [1307].

Berry *An origin name:* Dukedom of <u>Berry</u>, France *46°47'N 1°43'E*. 'Manor': One Ash *1665 Richard* by heiress about [1650]. *Figure 3* Overseas Connections refers.

Bertram St: Shrine near Ilam Hall *1350*. An Anglo-Saxon saint and hermit who converted the district to Christianity.

Bess of Hardwick: See *Talbot* and *Cavendish*.

Birch: *A residence name:* by a birch tree. OE: <u>bierce</u> = birch. *Robert* was the buyer of Holme Hall *2169* when *Joan Archer* (nee *Eyre*) died and the Court of Chancery ordered the sale.

Bird: *An occupation name:* 1. <u>Bird catcher</u> or 2. *A characteristic name:* '<u>bird brain</u>'. ME: <u>bridd</u> = a bird. Of Bakewell *2168*. Marriages: with the *Sheldons*.

Blackw(a)ell: *A residence name:* OE: <u>bloec</u> = black + <u>wella</u> = a stream or spring. 'Knight': Of Derbyshire returned to Parliament: *Richard* [1553]. Livery company: *George*, grandson of a Wendesley *2661* resident, member of the Worshipful Company of Skinners. Memorials: Church of St Michael, Taddington *1471 Sir Richard* died [1505] + wife + 6 sons + 5 daughters. Eyam Plague: *Margaret* was left for dead by her family but survived [1666]. 'Mesne manor': Blackwell *1272*. Compulsory sale ordered by *Charles II* [1660-85].

Blount: *An appearance name:* OF: <u>blond</u> = fair haired. **Public service**: 'Justices of the Peace' *Walter* for Staffordshire [1380], for Derbyshire [1388], *William* Lord Mountjoy for Derbyshire, Hertfordshire and Staffordshire *1532* 'Knights': Of Derbyshire returned to Parliament: *Walter* [1399], [1446], [1448],

[1450], [1452], [1454], [1460], *Thomas* [1420], *William* [1467], *James* [1472]. 'Sheriffs': Of Derbyshire: *Thomas* [1447], *William* [1470]; Steward of the High Peak [1451] *Walter Blount*. 'Feuding families'. 'Manors': Brushfield *1672* by heiress [uncertain date], Little Longstone *1871 Sir John* by *Isolda Mountjoy* heiress [15th century]; sold to *Richard Shakerley* [1474], Winster *2460 Sir John* (as Little Longstone).

Boden/Bowden: *A residence name:* OE: *boga* = bow [shaped] + *'dun'* = a hill. *John* (age 4 years) inherited Stanton *2563* estates from his uncle *John Alen* [1700]. However they were filched by the *Freemans*.

Botetourt: 'Baron' See *Somerset*.

Bouer: *A characteristic name:* OF: *beau* = fair + *fleur* = a flower Good looking. 'Mesne manor': Little Longstone *1871, Sir Thurston* [1399-1413].

Bourne: *A habitation name: beside a stream* 1. OE: *burna* = a stream *or* 2. *An origin name:* Bourne *0920*, Lincolnshire. 'Moiety manor': ¼ Monyash *1566 Dr Henry* about [1700].

Bower: See *De Bower*.

Bowles: *A characteristic name:* OF: *boule* = round. 'Manor': Abney *1979 Charles* by heiress [1789].

Bowman: *An occupation name:* OE: *boga* = bow + *mann* = man. *W & J H* last lessees of Ecton *0958* mines from *Duke of Devonshire* [1865-85].

Boyle: *An origin name: descendant of Baoighill*. Anglicised from the Gaelic; possibly via Ireland. 'Earl' of Burlington [1664]. 'Manor': Eyam *2176 Richard* by *Dorothy Savile* heiress of the *Marquis of Halifax* [1700].

Bradbury: *A residence name:* OE: *brad* = broad + *burrh* = a fort *or an origin name:* Bradbury *3128*, Yorkshire. Of Ollerset *0285* until about [17/05/1662] Also a Youlgreave *2064* branch of the family. Hall: Home of *Nicholas* + *Mary* about [1529]. Protestor: *Hugh de* against paying tithes to 'Lenton Priory' [1318]. See Blackwell *1272*. Dispute: *Nicholas* against *Ralph Mellor* concerning right of way to Beard *0184*. Marriage: *Edward* or *Edmund* to *Eleanor*, niece of *Grace Shakerley*, wife of 5th 'Earl' of Shrewsbury. Journalism: *William* of Bakewell *2168* founded Daily News, and Field, publisher of Punch. 'Literary Connections': *Freeman*.

Bradford: 'Earl' See *Bridgeman*.

Bradshaw(e): *A residence name:* OE: *brad* = broad + *sceaga* = copse *or an origin name:* Bradshawe *7312*, Cheshire. Family: Ancestor *Uchtred*, the Saxon Thane. Extinct [1735]. 'Manors': Abney *1979 Francis* purchased from *Nicholas Bagshawe* [1593]; Brushfield *1672* purchased [1658]; Litton *1675* purchased from *Bagshawes* [1620]. Hall: Eyam *2176*. Residences: *Francis* at Bradshaw Hall *2176* about [1630]. *George* at Eyam *2176* but he fled the Plague [1665]. 'Knight': Of Derbyshire returned to Parliament: *Roger* [1406]. 'Sheriffs': Of Derbyshire: *Francis* [1630*], *Henry* [1701], *John* [1717], *Joseph* [1776], *Francis* [1806], [1851] * See also *John Manners* for letter regarding grain shortage. Expulsion: From Peak lands by *King James I* [1622]. Regicide: *John* [1649]. Livery company: *Anthony*, grandson of *William* + *Anne Whinyates* of Chellaston *3830*, a member of the Ancient Guild of Goldsmiths. 19th century craftsman: 'Wheelwright' – no first name given. Marriages: *Henry* to *Catherine* daughter and co-heiress of *Ralph Winnington* about [1701]. *William* to *Anne Whinyates*.

Brampton: *A residence name:* OE: *broer* = gorse, broom + *'ton'* = a farmstead *or an origin name:* Brampton *3372*, North-east Derbyshire. 'Moiety manor': Tideswell *1575* by heiress [12th century].

Brereton: *A residence name:* OE: *brim* = briar + *'ton'* = a farmstead *or an origin name:* Brereton *0516*, Staffordshire. Of Hurdlow either *0260* or *1166*.

Bridgeman: *An occupation name: keeper of a bridge*. 'Baronet' [1660] 'Earl' of Bradford [1815]. 'Manor': Stoke *2376* by heiress of *Revd John Simpson*, *Elizabeth* [18th century].

Brindley: *A residence name:* OE: *berned* = burnt + *'ley'* = a clearing. Owner of Hartington cheese factory: *Thomas*. Memorial: *Thomas* Church of St Giles Hartington *1360*.

Brittlebank: *A residence name:* OE: *brytel* = brittle [unstable] + *bank*. 'Manor': Grindlow *1877* purchased [18th century].

Brown(e): *An appearance name: Hair, complexion or clothing* OF: *brun* = brown. 'Moiety manor': 3/12th Beeley *2667* purchased from *Gilberts* of Locko *4038* [1734]. Marriage: *Ford.*

Bullock: *An attribute name:* ME: *bullock* = exuberant. 'Manor': Stoke *2376* [16th century]. Residence: Ashford Rookery *1969.* 'Sheriff': Of Derbyshire: *John* [1616].

Bunting: *An appearance name: Short or Thick set.* Probably a Germanic language. Marriage: *Dorothy* of Youlgreave *2064* to *Christopher Bowers,* brother of the rector of Barlborough *4777* North-east Derbyshire about [1750].

Buxton: *An origin name:* Buxton *0673:* OE: *bugan* = to bow + '*ton*' = a farmstead.
'Manor': Youlgreave *2064* purchased possibly [17th century]. Gift: Font, St John the Baptist Church, Chelmorton *1169: Ralph* of Flagg *1368* [1630].

Carle(u)il: 'Baron' of Carlisle [1042-66] 'Earl' [1620] Forfeited [1715] 'Manors': Little Hucklow *1678* [18th century], possibly Longstone *1871.* Residence: Longstone Hall *1871.*

Carrington: *A residence name: Cara's* + '*ton*' *= a farmstead or An origin name;* Carrington *2155,* Lincolnshire. The self educated schoolmaster of Wetton *1059,* helper of *Thomas Bateman* with excavations at Wetton *1055* [1840s]. Fossils are engraved on the headstone of his grave at Wetton.

Carver or **Carr:** *An occupation name:* ME: *kerve* = to cut [wood] or OF: *caruier* = a ploughman. 'Sheriff': Of Derbyshire: *Marmaduke* following his name change to *Marmaduke Middleton Middleton* [1808].

Caschin: The Saxon lord of Eyam manor *2176* before the Norman Conquest [1066].

Cathcart: 'Baron' [1452-54], 'Viscount' [1776], 'Earl' [1814]. Hall: Throwley *1052* [16th century].

Cavendish: *A residence name* OE: *cafna* = bold + *bedisc* = enclosed pasture *or an origin name:* Cavendish *8046,* Suffolk. 'Earl' [1605], 'Duke' of Devonshire [1694]. NB The links listed below do not include family members only loosely connected with the Peak.
Churches: Builder Peak Forest *1179* chapel *Christian,* Countess of Devonshire [1659], 'Patron' Baslow *2572* [1811], Hartington *1360* [1693].
Public service: 'Custos rotulorum': [1615] *Sir William Cavendish* 1st 'Earl' [1551-1626]; 'Knights': Of Derbyshire returned to Parliament: *Henry* [1572], [1585], [1586], [1589], [1593], *William* [1620], [1623], [1625[, [1625] (same year), *Henry* [1660], *William* [1640-1707] [1661], [1679], [1679] (twice in the same year), [1680], [1694], [1697] *Charles* [1734], *William* born [1720] died [1764] [1741], [1747] builder of Chatsworth House; 1st Duke of Devonshire, *Frederick* [1747], *George* [1754], [1761], [1768], [1774]. *Richard* [1780], *George* [1784], [1790], *John* [1796], *George* [1797], [1802], [1807], [1812], [1819], [1820], [1826], [1830], [1831]. Members of Parliament: For Derby/shire *Henry* [1550-1616] [1572], *William* 2nd 'Earl' [1590-1628] [1614], [1621], [1624], [1625] *William* 4th Duke [1720-64] [1741]. 'Sheriffs': Of Derbyshire: *William* [1592], *Henry* [1608], *Henry* [1741]. 'Lords Lieutenant': Derbyshire: *William* [1638-41], *William* 3rd 'Earl' [1683], *William* (4th Duke) [1756], *George.* [1766], *William* (5th Duke) [1782], 6th Duke [1811], 7th Duke [1858] Ireland *William* [1737-44] Knight of the Garter [1756]. Memorials: Church of St Peter, Edensor *2468, Henry* died [1616] and *William* died [1625] in black 'marble' Lord *Frederick* assassinated [1882] in Phoenix Park, Dublin. Marriages: *Sir William,* his 3rd wife, to *Elizabeth Talbot/Bess* of *Hardwick,* her 2nd husband, [1545] *Sir William* was persuaded by *Bess* to leave Suffolk and settle at Chatsworth. *Mary* daughter of *Sir William* to *Gilbert* (**aged 14**) 7th Earl of Shrewsbury [1568]. Royal service: *Evelyn,* Duchess of Devonshire [1870-1960], Mistress of the Robes, Eyam Plague: [1665-66] *William* 3rd Earl of Devonshire [1617-84] provided food in return for coins left by villagers in vinegar at the isolated collection point. Authors: Life of Wolsey by *George Cavendish,* Chatsworth *Deborah,* [1992]. 'Literary connections'. 'Additional Information'.
Government officers: Financial secretary to the Treasury: [1916-21]; *Victor Christian* [1868-1938] *Andrew* 11th Duke [1920-2004] Minister of State, Governor General of Canada [1922-24] *Victor Christian* Secretary for the Colonies. Prime Minister: *William* [November 1756-May 1757]. 'Lord Lieutenant' and Governor General of Ireland [1755]. Knight of the Garter [1756]. 'Manors': Ashford *1969 Sir William* purchased from the *Nevilles* [1549/1550]*;* Beeley *2667 William* purchased [1747]; Blackwell *1272 Sir William,* gift of *Edward VI* [1552]; Brushfield *1672* purchased [1662]; Castleton *1583* [uncertain date] Royal demesne under the Crown; Chatsworth *2670* [1557]; Chelmorton *1169* leased [date uncertain]; Edensor *2468;* Eyam *2176* by heiress [1781]; Grindlow *1877 Sir William* gift of *Edward VI* [1552]; Hathersage *2381 William* purchased [1705]; Highlow *2180* purchased on the death of *Joan Archer*

(Eyre) as ordered by the Court of Chancery [1802]; Hope *1783*, leased from the Duchy of Lancaster; Little Longstone *1871 Bess of Hardwick* married [3/11/1541] purchased; One Ash *1665*; Stoke *2376 William* [16th century]; Taddington *1471* [uncertain date] Royal demesne under the Crown; Tideswell *1575* [1802]. Hall: Highlow *2180* purchased when the Court of Chancery ordered the sale on the death of *John Archer* (the name was changed from *Eyre*) about [1700].

Cearl: King of Mercia [7th century].

Chaworth: *A residence name:* OLG: *wort* = an open space [in a 'village'] 'Manor': Stoney Middleton *2375* [1086]. 'Knight': Of Derbyshire returned to Parliament: *Thomas* [1413]. 'Sheriffs': Of Derbyshire: *Thomas* [1424], *William* [1458], *George* [1513], *John* [1557].

Cheney: *An origin name:* Quesnay France *50°43'N 3°0'E* or *A habitation name:* Dweller by the oaks. OF: *chesnai* = oak. 'Manor': Beeley *2667* [1189-99], Monyash *1566* purchased in 'moieties' [1721] and [1736] from *Sir Talbot Clerke* and from *Dr Henry Bourne*. Battle: *John* struck by the axe of *Richard III* [1483-85] at the Battle of Bosworth Field [1485] and left for dead. *John* recovered to be made a peer and a 'knight' of the garter by *Henry VII* [1485-1509]. 'Sheriff': Of Derbyshire *Robert* [1775]. Residences: [18th century] Ashford in the Water *1969*, Monyash *1566*. *Figure 3.*

Chetal: Saxon Lord of Chatsworth Manor *2670* before the Norman Conquest.

Clegg *A residence name:* ON: *kleggi* = a haystack. Presbyterian minister: *James* successor to *William Bagshaw*, "Apostle of the Peak", [1628]. Joined his friends in coursing and fishing, played bowls and shovelboard; spent a festive evening in a tavern. Marriage: *Rebekah* to *Thomas Bateman* of Middleton by Youlgreave *1963* [1823].

Cle(a)rke: *An occupation name:* Either A member of the clergy or a learned person. 'Moiety manor': $^{1}/_{6}$th Monyash *1566 Sir Talbot* about [1700].

Clifford: *A residence name:* OE: *clif* = cliff + *ford* or *An origin name:* Clifford *4244*, North Yorkshire. 'Moiety manor': ½ Edensor *2468* [15th century] by heiress. *Cavendish* connection.

Co(c)kayne: *An imaginary origin name:* from legendary Cokaygne. Halls and residences: Harthill *2262*. 'Knights': Of Derbyshire returned to Parliament: *John* [1335], [1337], [1338], [1339], [1339] (same year), [1340], [1341], [1344], [1350], [1351], [1360], [1361], [1362], [1394], [1402], [1404], [1427], [1430], *Thomas* [1552]. 'Sheriffs': Of Derbyshire: *John* [1423], [1429], [1435], *John* [1521], *Thomas* [1530], [1550], [1569], [1570], [1580]; *Francis* [1590], *Edward* [1597]. *Thomas* voted for writs of 'Praemunire' and Provisors. Marriage: [1488] *Thomas* and his wife, *Agnes Barlow* living at Hartle *2764*. [1488] *Thomas* was killed in a fight with *Thomas Burdett* on his way to Youlgreave church *2164*. Battle: *Edmund* killed at the battle of Shrewsbury [23/07/1403]. Son of *Cecilia Vernon* and husband of *Sir Thomas Shirley's* daughter. Memorials: All Saints, Youlgreave *2064*. *Thomas* died [1488] 'Alabaster'. Authors: Hunting by *Thomas Cokayne*. *Sir Aston*, an enthusiast for the poems of his cousin, *Charles Cotton* [1630-87], writer of the Milward Sonnets [1658]. 'Literary connections'.

> *The land of Cokaygne*
> *Far in the sea to the west of Spain*
> *Is a country called Cockaygne*
> *There's no land not anywhere*
> *In goods or riches to compare*
> Verse 1 of a poem 190 lines in length [1315]

'Manors': Grindlow *0854 William* [17th century] by heiress, *Barbara Hill*; Hartle *2764 Edmund* [1377-99] by heiress; Middleton by Youlgreave *1963 Edmund* [1377-99] by heiress; sold [1598-99] to the *Fulwoods* to raise money.

Coke: An occupation name: seller of cooked meats. OE: *coc* = cooked. Of Trusley *2535*, South Derbyshire. 'Manor': Over Haddon *2066* [?17th century].

Colle: Saxon. Lord of Youlgreave Manor *2064* before the Norman Conquest. *Robert* gift to Leicester Abbey ('Dominican') [1154].

Colne: Saxon. Lord of Little Longstone. 'Manor' *1871* before the Norman Conquest.

Columbell: *An attribute name:* OF: *columbe* = a dove [peaceful]. Religious Persecution: *Roger Columbell*, a Darley Dale *2663* magistrate, arrested *Nicholas Garlick*, a Roman Catholic, at Padley Hall

[1537]. 'Moiety manor': *Roger* bought ¼ Wensley *2661* from *Lettuce de Wendesley (nee Needham)* [1603]. Livery company: *Roger* Guild of Merchant Tailors.

Copwood: *A residence name:* OE: copp = summit + wod = wild. Hall: Bubnell *2472* [1583] in the right his wife *Margaret* daughter of *Sir William Bassett* + *Anne Cokayne*.

Cotterell: *A residence name:* OF: cotier = cottager or 'cotter'. Land allocation: *Cotterell the Norman*, an 'Albigensian', given 2 'oxgates' in Taddington *1471* and Priestcliffe *1371* by *Henry III* [1235]. 'Moiety manor': ⅓rd Taddington *1471 William* [1272-1307] Royal demesne under the Crown. 'Manor': Taddington *1471 William* [1307-27].

Cotton: *A residence name:* OE: cot = a cottage + tun = a farmstead. *Charles* born [1630] at Beresford Hall *1259* died [1687]. *Impecunious poet, who hid from his creditors in a cave *1259* translator and author of the fly fishing chapter in the 5th edition of The Compleat Angler [1676]. 'Literary connections'. The principal author, *Izaak Walton* [1593-1683], was a frequent visitor to Cotton's house on the River Dove in Beresford Dale. Cousin of *Sir Aston Cokayne*. *Charles'* father eloped with a *Stanshope* daughter of Elvaston *4132*.

*Oh! My beloved Caves, from Dogstar's Heat
And all anxieties, my safe retreat,
What safety, privacy, what true delight,
In the artificial night
Your gloomy entrails make.

Retirement by *Charles Cotton*

Cowper: *An occupation name:* ME: couper = a cask [maker]. 'Baron' [1706], 'Earl' of Wingham *2547* and 'Viscount' Fordwich [1718] *1859*. Cowper Stone: *2583 Sir Edmund Cowper*, a Royalist [1642]. 'Mesne manor': Over Haddon *2066*.

Cox: of Derby. 'Manor': Grindlow *1877* [17th or 18th centuries] by purchase.

Cresswell: *A residence name:*OE: cressa = cress + wella = a spring or stream or *An origin name:* Cresswell *9739*, Staffordshire. Residence: Ford Hall *0882* early [16th century]. Heiress sold it to *Robert Ashton* [1648].

Crewe: See *Harpur*.

Cromwell: 'Viscount' Lecale [1624],'Earl' of Ardglass (54°16'N 5°37'W County Down, Ireland) [1645]. Marriages: Daughter to *Robert Meverell*. Countess of Ardglass, 2nd wife of *Charles Cotton*. She used to light a beacon to guide him home under cover of darkness after he had been hiding from his creditors. 'Manor': Tideswell *1575 Thomas* [1625-49] by *Meverll* heiress.

Curzon: *An origin name:* Courson *36°47'N 3°30'E*. Descent from *Roger De Courson*. 'Baron' [1761] (Scarsdale *4468*) 'Viscount' [1911]. *Figure 3* Overseas Connections refers.
'Manors': [11th century] Baslow *2572* (given to *Vernons*) [1330]; [18th century] Litton *1675* by purchase, [1719] Middelton by Youlgreave *1963* with *Bateman* by purchase.

Dakeyn(e)/Dakyn/Dakyns/Dakeyne/Dalkin/Dawkin/Deakin: *An attribute name:* thief [by implication]. OE: dawe = jackdaw. Residences: 'Manors' and Gradbach *9966*. Marriage: *John* to *Dorothy Needham* [1541], *Richard* to *Katherine Leslie*. 'Manors': Chelmorton *1169* [1327-77] [1461-83]; Hartington *1360* [1485-1509]. 'Granges' Biggin *1459* [1509-47]; Snitterton *2760* [1558-1603].

Dale: *A habitation name:* OE: doel and ME: dale = 'dale' or *An origin name:* Dale *4338*, South Derbyshire. Hall: Flagg *1368*. 'Sheriff' of Derbyshire: *Robert* [1786].

Daniel: *A Biblical name*. Marriages: Daughters and co-heiresses *Elizabeth* to *Thomas Meverell*. *Catherine* to *Reginald de Marchington*. *Johanna* to *John de Turvill* about [1357].
'Manors': Taddington *1471* [1199-1216] gift of *King John*; Tideswell *1575 Richard* [1216-72] by purchase; ownership was confirmed by *Edward I* [1272-1307].

De Blundevil: 'Earl' of Chester *Hugh*, major landowner in the Cheshire Peak at Domesday Survey. 'Castellan' of Peak Castle *1583 Randolph* [1215].

De Bower: *Thurstan* See Glossary: 'Bower'. Wealth: Prospered from lead mining. Founder member: Guild of St Mary [1384] and [1392], Tideswell *1575*. Died [1423] Memorial: St John the Baptist Church, Tideswell *1575*.

De Derley: *A habitation name:* Derbyshire + OE: *ley* = a clearing. 'Manor': Bakewell *2168* [1307-327]. 'Moiety manor': Nether Haddon 'township' *2266* [1272-1307].

De Eston: *An origin name:* Eston *5518*, Durham. 'Moiety manor': ½ Monyash *1566 Matthew* [1200].

Devonshire: Duke of, see *Cavendish*.

De Foleschamp and **De Folcham:** See *Foljambe*.

De Gerno(u)n: *An origin name:* Possibilities Gournay en Bray *49°29'N 1°44'E* or Gourdon *44°45'N 1°22'E*. Marriages: *Joanne*, one of *Sir John's* daughters, and a co-heiress, took Bakewell *2168* to her husband, *John Botetourt*. *Margaret* to *Thomas Foljambe* about [1256]. 'Justice itinerant: (in Eyre)' [1216-72] *Robert* or *Roger*. 'Manor': Bakewell *2168 Ralph* gift of *King John* [1199-1216]. Last of the senior line died without male heir: *Sir John* [1381] or [1383]. *Figure 3*, Overseas Connections, refers.

Degge: *An occupation name:* Sprinkler of water [Textile mills in Chapel en le Frith *0580*]. Hall: Bowden *0681* bought from the executors of *Nicholas Bowden* about [1668]. Sold to *Hibbersons*.

De Hockele: 'Moiety Manor': Taddington *1471 Michael* [1272-1307].

De Lisle: *An origin name:* Lisle *45°16'N 0°34'E*. 'Castellan': Peak Castle *1583 Bryan* [1228, 1231]. *Figure 3*, Overseas Connections, refers

De Ludank: *An origin name:* Either Lude Valley *47°39'N 0°09'E* or Le Lude on the River Loire. *Walter* a 'Lollard', possibly meeting at 'Lud's Church' *9865* [14th century]. *Figure 3*, refers.

De Malbanc: Gift: *William* granted Alstonefield *1355* by *King William I (The Conqueror)* [1086]. Founder: Combermere ('Cistercian') Abbey [1133] *5844*: *Hugh* [1130] 'Baron' of Wych Malbanc *6552*.

De Montfort: 'Castellan': Peak Castle *1583 Simon* [1263].

Denman: *A residence name:* OE '*dun*' = a hill + *man*. Marriage: *Joseph MD (Medicinae Doctor)* of Bakewell *2168* 'Justice of the Peace', married *Fynney* heiress and gained Stoney Middleton estate *2375* as distinct from the manor [1761]. Family professions: Peak Castle *1583 Hugh* [1204]. See also *Neville*.

De Nov(n)ant: Bishop of Lichfield *Hugh* [1191]. Gifts: Hope *1783* and Tideswell *1575* by *King John* [1199-1216]. 'Castellan': Peak Castle *1583 Hugh* [1191].

De Paunton: *A residence name:* Welsh: *pant* = valley + OE: '*ton*' = a farmstead. 'Moiety manor': Tideswell *1575* [12th century] by heiress, *Paulina Lameley*.

Dering: *Sir Chomley* killed in a duel by *Major Richard Thornhill* of Highlow Hall *2180* after dinner at "The Ivy" Hampden Court *1568* [07/04/1711].

De Salocia: 'Moiety manor': ½ Monyash *1566 Robert* [1200].

De Stokes: Probably *an origin name:* Stokesley *4208*, North Yorkshire. 'Manor': Grindlow *1877 Matthew de* [12th century].

De Turvill: *An origin name:* Either Tourville la Riviere *49°20'N 1°07'E* or Tourville les Ifs *49°42'N 0°24'E*. Marriage: *John* [14th century] to *Johanna Daniel*. *Figure 3*, Overseas Connections.

De Vesci: *Elizabeth* married a *Bradshaw* about [1700].

Devonshire: See *Cavendish*. The name probably originated because Derbyshire was misread by a copyist, an easy mistake because [17th] century handwriting had many looped letters.

Dymoke: *An occupation name*. 'Dymoke' Estates: Hassop *2272* purchased from *Sir Robert Plumpton* by *Catherine* (nee *Dymoke*) wife of *Stephen Eyre* [1498]. Her wealth was the basis of the subsequent wealth of the *Eyres*.

Edensor: *A residence or origin 2469 name:* Eden's + OE: *ofer* = a bank Philanthropist: *Richard* gave money to Hartington *1360* poor for bread [1764]. Memorial: *Richard* Church of St Giles, Hartington *1360*. 'Manors': Hartle *2764* [11th century]; Middleton by Youlgreave *1963* [11th century]. 'Mesne manors': Little Longstone *1871* [13th century]; Tissington *1752* by co-heiress *of William Savage* [1259]. Other heiress beneficiary, *Meynell*.

Eric of Norway: After the murder of 'Earl' *Uhtred* in [1016] he was given the 'earldom' of Northumbria and presumably lordship of Elton 'manor' *2260* by Cnut [1017-35]. He held the lands [1018-23]. *Eric* was succeeded by *Siward*, a Dane.

Ernvi: Saxon. Lord of Hucklow 'Manor' *1777* before the Norman Conquest [1066].

Evans: Welsh given name: *Ifan*. 'Manor': Bamford *2083 Francis* [1802].

Eyre: Either *a characteristic name:* OF: *errer* = to wander (from *Eyre 4152, Skye*) or one changed by *William the Conqueror* when a man called Truelove helped the king after a fall from a war horse; "True love you have shown to me henceforth your name will be Eyre". 'Earl' of Newburgh, *2318* Scotland [1660]. Lords of 20 manors in the Peak and elsewhere. Arguably connected with Jane Eyre by *Charlotte Bronte*. 'Sheriffs': Of Derbyshire: *Robert* [1481], *Thomas* [1621], [1658], *William* [1691], *Henry* [1723]. Religious persecution: *Robert* of Bubnell *2472* searched Harwood 'Grange' *3168* for a 'recusant'. Royal connection: [13th century] *William* in charge of the King's Hope Valley *1683* venison and he held lands in capite. Marriages: *Nicholas* to ? *Archer* of Highlow *2180* [1360] *Stephen* to *Catherine Dymoke* [1498], grandson of *Catherine, Rowland,* to the prodigiously rich *Gertrude Stafford, Robert* to *Anne Wells, Robert* to *Joan Padley* – 10 children, *Robert* to *Dorothy Columbell* – 6 sons, 7 daughters, *Dorothy*, Countess of Newburgh, to *Colonel Charles Leslie*. Pre-arranged proposal *Arthur* of Padley *2579* to *Margaret Plumpton* in consideration of 250 marks to be paid in 50 shilling instalments for her keep. (Letter from *Robert Eyre* to *Sir Robert Plumpton*. [St Valentine's Day 1499-1500]. Last of the line: *Arthur* (one of the Padley *Eyres*) died [1853]. The title was inherited by *Princess Giustiniani*, a descendant of the 4th Earl of Newcastle who died in [1768]. Memorials: All Saints' Church, Hassop *2272 Thomas* died [1833]; Church of St Michael, Hathersage *2380, Robert* died [1459] his wife and children, *Ralph* died [1493] and his wife nee *Joan* of Padley *2579 Robert* about [1500], *Sir Arthur* about [1560] *with his wife*; Church of St Giles, Longstone *1871 Roland* died [1624]. Vicar: Birchover *2462 Rev Thomas* died [1717]. Carver of Rowtor Rocks and builder of Rowtor Chapel *2462*. Family size: *Stephen,* bailiff of Ashford manor *1969* for *John Neville* [1440s], **11th** son of *Ralph + Joan*. Coal man: *Charles* in Brough *1882* [19th century]. Battles: *Robert* died [1459] fought at Agincourt [1415]. Royalist Cavalier *Rowland* against the Parliamentarians [1643]. Converted Hassop Hall *2272* into a barracks. He was compelled to pay £21,000 to redeem his property. *Colonel Thomas Eyre* died [1645] at the battle of Newark. [1643]. Translator: *Thomas* Christian Piety by *Gobinet* [1613-99], French religious writer. Halls: Holme *2169* by heiress *Anne Wells* on marriage to *Robert* Highlow *2180*, North Lees *2383* left hastily at the English Revolution [1688], Moorseats *2288*, Offerton *2181,* Rowtor *22362*, Shatton *1982*. 'Manors': Calver *2374* [1558-1603] by purchase; Castleton *1583* [uncertain date] leased; Haddon *2366* held for *Charles I* [1625-49]; Hassop *2272 Catherine* [1498] purchased from the *Plumpton* family and again in [1611]; Hathersage *2380* [16th century]; Highlow *2180 Nicholas* by marriage to *Archer* heiress about [1360]; Padley *2579 Sir Robert* [15th century] by marriage to *Joan Padley,* heiress; Rowland *2172 Rowland* [1558-1603] by heiress; Thornhill *1983* [1400]; Tideswell *1575* [1654] purchased from *Thomas, Lord Cromwell;* Wormhill *1274* [1489] purchased + annual payment of 3d (2.4d = 1p). 'Mesne manor': Chelmorton *1169* [16th century].

Farrar: *An occupation name:* OF: *ferreor* = iron [worker]. *Rev Frederick* died [1819], founder of the library in the Church of St Edmund, Castleton *1583*.

Ferne: *A residence name:* OE: *fearn* = fern. 'Moiety manor': ½ Snitterton *2760 Henry* [17th century] purchased.

Ferrars De: *An origin name:* Ferrieres sur Risle 48°03'N 0°51'W. *Henry*, founder of Tutbury Abbey [1080] *2129*, a Domesday commissioner with 114 lordships in Derbyshire and 7 in Staffordshire given by *William I* in return for protecting royal sources of wealth; *Robert* 'Earl' of Derby [1138]. 'Castellan': Of Peak Castle *1583 William* [1228]. Marriage: *Gundred* to *Sir Ralph Foljambe* [12th century]. *Figure 3*, Overseas Connections, refers. 'Manors': All [1086] Birchover *2462*; Edensor *2468;* Elton *2260*; Gratton *1960*; Hartle *2764*; Little Longstone *1871*; Stanton *2462*; Tissington *1752*; Winster *2460*; Wormhill *1274*; Youlgreave *2064* forfeited by *Robert de* – 8th Earl of Derby - for disloyalty to the Crown at the Battle of Chesterfield [1265]. Total: 114 manors in Derbyshire. *Figure 3*, refers.

Fidler: *Samuel* of Longnor *0864* died [1780] aged **105.**

Fiennes: see *Fynney*.

Fitz Alan-Howard: 'Duke' of Norfolk [1483]. Roman Catholic Yorkists. *Murray* owner of Derwent Hall *2383*. School and chapel: combined [1883]

Fitzherbert/FitzHerbert: *A patronymic name: Son* of Herbert.* *Scandinavian practice.
'Sheriffs': Of Derbyshire: *Nicholas* [1448], *William* [1456], *Nicholas* [1466], *Francis* [1498 & 1499], *John* [1602], [1624], [1626], *Richard* [1654], *Henry* [1815], *William* [1866]. Member of Parliament: For Derbyshire: *Sir Henry* [1284-1307]. Marriages: *William* to *Rachel Bagshawe*, heiress of The Ridge *Bagshawe* estates. *Richard* to *Anne Shallcross*. Religious persecution: *Thomas*, died [1591] husband of *Anne Eyre*, knighted by *Edward VI* but imprisoned by *Elizabeth I* for 'recusancy'. Padley estate *2579* looked after by brother *John* until his own trial, at which he was sentenced to death but commuted to a £10,000 fine and imprisonment in lieu of execution. Memorials: Church of St Mary, Tissington *1752*, *Francis* died [1619] and his *wife*, *Sir John* died [1643] and his *wife*, *Mary* died [1677], *Martha* died [1699]. Authors: *Judge*, Natura Brevium, born at Tissington Hall [1458], *Richard Greaves*, Spiritual Quixote, former resident of Tissington Hall.
'Manors': Middleton by Youlgreave *1963 Ralph* [1086]; Padley *2579 Thomas* [15th century] by heiress; Tissington *1752* purchased from the impecunious *Cokaynes* about [1599] initially a 'moiety' in the dowry of *Cicely Francis*, wife of *Thomas*.

Fitzhubert: *A patronymic name: Son* of Hubert.* * Scandinavian practice.
'Manors': All [1086] *Ralph* Bamford *2083*, Hathersage *2380*, Middleton by Youlgreave *1963*. Total in Derbyshire [1086] = 24.

FitzWaltheof: *A patronymic name. Son of Waltheof*, a Scandinavian family name, father of *Uchtred*.
'Manors': Brushfield *1672*, *Robert* [1086]; [14th century] by heiress to *Blounts* [15th century]. *Robert* son of *Waltheof*, the Saxon to whom *William I* gave the 'Earldoms' of Huntingdon and Northampton, was later imprisoned for plotting against his benefactor and executed at Winchester [1075].

Foljambe: *An attribute name:* OF: *fol* = foolish + *jambe* = leg [leg disability]. Adherents to House of *Rollo** since the subjugation of Normandy [905]. ***Rollo/Rolf/Hrolf/Rou*** was the 1st Duke of Normandy, a Viking, who accepted Christiantiy, died [930]. 'Normans': *Godfrey* descended from *Ragnar Lodbrok(g)* King of Denmark and Sweden who was killed attempting to invade England [794]. Battle: *Godfrey* fought with *William the Conqueror* at Hastings [1066]. 'Knights': Of Derbyshire returned to Parliament: *Thomas* [1296], [1301], *Henry* [1304], *Thomas* [1308], [1310], [1314], *Godfrey** [1338], [1348], [1364], [1369], [1371] (twice), *Godfrey*, Puisne of King's Bench [1344] died [9/9/ either 1377 or 1388] leaving daughter *Alice* (1 year old). *Godfrey's* lands were assigned to his widow *Margaret Thomas* [1390], [1391], *Godfrey* [1557] at the 'Field of the Cloth of Gold'.
'Sheriffs': Of Derbyshire: *Godfrey* [1520], [1525], [1537], *Godfrey* to daughter of *Uchtred* [11th century]. Sir *Ralph*, son of *Godfrey*, to *Gundred de Ferrars*. *Thomas* to *Margaret de Gernon* of Bakewell about [1251]. *Alice* (age 14 years) daughter of *Sir Godfrey* and *Margaret* to *Robert Plumpton* [1401]. Covenant of marriage for the *ward* of *Sir John Leake* and subsequently *Sir William Plumpton* made out when she was **11 months old**. *Frances*, died aged 37, to *John Twigge*, sheriff, about [1750]. Founders: 'Chantries': Tideswell *1575 John* [1377-99]; Bakewell *2168 Sir Godfrey* [1344]. Guild either [1327-77] *Edward III* or [1377-99] *Richard II*. Family branches: Tideswell *1575*, Wormhill *1274*. Monuments: All Saints' Church Bakewell *2168*, *Sir Godfrey* died either [1366] or [1377] and his wife *Avena* died [1385] 'Alabaster', Tideswell, St John the Baptist *1575 John* died [1358 or 1383]. 'Chantry': Bakewell *2168* founded by *Sir Godfrey* and his wife. *Opposer of 'annates'. 'Manors': Castleton *1583* [date uncertain] leased; Edensor *2468* [11th/12th centuries]; Elton *2260* [1327-77]; Hassop *2272* [11th century]; Little Hucklow *1678* [date uncertain]; Stanton *2563* [1327-77]; Tideswell *1575*; Wormhill *1274* [12th century] *Sir John* died [1245]. The family virtually ceased to be Peak landlords by the [17th century].

Ford: *A residence name:* OE: *ford* or *An origin name: 0654*, Staffordshire or *0882*. Residence: [1304] Ford Hall *0782*. Bailliffs of 'Forest': [1304]. See *Thomas Foljambe*. Marriage: Heiresss to *Browne* of Marsh Hall *0479*, North-west Derbyshire.

Fox: *A charactierstic name:* ME = *foxy* [cunning]. Hazlebadge Hall *1780* [18th/19th centuries]. Inventor: *Samuel* Ribbed folding umbrella frame [1850] born Bradwell *1781*.

Franceys: *An origin name:* OF: *franceis* = Frenchman. 'Manor': Over Haddon *2066 Gilbert le* [?14th century] by heiress.

Francis: *An origin name:* OF: *francois* = Frenchman. Marriage: *Cicely* to *Thomas Fitzherbert* [14th century].

Freeman: *An attribute name:* OE: *freomann, frigmann* = freeman. Residence: Wheston Hall *1376* about [1690]. Marriages: [Medieval period] to *Alens*. Crime: Divested the infant *John Bo(w)den* of the Wheston Estates about [1700]. Left the estates to the *Maxwells*.

Fulwood: *A residence name:* OE: *ful* = muddy + *wudu* = wood *or An origin name:* Fulwood *3085*, South Yorkshire. 'Sheriff': Of Derbyshire *Sir George* [1611]. Civil War: Cavalier *Christopher* shot by Parliamentarian *Gell* for recruiting 1,000 Tideswell lead miners as a bodyguard for *Charles I* [1643]. Castle/fortified manor house built by *Sir George* [17th century] *1863*. 'Manor': Middleton by Youlgreave *1963* [1598-99] purchased from the impecunious *Cokaynes*.

Furnival(l): 'Baron' [1295] by *Edward I*. Title abeyant [1968]. Lord of Eyam. *Thomas* of Wigtwistle *2495* granted land to *Adam Wilson*, ancestor of Broomhead Hall *2496* family, his shield bearer (scutiger) for services during the Scottish Wars. 'Manors': Eyam *2176 Thomas* [1307] purchased from *Sir Roger Morteyne*; Stoney Middleton *2375 Thomas* [1272-1307] purchased from *Richard de Bernake* [1307]; transferred on the marriage of *Elizabeth* of Ashford in the Water *1969* to *Joseph 'Denman' MD* of Bakewell [1761].

Fynney: *A residence name:* OE: *fynig* = marshy place *or An origin name:* Danish: *Fyn* = Funen *55°15'N 10°20'E*. The senior branch of the family were 'squires' in Taddington Dale *1671*. Marriages: *Elizabeth* to *Joseph Denman* of Bakewell *2168* [1761]. Probably *Ann* to *J. Cook* of Alstonefield *1355* [1818]. 'Sheriff': Of Derbyshire: *Edward* [1690]. Halls: Ashford in the Water *1969* [16th century] and Flagg *1368*. Fynney Cottage *1871* possibly built by *John Fynney* [1575]. Residences: *James* resident of Little Longstone *1871* [1596] on his marriage to *Mary White* of Ashford Rookery *1969, George*, a surgeon, in Longnor *0864*, and also *Frederick Wyatt* and *Joseph Poole* [1840s]. 'Manors': Monyash *1566 Richard* [uncertain date], Stoney Middleton *2375* by heiress, possibly *Margaret Peploe* mother of *Elizabeth Fynney*.

Galliard: *A characteristic name:* ME: *galliard* = high spirited. 'Manor': Abney *1979 Joshua* [1593] by heiress *Elizabeth Bradshaw*.

Gargrave: *An occupation name:* ON: *gard* = guard + *greify* = steward *or An origin name:* Gargrave *9354*, North Yorkshire. 'Manor': One Ash *1665 Thomas* [1558-1603] by purchase.

Garlic(k): *An occupational name:* OE: *garleac* and ME: *garlek* = garlic. [grower or distributor]. Hall: Padley *2579 Nicholas*, Tideswell Grammar School Headmaster, martyred [25/07/1588] with *Robert Ludlam* and *John FitzHerbert*. He became schoolmaster of Tideswell *1575*; entered Roman Catholic priesthood after his marriage to daughter of *Richard Stafford* of Eyam *2176* and Tideswell *1575* was forbidden because *Nicholas* was a son of a 'yeoman'.

Gaunt: *John of* Duke of Lancaster. Castellan: Peak Castle *1583* [1372]. 'Manors': Both [1327-77] Castleton *1583* and Hope *1783*.

Gi(y)lbert: *An allegiance name:* *St Gilbert* of Sempringham *1132*, Lincolnshire [1085-1189] ('Premonstratensian') *or A characteristic name:* Germanic: *gisil* = noble + *berht* = bright of Locko *4038*, South Derbyshire. 'Knight': Of Derbyshire returned to Parliament *Henry* [1689]. Ore processing: *Thomas* leased Greenlowfield copper smelting mills *1555* [1740s]. Memorials: All Saints' Church, Youlgreave *2064 Robert* died [1492], wife and **17** children, *Frideswide* died [1603]. 'Manor': Eyam *2176* by *Mary Gilbert* heiress [1616]; Youlgreave *2064* [uncertain date] by *Rossington* heiress; Beeley *2667* [1734] by heiress, niece of *William Savile*. The manor was eventually divided into 12 lots and sold. 'Moiety manor': ⅓rd Monyash *1566* by heiress [17th century].

Gilbey: 'Baron' [1523] Vaux of Harrowden *0646*, Bedfordshire [1523]. 'Manor': Beeley *2667 Thomas* [1509-47] by heiress.

Gisborne: *An origin name:* Gisbo(u)rne *8248* North Yorkshire. Marriage: *Thomas John* to *Sally Krechmer* of St Petersburg *59°59'N 30°29'E*. Hall: Holme *2169* [uncertain date] *Thomas John* by purchase.

Gladwin: *A characteristic name:* OE: *gloed* = shining + *wine* = a friend. 'Moiety manor': ⅓rd Monyash *1566 Thomas* [1646] of Tupton Hall *3865*.

Godric: The Saxon Lord of Beeley manor *2667* before the Norman Conquest.

Goodwin: *George* lived in Long Clough *9873*, died [1783] aged **103**, buried Forest Chapel *9771*.

Gould: *John* of Alstonefield *1355*. Executed [1811] for accidentally killing his wife when attempting to abort their second child.

Goush(e)ill/Gonshill: *A residence name:* OF: gous = dog + OE: hyll = a hill. 'Manor': Hathersage *2380 Walter* [14th century].

Greaves: *An occupation name:* LG: greven = the residue after rendering meat for 'grease' and 'tallow'. 'Sheriff': Of Derbyshire *Joseph* [1765]. Homes in the Peak: After the sale of Hill Top to *Howard Savile*: Beeley *2667*, Birchover *2462*, Rowsley *2566*, Stanton Woodhouse. Sufferings: Under the Commonwealth [1649-59] for supporting the Stuarts. Author: Revd *Richard* Spiritual Quixote sometime resident of Tissington Hall *1752*, 'Natural World; Physical' 'Manor': Beeley *2667 John* [1560] purchased from *Nicholas*, brother of *Lord Vaux*; sold to *William Savile*.

Grey: of Codnor *4149*, South Derbyshire. 'Manors': Possibly Monyash *1566*; Stoke *2376* [12th/13th century].

Grimshawe: *A residence name:* OE: grima = ghost + sceaga = copse. Hall: Errwood *0175*. Built [1830]. Sold to Stockport Corporation [1930].

Gurneburn: Saxon Lord of Castleton Manor *1583* before Norman Conquest [1066] with *Hundine*.

Hall: *Elias*, Geologist buried in Castleton churchyard *1583*.

Hamilton: *A residence name:* OE: hamel = scarred + 'ton' = a farmstead. 'Manor': Over Haddon *2066 William de* [1286]. 'Moiety': ⅓rd Taddington *1471 William de* [1272-1307].

Hancock: *Elizabeth* buried her husband, and **six** children, during the Eyam plague [1665-66] but survived herself.

Hardwick: "Bess of" *Elizabeth Talbot*, Countess of Shrewsbury died [1607]. mother of the 1st Duke of Devonshire.

Harpur: *An occupation name:* ME: harp or *An origin name:* Harpur Hill *0671*, North Derbyshire. Builder: Alstonefield Hall: *1355 John* [1587]. Rebuilder: Warslow Hall *Sir George Crewe* (*Harpur-Crewe* family) of Calke Abbey *3721*, South Derbyshire *3722*. Market: Grant to *John* [1595]. Market Hall rebuilt by *Sir John Harpur Crewe* [1873]. 'Manor': Alstonefield *1355 John* [1595] died [1622]. Manorial court ordered 6 tenants, nominated by the bailiff, each to deliver a load of peat fuel annually to his manor house [1660]. 'Moiety manor': Wensley *2661* purchased from *Lettuce de Wendesley (nee Needham)*, wife of *Richard* [1591].

Hathersage: *A residence name:* OE: hoed = he-goat [ie steep] ridge. 'Manor': Hathersage *2380 Sir Matthew de* [1216-72] possibly by *Meynell* heiress. Franchise: Free 'warren' granted to *Matthew de* by *Henry III* [25/10/1248].

Hatfield: *A residence name:* OE: hoed = he-goat [ie steep] + feld = field or *An origin name:* Hatfield *6609*, South Yorkshire. Hall: Crowden, *0799* built [1692].

Helyon: *An origin name:* Ely *5380*, Cambridgeshire. Marriages: *Isabel*, heiress of Bakewell Manor *2168*, to *Humphrey Tyrell* 'Manor': Bakewell *2168 John* [14th century] by heiress *Alice Synburne*, daughter of *Sir Richard*.

Herbert: 'Earl' of Pembroke and Montgomery [1551]. 'Moiety manor': ⅓rd Monyash *1566* [1616] by co-heiress.

H(a)erthill: *A residence name:* OE: heorot = a hart + hyll = hill or *An origin name:* Harthill *4955*, Cheshire or *4980*, South Yorkshire. 'Manors': Hartle *2764* [11th/12th centuries] by heiress; Middleton by Youlgreave *1963* [1216-72].

Hibberson: *A characteristic name:* OG: hild = battle + behrt = brave. Bought Bowden Hall *0681* from *Degges* [17th century]. Sold to *Slacks*.

Hill: *Sergeant* Lawyer. 'Manor': Grindlow *1877* [17th century] *Barbara*, daughter and heiress of *William*, married *Edmund Cokayne*.

Hodgkinson: *A characteristic name:* ME: *hodge* = a glutton + *son*. 'Moiety manor': ½ Snitterton *2760* [1670] by *Sacheverell* co-heiress.

Hol(l)and: *A residence name:* OE: *hoh* = ridge + *land* [old land ie grassland that has recently been cultivated]. Battle: *Robert* probably at Crecy [1346]. 'Manors': Ashford in the Water *1969* Sir *Thomas* [14th century] by heiress, *Joan* "Fair Maid of Kent", daughter of *Edmund Plantagenet*; Longendale *0397 Robert* until [1328].

Hope: *A residence name: 1783* S: *hob* = wild boar (habitat: valleys with water – Peakshole Water) or ME: *hop* = a valley. 'Mesne manor': Blackwell *1272*, gift of *Charles II* [1660-85].

Howe: *A residence name:* ME: *how* = small hill *or An origin name:* Howe *2799*, Norfolk. Plague: *Marshall*, gravedigger and survivor of the Eyam Plague [1665-66]. 'Manor': Middleton by Youlgreave *1963* [18th century] and with *Roper* [1771].

Hundine: The Saxon. Lord of Castleton 'Manor' *1583*, with *Gurneburn* before [1066].

Hunter: *An occupation name:* OE: *hunta* = (1) stags and wild boar [a nobleman], (2) birdcatcher or (3) poacher. Alderman M. Hall: Stoke *2376* used as summer residence away from his works in Sheffield [19th century]. See also Warslow *0858*.

Hurlock: *An occupation name:* lime worker. 'Manors': *Henry Francis* All by descent [1875]. Birchover *2462*; Elton *2260*; Gratton *1960*; Stanton *2563 Henry Francis* [1875] a *Thornhill* on his mother's side on the death of *William Pole Thornhill* [1875]. The manors were transferred to his sister's husband, *Major McCreagh*, on the death of *Henry Francis*.

Hurt: *A characteristic name:* ME: *hert* = hart [quick]. Hall: Castern *1252* [18th century]. 'Sheriffs': Of Derbyshire: *Charles* [1714], *Nicholas* [1756], *Francis* [1778], *Charles* [1796], *Francis* [1814], *Francis* [1860].

Hugh de Novant: Bishop of Ely. Given custody of Peveril (Peak) Castle after a quarrel between *Richard De Clare*, "Strongbow", and *Longchamp* about [1215].

Hyde: *An occupation name:* farmer of a *hide*. OE: *hi(gi)d* = 'hide'. Hall: Long Lee *0188*. Ghost of hall: *John*.

Ible: *A residence name: Ibba's valley 2457*. Moneyer: *Ibba* [951]. 'Knight': Of Derbyshire: *William* [1461].

Jewitt: *A local term of reproach.* Historian and archaeologist: *Llewellyn Frederick William*. Author: Ballads of Derbyshire [1867]. Hall: Winster *2460*. 'Literary connections'.

Joddrell: *An origin name* Joddrell *7971*. Military family from Agincourt [1415] until World War II [1939-1945]. Monuments: St Leonard's, now St James' Church, Taxal *0079*.

Jol(l)iffe: *A characteristic name:* OF: *jolif* = lively. 'Manor': Elton *2260* [17th century].

Kent: 'Earl' [1067], *Eudes* Bishop of Bayeux repeat creation [1226/7]. 'Moiety manor': ⅓rd Monyash *1566* [1616] by co-heiress *Joan*, "Fair Maid of", daughter of *Thomas* of Woodstock, grand daughter of *Edward I* [1272-1307].

Kniveton: *An occupation name: Cengifu's* (a woman's name) + '*ton*' = a farmstead *or An origin name:* Kniveton *2050*, South Derbyshire. 'Knights': Of Derbyshire returned to Parliament: *Henry* [1294], [1335], *William* [1603]. 'Sheriffs': Of Derbyshire: *Nicholas* [1467], [1490], [1494], *William* [1614], *Gilbert* [1623]. 'Manor': Little Rowsley *2566* Sir *William* [1558-1603] on marriage to *Matilda Rollesley*.

Lamb(e): *A characteristic name:* OE: *lamb* = lamb [inoffensive]. 'Baron' (Ireland) [1770], Melbourne 'Viscount' (Ireland) [1781], 'Viscount' (Great Britain) [1815]. 'Mesne manor': Over Haddon *2066* [uncertain date].

Lameley: *A residence name:* OE: *lamb* = lamb + '*ley*' = a clearing. 'Manor': Tideswell *1575* given by *King John* [1199-1216] to *Thomas de*. Descended to his son, *Monechias*, then his grand daughter, *Paulina*, who married a *De Paunton*.

Lancaster: 'Baron' [1299] *Henry*, 'Earl' [1361] *John of Gaunt*, 'Duke' [1362]. Investments: Enclosures and the conversion of arable to pasture [13th and 14th centuries]. 'Manors': Alstonefield *1355*; Winster

2460 Edmund [1216-72], Peak lead fields - Castleton *1582*, High Peak *0065 and* part Hartington *1360* [1640].

Langford: *A residence name* OE: *lang* = long + *forda* = ford *or An origin name:* Langford *8258* Nottinghamshire. 'Manor': Edensor *2569* [16th century].

Leake: *An origin name: from* Leek, Staffordshire *9856 or* East Leake *5526*, Nottinghamshire. *Sir John* Buyer of the wardship of a *Foljambe* heiress from *Richard II* [1377 -99] for 50 marks (£33). Wardship sold to *Sir William Plumpton* for 100 marks (£66) two months after the death of heiress' father who died aged 21 ie £33 profit.

Leche: *A professional name:* S: *leech* = medical practitioner. 'Knights': Of Derbyshire returned to Parliament *Roger* [1402], [1413], [1413] (twice in the same year), [1414]; *Edward* helped secure the Petition of Rights [1628]. Lord High Treasurer: To *Henry V*: *Sir Roger* [1414-22]. 'Manor': Chatsworth *2670* [15th century].

Lee: *An occupation name:* OE: *hleow* = a shelter for sheep [ie a shepherd]. Residents of The Greaves, Beeley *2667* [18th century].

Leslie: *An origin name*: Sc: *lesslyn* = Leslie *2401* or *5924*. Colonel *Charles*, husband of *Dorothy Eyre*, who bequeathed to him. Marriage: *Katherine* to *Richard Dakeyne* of Snitterton *2760* about [1580]. 'Manors': Calver *2374*; Hassop *2272*; Rowland *2172* and Thornhill *1983* on her death [22/11/1853] at Hassop Hall *2272*.

Levenot/Leofnoth: Saxon Lord of Edensor *2468* manor before the Norman Conquest.

Lewin/Leofwine: Saxon Lord of Hazlebadge 'Manor' *1780* before the Norman Conquest.

Litton/Lytton: *A residence name:* OE: *hydel* = torrent (River Wye) + '*ton*' = a farmstead.
Agisters' of forest: *Henry IV* [1399-1413]. Last of line: Died [1705]. Memorials: Church of St John the Baptist, Tideswell *1575 Sir Robert* died [1483] and his wife, *Isabel*. 'Manors': Tideswell *1575* [possibly 12th century]; Litton *1675* [1597] sold to the *Alsop* family.

Longford: *An origin name:* Longford *2037* South Derbyshire. 'Knights': Of Derbyshire returned to Parliament: *Nicholas* [1323], [1403], *Roger* [1406], *Nicholas* [1472]. Gifts: To Welbeck ('Pre-Monstratensian') Abbey, *5674* Nottinghamshire: *Oliver*, son of *Cecilia* co-heiress of *Matthew de Hathersage*, supplemented the gift of Derwent Chapel *2383* by the *Avenells* [12th century]. 'Sheriff': Of Derbyshire: *Ralph* [1501], [1536]. Marriages: *Oliver* to *Ercald* heiress; *Nigel* to *Cecilia De Hathersage*. 'Feuding families'. 'Moiety manor': ½ Hathersage *2380 Nigel* by heiress [14th century].

Longsdon: *A residence name:* OE *lang* = long + '*dun*' = a hill *or An origin name:* Longsdon *9554*, Staffordshire. Bakewell lawyer: *Longsdon Parva* [1199-1215] resident of Little Longstone *1871*. 'Moiety manor': Little Longsdon *1871* [12th century].

Lowe: Either *A residence name* OE: *hlaw* = a hill or *A characteristic name*; ME: *lah* = short [man] 'Manor': Gratton *1960 Francis* by heiress [1675].

Ludlam: *A characteristic name* OE: *hlud* = loud + *lamb* = inoffensive. Hall: Padley *2579*, *Robert* martyred [25/07/1588], Roman Catholic priest with *Nicholas Garlick*.

Lynford: *An occupation name* OF: *linier* = linen cloth + *forda*. Valet: To *Edward III* [1327-77]. 'Manors': Calver *2374 Thomas* [1422-61]; Monyash *1566 William de* [1340].

McCreagh: *Major A characteristic name:* G: *mag raith* = grace, prosperity. 'Manors': Birchover *2462*; Elton *2260*; Gratton *1960*; Stanton *2563* [1881] on the death of *Henry Francis Hurlock*, brother of *Major McCreagh's* wife. 'Mesne manor': Chelmorton *1169* [1853].

McDougall: *Sir Robert*. 'Benefactor: Large areas of Dovedale *1451* [1930s] and Ilam Hall *1350* donated to the National Trust.

Manners: *An origin name:* Mesnieres en Bray *49°44'N 1°29'W*. 'Earl' 'Duke' of Rutland [1703]. Divorce and re-marriage: *John*, 9th 'Earl', divorcee of *Anne Pierpont*, canon law set aside by Act [1670]. 'Law'. Public service: [1580] 'Custos rotulorum' *John Manners* died [1584] after hitch between Queen *Elizabeth I* and the Lord Chancellor over the appointment of *Sir John Zouch*. 'Knights': Of Derbyshire returned to Parliament: *George* [1593], *John* [1625], [1639], [1699]. 'Sheriffs': Of Derbyshire: *John* [1576],

[1585], [1594], *Roger* [1618], *John* [1632]. Founder of Bakewell 'School': *Lady Grace* [1636] and leader of armed attacks on lead miners by her Smerrill Grange *1962* tenants. Memorials: All Saints' Church, Bakewell *2168* , *Sir John* died [1584] with *his wife Dorothy Vernon* and *children, Sir George* died [1623] with *his wife* and *children;* Church of St Katherine, Rowsley *2566, Lady John Manners* died [1859].
Grain shortage: [1630-31] On behalf of *Charles I,* letter from *John Manners* to *Francis Bradshaw,* High Sheriff commanding that surplus grain (oats and oatmeal) be taken to Bakewell *2168* and Tideswell *1575* markets. 'Manors': Bakewell *2168*; Baslow *2572 John*; Haddon *2366*; Hartle *2764 John* [1599] purchase, Hazelbadge *1780*; Little *2566 Sir John* [1603-49], and Great Rowsley *2566*; Nether *2266* and Over Haddon *2066*; Stanton Lees *2563*; Youlgreave *2064* [1685] purchase from the *Buxtons*. The heiress, *Dorothy Vernon,* on her marriage to *John,* a simple 'squire', brought all the undated manors in [1575]. *Figure 3,* Overseas Connections, refers.

Marbury: *An occupation name:* OF: marbier = marble [worker] *or An origin name:* Marbury *5545,* Cheshire. *Columbell* lands (Wensley *2661*) brought by heiress on marriage. ? *Marbury* died soon afterwards; and given in his memory to the *Thacker* family.

Marchington: *A residence name:* OE: marchant = merchant + tun = a farmstead *or An origin name:* Marchington *1330,* Staffordshire. 'Moiety manor': ⅓rd Tideswell *1575, Reginald* [14th century] by co-heiress, *Catherine Daniel.*

Marshall: *An occupation name* either OHG: mare = a horse + scalc = a servant *or* OF: mareschal = marshall [military officer]. Marriage: *Barbara* of Tideswell *1575* to *Bernard Wells* about [1626]. Child care: When *Catherine Bradshaw* died in childbirth, *Barbara Wells* looked after her three small sons, *Henry, John & Francis + Bernard & Barbara Wells'* own children: *Mary, Anne & Bernard.*

Maxwell: *A residence name* Sc: mackeswell = spring or stream. Hall: Wheston *1376* inherited from the *Freemans* who obtained it fraudulently [early 18th century].

Melland: *An occupation name:* same as 'Millward'. 'Moiety manor': ½ Bamford *2083* [19th century].

Mellor: *An origin name*: Mellor *6530* or *9888,* Lancashire. Thomas died aged **103**. His memorial is in the church of St Giles, Hartington *1360.*

Metcalf: *An occupation name:* ME: metacalf = meat calf. *Captain Tom.* Hall: Winster *2460* [19th century].

Meverell: *A characteristic name:* OF: mievre = insipid *or An origin name:* Mereville 28°19'N 2°06'E. Of Throwley *1052,* Staffordshire. Redundant prior: *Arthur* vicar of Tideswell [1544-47] after Tutbury Priory dissolution *2129.* Marriages: *Thomas* to *Elizabeth Daniel* about [1327]; *Robert's* daughter (mother of *Elizabeth Heminge,* daughter of a Lord Chief Justice, to *Thomas,* Lord Cromwell. (Tideswell manor *1575* in her dowry); *Dorothy* to *Thomas Barlow* [1509-47]; *George* to *Constance Allen* of Whetsone *5597* [1509-47]; *Barbara* to *Thomas Statham* about [1707]. Quarrels: *Meverells* and *Bassets.*[1440s]. Crime: *Sampson* summoned for bigamy [1564]. Memorials: Holy Cross Church, Ilam *1350 Robert* of Throwley Hall *1052* died [1625], Church of St John the Baptist Tideswell *1575, Sir Sampson* died [1462].
'Manor': Tideswell *1575* [1558-1603] by purchase or gift. *Ottowell,* [1585-1648], physician and lecturer on anatomy. 'Moiety manor': ⅓rd Tideswell *1575 Thomas* [13th century] by co-heiresses. *Figure 3,* Overseas Onnections, refers.

Meynell: *An origin name:* Mesnil. There are several places with the same name north of Paris – Amelot, Aubry, Esnard, St Denis. 'Manors': Hathersage: *2380* possible demesne tenants of *Ralph Fitzhubert* about [1086]; Winster *2460* [uncertain date] by purchase. 'Moiety manor': Tissington *1752* by co-heiresses *of William Savage* [1259]. Other heiress beneficiary: *Edensor.*

Middleton: *A residence name:* OE: midel = middle + 'ton' = a farmstead *or an origin name* from one of 26 places in 18 counties named Middleton. Last of the male line: *Robert* died [1736]. Hall: Leam *2379.* 'Manor': Gratton *1960 Thomas* [1485-1509]. A possible Nottinghamshire branch of the family.

Milnes: *An occupation name:* OE: mylen = mill [worker]. Residents of Ashford Rookery *1969* [16th century].

Milward: *An occupation name:* OE: mylen = mill + ward = a keeper. 'Sheriffs': Of Derbyshire: *Colonel John* (Royalist) [1620], [1635] died [1670], *Henry* [1680]. Livery company: *John,* of Dove Dale *1451* and Snitterton *2760,* 'one of the captains of ye Cittie of London' governor of the silkmen of England,

Wales and Ireland. 'Moiety manor': ½ Snitterton *2760* purchased from *Sacheverells*. Transferred to co-heiresses [1670]. *Felicia* married *Charles Adderley* who sold it to *Henry Ferne*.

Mompesson: *An origin name:* Mont Pincon, *48°50'N 0°60'E*. Vicar of Eyam *2176* during the plague *William* [1665-66]. *Catherine* wife died [25/08/1666], the 220th victim of the plague. Mompesson Well *2277*. Their children, *George* and *Elizabeth*, were evacuated to Yorkshire. *Figure 3*, Overseas Connections, refers.

Moore: *A habitation name:* OE: <u>mor</u> = moor *or An origin name:* <u>Moore</u> *5584*, Cheshire. <u>Builder</u>: Winster Hall: *2460 Francis* about [1624] using Stancliffe quarries 'millstone grit'. <u>Married</u>: [26/04/1624] at Bakewell *2168*. Cotton '<u>Mill</u>' owners Bamford [1780] *2083*.

Morteyne: *An origin name:* Mortagne, *48°32'N 0°32'E*. 'Manors': [1199-1216] Eyam *2176* gift of *King John*; [1307] sold to *Thomas Furnival*; Foolow [1283] Seized on *William's* death *1976*. *Figure 3*, Overseas Connections, refers.

Morton: *A characteristic name:* OE: <u>mor</u> = marsh + '<u>ton</u>' = a farmstead *or An origin name: either* Derbyshire *4060*, Lincolnshire *0924 & 8091*, Norfolk *1217*, or Shropshire *2824*. <u>Forbidden marriage:</u> *Anne* of Hazleford *2379*, "The Maid of Derwent", prevented from marrying *Bernard Wells*, of Holme Hall *2169*, by his father, *Bernard*. She eloped with him [1618].

Mountjoy/Monjoy: *An origin name:* Montjoie (Monschau since 1920) *50°33'N 6°15'E*. 'Manors': Brushfield *1672* [12th century]; Little Longstone *1871* [1272-1307] gift of *Edward I* [1272-1307], brought by *Isolda Mountjoy*, heiress to *Sir John Blount* together with Winster *2460* [15th century]. 'Justice of the Peace': *William Blount, Lord Mountjoy* for Derbyshire, Hertfordshire and Staffordshire [1532]. *Figure 3*, Overseas Connections, refers.

Mulgrave: 'Earl' [1626] *Edmund Sheffield*. *An origin name:* <u>Mulgrave</u> Castle *8412*, North Yorkshire. Explorer of the Blue John Mine *1583* who entertained miners to dinner in the cavern.

Naule: <u>Blacksmith in Litton:</u> *1675 Robert* [about 1634].

Needham: *A residence name:* OE: <u>ned</u> = hardship + <u>ham</u> = a homestead *or An origin name:* <u>Needham</u> *2281*, Norfolk. <u>Marriage</u>: *Dorothy* to *John Dakyn* [1541]; they lived at Snitterton Manor House *2760*. *Ellis* the notoriouos manager of 'Cressbrook' Mill *1773*.

Neville: *An origin name:* Neu-ville (New town) *48°5'N 2°3'E*. 'Earl' of Westmoreland [1397] alternative date [1461]. 'Manors': Ashford *1969 John* [1408] by heiress. *Bess of Hardwick* [1549] persuaded *Sir William Cavendish* to buy it from the *Nevilles*; Eyam *2176 Thomas*, Lord Furnival, [1383] by heiress, *Joan*. *Figure 3*, refers

Newcastle: *Cavendish* 'Marquis' [1643], 'Duke' [1665].

Newdigate: *An origin name:* <u>Newdigate</u> *2042*, Shropshire. 'Sheriff': Of Derbyshire: *Francis* [1880]. <u>Hall</u>: Derwent *2383*.

Newton: *A residence name:* OE: <u>niowe</u> = new + '<u>ton</u>' = a farmstead *or An origin name* from one of 31 places in 23 counties most probably in Cheshire eg *5059 & 5274*. *William*, the carpenter-poet, builder of Cressbrook Mill *1772* destruction by fire [1783] made him and his wife destitute but *Anna Seward*, poet "Swan of Lichfield" and one of his godmothers found him employment in Monsal Dale Mill *1871*. "Minstrel/Poet of the Peak", born Cockey Farm, Abney *1979* [25/11/1750], died Tideswell *1575* [3/11/1830] aged **80.**

Norfolk: 'Duke' of See *FitzAlan-Howard*.

Norman: *An origin name for settlers:* <u>Norman</u>(dy) or Scandinavian Settlers called themselves: *noromaor* NB Normanwood *0078*. 'Moiety manor': ⅓rd Beeley *2667* [1734] purchased from the *Gilberts* of Locko *4038*.

Nussey: *An origin name: from* <u>Nussey</u> Green *0361*, North Yorkshire. *Ellen*, a friend of *Charlotte Bronte* [1816-55] and daughter of the vicar.

Oldfield: *A residence name:* OE: <u>eald</u> = old + <u>feld</u> = a pasture. Mother of *William Bagshawe*, "Apostle of the Peak".

Olivier: *An allegiance name:* <u>Olivier</u> was one of *Charlemagne's* paladins, faithful friend of *Roland*, to whom many romantic exploits were attributed. See *Rowland*. <u>Hall and residence</u>: Ashford in the Water *1969*.

Padley: *A residence name:* <u>Padda's</u> + OE: '<u>ley</u>' = a clearing. 'Knight': Of Derbyshire returned to Parliament *Roger* [1352]. <u>Builder of church</u>: *Joan* Stoney Middleton *2275* as a thank offering for delivering her husband at Agincourt [1415]. <u>Battle</u>: *Roger* knighted at Agincourt [1415] for taking prisoner a marshal of France. 'Manor': <u>Padley</u> *2579* [14th century].

Paunton: *A compound characteristic + residence name:* ANF: <u>paunch</u> = paunchy [large] + OE <u>tun</u> = a farmstead. 'Manor': Tideswell *1575* [16th-17th centuries].

Pegge: *An occupation name:* ME: <u>pegge</u> = peg [maker *and* vendor]. 'Manor': Hathersage purchased [16th century].

Pembroke: See *Herbert* and *FitzHerbert*.

Peploe: *A residence name:* OE: <u>pybbell</u> = pebble + <u>hlaw</u> = hill *or An origin name:* <u>Peplow</u> *6324*, Shropshire. *Margaret*, mother of *Elizabeth Fynney*. *Peploes* possibly bought Stoney Middleton *2375* from the *Ashtons*.

Peverell: *A characteristic name:* OF: <u>pevre</u> = pepper [peppery]. <u>Genealogy</u>: Either an illegitimate son, or brother, of *King William I*, William the Conqueror, Duke of Normandy or illegitimate son of *Maud*, daughter of *Ingleric* the Saxon whose husband was *Randulph Peverell* standard bearer to *Robert*, the father of *William I*. A prominent tenant of Castleton *1583* entrusted with protecting a source of wealth. 'Manors': Given to *William* by *King William I* (*The Conqueror*) [1086] but forfeited in [1154] for the alleged poisoning of *Ranulf*. Abney *1979*; Bakewell *2168*; Bradwell *1781*; Castleton *1583*; Chatsworth *2670*; Nether Haddon *2266* and Over Haddon *2066*; Hazelbadge *1780*; Highlow *2180*; Little Hucklow *1678*; Litton, *1675*; One Ash *1665*; Thornhill *1983*; Tideswell *1575*; Eyam *2176* [1100-35] gift of *King Henry I*. Total manors, including the Peak area gifts = 162. 'Honour'.

Pickford: *A residence name:* OE: <u>pic</u> = pike + <u>forda</u>. <u>Entrepreneur</u>: [1670] *Thomas* divested of his estate by *Oliver Cromwell* so he diversified into road repair using 'packhosres' to carry gritstone from Goytsclough Quarry *0173*. <u>Memorial</u>: 'cross': Sergeant *Joseph*, Notts & Derby Regiment, killed in action [12/10/1918] at Neuvilly 49°10'N 5°04'E, Church of St John the Baptist, Chelmorton [1200] *1169*. 'Manor': Sheldon *1768* [1216-72].

Piers Gaveston: 'Castellan': Peak castle *1583* [1307]. 'Manor': Castleton *1583* [1307-27] gift of *King Edward II*.

'Plantagenet': 'Earl' of Kent. 'Castellan': Peak Castle *1583 Edward* Prince [1250] *Joan* [1328]. 'Manor': Ashford in the Water *1969 Edmund* [1319] gift of *Edward II* [1307-27].

Plumpton: *An origin name:* <u>Plumpton</u> *3732*, Lancashire. <u>Supporters</u>: Lancastrians [15th century]. 'Sheriff': Of Derbyshire: *William* [1453]. <u>Wardship</u> of 1 year old heiress and arranged marriage to son of *Sir William Plumpton*: *Foljambe* bought it from *Sir John Leake* about [1388]. <u>Marriages</u>: *Robert* to *Alice Foljambe*, daughter of *Sir Godfrey* + *Margaret* [1401]. *Robert* pledged his daughter *Margaret* to *Arthur Eyre* in consideration of 250 marks (£165) and £2 50 to be allowed out of each instalment for her keep. Letter dated Valentine's day [1499-1500]. Daughter *Anne* married *Sir Thomas Fitzherbert*. 'Manors': <> Edensor *2468*; <> Hassop *2272* sold by *Sir Robert* to *Catherine Dymoke* wife of *Stephen Eyre* [1498]; Stanton *2563* [uncertain date] gift; <> Wormhill *1274*. 'Mesne manor': Chelmorton *1169*. <u>Key</u>: <> *Sir Robert* by heiress, *Alice Foljambe* (age 1 year) [1388].

Pole: *A residence name:* OE: <u>pol</u> = pool. <u>Member of Parliamant</u>: *John* of Hartington *1360* [1377].

Prime: *A characteristic name:* OF = excellent. 'Moiety manor': ½ Bamford *2083* [19th century].

Raven: Saxon Lord of Stanton *2563*. 'Moiety Manor' before the Norman Conquest.

Ridel: *An origin name:* either Rydale *5982*, Yorkshire or Rydal *3606*, Cumbria. <u>Children</u>: *Matilda*, mother of *Ralph Shirley*. <u>Marriage</u>: *Maud* to *Richard Bassett* [1100-54]; Hathersage *2380* estates in her dowry. 'Manor': Hathersage *2380* [11th century].

Robinson: *A given name:* <u>Diminutive of Robert</u>. 'Moiety manor': ½ Bamford *2083* [19th century].

Rocliffe: *A residence name:* ME: *rok* = a rock = OE: *clif*. 'Moiety manors': ½ Edensor *2468 Robert* [15th century] and ½ Stanton *2563* with *John Sotehill* [15th century] by 'rascality'.

Rollesley: *A residence name:* Latin: *rota* = a [round] wheel + OE: *'ley'* = a clearing. 'Manor': Little Rowsley *2566 Henry de* [1189-99], transferred to *Sir William Kniveton* on his marriage to the heiress *Matilda Rollesley* about [1600].

Roper: *An occupation name:* OE: *rap* = rope [maker]. 'Manor': Middleton by Youlgreave *1963* with *Howe* [1771].

Rossington: *A residence name:* OE: *rosing* = enclosure on a moor + *tun* = a farmstead *or An origin name:* Rossington *6298*, West Yorkshire. 'Manor': Youlgreave *2064* [uncertain date] between the *Shirley* and *Gilbert* ownerships.

Rowe: *A residence name:* ME: *row* [by] hedgerow or a row [of houses]. Memorial: Youlgreave *1963*, All Saints *Roger* died [1613].

Rowland: *A residence name 2072 or A loyalty name: Roland*, one of *Charlemagne's* generals, whose heroic exploits in the Battle of Roncesvalles *43°0'N 1°16'W* [15/08/778] defeated the Moors before he was killed. The Chanson de Roland was copied in England about [1150] *'Olivier'*. Residence: *Godfrey*, Longstone Hall *1871* [1403]. Raided by *Sir Thomas Wendesley* accompanied by the Vicar of Hope *1783* and accomplices who captured 'squire' *Godfrey*, imprisoned him in Peak Castle *1583*, starved him for 6 days and cut off his right hand [1403]. Marriage: *Godfrey's* heiress to *Staffords* of Eyam *2176*.

Rowlandson: *An allegiance name:* See *Rowland* of Bakewell *2168*. Tutor: To *William Bagshawe*, "Apostle of the Peak".

Russell: *An appearance name:* OF: *roussel* = red hair. Builder: Ilam Hall, remodeller of village *1350 Jesse Watts*, manufacturer [1821-26].

Rutland: 'Duke' of See *Manners*.

Sacheverell: *An occupation name.* ML: *sacer* = holy + *everra* = cleansed + *capella* = chapel. High standing with *Henry VIII* [1509-47], *Sir Richard* at the 'Field of the Cloth of Gold'. 'Knights': Of Derbyshire returned to Parliament: *John* [1448], [1449], *William* [1461], [1479], [1479] (twice in the same year), [1480]. 'Sheriffs': Of Derbyshire: *Henry* [1531], [1542], [1595], *Jacinth* [1622], *George* [1709]. Marriage: *John* to *Statham* heiress [Snitterton Manor *2760*]. Sacheneverell Cottage Birchover *2462*. 'Manors': Snitterton *2760* by heiress [15th century] sold ½ to *Colonel John Milward* and ½ to *Shores*. Stoke *2376* purchased from the *Bullocks* [1656].

Sanders: *Diminutive name of Alexander.* Crime: *Roger* was charged with poaching at Castleton [1199-1216]. 'Sheriff': Of Derbyshire and Nottinghamshire [1503] *Sir John* [1423-95]. Steward: High Peak *Sir John* [1485-1508]. 'Manor': Middleton by Youlgreave *1963* [18th century].

Savage: *A characteristic name:* OF: *sauvage* = savage. 'Manor': Tissington *1752* by descent; held until death of last male heir. *William* [1259].

Savil(l)e: *An origin name:* Sainville *48°25'N 1°54'E*. 'Sheriff': Of Derbyshire: *George* [1699]. Last of the line: *George* died [1734] Beeley Manor *2667* left to a niece who married a *Gilbert* of Locko *4038*. 'Manors': Beeley *2667 William* 2nd 'Marquis' of Halifax [1687] purchased from the *Greaves*; Eyam *2176* [1616] by heiress *Mary*, Countess of Pembroke, then transferred to Earl of Burlington by *Dorothy Savile* heiress [1700]. 'Moiety manor': ⅓rd Monyash *1566* [1638] purchased from the *Earl of Kent*. *Figure 3*, Overseas Connections, refers.

Scarsdale: 'Viscount' See *Curzon*.

Senior: *A characteristic name:* OF: *seigneur* = lord [peasant with airs and graces]. Memorial: *Robert* Church of St Michael, Hathersage *2380* about [1459]. 'Moiety manor': *Richard* ¼ Wensley *2661* purchased from *Lettuce de Wendesley (nee Needham)* [1603].

Sha(c)kerley: *An occupation name:* OE: *sceacel* = shackle [maker] + *'ley'* = a clearing. 'Manors': Calver *2374 Rowland* [1485-1509]; Little Longstone *1871 Richard* purchased from the *Blounts* [1474], sold to *Bess of Hardwick* about [1550].

Sharpe, Cecil James: [22/11/1858-23/06/1924] Folk music collector. Morris Dancing Winster *2460*.

Sheldon: *A residence name: 1768.* OE: *scylf* = shelf + *'dun'* = a hill. Theatre: *Gilbert*, had connections with the Sheldonian Theatre, Oxford. Politics: *Gilbert* used his homes as retreats during the Cromwellian Commonwealth Interregnum [1649-60]. Land: One Ash 'Grange' *1665* [1544] purchased from the *Beresfords*. Farms, arable and pastoral, and homesteads in the Elton *2260*, Gratton *1960*, Middleton *1963*, Youlgreave area *2064*. Marriages: *Birds* of Bakewell *2168* and *Simpsons*.

Shirley: *A origin name:* Shirley *2141*, South Derbyshire. OE: *shire moot* + *'ley'* = a clearing. 'Sheriff': Of Derbyshire: *Ralph* [1497], son of *Matilda Ridel*, a daughter of *Lord Hathersage*. Battles: *Sir Thomas* at Crecy [1346] and Poitiers [1356]; *Sir Ralph* at Agincourt [1415]; *Sir Hugh* at Shrewsbury [1403]. 'Forester in fee': Peak Forest: Edale portion, junior member [1509-47]. End of male line: [15th century]. Heiress married *John Sacheverell* of Ible *2457*. 'Feuding families'. 'Manors': Snitterton *2760* [uncertain date]; Youlgreave *2064* [1272-1307].

Shore: *A residence name:* OE: *scora* = a bank [steep slope]. 'Moiety manor': ½ Snitterton *2760* purchased from *Sacheverells* [17th century]; passed to the *Hodgkinsons* and then to the *Banks*.

Shrewsbury: 'Earl' of See *Talbot*

Shuttleworth: *An origin name:* from Shuttlewood *4672*, North-east Derbyshire. 'Manor': Padley *2579* [19th century] by heiress. 'Moiety manor': ⅓rd Bamford *2083* [19th century].

Simpson Revd *John*: 'Manor': Stoke *2376* [17th/18th centuries]. Heiress *Elizabeth* took it in her dowry on her marriage to *Henry Bridgeman*.

Siward: A Dane, 'Earl' of Northumbria [1023-43], successor to *Siward*. 'Manor': Wormhill *1274*.

Slack: *A residence name:* ON: *slakki* = a narrow valley *or An origin name:* Slack *9828*, West Yorkshire. Of Edale *1285*. Deputy officials for *Meverells* and *Shirleys* [1509-47]. Hall: Bowden *0681* purchased from *Hibbersons* [17th/ 18th century]. 'Manor': Thornhill *1983 Adam* 1602 purchased from the *Eyres*; sold [1611].

Slater Revd *Leonard*: Occupant of Bakewell Hall *2168* about [1890].

Sleigh: *An origin name*: ON: *sletta* = a level field. Several generations in Hartington *1360*. Charles Cotton Hotel was known as Sleigh Arms until about [1900].

Slingsby: *A habitation name:* ON: *slengr* = idle + *byr* = a farm *or An origin name:* Slingsby *6974*, North Yorkshire. Politics: *Sir Henry* allegedly stayed at Offerton Hall *2181* when trying to raise support for the Stuarts [1657-58].

Smith: *An occupation name:* OE: *smio* = to strike [metal]. ON: *smithr* OHG: *smid*. 'Manors': Snitterton *2760*, Stoke *2376*. Pastoral farming: *Thomas* of Blore *1349* selling 55 head of cattle and 75 head of sheep at Blore **annual** sale of store stock [8/10/1839 10 00 a.m.].

Somerset: 'Baron' *Botetourt* created [1305] Abeyant [1984]. Marriages: Daughter of *Joane + John Botetourt* married *Sir Richard Swynburne*. *Alice*, daughter of *Sir Richard*, married *John Helyon*. 'Manor': Bakewell *2168 John* [1383] by co-heiress, *Joane De Gernon* on the death of her father, *Sir John De Gernon*.

Sotehill: OD & ON: *sati* = a well known person + OE: *hyll*. 'Moiety manors': ½ Edensor *2468 John* [15th century]; ½ Stanton *2563 Henry* with *Brian Rocliffe* [15th century] by 'rascality' of *Sir William Plumpton*.

Spencer: *An occupation name:* ME: *spense* = a larder [servant]. 'Manor': Padley *2579* date uncertain [? 18th century] by heiress.

Stafford: *A residence name:* OE: *steo* = a landing place + *forda or An origin name:* Stafford *9223*. *Toenei*, cousin of *William I*, changed his name to *Stafford*. Marriages: To *Godfrey Rowland's* heiress. Prodigiously rich *Gertrude* to a grandson of *Catherine Eyre*. Gifts: 13 manors in Derbyshire and 131 in other counties by *William I* about [1066]. 'Manors': * Bretton *2078*; * Calver *2374*; Foolow *1976* probably purchased from *William de Morteyne* [1283]; Rowland *2172*. *Gifts of *King John* [1199-1216]. 'Moiety manor': ?⅔rd Tideswell *1575* representative of *De Marchington* and *De Turvill* [1377-99].

Stanley: *A residence name:* OE: *stan* = stone + *'ley'* = a clearing *or An origin name:* Stanley *4140*, South-east Derbyshire or Staffordshire *9252*. Vicar: Eyam *2176 Thomas* [1644-60] until removed and demoted to curate for dissent. He subsequently served under *Mompesson* during the plague [1665]. 'Manor': Longendale *0397 Sir William* of Holt *0069* granted by *Henry VII* [1487] held until [1495].

Stanshope: *A residence name:* OE: <u>stan</u> = stone + <u>hop</u> = an enclosure. [17th century] inherited Beresford *1259* 'manor' and hall when the last of original *Beresford* family died. A *Stanshope* daughter eloped with the father of *Charles Cotton*.

Statha(u)m: *A residence name* OE: <u>staed</u> = a landing-stage. 'Knight': Of Derbyshire returned to Parliament *Ralph* (Supported, with *Edward Appleby*, the impeachment of a minister of the Crown for malpractice [1376], [1365], [1372], [1376], [1378]. 'Sheriffs': Of Derbyshire: *John* [1445], *Henry* [1475], *Wigley* [1726]. <u>Marriages</u>: *John Sacheverell; Sir Robert* to *Elizabeth* heiress of the *Vavasours* [1327-77], *Thomas* to *Barbara Meverell* about [1707]. <u>Memorial</u>: Church of St John the Baptist, Tideswell *1575, Thomas*. 'Manor': Litton *1675* [1707] purchased from the *Uptons*.

Stevenson: *An allegiance name:* <u>Stephen</u> the first Christian martyr. <u>Builder of private residence</u>: Now the Peacock Hotel *John*, "man of affairs" to *Grace, Lady Manners*. <u>Hall</u>: Long Lee *0188 John*, the name over the entrance [1652]. 'Manor': Elton *2260* [1558-1603].

Stratford: *A residence name:* <u>by a ford</u>. 'Manor': Calver *2374* [1485-1509].

Strelley: *An origin name:* <u>Strelley</u> *5042*, Nottinghamshire. <u>Courtiers</u> of *King John* [1215]. <u>Brough mill</u>: *1882* in return for attending the king on horseback, whenever he came to Derbyshire carrying a heron falcon. 'Knight': Of Derbyshire returned to Parliament: *Robert* [1407], [1420]. 'Sheriff': Of Derbyshire: *Robert* [1446], [1452], [1464], *Nicholas* [1529], [1538]. 'Manor': Hazelbadge *1780* [1327-77] by heiress; sold to *Vernons* [1421] by *Sir Robert Strelley*.

Streona: *Edric* ealdorman of Mercia about [990].

Sutton: *A residence name*: OE: <u>sud</u> = south + '<u>ton</u>' = a farmstead *or An origin name:* most likely places Nottinghamshire *6784 & 7637*, Staffordshire *7622*. <u>Last of the line</u>: *Thomas* died [about 1611] aged **84.** 'Sheriffs': Of Derbyshire: *Henry* [1551], *James* [1842]. 'Mesne manor': Over Haddon *2066* [uncertain date]; a branch of a Cheshire family

Swain/Swein, Sweyn Forkbeard: A Danish 'thane'/thegn, Lord of Abney Manor *1979* King of Denmark [?986-1014], father of *Cnut/Canute* died [1013]. Conquered England forcing *Ethelred II*, the Unready, [979-1013] to flee in [1013]. King of England for a few months prior to his death in [1013]. Swain's Head and Greave *1397* See also 'Beorn'. 'Manor': Abney *1979*.

Swinburne: *A residence name:* OE: <u>swin</u> = swine + <u>burna</u> = a stream. 'Manor': Bakewell *2168 Sir Richard* [14th century] by heiress, daughter of *John Botetourt*.

Swynfen: *Margaret* married *Sir William Vernon* [1422-61].

Talbot: *Possible hunting connection; talbot is the name of a hound in Chaucer* [1386]. 'Earl' of Shrewsbury [1442] England; [1446] Ireland; [1784] Great Britain. <u>Battle</u>: *Sir John* defeated by *Joan of Arc* at Patay [1429]. <u>Marriages</u>: *Gilbert* (**aged 14**) to *Mary Cavendish* [1568]. *Elizabeth* (*Bess of Hardwick*) [1518-1608] (2nd husband) *Sir William Cavendish* (4th wife) [1545]. <u>Conflicts</u>: 360 poor Tideswell *1575* cottagers complained about enclosures by the *Earl of Shrewsbury* [1576] depriving them of pastures. *Wilson* of Broomhead Hall *2496* led Bradfield *2692* freeholders against *Gilbert* in a campaign against tithes. 'Manors': Bamford *2083* possibly purchased [14th century]; Baslow *2572*; Brushfield *1672* [1537] gift of *King Henry VIII**; Eyam *2176 Sir John* [1406] (1st Earl born [1388] died [1453]); Monyash *1566* [1460]; One Ash *1665 Francis* [1509-47] gift of *Henry VIII*, and Padley *2579* [uncertain date]. * Dissolution of the monsteries beneficiaries. 'Mesne manor': Chelmorton *1169* [1509-47] gift of *King Henry VIII*.

Thacker: *An occupation name:* ON: <u>pak</u> = thatch. Received *Columbell* lands by gift from *Marbury* widow about [1673]. He sold them in parcels some of which were purchased by *Richard Arkwright*.

Thomas, Eustace: A Manchester business man. First Derwent watershed bog trotter; 38 miles in 11.5 hours [1918]. Designer of the Thomas stretcher after an accident on Laddow Rocks *0501* [1928].

Thornhill: *A residence name: 1983* OE: <u>torn</u>= thorn + <u>hyll</u> = a hill. 'Sheriffs': Of Derbyshire: *Bache* [1776], *William* [1836]. <u>Marriage</u>: *John* of Thornhill *1983* to *Marian Heaton* [1279]. <u>Crime</u>: *Major Richard* tried at the Old Bailey for killing *Sir Chomley Dering* in a duel after he suffered an unprovoked attack after both had dined at The Ivy, Hampden Court [7/4/1711]. Memorial: Holy Trinity *Church, Stanton in the Peak *2464*, *Henry Bache* died [1822]. Gifts: Bells to Youlgreave Church. *2064* & * [1839] Stanton Church. 'Manors': Birchover *2462* [date uncertain]; Elton *2260* [17th century]; Gratton *1960 John* [1723] by purchase; Middleton *1963*; Stanton *2563 John* [1698] by *Bache* heiress; Thornhill *1983* possibly [12th century] on the death of *William Pole Thornhill*, transferred to *Henry Francis Hurlock* [1875]; Winster *2460*; Youlgreave *2064*. All the manors were in Youlgreave 'Parish'

Thorp(e): *A residence name: 1550*. ON: torp = hamlet or village. 'Manor': Hathersage *2380* by purchase [1450].

Tibetot: *An allegiance name: Thibaut IV (II of Champagne)* almost established a kingdom in England [1102 -52]. 'Manor': Elton *2260* [12th century] and possibly Stanton *2563* [12th century].

Tiptoft: Probably *Tibetot* anglicised. 'Manor': Padley *2579* [uncertain date].

Topcliffe: *A residence name:* OE: topp = top = clif *or An origin name:* Topcliffe *3976*, North Yorkshire. Espionage: *Richard* The spy whose evidence led to the martyrdom of Roman Catholic priests *Nicholas Garlick* and *Robert Ludlam* and to *John FitzHerbert* dying in prison [1588].

Tracey: *An origin name:* Tracy le Mont *49°28'N 3°01'E*. 'Manor': Calver *2374* [1485-1509].

Turner: of Derby. 'Moiety manor': ½ Snitterton *2760* by heiress [17th century].

Turvill: *An origin name: possibly* Tourville la Riviere *49°20'N or* Tourville les Ifs *49°42'N 0°24'E*. 'Manor': Tideswell *1575* by co-heiresses [1216-72]. *Figure 3*, Overseas Connections refers.

Twigge: *An appearance name:* OE: = thin. *John* resident of Holme Hall *2169* about [1750]. Marriage: Wife one of the last of the *Foljambes*.

Tyrell: *A characteristic name:* stubborn. 'Manor': Bakewell *2168 Humphrey* [14th century] by *Isabel Helyon*, heiress of *Humphrey* + *Isabel* who took Bakewell *2168* to *Sir Roger Wentworth*.

Uchtred/Uhtred/Uhtread: A Saxon 'Thane' (thegn) Earl of Northumbria. Joined with *Edmund* to devastate Cheshire, Staffordshire and Shropshire. He was murdered by *Thurbrand the Hold* [1016] 'Hold'. The earldom of Northumbria was given to *Eric of Norway* by *Cnut/Canute*: [1017-35]. *Eric* was an ancestor of the *Bradshaw* family and possibly became lord of Elton Manor *2260*. Marriage: A daughter, or grand daughter, to a *Foljambe* about [1066].

Upton: *A residence name:* OE: up = upper + 'ton' = a farmstead *or An origin name:* Upton *4069*, Cheshire or *7354* or *7476* Nottinghamshire. 'Manor': Litton *1675* from the *Bradshawes* [1686].

Vaux: See *Gilbey*.

Vavasour: 'Baron' [1299] *Originally a* status *name:* OF: vavasour = below a baron. [1160-1230] a prosperous Yorkshire, Roman Catholic family; owners of Peter's Post section of Thevesdale quarry, Tadcaster *4843* which supplied stone for York Minster [13th century]. 'Manor': Hazelbadge *1780* [1307-27] until transferred on the marriage of *Elizabeth* to *Sir Richard Strelley* [1327-77].

Vernon: *An origin name:* Chatellerie de Vernon *49°6'N 1°28'W*. 'Duke' of Rutland [1703] Hazlebadge branch of family extinct [end of 17th century]. 'Knights': Of Derbyshire returned to Parliament; *Richard* [1389-1451], [1422], [1426], [1433]; (Speaker and Member of the Parliament of "Bats" [1426], *Fulk* [1436], *William* [1441], [1449], [1450], [1467], {Married *Margaret Swynfen*}, *Henry* [1477], *George* [1541] "King of the Peak", *George* [1831]. 'Sheriffs': 1. Of Derbyshire: *Sir Richard* [1425], *Henry* [1504], *John* [1523], [1524], [1527], *Edward* [1627], *George* [1664]. 2. Of Staffordshire *Sir Richard Vernon* [1416], [1427]. Stewardships 1. [1424] High Peak and 2. *John Mowbray's* 'Duke' of Norfolk, Derbyshire estates *Sir Richard*. Marriage: *Dorothy* to *John Manners* [1567]. Memorials: All Saints, Bakewell *2168 John* died [1477], *Sir George* died [1567], "King of the Peak" + two wives. 'Chantry': at Bakewell *2168* founded by *Vernon* family. 'Feuding families'. Hall: Haddon *Richard de* given a licence to fortify his house [1199]. Battles: *Sir Richard* beheaded as a traitor after the battle of Shrewsbury [23/07/1403]. *Cecilia Vernon*, mother of *Sir Edmund Cokayne* who was killed at Shrewsbury. 'Manors': Bakewell *2168 Sir Henry* [1502], purchased from *Sir Roger Wentworth*; Baslow *2572* gift of *Henry de Curzon* [1330]; Haddon *2366*; Great Rowsley *2566*; Hartle *2764* purchased from the impecunious *Cokaynes*; Hazelbadge *1780 Sir Richard* [1421] purchased from *Sir Robert Strelley*; Nether Haddon *2266* [1327-77] purchased; Over Haddon *2066 William* [1195], son of *Warine*, by heiress on marriage to *Avicia,* daughter of *William de Avenel*; Stanton Lees *2563.* 'Moiety manor': ⅓rd Tideswell *1575. Figure 3*, Overseas Connections, refers.

Verus: *Caesar Julius* Builder or re-builder of Brough [AD158] *1882.*

Vicars: *George.* The Eyam *2176* tailor bitten by the rat flea, *xenopsylla cheopsis* (or *yersinia pestis*), which jumped out of the bale of cloth delivered from London [1665]. 'Delta 32', *Margaret Blackwell*, 'Earl' of Devonshire, *Elizabeth Hancock, Marshall Howe.*

Wake: *A characteristic name:* ON: *vaka* = vigilant. 'Manor': Little Hucklow *1678 Bernard* [date uncertain].

Wallesby: *An origin name:* ANF: *waleis.* 'Moiety Manor': ⅓rd Bamford *2083* [19th century].

Ward: *An occupation name:* OE: *weard* = a guard. *John*, deerkeeper to the Lord of Haddon *2366* [1527]. He was dismissed six times and died drunk. His son succeeded him. *Bert. (G H B)*, organiser of the Mass Trespass [1932] when the 9th Duke of Devonshire turned his gamekeepers on the trespassers. Ward's piece *1585.*

Warner: *John.* physician, sold the 'Chantry' of Snitterton *2760* to *Richard de Wendesley* [1531].

Warren(e): 'Earl' of Surrey *An occupation name;* OF: = breeder of game 'warren'. 'Castellans': Of Peak Castle *1583*: *William* [1289], *John* [1310]. Execution: *Alice*, daughter of *William*, sister and heir of *John* was executed when Arundel Castle was granted to *Edmund*, Earl of Kent, son of *Edward I* [1326]. 'Manor': Castleton *1583* [1307-27].

Watson: *A given name:* ME: *Diminutive of Walter.* Founder: Black marble works at Ashford-in-the-Water *1969 Henry* [1748]. Inventor: Water-powered multiple stone saw [1748]. Mine owner and entrepreneur: Blue John mine at Castleton *1583* [1756]. Memorial: Ashford in the Water, Holy Trinity Church *1969 Henry* died [1780].

Wells *A habitation name:* OE & ME *wella* = a stream. Hall: *Bernard* built Holme Hall *2169* [1626]. Marriages: One of his co-heiresses, *Anne*, to *Robert Eyre* of Highlow *2180.* He forbade his son, *Bernard*, to marry *Anne Morton* of Hazleford *2379,* "The Maid of Derwent". They eloped but *Bernard* drowned in a stream according to *W Wood* in Traditions of the Peak [1862]. Memorials: *Bernard* died [1658] Bakewell Church of All Saints. His son, also *Bernard*, died [1618] Church of St Lawrence, Eyam *2176.*

We(a)ndesley/Wensley: *A residence name:* 2681 *Wendel's* + OE: '*ley*' = a clearing. 'Knight': of Derbyshire returned to Parliament: *Sir Thomas de* [1382], [1384], [1398], [1391]. Crimes: Aided by the *Vicar* of Hope *1783* and accomplices, raided Longstone Hall *1972*, captured *Godfrey Rowland*, imprisoned him in Peak Castle *1582*, starved him for 6 days, then cut off his right hand [1403]. *Richard* summoned for bigamy [1564]. Battle: *Sir Thomas,* a Lancastrian, killed at Shrewsbury [23/07/1403]. 'Bakewell'. Last of the line: *Richard de* purchased Chantry of Snitterton *2760* from the *Warners*. Property dealings: Buy to let: Snitterton Manor House *2760* eg to *Foljambes* and *Harpurs.* Lettuce Wendesley (nee Needham) sold moiety of Wensley *2661* to *Harpur* [1591], then ¼ of the remainder to *Richard Senior, Roger Columbell,* ½ to *Sir John Manners.* Purchase: Snitterton 'chantry' at the Dissolution of the Monasteries about [1531]. Memorial: All Saints, Bakewell *Sir Thomas 2168,* who died at the battle of Shrewsbury [1403] 'Alabaster'.

Wentworth: *A residence name:* OE: *wintra* = winter + *word* = enclosure *or* OLG '*wort*' = an open space in a village *or An origin name:* Wentworth *3898*, South Yorkshire. 'Manor': Bakewell *2168 Sir Roger* [14th century] by heiress, daughter of *Humphrey + Isabel Tyrell.* [1502] sold to *Sir Henry Vernon.*

Wenunwyn: Lord of Powisland. 'Manor': Ashford in the Water *969* gift of *King John* [1199]. His son, *Griffin*, founded 'chantries' at Ashford *1969* [1257] and Great Longstone *2071* [1251].

Whinyates: *A residence name*: OE: *wind* = windy + *pass.* Of Chellaston *3830*, South Derbyshire. Marriage: *Anne* to *William Bradshawe.*

White: *An appearance name:* OE: *whit* = white [hair]. Hall: Ashford in the Water *1969.* Marriage: *Mary* to *James Fynney* [1596].

William I: King [1066-87] The Conqueror. Royal 'demesne' 'manors': Ashford *1969*, Baslow *2572*, Beeley *2667*, Blackwell *1272*, Calver *2374*, Chelmorton *1169*, Eyam *2176*, Grindlow *1877*, Hassop *2272*,

Hope *1783*, Monyash *1566*, Nether Haddon *2266*, Little Rowsley *2566*, Rowland *2172*, Sheldon *1768*, Snitterton *2760*, Stoke *2376*, Taddington *1471*, Tideswell *1575*.

Wilson: Residence Broomhead Hall *2496*. Conflicts: Leader of Bradfield freeholders' *2692* compaign against 'tithes' and *Gilbert*, Earl of Shrewsbury. *Christopher* fined for failing to attend *Charles I's* coronation and be knighted [1600]; captain in the Parliamentary Army.

Winnington: *An origin name:* Winnington *6474*, Cheshire. Marriage: *Catherine* to *Henry Bradshaw*, daughter and co-heiress of *Ralph Winnington*. Hall: Offerton *2181*.

Wirgman: Builder: Hartington School: *1360 Augustus* about [1850]. Vicar: *Augustus* Church of St Giles, Hartington *1360* about [1850]. Memorial: Church of St Giles, Hartington *1360*, *Augustus*.

Woderofe/Woodroffe: *A characteristic name:* O & ME: *wod* = frenzied. High Peak 'forester in fee' *Robert* [1440]. Residents of Hope *1783*.

Wright: *An occupation name:* OE: *wyrta* = a craftsman. Residences: Longstone Hall *1871* about [1319], Eyam Hall *2176* [1735-present day]. Memorial: Church of St Giles, Longstone *1871*. 'Moiety manor': Beeley *2667* manor purchased from *Gilberts* of Locko [1734].

Wudia/Wodie: Saxon lord of Stanshope 'manor' *1354*.

Richard Arkwright 1732-92
Industrialist, Investor &
Inventor

"George Eliot" 1819-80
Dove Dale in "Adam Bede"

D H Lawrence 1885-1930
Griffe Grange and Ible in
"Wintry Peacock"

Creative Contributors to the Peak Heritage

Figure 3 Overseas Connections

```
                                            Antwerp/Anvers
                    FLANDERS                 Danvers
                            Quesnay
                             Cheney      Montjoie
                                          Mountjoy

         PICARDY
                        Mesnieres
                         Manners
     Tourville           Gournay
      Turvill            Gernon
         1,Bernay        Vernon
          Balguy         Vernon
              Ferriere
               Ferrars
           Mont Pincon
            Mompesson
   NORMANDY
            Mortagne
             Morteyne
                            Sainville
                             Savile
                              PARIS

     2. Bernay                Neuville
       Balguy                  Neville

     BERRY              BURGUNDY
     Berry
                                Citeaux
                               Cistercians

                                Cluny
                              Benedictines
```

Names of families are in *italics*, names of provinces in CAPITALS.

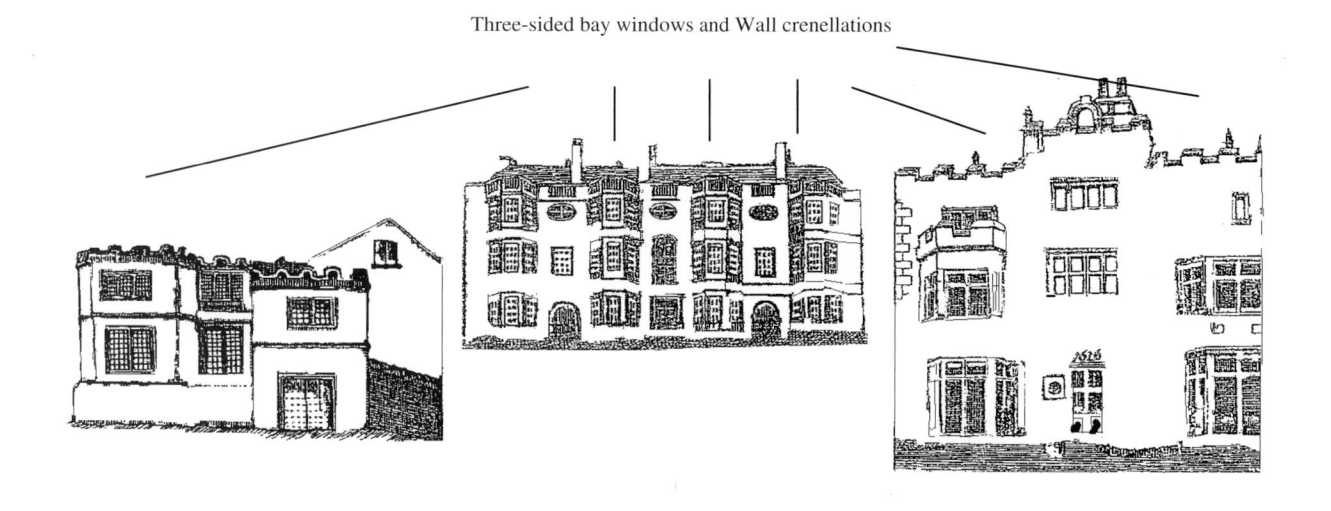

Three-sided bay windows and Wall crenellations

Highlow. Built in the 16th century. Eyre family property until **bought** by the Duke of Devonshire

Hassop. **Given** in 1853 by Dorothy Eyre to her husband, Colonel Leslie.

Home. Built 1626 by Bernard Wells. In Anne Wells' **dowry** when she married Robert Eyre

<u>Some Eyre Family Halls</u>

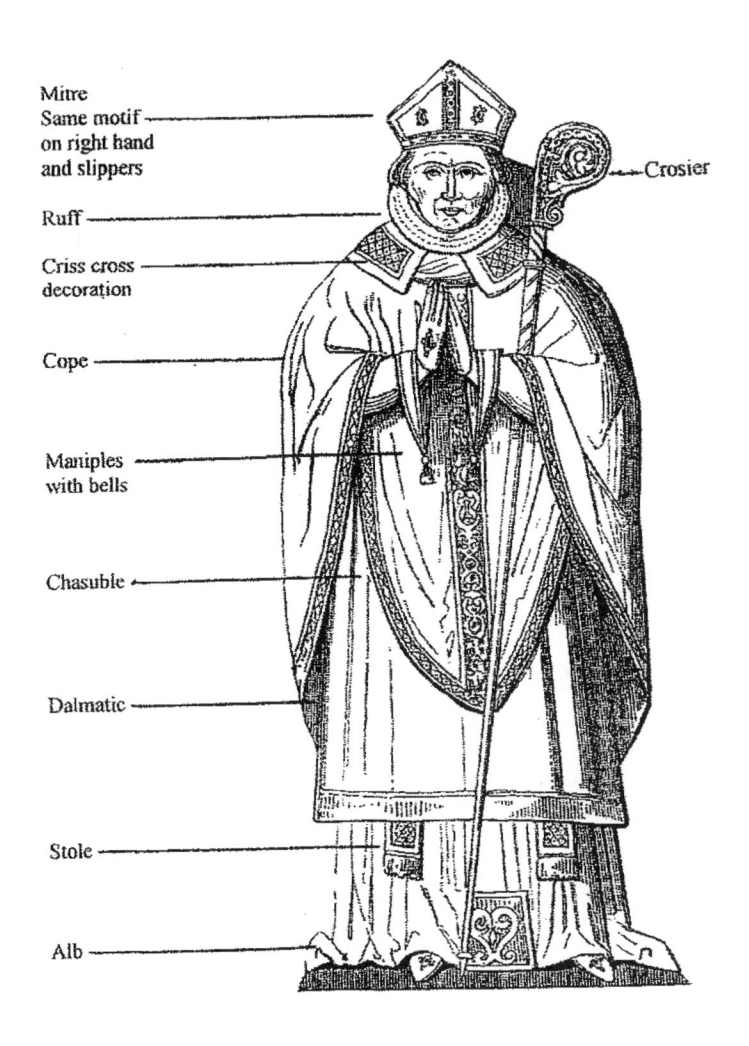

Robert Pursglove. Born in Tideswell. Died 1579. Founder of Almshouses and Tideswell Grammar School. Bishop of Hull 1560.
In the Church of St John the Baptist, Tideswell, there is a large engraved brass memorial plate of him wearing his vestments.

PEAK PLACES

Entries in this chapter provide more input into the Peak History network. Where the requisite information is available, entries use a possible meaning of a place name to gain some insight into its origin. Names and people connected with it, their land, buildings and resources facilitate tracing its subsequent development. As in the Natural World chapter, name and origin connections are under-lined in order to show their relationship. The majority of these places are still inhabited. The evolution of languages, and local dialects, caution against treating explanations of place and site name origins as definitive. *Figure 4*, Languages and Peak Place Names refers. Dates in the past, when these places were mentioned in documents, because land ownership and use changed, or prominent people associated with them, enables the past importance of places to be assessed.

In the absence of a single male heir, daughters became heiresses because inheritances were divided equally between them. Even when there was a male heir, daughters could still expect to receive land from fathers and elder brothers. In the absence of any heirs or heiresses property descended to nearest relations.

Abney: *1979. Abba's* well-watered land. Habenai [DB], Abbenaia [1200 *John*]. 'Manor': *Swain/Swein/Sweyn*,the Saxon; [1086] *William Peverell*; [1307-27] *Archers*; [1377-99] *Bagshawes*; [1593] *Francis Bradshaw* by purchase; [1597] *Alsop* by purchase from *Littons*; [1735] *Joshua Galliard* by *Vescis* heiress; [1789] *Charles Bowles* by heiress. House: A *Bagshawe* residence. Birthplace: Cockey Farm *1979 William Newton*, "Minstrel/Poet of the Peak" [25/11/1750] and builder of Cressbrook Mill *1773*.

Alport: *2164*. S: *ald* = old + Latin: *porta* = a gate [to a settlement – Youlgreave *2064*. Aldeport [1276 Edward I]. Christian worship: Nonconformist services held in a barn in a narrow part of the River Bradford valley after the Restoration of *Charles II* [1660] *2264*. Rock: 'Duke's red marble'.

Alport 'Castles': *1491*. S: *ald* = old + Latin: *porta* = a gate [River Alport valley route across the moor]. A large landslip. See also *0062*. Not 'castles' built by man. Farm *1391* Meeting place for 'Covenanters' evicted after the Act of Uniformity [1662] and for a Methodist 'Love feast' held annually since [1745].

Alsop en le Dale: *1655. In Aelle's* OE: *dael* = a 'dale' Elleshope [DB], Aleshop [1241 *Henry III*]. Hall: [16th century]. Normans: Doorway to the Church of St Michael and All Angels. Persecution: *Thomas Becon*, [1512-67] a Protestant, campaigner for girls' schools, sheltered in the church during Queen Mary's reign [1553-58].

Alston(e)field: *1355. Aelfstan's* + OE: *feld* = a field. Alstanesfeld [DB], Aenestanefelt [1179 *Henry II*]. 'Parish', 'Forest', and township. 'Manor': *William Malbanc*, + a baron of the *Earl of Chester*; + *Edmund Lancaster* [1216-72], NB [1270s] 3 lords simultaneously, *Vincent Mundy* about [1570], *John Harpur* [1595], *Sir George Crewe* (*Harpur-Crewe* family) rebuilder of Warslow Hall [1830] *0858*. Hall: [1587]. Church: Dedication by *St Oswald*, Archbishop of York of a church [892]. Stone coffins in the Church of St Peter. Built probably about [1100]. Abbey Endowment: Combermere *5844*. Pre-history: 'Neolithic' or 'Bronze Age' hammer found. Normans: Doorway of the church. Market: Charter [1308 *Edward II*]. Held regularly until about [1500]. Grant; To *John Harpur* [1595]. 'Guild': [1549]. Enclosure: Manorial waste land [1836]. 'Hawkers': under pressure from shopkeepers who paid higher taxes, petitioned against a proposal to abolish their licences [1782-83].

Alton: S: *ald* = old + '*ton*' = a farmstead. The coal seam surfacing at Chatsworth *3664* for 'adit' working.

Aldwark: *2357*. S: *ald* = old + *weorc* = work [building the fort] Aldeuuere [DB], Adewerk [1226 *Henry III*]. Pb 'Grange': *2358*.

Andle Stone: *2462*. Height: 5 metres (15 feet) Dialect: = anvil [shaped]. ? 'Bronze Age' circle

'Arbor' 'Low': *1663*. OF: *herbier* = grassy + OHG: *hlais* = a grave 'Bronze Age' or 'Neolithic' sanctuary. A 'henge' stone circle. Rocks: 'Barytes', 'Derbyshire Diamonds', 'Porphyry'.

Arrock: *1869*. Welsh: *arg* = bright [marble]. Rock: 'Marble' for *Henry Watson's* memorial in Holy Trinity Church, Ashford in the Water *1969* was quarried here. River Wye mill.

Ashford in the Water: *1969.* Either 1. OE: aesc = 'ash' tree + forda (River Wye) or 2. Black [like cinder ash] argillaceous limestone in the shale beds. Aisseford [DB]. Pb 'Manor': [1086] Royal 'demesne'; [1199] *Wenunwyn*, Lord Powisland; [1319] *Edmund Plantagenet* 'Earl' of Kent; *Sir Thomas Holland* by heiress *Joan*, "Fair maid of Kent"; [1408] *John Neville*, Earl of Westmoreland by heiress; [1550] *Sir William Cavendish* by purchase. Hall: Rookery [16th century]. Residence of *Milnes, Fynneys, Cheneys and Lord George Cavendish* [1874]. 'Portway': → Eyam *2176* via Great Longstone *2071*. In the early [19th century], at the junction of the Wye Valley *2168* and Edensor *2468* 'turnpikes'. Normans: 'Typanum' in Holy Trinity Church. 'Chantry': founded by *Griffin*, son of *Wenunwyn*. Rocks: 'Marbles': 'Anthraconite','Black Bird's Eye', 'Rosewood'. 'Chapel of ease' to Bakewell until [1872] Maiden garlands for unmarried girls [1750-1800]. Communications: Stage Coach House [1840]. Local rivalry: [1616] *Lord Cavendish* led his tenants against Monyash *1566*

Ashop: river *1289.* OE: aesc = 'ash' + hope = a valley. Aeschop. Essop [1215 *John*], Asshope [1229 *Henry III*].

Ashopton: *1986.* OE: aesc = 'ash' + hope = a valley (River Derwent) + 'ton' = a farmstead. Gift: *Sir William Avenell* to Dunstable Priory ('Dominican' friars) *0221* [1189-99]. Day trips: The Ashopton Inn (The Snake) was a day trip destination for Sheffield excursionists in old London omnibuses in [1874].

Aston: *1884* [DB] Estune bees. OE: east + 'ton' = a farmstead. Manor House: One of the *Balguy* residences dated [1578]. 'Bronze Age': Log boat found.

Bagshaw: *2168.* OE: bacga = badger + scaega = copse or thicket. Hall: [1684] A *Bagshawe* residence. Cavern *1680*, Dale *1566*.

Bakewell: *2168.* Be(a)deca's + OE: well = spring or stream or bad-kwell = bath spring. Badecanwiellan [924], Badecanwelle [949], Badevella [DB]. Pb 'Romans': Bath fed by warm thermal springs resulting from underground volcanic activity. 'Chalybeate' wells dried up. Anglo Saxons: [8th century] Anglian 'cross'. Site of a Saxon Church. Saxon coffins. Gift: 'Collegiate church' to the Dean and Chapter of Lichfield by *King John* [1192]. Bath House: [1697] built by Duke of Rutland in attempt to compete with 1st Duke of Devonshire's in Buxton. Battle: *Edward the Elder* held Castle Hill earthwork against Danish invaders [924]. Earthwork: Castle Hill built [920] by *Edward the Elder*, son of *Alfred the Great*. Memorials: *Sir Godfrey Foljambe* died [1366], founder of 'chantry' [1344], *Avena*, his wife (formerly *Ireland* of Hartshorne *3221*), died [1385]; *Sir Thomas Wendesley* killed [1403]; *John Dale*, barber-surgeon and two wives, *Basset Copwood* of Bubnell *2472*. 'Alabaster'. 'Manor': [1086] *William Peverell* forfeit to the Crown; *Ralph De Gernon* given by *King John*; [1383] *John Botetourt* by heiress, *Joane de Gernon*, wife; *Sir Richard Swynbourne* by heiress; *John Helyon* by heiress; *Humphrey Tyrell* by heiress; *Sir Roger Wentworth* by heiress; [1502] *Sir Henry Vernon* by heiress; [1565] *John Manners*, Duke of Rutland by purchase. Communications: 'Packhorse roads' and bridge [1664] from Hartington *1360* and Edensor *2468*. 'Portway' → Alport *2164*. Post horse route Chesterfield *3871*→ Bakewell *2168*→ Manchester *8397* [17th century] 'Turnpike [1815] → Buxton. 'Railway' Chinley *0382* → Derby *3435* [19th century]. 'Saltway' from Cheadle *0043* via Haddon *2366*. Stage coach Sheffield *3587* → Bakewell *2168* → Buxton *0673* as late as [1895]. White Horse Inn (Rutland Arms) [1804] rebuilt by fifth *Duke of Rutland* for coach travellers. [1828] was the height of coaching era. Hall: Bagshaw Hall built by *Thomas* [1684] died [1721]; tenants *Barkers* of Darley *2763*; *Revd Leonard Slater* about [1890]. Commerce: Market granted [1330]. Manufacturing: Elaborate Saxon stone crosses. *Ralph de Gernon* [1254]. Cotton mill started by *Richard Arkwright*. [1844] 10 hosiery machine frames. Philanthropy: St John's almshouses. Prominent inhabitants: *Bagshawe*. Pudding: Probably dates from [1859]. Rocks: 'chalcedony', 'clay', 'opal', 'wad'. [1393] minerals leased to *Stephen de Schaynton*.

Ballidon: *2055.* OE: baelg = bag [shaped] + 'dun' = a hill. Belidene [DB]. Quarry: 'Fluorite'. Normans: Parts of All Saints' Church. 'Barrow': Stone 'cists' found.

Bamford: *2083.* OE: beam [pedestrian plank] + forda. 'Manor': [1086] *Ralph Fitzhubert*; [1461-83] *Talbots*, 'Earls' of Shrewsbury; [1802] *Francis Evans*. 'Moieties': *Melland* and *Prime*; *Wallesby, Shuttleworth* and *Robinson*. Manufacturing: Corn until [1780] then cotton-mill on the River Derwent.

Barlborough: *4777.* North-east Derbyshire. *Dorothy Bunting* marriage.

Barleighford: *9464.* OE: barlic = barley + forda.

Bartomley: *9665.* OE: *barlic* = barley + '*ton*' = a farmstead + '*ley*' = a clearing. Romans: Jewellery – gold rings, gold chains with links of 'prez' found.

Baslow: *2572.* *Bassa's* + OHG: *hlais* = a grave. Basselau [DB]. Pb 'Manor': [1086] Royal 'demesne'; *Curzons*; *Avenells* of Haddon then [1195] *Bassets* by *Avenell* heiress; [1330] *Vernons* gift of *Henry De Curzon/Courson*; [1406] *Nevilles* 'moiety' then by heiress to *Talbots*; [1565] *John Manners*, Duke of Rutland by heiress. 'Military History'. Coal mining: [17th century] and in World War I [1914-18] for Chatsworth greenhouses. Hall: Built [1907]; S Z Ferranti [1913]

Battle Stone: *1250.* The shaft of a cross [mid 11th century]. Local tradition: It marks a struggle between Saxons and Vikings/Danes.

Beeley: *2667.* The 'Greaves' *2668 Beage's* + OE: '*ley*' = clearing Beegeleg [DB] *Greaves* family. 'Manor': Godric the Saxon, [1086], Royal 'demesne'; [1189-99] *Warren De Beeleigh*; *Cheneys*; [1509-47] *Thomas*, Lord Vaux by heiress; [1560] *John Greaves* by purchase; [1687] *William Saville* by purchase; *Lees*; [1734] *Gilberts* of Locko *4038* by heiress, niece of *George Savile*; *Normans, Browns, Wrights* in 12 lots; [1747] *William Cavendish*, Duke of Devonshire by purchase. 'Normans': Doorway to the Church of St Anne. Rock: 'Millstone grit' for Chatsworth House. Hall and Hilltops: [17th century] *Greaves* family sold the property to *Howard Savile*. 'Chapelry'.

Beeston 'Tor': *1054.* OE: *byge* = trading + *stone* [post] at the confluence of the rivers Hamps and Manifold. Cave: St Bertram's. 49 Anglo Saxon silver pennies were found.

Benty 'Grange': *1464.* OE: *beonet* = 'bent grass'. Tumulus: Skeleton, silver edging and ornaments of a leather cup were found. Saxon helmet with a Christian cross and a boar on the crest [7th century].

Beresford: *1259.* OE: *bera* = bear + *forda*. Pre-history: Barbed flint arrow head found. Mineral ore: Copper. Hall: Built [16th century]. Last of *Beresford* line died [17th century]. Inherited by *Stanshopes* of Elvaston *4132* [1825] purchased by Marshal Lord *Beresford*, victor of Albuera [1811] and bequeathed to Mr *Beresford – Hope*. Demolished and materials recycled about [1850]. 'Chantry': Founded [1511]. 'Limestone': Quarried extensively in the [17th century]. Recreation: *Charles Cotton's* bowling green.

Biggin: *1559.* OSca: *byggia* = a building. [18th century] Georgian house.

Biggin Dale: *1457.* 'Packhorse' route → Hartington *1360*.

Big Low: *9577.* Coal: Thin seam mined when supplies of wood for Cheshire salt pans were exhausted.

Billinge Hill: *9577.* OE: *bile* = a headland + *hyll* = a hill *William Billinge* of Fawfieldhead *0763*. Coal: Thin seam mined when supplies of wood for Cheshire salt pans were exhausted. Rocks: 'Millstone grit' quarry.

Birchover: *2462.* OE: *bierce* = 'birch' + *ofer* = overgrown or *bricha* = newly cultivated ground Barcoure [DB], Birchoure [1226 *Henry III*], Byrch Over [*Daniel Defoe* 1660-1731] Pb 'Manor': [1086] *Henry De Ferrars*; *Thornhills*; [1875] *Henry F Hurlock* by descent; [1881] *Major McCreagh*. 'Druid': Stones. Rowtor Rocks Vicar: *Revd Thomas Eyre*. Rock: 'Millstone grit'. Mineral ore: 'Antimony' (according to Daniel Defoe).

Birchinlee: *1691.* OE: *bierce* = 'birch' + *lee* = a shelter for sheep. "Tin Town navvy" village for reservoir builders.

Blackwell: *1272.* OE: *blaec* = black + *wella* = a stream Blacheuuelle [DB]. Pb Saxons: 'Cross' remains. 'Manor': [1086] Royal 'demesne'; [1100-35]; Lenton Priory *5238* ('Cluniac') by gift of *Henry I*; [1552] *Sir William Cavendish*, gift of *Edward VI* [1547-53]. 'Mesne manor': *Blackwells*, Compulsory sale ordered by *Charles II* [1660-85]; *Hopes* gift of *Charles II*.

Blake (Black) **'Low':** *2170.* Tumulus: A girl with child and the tine of a stag's antler found.

Blore: *1349.* ME & ON: exposed hill [a windy place] Blora [DB], Blore [1227 *Henry III*]. Church: St Bartholomew [1519]. Monuments: *William Basset* died [1601], his wife died [1616] and son in law died [1640]. Hall: [15th century] (now demolished). Agriculture: Advertisement in The Derby Mercury for the **annual** sale of store stock on [8/10/1839] at 10 00 am. 55 head of cattle, 125 head of sheep.

Boothman's: *0271.* ON: *buth* = temporary shelter + OD: *mann*. Coal miners' Cottages.

Bowden: *0681.* OE: *boga* = bow [shaped] + *'dun'* = a hill. Residence: *Bowdens* from 13th century until the death of *Nicholas* [1668]. Purchased by *Degge*, then *Hibberson* and *Slack* families.

Bradfield, High, Low: *2692.* OE: *brad* = broad + *feld* = field Bradesfield [1188 *Henry II*] Bradefeld [1316 *Edward II*]. Cross: 'Celtic' [10th century]. Disaster: Great Sheffield Flood [1864] when the earthen dam of Dale Dike Reservoir collapsed while it was filling with water, 244 people died. School destroyed; rebuilt [1874]. Marriage: [1650s] *Elizabeth Berley (Captain Bess* – rescuer of her mortally wounded husband on battlefield) of Middlewood House to *Thomas Longsdon*, Parliamentary troop leader. Manufacturing: Frame knitting. Memorials: Church of St Nicholas; *John Morewood* died [1647], *James Rimington* died [1839]. Crime prevention: Body snatcher lookout on High Bradfield church tower.

Bradford: river *2064.* OE: *brad* = broad + *forda*. Recreation: Weirs for angling.

Bradley Howel: *0065.* OE: *brad* = broad + *'ley'* = a clearing + *hun-wella* = [by the] tributary streams (of the River Dane).

Bradshaw: *2176.* OE: *brad* = broad + *scaga* = a thicket Bradschlag [DB], Bradeshaghe [1246 *Henry III*]. Hall: [17th century].

Bradwell: *1781.* OE: *brad* = broad + *wella* = a stream (Bradwell Brook) Bradeuuelle [DB]. Pb 'Manor': [1086] *William Peverell* with Castleton *1583*. Persecution: 'Pipe veins'. The Romans sent renegade Christians to work in them. Inventor: Birthplace of *Samuel Fox*, inventor of grooved metal frames for umbrellas [1847]. Manufacturing: Beaver hats worn by miners. Cotton and silk weaving [18th & 19th centuries]. 'Earl' *Edwin* of Mercia killed on his way to Scotland [1071].

Bramley: *2473.* OE: *bram* = broom + *'ley'* = a clearing Brumelai [DB], Bromelege [1160 Henry II].

Bretton: *2078.* OF: *Breton* (*William the Conqueror's* mercenaries) + *'ton'*. = a farmstead. Brettone [1240 *Henry III*], Brecton [1301 *Edward I*].

Broadmeadow: *0855.* OE: *brad* = broad + *maedwe* = a meadow. Hall: *1163*.

Brookfield 'Manor': *2382.* OE: *brac* = a brook (Hood brook) + *feld* = field. Fortified house.

Brough: *1882.* Anavia [Romans], OE: *burg* = a fort. Burgus [1165 *Henry II*], Burg [1253 *Henry III*]. Fort: Built, or re-built, by *Caesar Julius Verus* after 'Brigantes' revolt of about [AD158]. Arnemetia goddess name on altar. Mill: (River Noe) Owned by the *Strelleys* about [1492] in return for attending the king on horseback whenever he came to Derbyshire carrying a heron falcon.

Brushfield: *1672.* Tumulus *1771.* *Beorhtric's* + OE: *feld* = field Brithicesfel, Brittrichisfield. Pb 'Manor': [1086] *Robert Fitz-Waltheof*; Abbey of Rufford ('Cistercian') *6464*; *Mountjoy* or *Monjoy*; *Blounts* by heiress; [1537] *Talbot, Earl of Shrewsbury* gift of *Henry VIII* [1509-47]; [1628] *Sir William Armine* by purchase; *Bradshaw* by purchase; [1662] *Earl of Devonshire* by purchase.

Bubnell: *2472.* *Bubba's* + OE: *hyll* = a hill. Bubenele [DB], Bobenhull [1283 Edward I]. Pb Hall: [1583] *Richard Copwood* dowry of *Margaret*, daughter of *Sir William Bassett* and *Anne Cokayne*. 'Manor': [1086] *William Avenell*; [1205] *Elizabeth Bassett* (formerly *Avenell*) allegedly paid *King John* 80 marks to remain a widow and retain Bubnell, [1205] *Vernons* (*Simon Bassett's* death) [1205], [1378] *Bassets* of Blore *1349* takeover by Baslow *2572*, [15th century] *William Eyre*.

Burton: *2067.* OE: *burgh* = a fort + *'ton'* = a farmstead. Burtune [DB],

Burton upon Trent: Staffordshire *2423.* Abbey ('Benedictine') founded by *Wulfric* [1004]. Lands: Mixon *0257*, Musden *1251*, Sugworth 'grange' *2389*.

Butterton: *0756.* OE: *butere* = butter [dairy cattle] + *'ton'* = a farmstead. Butterdon [1200 *John*], Boterdon [1236 *Henry III*]. Church: St Bartholomew built [1871-73].

Calais: *50°57'N 1°50'E Edward III* created a 'staple' for lead here. Captured by him [1347]. Recaptured by the French *Duke of Guise* [1558]. 'River Derwent'.

Calton Hill: *1171* and *1050.* OE: *calf* + *'ton'* = a farmstead + *hyll* = a hill. Rocks: 'Dolerite', 'amethyst', 'quartz'.

Calver: *2374.* OE: *calf* + grazing ridge. Caluoure [DB], Caloure [1199 *John*], Caulver [1650]. Pb Manufacturing: Cotton mill powered by the River Derwent, built with iron pillars and wooden floors.

Tumulus: Calver 'Low'. 'Manor': [1086] Royal 'demesne'; [1199-1216] *Richard Stafford*: [1422-61] *Thomas Lynford*; [1485-1509] *Rowland Shakerley*; *Traceys*; *Stratfords*; [1558-1603] *Eyres* and merger with Rowland *2172*. *Figure 13,* Water and Wind Mills, refers.

Carl('s) wark/Carl Wark: *2681.* ON: karl = a farm labourer + wark = a fort. Fort: Possibly 'Iron Age' or [5th or 6th centuries – 'Dark Ages'] 'millstone grit' facing walls, vallum width 6 metres (17 feet) x length 50 metres (150 feet), south side gate.

Castern: *1252.* Catt's thorn bush. Caetestherne [1002 *Ethelred II*], Catesturn [1227 *Henry III*], Casterne [1327 *Edward II*]. Hall: [18th century].

Castleton: *1583.* CL: *castellum* + OE: 'ton' = a farmstead. Castellum Willelm [DB]. Pb Ditch: Town/Grey - possibly an Anglo 'Saxon' fortification. 'Military History'. 'Normans': Peveril/Peak Castle, Chancel arch in the Church of St Edmund. 'Garlands'. Caverns: 'Blue John', Peak, Speedwell, Treak. Discovered by lead miners [1750]. Titan *A secret system of caves and conduits. In praise of limestone. W H Auden [1907-73].* Mineral ores: 'Galena', 'Pyrite'. 'Sphalerite'. Rocks: 'Blue John', (*Henry Watson*) 'Calcite', 'Fluorite', 'Sandstone' roofs on buildings. Horse breeding: Until about [1300], the King had a stud at Castleton. Memorial: *Robert & Jean Eyre* + **14** children. *Micah Hall* (attorney) died [1804], *Mawe,* mineralogist. 'Manor': *Gurneburn,* The Saxon with *Hundine;* [1086] *William Peverell;* [1154] forfeit to the Crown; [1199-1216] 'Barons'; [1307-27] *Piers Gaveston**; Earl Warrenne*;* [1327-77] *John of Gaunt; Dukes of Devonshire* under the Crown; leased to *Foljambes, Eyres and* others. * Gift of the King. *Figure 11,* Metal Ore Extraction and *Figure 12,* Rock Extraction, refer.

Caudwell Mill: *2566.* Dialect: caud = cold + OE: wella = stream. Water mill: Flour and ovender [19th century] on the River Wye. *Figure 13,* Water and Wind Mills, refers.

Charles Cotton's Fishing Lodge: Also known as *Izaak Walton's* Fishing Temple *1259.*

Chatsworth: *2670.* Chetal's/Ceatt's + OLG: wort = an open space in a village. Chetesuerde [DB], Chattesworth [1246 *Henry III*]. 'Manor': *Chetal* the Saxon; [1086]. *William Peverell; Leches;* [1550] *Agards* by purchase; [1557] *Sir William Cavendish* by purchase. House: Originally built by the *1st Duke of Devonshire* [1687-1707]. Mining: [1623-25] £10 spent on a coal mine. During World War I [1914-18] re-opened for heating greenhouses

> *CHATSWORTH! Thy stately mansion, and the pride*
> *Of thy domain, strange contrast do present*
> *To house and home in many a craggy rent*
> *Of the wild Peak; where new-born waters glide*
> *Through fields whose thrifty occupants abide*
> *As in a dear and chosen banishment,*
> *With every semblance of entire content;*
> *So kind is simple Nature, fairly tried!*
> *Yet He whose heart in childhood gave her troth*
> *To pastoral dates, thin-set with modest farms,*
> *May learn, if judgment strengthen with his growth,*
> *That, not for Fancy only, pomp hath charms;*
> *And, strenuous to protect from lawless harms*
> *The extremes of favoured life, may honour both.*
> *William Wordsworth* [1830]

Chellaston: *3830.* South Derbyshire. *Whynyates* family.

Chelmorton: *1169.* OE: cegel = a boundary + mearc = a mark + 'ton' = a farmstead. Chelmerdune, Chelmaredon, Chilmerdon [1236 *Henry III*] Pb. 'Manor': [1086] Royal 'demesne'. 'Mesne manor': [1509-47] *Talbots* gift of *Henry VIII; Eyres:* [1853] *Colonel Leslie* gift of his wife, *Dorothy Eyre.* Stone artefacts: Coffins and [15th century], low screen in St John the Baptist Church. Sepulchral slabs. 'Chantry': [1256] Permission was granted to add one to the church. Strip fields.

Chunal: *0391.* Ceola's + OE: halh = secret place [isolated]. Ceolhal [DB], Chelhala [1185 *Henry II*]. 'Manufacturing': [1874].

Citeaux: (Nuits Saint Georges) *47°08'N 4°57'E* Dukedom of Burgundy. Connected with the reformation of the 'Cistercian' monastic order about [1109]. *Figure 3,* Overseas Connections.

Cliff College: *2573.* Founded [1903] as Longcliff * Hall for training Methodist and other evangelists. *Reference to Froggatt Edge ('millstone grit').

Cluny: Dukedom of Burgundy *46°30'N 4°39'E.* 'Benedictine' Abbey [910].

Cockey Farm: *1979.* OE: cocc-hege = an enclosure for wild birds. Birthplace: *William Newton,* "Minstrel/Poet of the Peak".

Codnor: *4149* South Derbyshire. *Grey* family and Stoke manor *2376.*

Combermere Abbey: *5844.* Cheshire. Founded by *Hugh de Malbanc* [1133] ('Cistercian'). Gift: Wincle 'grange' *9665* and Alstonefield *1355.*

Conk(e)sbury: *2065.* Crane's + OE: burgh = a fort Cranchesberie [DB], Cankesburia [1318 *Edward II*], Conkesburgh [1339 *Edward III*]. Gift: To Leicester Abbey ('Augustinian' canons).

Coombs 'Dale': *2274.* OE: cumb = a short valley + dael 'Barytes', 'Derbyshire Diamonds'.

Crag: Hall *9868.* Seat of *Earl of Derby* then residence of cotton mill managers [19th century].

Cressbrook: *1773.* OE: cressa = cress = broc = a brook. Manufacturing: Initially processed peppermint and distilled aromatic plants before becoming a cotton mill, nylon yarn [1965] (River Wye) Powered by water turbines [1890]. Built by *William Newton,* "Minstrel/Poet of the Peak" [1783], rebuilt after fire [1785]. 200-300 orphans living and working there. Bought [1835] by McConnell & Co *Ellis Needham,* notorious manager. Hall: [1835]. *Figure 13,* Mills, refers.

Cromford → High Peak Railway: *1661* → Cromford *2956.* Not all the tracks (now removed) were in the Peak National Park area. Construction began [1825]. *Figure 14,* Railways, refers.

Crowdecote: *1065.* OE: crawa = a crow + cote = a shelter. 'Saxon': Relics. cote = a shelter

Crowden: *0799.* OE crawa = a crow + 'dun' = a hill. Hall: Built [1692] *Hatfield* family.

Cucklet [arch] **Rock:#** *2176.* Dialect: [wind noise like the] cackle [of a hen]. "Church"* during Eyam Plague [1665].

> *Here a rude arch, not form'd by mortal hands,*
> *Th'unconsecrated church* of Cucklet stands;*
> *To this sequester'd spot, where all might seem*
> *The sweet creation of a poet's dream,*
> *Mompesson saw his suffering flock repair,*
> *Daily as toll'd the sabbath bell for prayer,*
> *When through th'afflicted village, wild with dread,*
> *And lost to hope, the plague contagion spread:*
> *Here from a rocky# arch, with foliage hung,*
> *Divinest precepts issue from his tongue;*
> *To all, his kindly aid the priest affords,*
> *They feel his love, and live upon his words.*
>   *Ebenezer Rhodes* [1762-1839].

Cutthroat Bridge: *2187.* Built [1820s] A man was found nearby with his throat cut [1635].

Dane, river: *9564.* OE: denu = deeply wooded valley or ONo: dave = tickling pool. Dauen [1220 *Henry III*], Davere [1248 *Henry III*], Daan [1295 *Edward I*] Devene, Deuene [1443 *Henry VI*], Dene [1487 *Henry VII*]. Power: For Gradbach Mill *9966. Figure 13,* Water and Wind Mills, refers.

Derwent: *2383.* MW: derv = oaks river or dwr-gwent = fair water. Deorwentan [1000]. Chapel: Gift of *King John* to Welbeck Abbey *5674* ('Pre-Monstratensian' monks) [1199-1216], Abbey Bank *1791,* Abbey Brook *1892.* Hall: Built by *Henry Balguy* [1672] to hoard gold requisitioned by *Charles II*; submerged by reservoir [1943]. One of the *Balguy* and *Newdigate* family residences. Owned by the *Duke of Norfolk* [1874]. [12th century] 'oak' carvings. River and valley: First leg of the rivers Derwent, Trent, and Witham route to Boston or Hull for (a) coastal shipment to London and Southern England, (b) across the North Sea - English Channel to the Calais 'staple' and, (c) York and Northern Europe. [1752]

'Justices of the Peace' accepted responsibility for bridges. Water power: for Bamford *1969*, Calver [1785] *2374*, Hathersage *2380 and* other mills. *Figure 13*, Water and Wind Mills, refers.

Dieulacres Abbey: Staffordshire *9857*. ('Cistercian') Founded [1214]. Gift: Swythamley 'grange' *9764*.

Doctor's Gate: *0893*. 'Roman Roads' Named after *Dr John Talbot*, vicar of Glossop [1495-1550].

Doll 'Tor': *2463*. 'Bronze Age' stone circle.

Dore and **Chinley** Sheffield → Manchester 'Railway': [1894] *2879 John Ruskin's* letter to Manchester City News [2/04/1884] 'The proposed railway will poison the air'. *Figure 14*, refers.

Dove, river: *1451*. CW: *gwy* = water or MW: = dark (overhanding trees) Dufan, Dulle [1228 *Henry III*]. 'Agriculture': Dairying on the banks [1686]. 'Manufacturing': Cotton mills on the banks at the end of the [18th century]. 'Recreation': Angling weirs.

The rapid Garonne and the winding Seine
Are both too mean,
Beloved Dove, with thee
To vie priority:
Nay, Tame and Isis, when conjoin'd, submit,
And lay their trophies at thy silver feet.

Charles Cotton

Dunford Bridge: *1502*. River Don + OE: *forda*. Communications: Station on the Manchester → Sheffield → Lincolnshire 'Railway' [1874]. *Figure 14*, Railways, refers. Hunting and Shooting: Home beagle pack [1902] 400 grouse killed in one day [1849].

Dunstable Priory: Bedfordshire *0221*. ('Augustinian'). Gift: Ashopton *1986* possibly by *Sir William Avenell*.

Earl/Church* Sterndale: *0967*. *Earl's* + OE: *styrna* = stern + *dael* = a dale. See also King Sterndale. Rocks: 'Calcite', 'olivine'. '*Chapelry': Former 'Norman' one of Hartington *1360*.

East Moor: *2970*. Forest clearance in 'Neolithic', 'Bronze Age' and 'Iron Age'

Ecton: *0958*. *Ecca's* + *tun* = a farmstead Echentone [DB], Echeton [1165 *Henry II*]. Bitumen: 'Elaterite'. *Figures 11, 12 & 28*, Metal Ores, Rocks, Fire and Light, refer. Mineral ores: Possible first worked by United Societies with whom *Prince Rupert* [1619-82], nephew of *Charles I* was associated. Gunpowder first used [1670], [1686] Worked by *William Courtenay*, de jure Earl Devon [1628-1702] and Dutchmen. Re-discovered [1720] by a Cornish Miner. [1739] Workers 300 men, women, boys and girls. Men dug the ores, women broke ores, boys wheeled to shed, girls 8-11 years old sorted it. [1780s] Estimated annual output 600 tons. Revenues from mining were used by 5th *Duke of Devonshire* to build Buxton crescent about [1780]. Last lease by the *Duke of Devonshire* [1885]. 'Arsenopyrite', copper ores 'Azurite', 'Bornite', 'Chalcanthite','Chalcocite', 'Chalcopyrite', 'Cuprite', 'Malachite'. Rock: 'Calcite'.

Ecton Low: *0957*. *Ecca's* + 'ton' + OHG: *hlais* = a grave. Oval 'barrow' and 'tumuli'. Burnt bones [suggesting cremation] found in a large urn.

Edale: *1285*. OE: *eg-dael* = land by a stream (Grinds Brook). Aidele [DB] bees, Eydale [1305 *Edward I*], Edale [1362 *Edward III*]. Forestry: Developed from the 'booths' rented by foresters – Barber *1184*, Grindsbrook *1286*, Nether *1486*, Ollerbrook *1285*, Upper *1085*. 'Manufacturing': Lace thread cotton mill powered by Grinds Brook. 'Recreation': Start of Pennine Way completed [1965]. 'Bog trotting' after about [1952]. Chapel: Built [1633] by 11 'yeomen' and 2 widows to avoid the long walk over Mam Tor *1283* to Castleton church *1583*. Rebuilt [1810]. Communications: Centre for five 'packhorse' trails. Railway [1894]. 'Cross': [12th century or 1610] Meeting point of Peak Forest Wards: Ashop, Edale, Champayne, Longendale. *Figure 13*, Water and Wind Mills, refers.

Edensor: *2569*. *Eden's* + OE: *ofer* = bank. Edbesovre [DB]. 'Manor': *Levenot*, the Saxon [1086] *Henry De Ferrars*; *Foljambes*; [1388] *Sir Robert Plumpton* by heiress; 'Moieties' by heiress ½ *Robert Rocliffe*; *Cliffords* by heiress ½ *John Sotehill*; *Henry*; *Langfords* then ½ + ½ *Bess of Hardwick/Duke of Devonshire*. Village: Moved to the present site by the 6th *Duke of Devonshire* [1839]. 'Turnpike': About [1810]. Memorials: Brass: *John Beton* died [1570] confidential servant to *Mary Queen of Scots*. 'Black marble': Pillars and slab to *Henry Cavendish* died [1616], *William Cavendish* died [1625]. Grave: *Kathleen*

Kennedy, wife of 'Marquis' of Hartington and sister of President of USA *John F Kennedy* killed in air crash in France [1948].

Elder Bush Cave: *0995.* Remains of bison, cave bear, cave lion, hyena, woolly rhinoceros and, in 'travertine', impressions of Montpelier maple *acer monspessulanun* and hazel *corylus avellana*.

Elkstone: *0559.* Eanlac's or OE: eolh = #elk + 'ton' = a farmstead. #Grazed Late Glacial Ice Age vegetation 20,000-8,000BC.

Elton: *2260.* OE: eolh = elks + 'ton' = a farmstead Pb *Bardolf, Tibetot, Foljambe and Stephenson* families. 'Manor': *Uchtred* the Saxon; [1086] *Henry De Ferrars*; *Bardolfs**; *Tibetots**; [1327-77] *Foljambes*; [1558-1603] *Stevensons of Rowlee 1589*; 'Moieties' *Thornhill* and *Joliffe*; *Thornhills*; [1875] *Henry Francis Hurlock of Thornhill 1983* by descent; [1881] *Major McCreagh* by sister of *Francis Hurlock*. Hall: [1668]. School:[1862]. Mineral: 'Wad' *Held from the Crown by a render of gilt spurs. *Figure 11,* Metal Ores, refers.

Errwood Reservoir: *0175.* OE: err = to ramble (River Goyt) + wudu = wood. Hall: [1830s] in Italianate style; comprising a hall, private school, servants' cottages, water mill and coal mine. Submerged [1934]. Previous occupants: *Grimshawe* family.

Etherow, river: *1299.* OE: edre = a water course + hoh = projecting ridge Ederhau [1226 *Henry III*], and [1285 *Edward I*].

Eyam: *2176.* OE: eyum = land between two streams* – (Hollow Brook and Jumber Brook). Aiune [DB]. Pb 'Saxons': [9th century] 'cross'. 'Normans': 'Font' in the Church of St Leonard. 'Military History'. Buildings: 'Gritstone' with stone flag roofs. Elaborate sun dial on church made locally [1775]. Hall: Demolished by *Francis Bradshaw*, husband of *Anne Stafford*, Rebuilt [1676]. Occupied by the *Wright* family since [1735]. 'Agriculture': *Land reclaimed for pasture, oats and potatoes.
Plague: [1665] A plague resistant gene, 'Delta 32', is believed to account for the survival of some of the population – 433 – when many succumbed to *yersinia pestis* in a bale of cloth from London. Seven members of the *Hancocke* family who lived at Riley Farm. *2275 William Mompesson, Thomas Stanley, George Vicars.* Mineral ores: 'Anglesite', 'Galena', 'Goethite', 'Heminorphite', 'Limonite', 'Smithsonite'.
Rocks: 'Calcite', 'Chalcedony', 'Fluorite', 'Opal'. *Figures 11 & 12,* Metals, Rocks refer. 'Portway':→ Ashford in the Water *1969* via Great Longstone *2071*; *Figure 15,* Routes, refers. 'Manor': [1086] Royal 'demesne'; [1100-35] *William Peverell* gift of *Henry I*; [1199-1216] *Morteynes* gift of *King John*; [1307] *Thomas,* Lord Furnival by purchase; [1383] *Thomas Neville* by heiress, *Joan*; [1406] *Sir John Talbot* by heiress, *Maud Neville*; [1616] *Mary, Countess of Pembroke* gift to her relatives, the *Savilles*; [1700] *Richard Boyle,* Earl of Burlington By heiress, *Dorothy Savile*; [1781] *Cavendishes* by heiress.

Fenny Bentley: *1750.* OE: fenny = boggy (Wash Brook) + 'bent [grass'] + 'ley' = a clearing Benelege [DB], Fennibenetlegh [1272 *Edward I*]. Manor house: [17th century] *Beresford* home, frequemtly visited by *Izaak Walton*. 'Alabaster'.

Fernilee: *0178.* OE: fearn = fern + 'lee' = a shelter. Ferneleia [1188 *Henry II*], Fernlee, Fernilegh [1283 *Edward I*], Firnil [1285 *Edward I*], Ferneley [1484 *Richard III*]. Coal: Mine [1610]. Manufacturing: Gunpowder. Explosion [1909]. Closed [1920].

Fin Cop: *1771.* OE: fin = a heap of wood or fina = a woodpecker + Dialect: cop = top. Hill fort: Probably 'Iron Age'.

Five Wells: *1271.* OE: fif = five + wella 'Bronze Age': Chambered long 'barrow'.

Flagg: *1368.* ME: flag = turf or sod. Flagun [DB], Flagge [1284 *Edward I*], Flagh [1315 *Edward II*]. Pb Hall: Possibly built by *Dales*. Turf: Uses: fuel and a covering of the stones and rocks on 'Roman' roads. 'Portway':→ Monyash *1566*. Harrier hunting: Long legged mountain hare *lepus timidus*. Flagg Moor *1367*. Philanthropy: *Dale's* gifts to the poor of Parwich *1854*.

Flash: *0267.* OD: flask = a swamp. 'Merchandising': Centre for pedlars/fudge-mounters, 'badgers', who spoke their own dialect slang and "minted" their own coins, sold mohair, twist (tobacco), silk, on their rounds slept in barns and 'cotes', begged for food. 'Manufacturing': Silk buttons taken by a 'Methodist', *James Wardle,* to Leek *9856*. Mineral: 'Haematite'. *Figure 11*.

Foolow: *1976. Foo's* + OE: *low* = a hill Foulove [1284 *Edward I*], Fuwwelowe [1338 *Edward III*]. Pb Wet point settlement site with 3 wells. Manor: *Morteyne*; [1199-1216] *Staffords* gift of *King John*. Manor House: [17th century]. Rocks: Knoll reef 'limestone'. Population decline: Lead mining contraction [1796]. Recreation: Remains of a bull ring.

Ford: *0653.* OE: *forda* Forne [DB], La Forda [1127 *Henry I*], Forda [1242 *Henry III*]. Hall: Early [17th century]. Home of 6 year old orphan, later *Colonel Bagshawe*, with *Robert Clive* in India having an ensign commission given [1740] by 3rd *Duke of Devonshire;* Repairs, sowing of acorns from Stanton Woodhouse *2564* [1758]; *Willam Henry Greaves Bagshawe JP* [1892]. Poor Relief: Leek Quakers used income from their farm for poor friends [1694].

Friden: *1660. Frigg,* the wife of the Nordic god *Odin* + OE: *dun* = a hill. Rocks: 'Barytes', 'Chalcedony', 'Derbyshire Diamonds','Jasper', 'Quartz', 'Silica sand'/clay for refractories.

Fynney: *1871.* OE: *fynig* = a marshy place. Cottage: *Fynney* family.

Garendon Abbey: *5020.* Leicestershire. Founded by *Robert,* Earl of Leicester [1133]. ('Cistercian') Biggin 'Grange' *1559.* Land in Hartington *1360.*

Gateham 'Grange': *1156.* OE *gat* = goat + *ham* = a homestead. 'Grange'. Gift: Probably to Combermere Abbey *5844* ('Cistercian').

Gautries Hill: *0980. Gouti's* + W: *trier* = a homestead.

Gib Hill: *1563 .* 'Round barrow': Contained stone 'cists'.

Ginclough: *9567.* Abbreviated OF: *engin* = gin (a hoist driven either by human or animal means) + OE: *cloh* = a 'clough' = a narrow valley.

Glossop: *0393.* North-west Derbyshire. *William Bagshawe*, "Apostle of the Peak", vicar excluded by the Act of Uniformity [1662].

Gospel Hillock: *1771.* OE: *godspell* + *hilloc*. Tumulus: Possibly the grave of a missionary to the Saxons.

Goyt, River: *0173.* OE: *gota* = a watercourse Goyt's Moss *0172.* Guit [1244 *Henry III*], Gwid,Gwit, Goyt [1285 *Edward I*]. Coal: Mines in the valley for 300 years. Derwent River *2475.*

Gradbach: *9966.* OE: *graede* = grassy (River Dane valley) + *baec* = stream. Hall: 17th century]. Mill: [1640] Corn (River Dane); Rebuilt after fire by *Sir Thomas Dakeyne* of Darley Dale *2663* [1785] flax [1785-1837], silk [mid-nineteenth century], saw [late nineteenth century]. *Figure 13.*

Grangemill: *2455.* Latin: *granum* = grain + *mola* = a mill (Ivonbrook).

Gratton: *1960.* OE: *greate* = great + *'ton'* = a farmstead. Pb 'Manor': [1086] *Henry De Ferrars*; [1485-1509] *Thomas Middleton*; [1675] *Francis Lowe* by heiress; [1723] *John Thornhill* by purchase; [1875] *Henry F Hurlock* by descent; [1881] *Major McCreagh* by heiress.

Great Hucklow: *1777.* OE: *greate* = great (to distinguish from Little Hucklow *1678*) + *Hucca's* + OE: '*low*' = a hill. Hochelai [DB], Hukelowe [1265 *Henry III*]. Pb Mineral ore: Lead. Rock: 'Fluorite'. Recreation: Gliding club founded [1934]. 'Literary connections'.

Great Longstone: *2071.* OE: *greate* = great (to distinguish from Little Longstone *1871*) + *lang* = long (3 km) + *stan* = a ridge (Longstone Edge *2073*). Pb Communications: 'Portway': From Ashford in the Water *1969* → Eyam *2176;*'Turnpike' [1765] Hassop *2272* → Newcastle under Lyme *8445* for 'chert'. Hall: Hunting seat for *Henry VII* [1485-1509]. Rebuilt [1747] *Wrights, Godfrey Rowland, Thomas Gregory* NB Three bays of brick. 'Manufacturing': Flemish weavers settled and started the stocking industry, Shoes - Inn named after *St Crispin* patron saint of shoemakers. Memorial: Church of St Giles [13th century]; rebuilt [1873] *Gertrude + Rowland Eyre; Wrights* [1873]. 'Parishes': Alstonefield *1355*; later a separate ecclesiastical one [1737]; civil [1866]. Rock: 'Chert' for pottery carried to North Staffordshire by 'turnpike' after [1760]. 'Military History'.

Grindleford: *2477.* OE: *grindle* = a narrow ditch or stream or *rindle Grindstone* place + *forda* (Burbage Brook).

Grindlow: *1877.* OE: *green* + '*low*' = a hill Greenlawe [1195 *Richard I*]. Pb Compare Grind Low, Grindon and Grindsbrook. 'Manor': [1086] Royal 'demesne'; *Matthew De Stokes*; [1199] Lilleshall Abbey *7315* ('Augustinian'*) by gift of *Matthew De Stokes* confirmed by *King John*; [1552] *Sir William Cavendish* gift of *Edward VI*; [1641] *Cavendish*, Earl of Newcastle: *Sergeant Hill*; *William Cokayne* by heiress; *Cox* of Derby by heiress; *Brittlebanks* by purchase; *Bagshawes*. *Chapel: Probably built by them. 'Grange'.

Grindon: *0854.* ON: *grennen* = to grin/snarl [winter winds at 330 metres altitude] + OE: '*dun*' = a hill Grendone [DB]. Mineral ores: Copper, lead. Church: [12th century]. 'Normans': 'Font'.

Grindslow 'Knoll': *1086.* ON: *grennen* = to grin/snarl [winter winds at 550 metres altitude] + *hlaw* = 'low'= a hill. Source of peat fuel for Edale *1285* inhabitants who had the right of 'turbary'. Peat was carried on sleds down Sled Road.

Haddon: *2366.* OE: *haep* = heather covered + '*dun*' = a hill Uverhaddon [DB], Ufrehedon [1206 *John*]. Hall: Originally [12th century] on a site with river [Wye] and cliff defences. *Avenell* and *Manners* families. See also Nether Haddon *2266* and Over Haddon *2066*.

Hallam Moors: *2386.* OE: *heall* = a rock or stone. Hunting: On foot. 'Commemoration': *Hallam*

Hamps, river: *0953.* MW: *hamhesp/hanespe* = dry in summer (disappearing river) Hanse* [1200]. Pastoral farming: Cattle bred on the banks.

> *Hanse*, that this while suppos'd him quite out of her sight,*
> *No sooner thrusts his head into the cheerful light,*
> *But Manifold, that still the runway doth watch,*
> *Him, ere he was aware, about the neck doth catch;*
> *And as the Angry Hanse would from her hold remove,*
> *They, struggling, tumble down into their lord, the Dove.*
>
> *Michael Drayton; Poly-Olbion* [1612].

Hammerton: *1573.* OE: *hamor* = hammer + '*ton*' = a farmstead. Farmstead and smithy on the site.

Harthill Moor: *2262.* OE: *heorot* = hart + *hyll* = a hill cf Hartington Hortil [DB], Herthil [1176 *Henry II*] + *0189*. Pb Stone circles.

Hartington: *1360.* OE: *heorot* = hart + '*ton*' = a farmstead. Horetedun [DB], Hertendon [1200 *John*], Hertindon [1251 *Henry III*]. Pb Hall: [1350] Rebuilt [1611] by *Thomas Bateman*, 'yeoman' farmer. Youth Hostel [1934]. Processing: *Thomas Brindley* started the cheese factory. Communications: 'Packhorse' route → Biggin Dale *1457*. Battle: Skirmish during the Civil War [1643]. Memorials: Church of St Giles: *Thomas Brindley*, founder of the cheese factory; *Sleigh* family; *Augustus Wirgman*, the [19th century] vicar who provided a school; Centenarian *Thomas Mellor* died aged **103**. Philanthropist *Richard Edensor*. Mineral ore: 'Wad'. 'Manor': Duchy of Lancaster [1360-early 17th century].

Hassop: *2272.* *Haett's* [small] valley. Hetesope [DB], Hatsope, [1236 *Henry III*]. Pb Chapel: Roman Catholic alongside the hall held by *Eyres* for *Charles I*. Church: Roman Catholic *Eyre* family built All Saints' [1816]. *Stephenson* family. Communications: Turnpike' [1765] from Newcastle under Lyme *8445* via Monyash *1566*. 'Railway' station on the Dore *3081* → Chinley *0382* line for the convenience of the *Duke of Devonshire*. 'Manor': [1086] Royal 'demesne'; *Foljambes*; [1388 or 1399] *Sir Robert Plumpton* by heiress; [1478] *Sir William & Robert Plumpton* leased to *Stephen Eyre*; [1498] *Catherine Eyre* (formerly *Dymoke*) by purchase; [1853] *Colonel Charles Stephen Leslie* gift of his wife *Dorothy Eyre* [1975] *Thomas H Chapman* by purchase.

Hathersage: *2380.* OE: *hoed* = he-goat [ie steep]. Hereseige [DB], Hauersheg [1200 *John*], Haursech [1242 *Henry III*], Hathersegge [1264 *Henry III*]. 'Robin Hood': *Little John* may be buried in the church yard of St Michael about [1381]. Manufacturing: Needles and hooks factory started by *Christopher Schutz*, a German immigrant [1566]. Umbrella frames - Hood Brook and River Derwent for water wheels. *David Mellor* [05/10/1930-07/05/2009] Cutlery. Processing: Lead mill. Memorials: *Eyre family*: *Robert* died [1459], *Ralph* died [1493] and *wife, Robert, wife and children* about [1500], *Sir Arthur* about [1560]. 'Manor': [1086] *Ralph Fitzhubert*; *Ridels*; [1216-72] *Matthew De Hathersage* possibly by *Meynell* heiress; Moieties *Nigel De Longford* and *Walter De Gousell*; [1450] *Thorpes* by purchase; *Eyres* by remainder; *Pegges* by purchase; [1705] *Cavendish* by purchase. *Figure 13*.

You gentlemen that here wish to ring
See that these laws you keep in everything;
Or else be sure you must without delay,
The penalty thereof to the ringers pay.
First, when you do into the bellhouse come,
Look, if the ringers have convenient room,
For if you do be an hindrance unto them,
Fourpence* you forfeit unto these gentlemen.
Next if you do here intend to ring,
With hat or spur do not touch a string;
For if you do, your forfeit is for that,
Just fourpence^y down to pay, or lose your hat.

If you a bell turn over, without delay
Fourpence* unto the ringers you must pay;
Or if you strike, misscall or do abuse,
You must pay fourpence* for the ringers' use.
For every oath here sworn, ere you go hence,
Unto the poor you must pay twelve pence^#
And if that you desire to be enrolled
A ringer here, these orders keep and hold.
But whose doth these orders disobey,
Unto the stocks we will take him straightway
There to remain until he be willing
To pay his forfeit, and the clerk a shilling^#

Ringers' Rhyme [1660] on the south wall of St Michael's, Hathersage belfry.
*Fourpence = 4d = 2p   #Twelve pence = 1 shilling = 5p

Hay Cop: *1773.* OE: <u>hay</u> = an enclosure* + Dialect: <u>cop</u> = top *Enclosed flat topped 'barrow'. <u>Archaeology</u>: Drinking vessel found and also a child's skeleton. 'Life expectancy'.

Hazelbadge: *1780.* OE: <u>haesel</u> = hazel + <u>becc</u> = swiftly flowing stream (Bradwell Brook) Hesel<u>bec</u> [DB], Hasel<u>bech</u> [1252 *Henry III*]. Pb <u>Families</u>: *Vernon* and *Swynnerton/Swynfen*. '<u>Manor</u>': *Lewin* the Saxon, [1086] *William Peverell*; [1307-27] *Vavasours*; [1327-77] *Strelley* by heiress; [1421] *Sir Richard Vernon* by purchase from *Robert Strelley*; [1565] *John Manners* by heiress. <u>Hall</u>: [16th century] Shooting box for the lords of Haddon. *Adam Eyre* [1647] bought pepper and aloes in Sheffield. <u>Rocks and Mineral ores</u>: 'Fluorite', 'sphalerite'. *Figures 11 & 12* refer.

Hazelford: *2379.* OE: <u>haesel</u> = hazel + <u>forda</u>. <u>Hall</u>: [17th century].

Highlow: *2180.* OE: <u>heah</u> = high + <u>hlaw</u> = 'low' = a hill. Heglave [DB], Heyelawe [1232 *Henry III*], <u>Heelowe</u> [1265 Henry III]. '<u>Manor</u>': [1086] *William Peverell*; [1307-27] *Archers*; [1327-77] *Nicholas Eyre* by purchase; [1802] *Cavendish* by purchase on the death of *John Archer* (name changed from *Eyre*) when the Court of Chancery ordered its sale. <u>Residence</u>: *Eyre* family from [14th century] until [1802]. <u>Hall</u>: [16th century].

High Peak Forest: Divided into wards: Ashop and Edale, Champayne, Longendale. 'Crosses'.

High 'Rake': *2073.* Stoney Middleton *2375* → Great Hucklow *1677* →. *Figure 15*, Routes, refers.

Hinkley Wood: *1250.* <u>Hinka's</u> + OE: <u>'ley'</u> = a clearing. Remains of early man found.

Hitter Hill: *0866.* 'Barrow' excavated [1862] Skeletons and urns found.

Hollins Cross: *1384.* 'Coffin route'.

Hollinsclough: *0666.* OE: <u>hol(h)</u> = deep + <u>cloh</u> = a 'clough' Holisurde [DB]. 'Manor', 'Rake'.

Hollins Hill: *0667.* Where inhabitants of the district camped for 3 weeks because they wanted to be safe from Napoleon's threatened invasion [1806]. 'Military History'.

Holme: *2169.* A member of the Danish *'hold'* class or S: = a low hill <u>Holm</u> [DB] Holum. <u>Hall</u>: Built by *Bernard Wells* [1626]; one of his co-heiresses, *Anne*, married *Robert Eyre* of Other owners: *John Eyre* (sale ordered by Chancery), *Robert Birch, Barker, Thomas John Gisborne* (married *Sally Krechmer* of St Petersburg), *John Twigge* ('sheriff' [1767]) + *Frances Foljambe*, his wife. TV Mast: *0804*. Also *1005*.

Hope: *1783* and *1255*. ME: *hop* = a valley. A *tributary valley [Peakshole Water]. [658, 926, & DB] bees Hope. 'Manor': *1783* One of *Balguy* family residences [1086] Royal demesne; [1327-77] *John of Gaunt, Duke of Lancaster*; *Cavendish* lease. Saxons: Remains of a 'cross'. 'Forest': 50% of the manor's 16,200 hectares (40,000 acres) occupied by forest [1874]. Communications: 'Packhorse' trail on the north side ridge overlooking the river valley.

Hope Cross: *1687*. Communications: 'Roman' road on a ridge. Cross roads of Ashop valley and 'Jaggers' Clough 'Packhorse' routes. *Figure 15*, Route Planning, refers.

Hulme End: *1059*. OD: *hulm* = a small piece of land by a stream [River Manifold]. Hulm [1278 *Edward I*]. 'Romans': Coins of *Emperor Lucius Septimus Severus* [193-211] who came to England with his wife to campaign against Caledonian Scots [208] and died in York [211].

Hurdlow: *0260* & *1166*. OE: *hord* = treasure + *hlaw* = 'low' = a hill. Hordlawe [1244 *Henry III*], Hordlowe [1251 *Henry III*]. *Brereton* family. 'Grange'.

Ible: *2457*. *Ibba's* + OE: *holu* = valley. Ibeholon [DB], Ibole [1288 *Edward I*] Pb. *Shirleys, Sacheverlls* by *Shirley* marriage; [1498] *Vernons* by purchase. The setting for Wintry Peacock by *D H Lawrence*. Rocks: 'Dolerite', 'Toadstone' *Figure 12*, Rock Extraction, refers.

Ilam: *1350*. W: *hil* = a trickling/disappearing stream [River Manifold]. Hilum [1002], Ylum [1227 *Henry III*]. Shrine: *St Bertram*. Bronze Age: 'Celt' found. Hall: Built [1821- 26] by a wealthy manufacturer, *Jesse Watts Russell*,on the site of an earlier hall; [1934] given to the National Trust by *Sir Robert McDougall*. Village: Planned and remodelled by *Jesse Watts Russell*. Literati: *William Congreve* [1670-1729] composed Old Batchelor in the grotto. Sheep Dog Trials: Dovedale. 'Saxons': 'Crosses' in the churchyard. 'Normans': Parts of Holy Cross Church. Memorials: *Robert Meverell* died [1625] in Holy Cross Church.

Kenslow: *1761*. ON: *kyn* = kindred + OHG: *hlais* = a grave. Tumuli cluster ' Iron Age' knives found.

Kettelshulme: *9879*. *Ketil's* + OD: *hulm* = a small piece of land by a stream [Goathole Brook]. Ketelshulm [1285 *Edward I*]. 'Glebe': House built [1911] to serve as vicarage for a church which was not built.

Kinder: *0888*. S: *Kynder Scut*, Chendre [DB], Kynder [1285 *Edward I*]. Scowt [1614] Recreations: Grouse shooting and Pennine Way walking. Walking 'groughs' in the dark peat moss. *Agatha Christie* [1890-1976]'Bog trotting' Route from Marsden, Yorkshire *0411* → Edale *1285*. Rock: 'Travertine' Hamlet: *0488*. Large calico printing works [1874].

King's Sterndale: *0972*. OE: *cyning* = king + *styrna* = stern + *dael* = 'dale'. Sternedale [1251 *Henry III*], Sternedal [1263 *Henry III*]. 'Earl Sterndale *0967*'.

Ladybower and Derwent Valley Reservoirs: *1886*. Dam Buster Bouncing Bomb Testing: [1943] Designed by *Sir Barnes Nevill Wallis* [1887-1979]. Reservoirs: Howden and Derwent Dams constructed [1912-16]. Derwent Hall was submerged by filling the Ladybower reservoir [1943].

Lathkill, River: *1865*. ON: a narrow valley with a barn Layth Kill [1520 *Henry VIII*]. NB Lathikin = a wooden bowl used in lead mining. Lathkill [1577] Mineral ore: Lead. Remains of a mining 'sough'. Recreation: Many weirs to improve angling. Rock: 'Tufa'.

Launde Priory: Leicestershire *7904*. ('Augustinian'). Founded by *Richard and Maud Basset* about [1125]. Endowment: Hathersage *2380*. 'Gifts'.

Lawrence Field: *2579*. Deserted village. Two stone buildings with 'enclosures' of the inner garden and an outer strip field.

Leam: *2379*. OE: *leah* = a clearing (dative plural). Hall: Possibly [17th century].

Leicester Abbey: *5805*. ('Augustinian'). Founded by *Robert le Bossu* [1143]. Gift: Conkesbury to the Abbey by *Sir William Avenell* between [1189 & 1199]. 'Grange': Meadow Place *2065*. *Figure 6*, Granges, refers.

Lenton Priory: *5238.* Nottinghamshire. ('Cluniac'). Gift: Blackwell manor *1272*. The monks had a 'tithe' on lead. Monks Dale *1375* named after them. Roof lead for Lincoln Cathedral bought at Lenton market [1209].

Letts 'Low': *0859.* Probable corruption of [prickly] *lettis*/lettuce *lactuca seriola* which grows on waste ground. 'Bronze Age': Tumulus. Daggers found. *Figure 22*, Bronze Age Sites, refers.

Lilleshall Abbey: *7315* Shropshire. Founded [mid 12th century] by Arrousian order then absorbed by the 'Augustinians'. Gift: Grindlow *1877* by *King John* [1199-1216].

Little Hucklow: *1678.* OE: *lytel* + *Hucca's* + *hlaw* = 'low' = a hill (before mining waste hillocks). Pb *Bagshawe* residence. 'Manor': *Ernvi* the Saxon; [1086] *William Peverell*; [1272-1307] *Archers*; *Foljambes*; *Carleils*; *Bernard Wake*. Great Hucklow *1777*

Little Longstone: *1871.* OE: *lytelI* = little + *lang* = long + *stan* = stone Pb Hall: Brick built [1747] *Carleil* residence. 'Manor': *Colne* a Saxon [1086] *Henry De Ferrars*; *Robert Fitz-Waltheof*; [1272-1307] *Mountjoys*; *Sir John Blount* by heiress, *Isolda Mountjoy*; [1474] *Richard Shakerley* by purchase; *Bess of Hardwick/Cavendish* by purchase. 'Moiety': [12th century] *Longsdons*. 'Mesne manor': [13th century] *Edensors*; [1399-1413] *Sir Thurston Bouer*.

Litton: *1675.* OE: *lictum* = burial ground + '*ton*' = a farmstead. See also '*Litton*' in People for alternative meaning of the name. Pb Litun [DB], Litton [1273 *Edward I*], Lutton [1302 *Edward I*]. 'Manor': [1086] *William Peverell*; *Littons*; [1597] *John Alsop* by purchase from *Rowland Lytton*; *Nicholas Bagshawe* by purchase (used as a residence); [1620] *Francis Bradshaw* by purchase; [1686] *Upton* by purchase; [1707] *Statham* by purchase; *Curzons* by purchase. Manufacturing: Cotton mill [1782] on the River Wye. Employed orphans, some as young as 7 years old from London. *Ellis Needham* was a harsh owner. [1844] 80 machine hosiery knitting frames. Birthplace: *William Bagshawe*, Apostle of the Peak [17/01/1628].

Locko Park: *4038.* South Derbyshire. Base of the *Gilbert* family. Beeley manor [1784] *2667*.

Lomberdale: *1963.* Dialect: *lomb* = gentle flow of water (River Bradford) + '*dale*'. Hall: Home of *Thomas Bateman,* the antiquarian [19th century].

Longendale: *0799.* OE: *lang* = long (8 km)+ *dael* = 'dale'. 'Manor': *Robert* Lord Holland until [7/10/1328], *Lovells* until [1485] (NB Battle of Bosworth), Crown confiscation, *Sir William Stanley* of Holt, probably *0738*, Norfolk by grant [1487] until [1495]. Shooting: Grouse. Reservoirs: In the Peak Park area Valehouse; Rhodeswood 1,3 million cubic metres (48 million cubic feet); Torside 65 hectares (160 acres) 6.6 million cubic metres (240 million cubic feet); Woodhead 6 million cubic metres (200 million cubic feet).

Longnor: *0864.* OE: *long* + *ofer* = a ridge. Langenoure [1227 *Henry III*], Longenoure [13th century]. Church: Possibly [12th century]. Communications: Turnpike [18th century]. Schools: Girls' and boys' boarding [1840s]. Longevity: *William Billings* died [25/01/1791] aged **112.** Memorial: Church of St Bartholomew [1223] *William Billings* 'Military History'.

Longshaw: *2581.* OE: *lang* + *scaega* = copse. Shooting lodge: For the Dukes of Rutland [1827].

Losehill *1585.* OE: *losian* = to perish + *hyll* = a hill. Legend: Losers of the bloody 'Dark Age' battle camped here; possible defeat of *King Cuicholm/Ceawlin* [560-91] of Wessex by *King Edwin* of Northumbria [?585-633]. Winners camped on Win Hill *1885*. Hall: *1583*.

Lud's Church: *9865.* Natural chasm probably caused by landslip 18 x 3 x 61 metres (60 x 10 x 200 feet) Possible 'Lollard' Meeting Place. Named after Pastor *Walter De Ludank* [14th century] whose granddaughter was killed in a raid by royal troops.

Lumford: *2169.* Dialect: *lum* = a place for the collection of water [from a quarry or mine]. Cottages and River Wye mill built by *Richard Arkwright*. 'Hold'.

Lutudarum: The name of a Roman emporium stamped on lead pigs found in North-east Derbyshire. Tapton *3972* may have been the site.

Lyme: *9682.* Latin: *limes* = a boundary [of Macclesfield Forest]. Gifts: Land. 1. *Edward III* to *Richard Danvers* (D'Anvers - French = Antwerpen - Flemish) [1346]. Hall: built by *Sir Piers Legh* died [1399].

2. Property by *Richard Legh,* 'Baron' Newton [1892] to the National Trust [1946]. Marriage: Heiress daughter of *Sir Thomas Danvers* to *Sir Piers Legh* [1388]. 'Battle of Blore Heath'. 'Crime'

Macclesfield Forest: *9671*. *Macca's* + OE: *feld* +ML: *forestis* Maclesfield [DB]. 'Saxons': Artefacts found. Royal 'forest': [1237]. Kings hunted here for meat until the [14th century]. Originally created by the Norman *Earls of Chester*. Chapel: Toot Hill. Rebuilt [1834] *9772*. Crime: Formerly a home of brigands and highwaymen. Wildlife: Badgers, red and fallow deer, foxes, geese, ducks, pheasants, ravens.

Magpie Mine: *1768*. Sheldon. Lead. Closed [1883] after the low return on the excessive investment in a 176 metres deep x 3.5km long (192 yards x 2 miles) 'sough' by *John Fairburn* of Sheffield. *Figure 11*, Metal Ore Extraction, refers.

Malcoff (e)/Malcalf: *0782*. Preaching place for *William Bagshawe,* Apostle of the Peak.

Mam Tor: *1283*. Dialect: *mam* = mother + OE: *torr* = rock, 'Shivering Mountain' in warm weather. 'Castles' Probable 'Iron Age' or'Celtic' Fort with 'Bronze Age' 'round barrows' within the enclosure. Rocks: 'Sandstone' overlying and slipping over shale during weathering. Hydrocarbon: 'Carbonite'. *Figures 12 & 29*, Rocks, Fire and Light, refer.

Manifold River and Valley **Railway:** *1059*. OE: *manigfeld* = many folds (meanders). Recreation: Name of a trail on the course of the former 'railway'. Angling. Power: For Wetton corn mill [1577] *0956*. *Figure 13*, Water and Wind Mills, refers.

Middleton by Youlgreave: *1963*. OE: *middel* = middle + '*ton*' = a farmstead. Middeltune [DB]. Pb Rocks: 'Barytes','Calcite'. Castle/fortified manor house. 'Bronze Age': Bowl found. *Figure 22*, refers. Communications: 'Portway' →Monyash *1566*. 'Manor': [1086] *Ralph Fitzherbert*; *Edensors*; [1216-72] *Herthills*; [1377-99] *Edmund Cokayne* by *Herthill* heiress; [1598-9] *Fulwood*;[1719] *Curzon* and *Bateman*; *Sanders, Viscount Howe*; [1771] *Howe* and *Roper*; [1800] *Thomas Bateman* by purchase.

Milldale: *1454*. OE: *mylen* = mill (River Dove) + *dael*. 'Methodist' Chapel: [1815]. The date on the wall refers to the permanent building not its predecessor. 'Packhorse': Way → Alstonefield *1355*.

Millers Dale: *1373*. Milndale [1630 *Charles I*], Millhousedale [1633 *Charles I*]. Rock: 'Amethyst quartz'. Recreation: Angling. Communications: 'Railway' station [1863-1968]. Lime kilns: Built 1879-80. 'Slotch' and 'crozel'. *Figure 14*, Railways, refers.

> *That valley where you might expect*
> *to catch sight of Pan, Apollo and the Muses,*
> *is now desecrated in order that a Buxton fool*
> *may be able to find himself in Bakewell*
> *at the end of twelve minutes.* (by rail)
>
> *Fors Clavigera by John Ruskin.*

Minories London EC3: Convent of the Minorities/Minoresses ('Poor Clares') *3582*. Income: Hartington church *1360*. Patron of St Giles Church before [1534] Abbess.

Mixon: *0457,* **Old Mixon Hay:** *0257*. OE: *mixen* = dung from a cowshed. Ownership: Land and mill (River Hamps) by Burton upon Trent Abbey *2423* ('Benedictine').

Monsal: *1871*. OE: *halh* = a valley (River Wye) Morleshal [1200 *John*].

> *And Monsal, thou mine of Arcadian treasure,*
> *Need we seek for Greek islands and spice-laden gales,*
> *While a Temple like thee, of enchantment and pleasure,*
> *May be found in our own native Derbyshire dales.*
>
> *Eliza Cook* [1812-99]

Monyash: *1566*. OE: *manig* = many + *aesc* = 'ash' tree. Maneis [DB], Moniasse [1200 *John*], Moniasche [1316 *Edward II*]. Pb Merchandising: Market charter granted [1340]. Steward of Haddon Hall *2366* bought eggs 27/12/1549. Communications: 'Packhorse' route. Normans: Church of St Leonard – a 'chapelry' of Bakewell about [1198]. Nonconformists: A Quaker Centre, Birthplace of *John Gratton* [1640]. Stopover [1769]. *Richard Boardman*, evangelist en route to North America held meeting at which the mother of prominent Wesleyan Methodist, *Jabez Bunting* [1779-1858] became a follower of Jesus Christ

Mineral ore: Lead. Rocks: 'Blue calcite'. Derby fossil 'limestone'. Lime kiln for limestone [calcite] processing. *Figure 12,* Rock Extraction, refers. Manufacturing: Candles, flint tools, rope.
'Manor': [1086] Royal 'demesne'; [1200] 'moieties' *Robert De Salocia, Matthew De Eston*; [1340] *William De Lynford* valet of *Edward III*; *Talbot,* Earl of Shrewsbury; [1616]. Three 'moieties' Earls of Arundel, Kent and Pembroke by co-heiresses; [1638] 1st ⅓rd *Savilles* then *Gilberts* by heiress; [1738] *Edward Cheney* by purchase; 2nd and 3rd ⅓rds [1640] *John Shallcross* by purchase; [1646] *Thomas Gladwin* by purchase; *Sir Talbot Clerke* and *Dr Henry Bourne* by co-heiresses; [1721] *Edward Cheney* by purchase from *Sir Talbot Clerke*; [1736] *Edward Cheney* by purchase from *Dr Henry Bourne*; *Richard Fynney.*

Hills* and valleys# are what you see
It's mother nature's gift for thee
With bustling waters passing through.
This heaven was made for all of you.

Samantha Hadfield

- Line 1   High Low 312 metres Dyke Head 316 metres* Lathkill Dale#
- Line 3   The source of the River Lathkill is underground> *1765*

Moor Hall: *1668.* OE: mor. The ancestral home of the *De Gernon* family.

Mouse/moss 'Low': *0853.* OE: mus = mouse or mos = moss + hlaw = 'low' = a hill. 'Bronze Age': Drinking cup, skeleton and arrows found.

Musden: OE: mus = mouse [infested] + dun = a hill Musden. **'Low':** *1250.* Mudesen 'Grange': *1251.* Land owned by Burton upon Trent Abbey *2423* ('Benedictine').

Needham: *1165.* OE: nied/nyd/neod = need + ham = homestead. Nedham [1244 *Henry III*]. 'Grange'.

Nether Haddon: *2266.* OE: niothera = nether/below + haep = heather + 'dun' = a hill Pb 'Manor': [1086] Royal 'demesne'; *Peverells*; [1154-89] Itinerant Justice *William Avenell* (held by 'knight' service; [1189-99]. Roche Abbey gift of *Sir William Avenell*; [1509-47] *Francis Talbot,* 5th Earl of Shrewsbury; [1558-1603] *Sir Thomas Gargave* purchase from *Gilbert Talbot,* 7th Earl of Shrewsbury; about [1600] *Richard Berry,* physician to *Oliver Cromwell,* by heiress. Moiety: [1378] From *Bassets* to *Vernons* 'Parish' church: Haddon Hall chapel *2366.*

New Engine* Mine: *2177.* Mineral ore: 'Heminorphite'. Deepest mine in Derbyshire 333 metres (1,092 feet). *New pump engines made this greater depth possible. Worked until [1884].

Newhaven: *1660.* Coaching inn: Built by the 5th *Duke of Devonshire* [1802].

Nine Ladies: *2563.* 'Bronze Age' Stone circle – Cork, Gorse, Heart stones. Diameter 10 metres (35 feet).

North Lees: *2383.* ON: northr + OE: 'lee' = a shelter. Hall: Built by *William Jessop* [16th century] of Broom Hall, Sheffield. Restored [1959]. Interior plaster ('limestone') decoration. Family associations: *Eyre* [17th century] tenants. Possibly Thornfield Hall in Jane Eyre. **Old Lees** *2081.*

Oakenclough: OE: ac = 'oak' + cloh = 'clough'. Hall: *0563.*

Odin Mine: *1383* 'Sitch': *1483.* Odin, in Norse mythology, the supreme creator god.

Offerton: *2181.* Offa's or OE: offerre = to present + 'ton' = a farmstead Offretune [DB], Offerton [1220 *Henry III*]. Hall: [16th century]. *Eyre* family. Rock: 'Sandstone'.

Ollerbrook 'Booth': *1285.* OE: alor = 'alder' [trees] + broc = a brook.

Ollset/Ollerset: *0285.* OE: alor = 'alder' [trees] + settan = planted. Hall: [1529] built by *Squire Newton*; ruins [1892].

One 'Ash': *1665.* OE: an = one + aesc = 'ash' tree Aneise [DB] = single ash. Oneash [1544] 'Manor': [1154-89] *Avenells*; [1189-99] Roche Abbey ('Cistercian') *5489* grange* gift of *Sir William Avenell*; [1509-47] *Francis Talbot* gift; about [1600] *Sir Thomas Gargrave* purchased from *Gilbert Talbot*; *Richard Berry,* physican to *Oliver Cromwell* by heiress; *Cavendish.*place of confinement for unmanageable monks from Roche abbey *5489.*

Onecote: *0455.* OE: <u>an</u> = one + <u>cote</u> = cottage/shelter/fold for sheep Anecote [1199 *John*], <u>Onecote</u> [1272 *Henry III*]. <u>Communications</u>: 'Turnpike' [18th century]. <u>Ownership</u>: Burton upon Trent Abbey *2423* ('Benedictine').

Otterbrook 'Booth': *1285.* OE: *oter* = <u>otter</u> + *broc* = <u>brook</u> + ON: *buth* = <u>booth</u> = a shelter.

Over Haddon: *2066.* OE: *ofer* = over + *haep* = heather + '*dun*' = a hill Pb <u>Mineral ore</u>: Lead in the River Lathkill valley. '<u>Manor</u>': [1086] *Peverells*; *Avenells*; [1195] *William De Vernon*; *Gilbert le Franceys*; [1565] *John Manners*, Duke of Rutland by heiress. '<u>Mesne manor</u>': *Suttons*; *Cokes* of Trusley; *Lambs*, 'Viscounts' Melbourne; 'Earls' *Cowpers*.

Overton Hall: *0078.* OE: *ofer* = over + '*ton*' = a farmstead. <u>Owners</u>: *Downes* family had the right to hang anyone caught hunting in the High Peak forest.

Padley: *2579.* *Padda's* + OE: '*ley*' = a clearing. '<u>Manor</u>': *Bernakes*; *Padleys*; [1422-61] *Sir Thomas Eyre* by heiress; *Sir Thomas Fitzherbert* by heiress; following *Fitzherbert* expulsion temporary possession by *Tiptofts*; then *Talbots*; *Ashton* by purchase, *Spencers* heiress, *Shuttleworths* heiress. <u>Hall</u>: and Roman Catholic martyrs' Chapel – *Nicholas Garlick* and *Robert Ludlam*.

When Garlick did the ladder[*] kiss
And Sympson after hie,
Methought that there St Andrew was
Desirous for to die.

When Ludlam looked smilingly
And joyful did remain,
It seemed St Stephen[#] was standing by
For to be stoned again

Local ballad

Line 1 [*] Ladder of the scaffold. Line 7 [#] The first Christian martyr

'Panniers' Pool: *0068.* '<u>Packhorse trains</u>: Watering hole for at Three Shires Head (Five trail junction).

Parsley Hay: *1563.* OE: *petersilie* = cow parsley *anthricus sylvestris* + *hay* = an enclosure. <u>Tumulus</u>: '<u>Railway</u>' Junction: High Peak railway and Ashbourne → Buxton railway. [1890s-1967]. <u>Rock</u>: 'Pink birds eye marble'.

Parwich: *1854.* Latin: *par* = equal + Latin: *vicus* = a trading centre and OE: *wic* = *farm/dwelling/ hamlet/'village'/manufacturing centre. <u>Peuerwich</u> [966], Pevrewic [DB] bees. Pb '<u>Manor</u>': [1561] *Levings* <u>Hall</u> [1747]. '<u>Normans</u>': Church of St Peter. Doorway, chancel arch and 'typanum' with farm animals. *Figures 7* Church Grpahics and *25* Domesday Survey, refer.

Peak Castle: See *Peveril*.

Peak Forest: *1179.* <u>Chapel</u>: St Charles the Martyr (extra parochial and extra episcopal) used for an annual average of 60 run away marriages until curtailed by Fleet Street Marriage Act [1753]. The 'Gretna Green of the Peak' could be reached from Buxton using Batham Gate Roman road *0876*, by Chapel en le Frith cotton, paper and printing workers, Eyam *2176* and Hucklow *1777* miners and Foolow *1976* quarry workers as well as being accessible from Bakewell *2168*, by the Monsal *1771*, Millers *1373*, Monk's *1374*, Peter *1275*, Hay *1276*, Dam *1178* linked 'dales' route. <u>Rocks</u>: 'Dolerite', 'Toadstone'.

Peveril: *1582.* Peuerel [1246]. <u>Castle</u>: Saxon and [11th century], roofed with Derbyshire lead and named after *William Peveril*, bailiff of the Royal 'Desmesne' 'Manors' in North-west Derbyshire.

Pilhough: *2564.* Dialect: *pill* = bare + *hoh* = spur.

Pilsbury: *1163.* *Pil's* + OE: *burg* = a fort. Pilesberie [DB]. '<u>Motte and bailey</u>': 'Castle' hills.

Pilsley: *2471.* *Pil's* + OE: '*ley*' = a clearing. Pirelaie [DB], Pilisleg [1205]. '<u>Manor</u>': With Edensor *2569*.

Pott Shrigley: *9479.* *Pott's* + OE: *shrike* (butcher bird) + '*ley*' = a clearing (in Macclesfield Forest). Schriggel [1285 *Edward I*], Schiggeleg [1288 *Edward I*], Shriggelepot [1348 *Edward III*], Potte Shryggelegh [1354 *Edward III*], Potte et Schrygelegh [1357 *Edward III*], Potte et Shriglegh [1393 *Richard II*]. <u>Family</u>: *Downes* owners of Shrigley Park, [1492]; *Geoffrey* of London's bequest to found 'chantry' and maintain 2 priests, unconnected with any Cheshire gentry families, their nomination to be by the owner of the park. <u>Hall</u>: [1824] built and owned by *Turner* of Blackburn *6827*. <u>Crime</u>: Only daughter, *Ellen Turner*, abducted from school in Liverpool by *Edward Gibbon Wakefield*, coloniser, [1796-1862]; secretly married at Gretna Green *3268*.

Priestcliffe: *1371*.   OE: <u>preost</u> = priest + <u>clif</u> = a cliff.   Presteclive [DB].   <u>Rocks</u>: 'Derbyshire diamonds' in weathered 'toadstones'.

Pym Chair: *0986, 9576*.   Dialect: <u>pill</u> = to rob + OF: <u>chaiere</u> Highwaymen's look-out.

Raper Lodge: *2165*.   MD: <u>reeper</u> and MLG: <u>reper</u> = a roper [rope maker].

Ravensdale: *1773*.   OSca: <u>hran</u> = raven + OE: <u>dael</u> = 'dale' Rauenes [DB], Ravenesdale [1251 *Henry III*].

Ridge: *0062*.   OE: <u>hrycg</u> = ridge.   <u>Hall</u>: Demolished, formerly one of the *Bagshawe* residences. <u>Rock</u>: 'Sandstone' quarry.   *Figure 12,* Rock Extraction, refers.

Roche Abbey: *5489*.   South Yorkshire. ('Cistercian') Sancta Maria de <u>Rupe</u> = Roche, Founded by *Richard De Bully* [1147].   <u>Gift</u>: One 'Ash' 'Manor' *1665* by *Sir William Avenell* [1189-99].

Rowland: *2172*.   OSca: <u>ra</u> = roe + <u>lundr</u> = wood.   Ralunt [DB], Raalund [1169 *Henry II*].   Pb 'Manor': [1086] Royal 'demesne'; [1199-1216] *Staffords*; [1558-1603] *Rowland Eyre* by heiress; [1853] *Colonel Leslie* inherited from his wife, *Dorothy Eyre*.   'Parish': Bakewell *2168*.

Rowlee Pasture: *1589*.   *Hropwulf's* + OE: '<u>lee</u>' = a shelter for sheep to stand under.   *Stephenson* family and Elton manor *2260*.   *Figure 9*, Ubiquitous Farming, refers.

Rowsley: *2566*.   *Hropwulf's* + OE: '<u>ley</u>' = a clearing.   Reuslege [DB], Rolvesle [1204 *John*].   <u>Birthplace</u>: *Thomas Bateman*, the antiquarian [8/11/1821].   <u>Integrated transport</u>: Boarding point for omnibuses meeting trains about [1874].   'Manor': [1086] Royal 'demesne'; [1189-99] *Henry De Rollesley*; [1558-1603] *Sir William Kniveton*; [1625-49] *John Manners*, 'Duke' of Rutland by purchase.

Row<u>tor</u> rocks: *2261*.   *Hrowulf's* + OE: '<u>tor</u>' = a bare, rocky hill.   Rocking stones of eroded 'millstone grit'.   'Druid': Vague connections.   <u>Rock carvings</u>: *Revd Thomas Eyre* died [1717].

Rufford Abbey: *6464*.   Nottinghamshire.   ('Cistercian').   <u>Gift</u>: Free 'warren' Brushfield Manor *1672*.

Salterford: *9876*.   OE: <u>sealt</u> + <u>forda</u> 'Saltway' or salt sellers' ford.   Saltreford [DB], <u>Salterford</u> [1241 *Henry III*].   <u>Hall</u>: Built [1733].   Leased for use as an agricultural training college [1895].

<u>Scalderditch</u> *1159*.   OE: <u>sceldu</u> = shallow + <u>dic</u> = a ditch.

Sharp 'Low' *1652*.   OE: <u>scearp</u> = sharp + <u>hlaw</u> = 'low' = a hill.   <u>Tumulus</u>: A skeleton of a young person, possibly 'Celtic', was found by *Thomas Bateman*, the antiquary.

Sha<u>tton</u>: [DB] Scetune bees OE: <u>sceat</u> = tongue of land in a corner *1881* between River Derwent and Overdale Brook; *1982* between the River Noe and Deep Dalebrook + '<u>ton</u>' = a farmstead.   Scetune [DB], <u>Scatton</u> [1230 *Henry III*].   <u>Hall</u>: *Eyres*.

Sheldon: *1768*.   ME: <u>schele</u> = shed + '<u>dun</u>' = hill.   Pb Scelhadun [DB], Schelehaddon [1230 *Henry III*]. <u>Mineral ores</u>: 'Cinnabar', 'sphalerite' Cornish miners.   <u>Rocks</u>: 'Black birds' eye marble', 'Rosewood marble' 'Manor': [1086] Royal 'demesne'; [1216-72] *Pickfords* by alienation; passed with Ashford in the Water *1969*.   Figures 11, 12 & 21; Metals, Rocks, Incomers refers.

Shireoaks: *0783*.   OE: <u>scir</u> = 'shire' + <u>ac</u> = 'oak'.   'Oak' trees on a 'shire' boundary.   'Packhorse' Route → Ford *0882*.

Slack: *0781*.   ON: <u>slakki</u> = a shallow valley or dell .   <u>Hall</u>: [1727].

<u>Slaley</u>: *2757*.   D: <u>slaf</u> or OE: <u>slaef</u> = muddy + '<u>ley</u>' = a clearing.

Smerril: *1962*.   OE: <u>smeorn</u> = butter + <u>rill</u> = small stream/rivulet.   Smerehull [1272 *Henry III*].   'Grange': owned by *Lady Grace Manners* [1650]

Snake Pass: *0892*.   OE: <u>snaca</u> Altitude 612 metres (1,229 feet).   'Turnpike'.

Snitterton: *2760*.   *Snytra's* + OE: '<u>ton</u>' = a farmstead.   Sinitretone [DB], <u>Sniterton</u> [1232 *Henry III*].   Pb 'Chantry': Sold by *Warners* to *Richard De Wendesley* [1531].   <u>Hall</u>: [16th century].   'Manor': [1086] Royal 'demesne', 'berewick' of Matlock; *Shirleys*; *John Sacheverel* of Ible *2457* By heiress who sold in moieties; ½ *Milwards* by purchase; [1670] *Charles Adderley* by heiress; *Henry Ferne* by purchase; *Turner of Derby* by heiress; *Arkwright* by purchase; other ½ *Shores*; *Hodgkinsons, Banks*.

Soles Hill: *0952*. OF: <u>soule</u> = [sandal] sole-shaped Animals' wallowing place (River Hamps).

Sparrowpit: *0880*. Dialect: <u>sparrow</u> = small + OE: <u>pytt</u> = a pit = excavation usually filled withwater (reservoir). 'Barrow'. Cottages: Rubble walls and stone "slates". Turnpike' → Sheffield [1759].

St Mary de Pratis: ('Benedictine') [1160]. Lands: In Haddon *2366,* Middleton Moor *1963,* Stanton *2464,* Winster *2460,* Youlgreave *2064.*

Stanage Edge: *2384*. OE: <u>stan</u> = stone + <u>ecg</u> = an edge. Rock: 'Millstone grit'. 'Romans': The Ridgeway, a Roman road → Hathersage *2381*. Pole: Erected to guide 'Jaggers' [1550] *2484*.

Stanshope: *1354*. OE: <u>stan</u> = stone + <u>hop</u> = a valley [Pasture Lane]. Stanesope [DB] 'Manor': Royal 'desmesne' [1087]. 'Grange'. Hall: [17th century] *1254*.

Stanton in the Peak: *2464*. OE: <u>stan</u> = stony + '<u>ton</u>' = a farmstead Pb. Halls: [16th century and 1667] Quarry: 'Millstone grit'. Ecclesiastical artefact: Italianate bronze 'stoup' [1596] in Holy Trinity Church. Memorial: *Henry Bache Thornhill* died [1822]. Trees: 'Elm', 'walnut' and 'yew'
'Manor': *Raven* the Saxon, [1086] *Henry De Ferrars*; ? *Bardolfs*; ? *Tibetots*; [1327-77] *Foljambes*; *Plumptons* by gift; *Sotehill* and *Rocliffe* by rascality; *Baches* by purchase; [1698] *John Pole Thornhill* by heiress; [1875] *Henry Francis Hurlock* by descent; [1881] *Major McCreagh* by heiress.

Stanton Lees: *2563*. OE: <u>stan</u> = stony + '<u>ton</u>' = farmstead + '<u>lee</u>' = a shelter for sheep to stand under. Quarry: 'Millstone grit'.

Stanton Moor: *2463*. OE: <u>stan</u> = stone + '<u>ton</u>' = a farmstead 'Bronze Age': Enclosed cremation cemetery. *Figure 22*, Bronze Age, refers. Tower: *2563* erected by *Thornhill* family as a memorial to *Charles,* 2nd Earl Grey instigator of the First Reform Bill [1832] [1764-1845] 'Cairn'.

Stanton Woodhouse: *2564*. OE: <u>stan</u> = stone + '<u>ton</u>' = a farmstead + <u>wud</u> = wood + <u>hus</u> = house Family: [Late 16th century] *Alen/Aleyne*. Hall: A shooting box (wood house) for the *Manners* Family [19th century]. Acorns gathered for Ford Hall *0653* [1758]

Steep 'Low': *1256.* OE: <u>steap</u> = steep + <u>hlaw</u> = 'low' = a hill Gibbet. 'Saxons': Evidence of secondary Saxon burials above 'Iron Age' ones.

Stoke: *2376*. OE: <u>stoc</u> = a place. 'Manor': [1086] Royal 'demesne'; *Greys* of Codnor *4149*; [1473] *Thomas Barlow* by purchase; *William Cavendish*; *Bullocks*; [1656] *Sacheverells* by purchase; *Simpsons*; *Bridgemans,* Earls of Bradford by heiress. Hall: [1557] *Barlow* family.

Ston(e)y Middleton: *2275*. OE: <u>stan</u> = stony + <u>middel</u> = middle + '<u>ton</u>' = a farmstead Pb Hall: Probably [16th century]. Residence of *Lord 'Denman'* [1874]. Building: Tepid baths erected by *Lord Denman* over springs known to the Romans; unsuccessful attempt to compete with Buxton. Mineral ore: 'Galena' Rock: Clay. Processing: 'Limestone' burning - for making lime [1788]. Hydrocarbons: Natural gas and oil. *Figures11, 12 & 28*, Metals, Rocks, Fire, refer. 'Manor': [1086] *Chaworth*; *Bernakes*; [1272-1307] *Thomas,*Lord Furnival; [1383] with Eyam *2176*, Estate: [1761] *Dr Joseph Denman* of Bakewell *2168* dowry of *Elizabeth Fynney* of Ashford in the Water *1969*. No children passed to *Thomas Denman*, Baron [1834] Lord Chief Justice of England [1832], Speaker of the House of Lords [1835]

Stonyway: *9972*. Toll "booth" for Macclesfield → Cat and Fiddle → Buxton 'turnpike'.

Swainsley: *0957*. OD: <u>Sven's</u> or ON or OSw: <u>Sveinn's</u> + '<u>ley</u>' = a clearing. Hall: Built by a London lawyer [1867].

Swythamley: *9764*. OE: <u>swy</u> = a pig + <u>ham</u> = a homestead + '<u>ley</u>' = a clearing. Swuthamlee, Swythumley, Swythomlee. Hall: Dieulacres Abbey *9857* hunting lodge. Rebuilt by *Brocklehursts* [19th century]. 'Grange': Dieulacres Abbey *9857* ('Cistercian'). After dissolution [1534] *John Witney.* [1540] granted to *Traffords* by *Henry VIII*. Mineral: 'Haematite'. *Figure 11*.

Taddington: *1471*. *Tada's* + '<u>ton</u>' = a farmstead. Tateringctun [840], Tadintune [DB], Pb Tatinton [1200 *John*], Tatinton [1263 *Henry III*], Tatingtone [1275 *Edward I*]. 'Manor': [1086] Royal 'demesne'; [1199-1216] *Daniels* gift of *King John*; [1272-1307] 'moieties' *Michael De Hockele, William Cotterell,*

William De Hamilton; [1307-27] *William Cotterell* under the Crown. Memorial: *Blackwells* [15th century]. Longevity: *William Hexed* died aged **218**.

Taxal: *0079*. *Tatuc's* OE: halh = alluvial land by a river [Goyt] or *taki* = surety/bail. Tackishalch [1273 *Edward I*], Takeshale [1274 *Edward I*], Tackesal [1285 *Edward I*], Tackesal [1285 *Edward I*], Tacsal [1288 *Edward I*], Landowners: *Joddrell* family, warriors at Agincourt [1415]. *Downes* family from Shrigley *9479*. They had right to hang anyone caught hunting in High Peak Forest. Religious persecution: [1792] 20 estate cottages demolished by staunch Anglican, *Edward,* to avoid 'Methodist' miners' tenancies. Royal connection: *Michael Heathcote* [1690-1763], Gentleman of the pantry and yeoman of the mouth (food taster) to *George II* [1683-1760]. Memorials: In the Church of St James/St Leonard to *Michael Heathcote* Gentleman of the Pantry and Yeoman of the Mouth to *George II* [1690-1763] and *Joddrell*. 'Battle of Blore Heath'.

Thornhill: *1983*. OE: thorn = thorn + hyll = a hill Thornhull [1230 *Henry III*] 'Manor': *?William Peverell*; *Thornhills*; [1404] *Eyres*; [1602] *Adam Slack*; [1611] *Eyres of Hassop*; [1853] *Colonel Charles Stephen Leslie* inherited from *Dorothy Eyre*, his wife.

Thorpe: *1550*. [DB] ON: torp = a farm/hamlet **Cloud** OE: clud = a hill. Carboniferous reef knoll. Manor: [17th century] *John Milward's* father by purchase from *Cokaynes*. 'Normans': Tower and nave in the Church of St Leonard. Plague: [1538].

Thor's Cave: *0954*. OE: *Thor* = god of thunder or '*tor*' = a hill + Latin: cava. 'Bronze' and 'sandstone' vessels. Pottery: 'Samian' and Roman.

Throwley: *1152*. OE: thrawan = twisted + '*ley*' = a clearing. Hall: [16th century] with 'Pele' tower. Owned by *Earl Cathcart* [1874]. 'Saxons': Remains.

Thursbitch: *9975*. OE: thyrs = giant + bitch = 'beech'.

Tides 'Low': *1578*. *Tidi's* = OE: hlaw = 'low' = a hill 'Round Barrow'.

Tideswell: *1575*. *Tidi's* + OE wella = stream or spring. Tidesuuelle [DB], Tiddeswell [1230 *Henry III*]. Pb 'Parish': [1086] A 'berewick' of Hope *1783*, became a parish in its own right [1245 or 1252] following a visit by Papal Commissioners. *Daniel* family. Grammar school: Founded [1558] by *Bishop Robert Pursglove*.Closed [1927]. Manufacturing: Hand woven silk scarves outsourced by a Macclesfield company. Merchandising: Market charter granted to *Bramptons* [1250] ?*Thomas Armiger*. Fairs Five every year. Geology: Volcanic sill in quarry. Strip farming: Enclosing walls around individual strips. Memorials: *John Foljambe* died [1383]; *Thurstan de Bower* died [1423]; *Sampson Meverell* died [1462]; *Robert Lytton* died [1483]; *Bishop Robert Pursglove* died [1579]. Local wood carvings in the church of St John the Baptist. 'Alabaster'. Ballad: Tideswell in Uproar. Visit of the future king *George IV* [1806]. 'Manor': [1086] Royal 'demesne'; *William Peverell*; [1199-1216] *Thomas Armiger* or *Thomas* then *Monechias Lameley* gift of *King John*; 'Moieties' *De Paunton* and *De Brampton*; [1216-72] *Richard Daniel* by purchase; *Thomas Meverell* by co-heiresses; 'Moieties' *Reginald De Marchington* and *John De Turvill*; [1377-99] *Stafford* of Eyam *2176* probably as agents for *Marchingtons* and *Turvills*; [1558-1603] *Meverells* by gift or purchase; [1625-49] *Thomas,* Lord Cromwell, Earl of Ardglass by heiress; [1654] *Eyres* of Highlow *2180*; [1802] sale ordered by the Court of Chancery; purchased by *Cavendish*.

Tintwistle: *0297*. OE: twisla = fork of a river [River Etherow and Arnfield Brook]. Tengestvisie [DB], Tyengetwisell, Tyngetwisel [1286 *Edward I*]. 'Palaeolithic': Leaf shaped arrow flint head found. 'Bronze Age': Mace head. Christ Church: Built [1837].

Tissington: *1752*. OE: *Tidsige's* + '*ton*' = a farmstead. Tinzinctum [DB], Tiscontona [1141 *Stephen*], Ticintona [1154-98 *Henry II & Richard I*], Tyscinton [1242 *Henry III*]. Pb Author: Revd *Richard Greaves*, author of Spiritual Quixote once lived in the hall. 'Recreation': Trail on the track of the former Ashbourne → Buxton 'Railway' 'Normans': 'Font' in the Church of St Mary. Hall: Built [1609] Served as Royalist headquarters [1644]. Enlarged [1896] 'Military History' 'Manor': About [1086-1100] *Henry De Ferrars*; [1100-1259] *William Le Savage*; [1259] *Edensor* and *Meynell* families by heiresses; *FitzHerbert*

Treak Cavern: *1383*. Dialect = to wander idly [the underground water]. Discovered by lead miners.

Tunstead: *1074*. OE: '*ton*' = a farmstead. Birthplace of *James Brindley* [1716-72] engineer for the Bridgwater Canal; the first in England.

Tutbury: Staffordshire *2129*. ('Benedictine') 'Priory' founded by *Henry de Ferra(e)rs* [1080]. A dependency of St Pierre sur Dives Normandy. *49°01'N 00°02'W*. Grant: Tithes from Tissington *1752* [11th century].

Upper Cupola: *2175*. OE: <u>yppe</u> = raised place + <u>cuppe</u> = cup. 'Cupellation'. Rock: 'Fluorite' quarry.

Upper Hulme: *0160*. OE: <u>yppe</u> = raised place + ODa: <u>hulm</u> = small piece of landby a stream (River Churnet). 'Romans': Road north east → Buxton. Manufacturing: 'Flax' mill.

Vale Royal Abbey: Cheshire *6060*. ('Cistercian') Foundation [1277]. Land and Church of St Edmund, Castleton *1583*.

Via Gellia: *2656*. Constructed by *Philip Gell* in a 2 miles long ravine. [18th century].

Viator bridge: *1354*. Named after a character in The Compleat Angler by *Izaak Walton and Charles Cotton*.

Ward's Piece: *1585*. Commemorates *Bert Ward* leader of the mass trespass [1932].

Wardlow: *1874*. OE: <u>weard</u> = [protective] watch + <u>hlaw</u> = '<u>low</u>' = a hill. Wardelowe [1258 *Henry III*], Wardlowe [1275 *Edward I*] Pb. 'Bronze Age': Fragments of an incense cup, flints and Burnt bones.

Warslow: *0858*. <u>Waer's</u> + OHG: <u>hlais</u> = '<u>low</u>' = a burial mound ['tumuli' nearby]. Wereslei [DB], Warthsale [1146 *Stephen*]. 'Manor': Lord agreed enclosure of waste land by tenants for conversion to arable. Hall: *0959*: Rebuilt by *Sir George Crewe* (*Harpur-Crewe* family) [1830] as a residence for Alstonefield estate agent, *Richard Manclark* died [1850] and as a summer residence for the *Crewe* family. See also *Hunter*. After [1850] it was used as a shooting lodge. Mineral ores: Copper, lead. Rocks: 'Calcite'. Communications: 'Turnpike' [18th century]. Ecclesiastical 'Parish': Separate [1785]. Joint with Elkstone *0559* [1902].

Waltham Abbey: *3800*. Hertfordshire. Roofed with Peak lead [1177-83].

Welbeck Abbey: *5674*. Nottinghamshire. ('Pre-monstratensian'). Gift: Derwent Chapel by *King John*. Founded by *Thomas de Cuckeney* [1154-89].

Wensley (Wendesley): *2661*. <u>Wendel's</u> + OE: '<u>ley</u>' = a clearing Pb. Church: St Mary's [1843]. 'Moiety Manor': Purchased by *Sir Richard Arkwright* [18th century]. Wesleyan 'Methodist': Local Preachers' Mutual Aid Association founded [1849], renamed Leaders of Worship and Preachers Trust [2005].

Wetton: *1055*. OE: <u>waet</u> = <u>wet</u> + '<u>ton</u>' = a farmstead Wettindun [1252 *Henry III*], Wetton [1327 *Edward III*]. Archaeological discoveries: Armlet made from 'bronze' wire. Anglo-Saxon and Roman remains. Mineral ore processing: Possible Roman lead smelting settlement at Borough Fields. Church: St Margaret's rebuilt [1820].

Wetton 'Low' *1154*. 'Neolithic' round burial mound excavated [1848]. In the area 23 barrows were opened by *Bateman, Carrington and Garner* 15 were 'Palaeolithic' or 'Neolithic'.

Wet-'Withi(e)ns': *2376*. OE: <u>waet</u> = wet + <u>with</u> = a strong flexible twig of 'willow'. 'Bronze Age': Stone circle.

Wheston/Whetstone: *1376, 0170*. OE: <u>hwetstan</u> = a whetstone* [for scythe sharpening]. Whestan [1231 *Henry III*]. *Warslow *0858* local word for whetstone = bullstone. Pb Hall: [18th century]. Strip farming: Enclosing walls around individual strips.

White 'Rake': OE: <u>hwit</u> *1974*. Mineral ores: Lead, copper and zinc.

Wildboarclough: *9868*. OE: <u>wil</u> = trap + <u>bar</u> = boar in a <u>cloh</u> = a 'clough'. Wildeborclogh [1357], Wylborlogh [1409 *Henry IV*], Wilberclogh [1503 *Henry VII*], Wideborclogh [1520 *Henry VIII*], Wisberslough [1639 *Charles I*]. Coal: 'Bell pits' [17th century]. Church: St Saviour built [1901] by 16th *Earl of Derby* in thanksgiving for the return of his sons from the Boer War [1899-1902]. Cotton: Decrease in cotton printing (Clough Brook) led to unemployment [1861]. Silk: Further decrease in employment due to recession in silk trade [1871].

Wilne Ferry: *4530*. Nottinghamshire. The confluence of Rivers Derwent and Trent. One writer states that it is the 'Limit of River Trent navigation' but makes no reference to the draught of vessels. Possible route via River Derwent of lead exports → Boston *3244*.

Wincle *9665*. *Wineca's* hill. Wynchull [1285 *Edward I*], Wynkehull [1291 *Edward I*], Wynkhull [1354 *Edward III*], Wincell [1543 *Henry VIII*], Wyncle [1544 *Henry VIII*], Wyncull [1547 *Henry VIII*]. 'Bronze Age': Cremation urn. 'Romans': Hoard of gold jewellery. 'Grange': Gift of *Ranulph III*, 6th 'Earl' of Chester, 1st 'Earl' of Lincoln [1170-1232] to Combermere Abbey ('Cistercian'). 'Manufacturing': Stoppage at the cotton mill (Hog Clough) [1851]. Employment decreased due to a recession in the silk industry [1871]. Church: St Michael's built [1820]. Parish: Prestbury *8976*.

Windy 'Knoll': *1383*. Hydrocarbons: 'Elaterite', 'olefinite'. Mineral ores: Iron 'pyrites'.

Winster: *2460*. OE: *Wine's* + *thryne* = a thorn bush. Winsterne [DB], Winesterna [1121 *Henry I*] Pb 'Manor': [1086] *Henry De Ferrars*; [1216-72] *Edmund*, Earl of Lancaster temporary possession; *Mountjoys*; *Sir John Blount* by heiress; *Meynells* by purchase; [1558-1603] Freeholders. Mineral ores: 'Goethite', 'Limonite'. Chapel: Gift to Abbey of Leicester ('Augustinian') *5805* by *Henry II* [1154-89]. Hall: Tenanted by *Llewllyn Jewitt*, antiquarian. Built [1624] using Stancliffe 'millstone grit' *2563*. Church: St John the Baptist [1721]. Pancake Races. *Figure 11*.

Wishing stone: *1376*.

Wolfscote 'Grange': *1358*. OE: *wulf* = wolf + *cote* = a shelter against wolves.

Woodhead: *0900*. Railway tunnels: *1301* First tunnels constructed [1845 & 1852] 4,846 metres (5,300 yards) for the Manchester, Sheffield → Lincolnshire Railway. Reservoir: *0899* 6 million cubic metres (200 million cubic feet) capacity. Church: St James' [18th century].

Wormhill: *1274*. OE: *wyrm* = worm + *hyll* = a hill Wruenele [DB], Wrmenhulle [1226 *Henry III*], Wurmehill [1227 *Henry III*]. 'Manor': *Siward* the Saxon; [1086] *Henry de Ferrars*; *Sir John Foljambe* (Last *Foljambe* resident *Sir Godfrey* [died 9/9/1388]; held portion of forest on Horseback attended by a boy; leased 10 acres (4 hectares) to *Nicholas and Letitia Stanedon* for one rose payable at the nativity of St John the Baptist), [1392] *Sir Robert Plumpton* by heiress but sold to cover legal expenses against *Empson, Henry VII's* miscreant lawyer; [1489] *Catherine Eyre*; held portion of forest for annual payment of 3d (= 1p) + knight service [1625-49] *Adam/William Bagshawe*. Hall: [1697] *Francis Westby Bagshawe JP DL* [1890]. Rock: 'Dolerite'. Preacher: *William Bagshawe*, "Apostle of the Peak", [1628-1702], preached his first sermon here. Church: St Margaret's west tower with medieval base.

Wye/Wey, river: *2267*. OE: *wye* = vigorous [man].Wey [1235 *Henry III*], Weye [1286 *Edward I*]. 'Romans': Road nearby. River valley used for their invasion. Communications: 'Turnpike' along the valley [1810]. Recreation: Angling. Water Power: For Caudwell *2566*, Cressbrook *1772*, Litton *1573*, Lumford *2168* and 16 other mills.

Youlgr(e)ave: *2064*. OE: *geolu* = yellow + *graf* = grove. Giolgrave [DB], Hyolgrave [1208 *John*], Yolegrave [1259 *Henry III*], Yolgreue [1285 *Edward I*]. Pb 'Manor': *Colle* the Saxon; [1086] *Henry De Ferrars*; [1272-1307] *Shirleys*; *Rossingtons*; *Gilberts* by heiress; *Barnesley* by heiress; *Buxtons* by purchase; [1685] *Manners*. Old Hall and Old Hall farm [1650]. 'Grange' 296 hectares (731 acres) 'Normans': Parts of All Saints' Church. Font [1200] dedication of church aisle [1904], *Thomas Cockayne* died [1488], *Robert Gilbert and family, Sir John Rossington*. Mineral ores: 'Haematite', lead, 'Wad'. Rocks: 'Calcite', 'Stucco'. *Figures 11 & 12*, Metal Ores, Rocks, refer. Unusual 'stoup' projecting from the font side supported by a salamander. Memorials: *Charles I*.

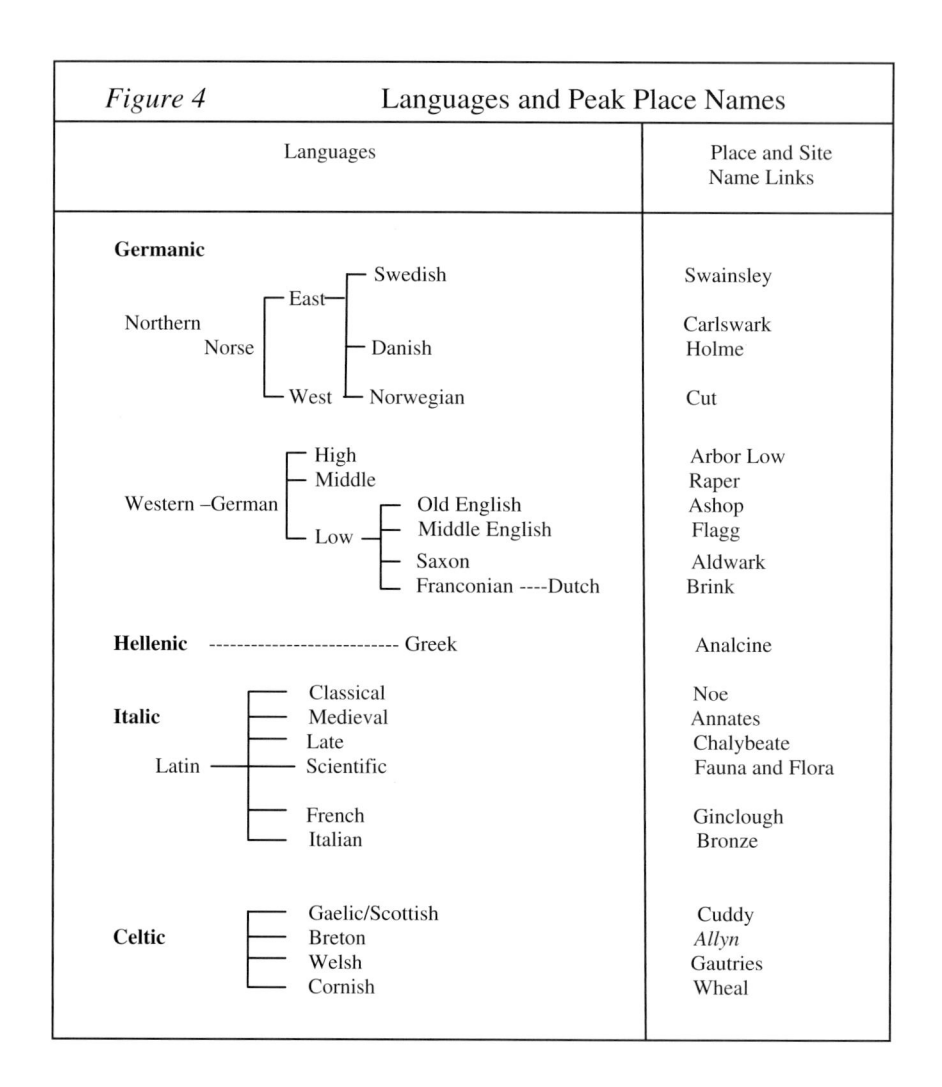

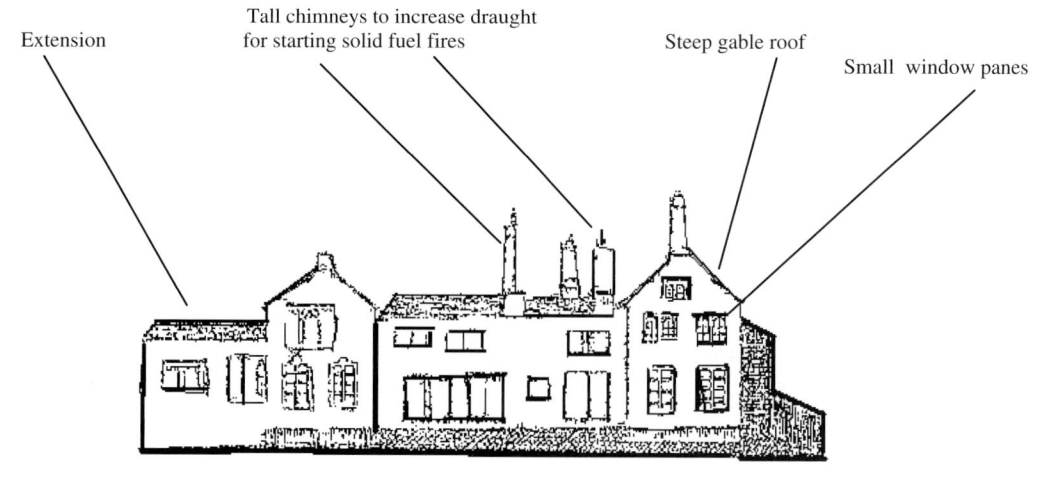

Figure 4 Languages and Peak Place Names	
Languages	Place and Site Name Links
Germanic Northern Norse — East — Swedish — Danish — West — Norwegian	Swainsley Carlswark Holme Cut
Western – German — High — Middle — Low — Old English — Middle English — Saxon — Franconian ----Dutch	Arbor Low Raper Ashop Flagg Aldwark Brink
Hellenic -------------------------- Greek	Analcine
Italic Latin — Classical — Medieval — Late — Scientific — French — Italian	Noe Annates Chalybeate Fauna and Flora Ginclough Bronze
Celtic — Gaelic/Scottish — Breton — Welsh — Cornish	Cuddy *Allyn* Gautries Wheal

Extension — Tall chimneys to increase draught for starting solid fuel fires — Steep gable roof — Small window panes

Stanton Moor Shooting Lodge

Three distinguished members of the Greaves family originated from here
John, a linguist, Thomas and another Thomas, a poet.

CHURCH and CHAPEL

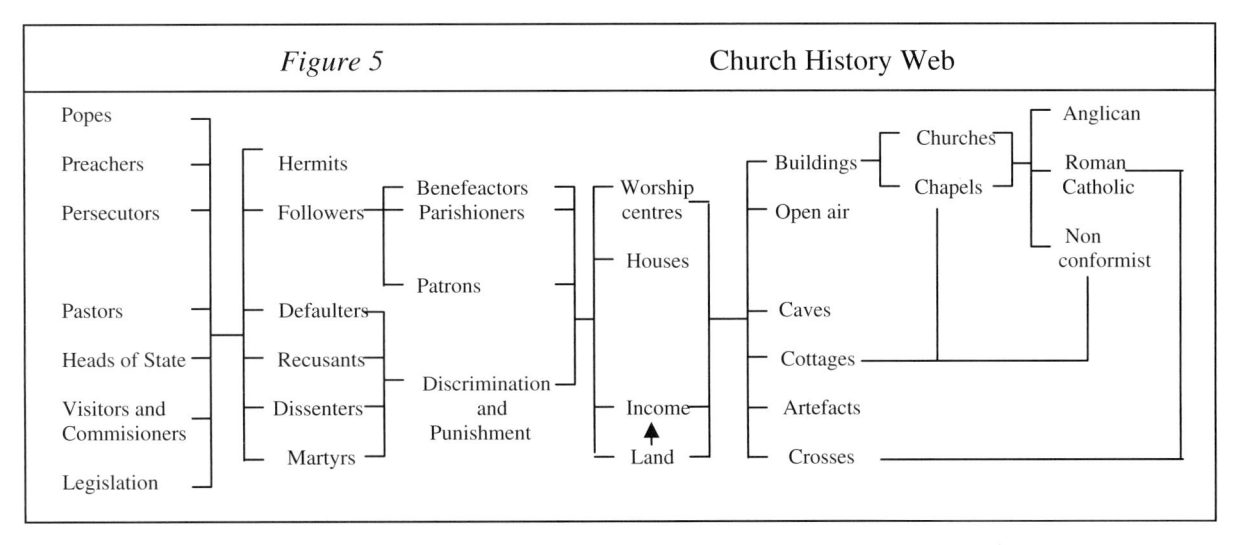

Figure 5   Church History Web

Popes — Preachers — Persecutors — Pastors — Heads of State — Visitors and Commisioners — Legislation — Hermits — Followers — Defaulters — Recusants — Dissenters — Martyrs — Benefeactors — Parishioners — Patrons — Discrimination and Punishment — Worship centres — Houses — Income ↑ — Land — Buildings — Open air — Caves — Cottages — Artefacts — Crosses — Churches — Chapels — Anglican — Roman Catholic — Non conformist

The word 'chapel' in *Figure 5*, Church History Network, is applied to Anglican, Roman Catholic and Non-conformist buildings. Chapel Gate *1083* was not a building but a footpath to Chapel en le Frith.

Anglican Churches: *16th* century Meerbrook [1562] *9860*, Taxal *0079*, Warslow *0858*, **17th** century Wincle *9665*, **18th** century Stoney Middleton *2375*, Winster *2460*, **19th** century: Bamford [1861] *2083*, Baslow *2572*, Biggin [1848] *1559*, Blackwell [1826] *1272*, Curbar [1868] *2574*, Edale [1885] *1285*, Edensor [1867] *2468*, Elton [1812] *2260*, Grindon [1848] *0854*, Hassop *2272*, Hollinsclough [1840] with school *0666*, Over Haddon *2066*, Rowsley *2566*, Sheen [1852] *1161*, Stanton in the Peak *2464*, Warslow [1820] *0858*, Wensley *2661*, Wormhill *1274*, **19th** century *additions and restoration* Alsop en le Dale *1655*, Ashford in the Water *1969*, Beeley *2667*, Castleton *1583*, Edale *1285*, Eyam *2176*, Hathersage *2380*, Parwich *1854*, Sheen *1161*, Taddington *1471*, Taxal *0079*, Tissington *1752*, Wormhill *1274*, Youlgreave *2064*, **20th** century Grindleford *2477*. 'Advowson', 'Impropriator', 'Limestone', Millstone Grit'.

'Annates': *Sir Godfrey Foljambe* died [1377].

Beating of the bounds: Gospel reading Gospel 'Greave', Ashford in the Water *1969*.

'Chantries': Ashford in the Water *1969 Griffin*, son of *Wenunwyn* [1257], Bakewell *2168*. 1. [15th century] *Vernon*. 2. Sir Godfrey Foljambe and Anne, his wife, 'Gifts', Berristall [1548] *9478* Chelmorton [1256] *1170*, Fenny Bentley [1512] *James Beresford*, Monyash [1348] *1566*, Pott Shrigley *9479* [1492] endowed by *Geoffrey Downes*, [1548] three, Snitterton *2760*, Tideswell *1575*, *Thomas Foljambe, Richard de Wendesley, Warners,* Youlgreave *2064* by *Thomas and John Vernon* [1490s].

'Chapels: of ease': Derwent [1912-44] *2383*, Jenkin [1733] *9876*, Sheldon [15th century] demolished [19th century] replaced by a church building *1768*, Toot Hill *977*.

'Chapelries': Mother church 'Parishes' underlined and their chapelries in the High Peak 'Hundred' section of the Peak Park National Park in [1876]. **Eleven** <u>Bakewell</u> *2168* – Ashford *1969*, Baslow* *2572*, Beeley* *2667*, Chelmorton *1169*, Haddon *2366*, Harthill *2262*, Longstone# *2071*, Monyash *1566*, Sheldon *1768*, Taddington > *1471*; **Four** <u>Hathersage</u> *2381* - Derwent *2383*, North Lees *2383*, Padley *2579*, Stoney Middleton ^*2275*, **Three** <u>Youlgreave</u> *2164* – Elton *2161*, Rowtor *2362*, Winster *2460*, **Two** <u>Ashbourne</u> (not in the Peak Park) – Alsop en le Dale *1655*, Parwich *1854*, **One** Bradbourn (not in the Peak Park) *2052* – Tissington *1752*, <u>Castleton</u> *1582* – Edale [1633] *1285*, <u>Hope</u> *1783* – Fairfield *1783*, <u>Hartington</u> *1360* - Earl Sterndale *0966*, * with Calver *2374* and Curbar *2574*. # with Hassop *2272*, Monsal Dale *1871* and Rowland *2172*, < with Blackwell *1272*, Brushfield *1672*, Puttoe *1771* and Priestcliffe *1371*, ^ with Froggat *2476*, Heywood *2577*, Toadpoole *2477*. **None** Edensor *2469*, Eyam *2176*, Fenny Bentley *1360*. Peak Forest [1659] *1179* was outside the jurisdiction of a 'parish' and a diocese. *1179*, Macclesfield 'hundred' – Taxal, *0079*, Wincle *9665*, Bradfield *2692*, Totmonflow 'hundred' Longnor *0865*, Warslow

0858. *, #, <, ^. [1650] Parliamentary Commissioners' opinion fit to become a 'parish' either by amalgamation with other 'chapelries' or upgrading.

Colleges: Cliff *2573* founded [1904]; Shrigley Hall: Salesian Missionary College [1929-80].

Complaints: Rate of Easter **Dues** [1488] by parishioners of Bakewell *2168*, Hope *1783* and Tideswell *1575; Vicars* Rebellion at Bakewell [1327] by parishioners. *John Cantrell* vicar of Bakewell *2168*, 'scandalous and inefficient' – report of Parliamentary Commission [1650].

Congregational Buildings: Ashford in the Water *1969*, Bakewell *2168*, Little Longstone *1871*, Middleton by Youlgreave (Tomb of *Thomas Bateman*, the antiquary) *1963*, Monsal *1871*, Tideswell *1575*, Tintwistle [1839] *0297*, Wetton [1811] *1055*, Congregationalists and Presbyterians formed the United Reform Church in [1972].

'Crosses': Not all crosses in the Peak area had specifically Christian associations. Those made of wood have not survived. Alstonefield Church, *1351*, High Bradfield [10th century] *2692*, Wishing Stone and [14th century] Nativity and Crucifixion near Wheston Hall *1376*, Litton *1783*, Hope *1783*, Taddington 'Celtic' *1471* Whibbersley *2972*. **Boundary**: Bow Stones, Macclesfield Forest [11th century] *9781*, Edale wardship of High Peak Forest *1376*, Longendale wardship of High Peak Forest *1064, 1170, 0078*, **Celtic** Eyam (similar to Iona) *2176*, Taddington *1471*. **Commemorative**: Battle Stone [11th century] Saxon versus Viking battle, *1272*, Stoney Middleton Corn Law Repeal [1846] *2275*, St Bertram's Well *1350*, Taddington *1471* possibly Norman Monyash *1566*. **Consecration** of a church by a bishop; door jambs at Tideswell *1575*. **Crucifix**: [probably 14th century] Hermit's Cave *2362*. **Decoration**: Saxon helmet Benty Grange *1464*. **Lady**: Virgin Mary for pilgrims *1499, 1566, 1675, 2778*. **Market**: *1587*, Cleulow [made from new red sandstone] *9664*. **Meeting point**: Edale also known as Champion cross [made from millstone grit] at the Ashop and Edale, Champayne/Campana (= open country) and Longendale wards of Peak Forest *1285*, Glossop *0393* → Edale *1285* → Sheffield *3587 and* Saxon road *1880*, Robin Hood's *2071*, Great Longstone *2176*, Hollins Cross *1384*, Moscar [1702] *2388, 2566*, Rowsley *2972*, Whibberley *9566*. Butterton *0798*. **Memorial**: Hollins for *Tom Hyett 1384, James Platt MP* [1857] *0304, 1250*, "Eleanor" Cross for *Mrs Watts - Russell 1476, 1499*, New *2192, Duke of Wellington* [1769-1852] erected 1866] *2673*, Church of St John the Baptist, Chelmorton *1169, Pickford*. **Prospector**: (mark made on the surface) Cross Low *1655*. **Saxon**: *1285*, Bakewell *2168*, Eyam *2375*, Ilam *1350*, Wheston *1376*. **Wishing Stone**: *1355. Figure 7,* refers

Financial matters:
Bond: [1695] Bishop required £400 payment to allow 3 Elton *2260* residents to prospect for ore.
'Bounty': Queen Anne to: Elton [1725] *2260*, Hathersage [1813 & 1824] *2381*, Winster [1702] *2460* to augment the income of the benefice.
'Chapter' transactions: #Lichfield Agent Transferring rent collected on chapter's land and tenements in Bakewell *2168*, Hassop *2272*, Hope *1783*, Holme *2169*, Monyash *1566*, Tideswell [1415] by *John Dean*, vicar of Hope *1783*, Bishop *Muschamp* [1198-1315] authorised a permement arrangement for Lichfield chapter to receive from Hope 'parish' church *1783* payments for taper wax. 'Grants' Lease [1509], by the chapter of Tideswell *1575*, rectorial houses and 'glebe' lands to *John Sanderby* for an annual rent. Reallocation of grant [1494] Dean and chapter ordered its transfer to Beeley 'chapelry' *2667* instead Of Bakewell *2168*; Refund annually [1389] 10% of covenanted payment to the chapter by *Sir Thomas de Wendesley*.# Lincoln. Equity release [1245-53] Lease on Bakewell *2168* and Hope *1783* rectories by *Henry de Lexington*, Dean of Lincoln, to pay for 3 chaplains and prebendaries at Bakewell *2168*, [1310] and [1329]. Pension Annual payment to the Dean, also rector of Asbourne, by Fenny Bentley 'chapelry' *1750*.
Commutation: [1809] 20 hectares (50 acres) Land for enclosing at Elton *2260 and* Winster *2460* in lieu of 'tithes' for the Elton minister 'Tithes' payable in kind – commuted into a cash rental payment by leasing arrangements.
Compensation: by Commissioners of Plundered Ministers [1650] to *Robert Craven*, vicar of Great Longstone *2071*, by the Exchequer [1555] Pension for last priest of suppressed chantry (by *Edward VI*) Haddon 'chantry' *2366*, [1558] by Queen Mary *William Oldfield* of Bakewell *2168, John Wymeslowe* of Castleton Hospital *1583, Richard Rowson* of Haddon *2366, Richard Machyn* of Youlgreave *2064*. **Dues** Easter collections from parishioners for the incumbent. eg Bakewell [1348] *2168*, Beeley [1671] *2667*.
Endowments: cash rental income for a benefice or place of worship arising from a gift of land: *Sir Godfrey Foljambe*[1344] for Ashford in the Water *1969*, Bakewell *2168*, Bubnell *2472*, Chatsworth *2670*, *Griffin's* [1267] for Great Longstone *2071*, 'Oxgate'.

Entertainment: expenses [1606] Subsistence at Youlgreave *2064* for Visitation personnel. *Fees* paid: Youlgreave *2064* church wardens' accounts [1604-1752]. Frequent Bell ringers, dog whipper. Occasional Legal application for warrant versus Elton *2260*, Winster *2460* for refusal to pay 'tithes' Maintenance personnel for artefacts, buildings and grounds. Pest control. Visiting preachers.
Financial instruments: bought and sold. 'Advowson', 'Patron'. *Fixed asset income*: Rent from own 'endowed' land, 'glebe', acquired commutation, 'gift' or 'legacy', or another's land; [1393] *Ulfeton de Litton* given land at Litton *1674* by *Robert de Bayley* conditional on annual payment to Tideswell church *1575*, from pews [1632] *Ralph White* Ashford in the Water *1969*.
Grants: by Lichfield Dean and Chapter #Annually for: [1280] Minister at Great Longstone *2071* 50% stipend [1315] 'Chapelries' Baslow *2572*, Beeley *2667* (after [1494] by the vicar of Bakewell *2168*), Great Longstone *2071*, Monyash *1566*, Taddington *1471*; by King James I [1620] Minister at Great Longstone *2071*, by Parliament Elton [1725] *2260*, #Single payment, with penalty clause, for repairs [1418] Bakewell *2168*. *Gratuity*: [1650] from Beeley parishioners to Beeley *2677* 'curate'; [1688] from 'Earl' of Devonshire's agent to the vicar of Derwent *2383*. *Guarantors* of *Ralph White's* pew rent [1632] *George Johnson and Will Milnes*. *Impecunity*: [1330] No staff at Baslow *2572*, Chelmorton *1169*, Great Longstone *2071*, Monyash 1565; *Leases*: 'Commutation of tithes'. *Legacies*: #Annual payment for: mass at Baslow *2572* from *Eyres* of Hassop *2272*; minister at Alsop en le Dale *1655* from *Thomas Levinge* [1639], #Single payment for: a conformable minister Derwent *2383* from *Henry Balguy* [1685]. *Levy* on [1700] lead ore Eyam *2176*.
Public appeal: for subscribers. Quarter Session Brief = mandate [1805] for rebuilding Elton *2260*.

Garlands: *Annual*: Castleton *1583*. *Funeral*: Eyam *2176*, Hope *1783*, Ilam *1350*. *Maidens*: Ashford in the Water *1969*.

Gifts: *Bells*: Baslow *2572 John Manners* 3rd 'Duke' and 11th 'Earl' of Rutland [1696-1779], Beeley [?1558] *2267*, Chelmorton [1621-81] *1169*, Hope *1783* [1733] 6th bell from 'Duke' of Devonshire', Great Longstone *2071* [1873] *G T Wright*, Winster *2460* [1860] by 'Dukes' of Devonshire and Rutland, Youlgreave *2064* [1870] by *Thornhills*. *Chest* [1630] Chelmorton by *Ralph Buxton* of Flagg *1368*.
Collection boxes: [1662] Alsop en le Dale *1655*, [1685] Chelmorton *1169*. *Benefice/living* [1650] Edensor *2469* from the 'Earl' of Devonshire, 'Bounty', 'Tithes'.
Buildings: [1839] Holy Trinity Church, Stanton in the Peak *2464* by the *Thornhills*, Income from land dedicated to the Virgin Mary/Our Lady for the upkeep of a chapel or shrine Lady Clough *1092*, Lady'bower' *1886*, Ladywash *2176*. Rectory from Deans of Lincoln Fenny Bentley *1750*, Thorp *1550*; *Chest* for books from *Michael Buxton*, woollen draper of Manchester, to Chelmorton *1169*. *Dioceses*: Hope *1783* and Tideswell *1575* chapel by *King John* to *Bishop Non(v)ant* for assignment to either Coventry or Lichfield.
Cathedral: *Bishop Muschamp's* grant to Lichfield 20 marks (£13.20) annually from Hope *1783*, and its 'chapelries', for the provision of ale. 'Collegiate Church'.
Disadvantaged: [1602] Prisoners at the King's Bench, [1614] Disabled soldiers Youlgreave *2064*.
Monastic orders: 'Augustinian': Ashopton *1986*, Conkesbury *2065*, Grindlow *1877*, Hathersage *2380*, Swythamley *9764*, Winster Chapel *2460*, [Launde *7904*, Lilleshall *7315*, Dieulacres *9857*]. 'Benedictine': Mixon *0457*, Musden *1250*, Onecote *0455*, [Burton upon Trent *2423*, Tutbury *2123*]. *Bennett*.
'Cistercian': *William De Malbanc* Brushfield *1672*, Castleton Church *1582* [Vale Royal/Dermhall Abbey *6060* [1269] by *Prince Edward*]. Hartington *2380*, One Ash *1665*, Swythamley *9764*, Gateham *1056*, Wincle *9665* Alstonefield Church *1355* by *Hugh Malbank* to [Rufford *6464*, Garendon *5020*, Roche *5498*, Combermere *5844*]. *Figure 6*, 'Granges' refers. 'Cluniac': Blackwell *1272*, [Lenton *5238*] *Hugh Bradbury*. Dominican': Ashopton *1986*, *Robert Colle*, Youlgreave and its 'chapelries' + land at Middleton *1963* [Leicester *5805*]. 'Poor Clares' Hartington *1360* [1291] by *Edmund*, 'Earl' of Lancaster, Leicester and Derby profits from the chapel, [1375] by 'chapelry' chaplain 8 hectares (20 acres) + 2 'messuages'. 'Pre-monstratensian': Derwent Chapel *2383* [Welbeck *5674*]. *Gilbert* NB Dissolution of the monasteries by *Henry VIII* about [1534] and Monk's Road *0291*. 'Granges'.
Sun dial: (to encourage attendance on time) Wormhill *1274* [1628] *Robert Meverell*. 'Eyam' 'Poverty and Philanthropy'.

Guild chapels: Great Longstone [1486] *2071*, *Stephen and Katherine Eyre*, Tideswell *1575* Guild of St Mary Charters [1384] and [1392].

Hermitage: Probably Ankers Knowl *9773*, *2262*.

House churches: Presbyterian *William Bagshawe* Ford Hall *0882* NB Act of Uniformity [1662]. Some 'Methodist' churches began as cottage meetings.

Long lease lands: OE: *laes* Early [13th century] Bakewell *2168* and Hope *1783*, except Tideswell Chapel *1575*, to *Robert Lexington*, judge and prebendary of Southwell *7053*, Lease Lands, Flagg *1368*.

Memorials: ***Bakewell*** *2168 Latham Woodroofe*, [1648] servant to Earl of Rutland. ***Beeley*** *2667 John Calvert* [1710]. ***Blore*** *1349 William Basset and Joan* [1498]. ***Edensor*** *2468 John Beton* [1570]. ***Hassop*** *2272, Thomas Eyre* [1833]. ***Hathersage*** *2380, Eyres – Robert and Joan* [1463]; *Ralph and Elizabeth* [1493]; *Robert, Elizabeth, 4 sons, 2 daughters* [1500]; *Arthur and Margaret* [1560]. ***Hope*** *1783 Henry Balguy* [1685], ***Longstone*** *1971 Roland Eyre* [1624], ***Taddington*** *1471 Richard Blackwall and Dame Agnes, 6 sons, 5 daughters* [1505]. ***Taxal*** *0079 Michael Heathcote, Joddrells*. ***Tideswell*** *1575, Sir Thurstan de Bower and his wife, John Foljambe died* [1358], *Robert Lytton and Isabel, Sir Sampson Meverll died* [1462], *Robert Pursglove*. 'Cairns', 'Crosses', 'Latten'.

'Methodist': meeting places, churches and chapels: Allgreave [1871] *9766*, Alport Castles Farm ('Love Feast') *1391*, Alstonefield [1813] *1355*, Ashford in the Water *1969*, Ashopton *1986*, Bagshaw *0781*, Bakewell [1799] *2168*, Bamford [1811] *2083*, Barrow Moor [1844] *0564*, Baslow *2572*, Beeley *2667*, Biggin [1784] *1559*, Birchover [1867 {2 chapels}] *2462*, Bradwell *1781*, Brownhill [1790] *0859*, Butterton [1828] *0756*, Calton [1813] *1050*, Calver *2374*, Castern *1252*, Castleton *1583*, Chelmorton [1874] *1169*, Coatestown *0666*, Cowhay Head *0658*, Cressbrook *1772*, Danebridge *9665*, Earl Sterndale [1787] *0967*, Ecton [787] *0958*, Edale *1285*, Elkstone [1857] *0559*, Elton *2260*, Eyam *2176*, Fernilee *0878*, Flagg [1839] *1368*, Flash [1784] *0267*, Fleet Green *0561*, Foolow [1866] *1976*, Gradbach [1849] *9966*, Great Hucklow *1777*, Great Longstone *2071*, Grindleford *2477*, Gun End *9662*, Hardings Booth [1860s] *0664*, Hathersage *2380*, Hartington [1809] *1360*, Hazelbarrow [1818] *0163*, Heathcote [1829] *1460*, Heathy Lee [1832] *0463*, Hole Car *0565*, Hollinsclough [1786] Bethel chapel built by *John Lomas*, a 'jagger' [1801] *0666*, Hope *1783*, Hulme End [1787] *1059*, Kettleshulme *9879*, Little Hucklow *1678*, Litton *1675*, Longnor [1798] *0864*, Middleton *1963*, Milldale [1815] *1454*, Mixon [1863] *0457*, Monyash [1839] *1566*, Morridge End *0366*, Morridge Top *0365*, Newstone [1818] *0163*, Newtown [1810] *0562*, Onecote [1815] *0455*, Parwich [1829] *1854*, Peak Forest *1179*, Pott Shrigley [1861] *9479*, Reaps Moor [1809] *0861*, Rewlach [1785] *0961*, Ringinglow *2883*, Rowsley *2566*, School Clough *0763*, Sheen [1810] *1161*, Smedley Sytch [1765] *0662*, Sparrowpit *0980*, Stanshope *1254*, Stiff Close *0965*, Stonepithill *1062*, Taddington *1471*, Thornhill *1983*, Tideswell *1575*, Tissington [1956] *1752*, Upper Elkstone [1872] *0858*, Warslow [1814] *0858*, *Wensley [1829] *2661*, Wetton [1780] *1155*, White Knowle [1809] *0583*, Wilshaw Hill *0566*, Winster [1837] {3 chapels} *2460*, Woodlands [1866] *1489*, Youlgreave {3 chapels} *2064*. * Wesleyan Methodist Local Preachers' Mutual Aid founded. 'Publications'.

Music: ***Choirs***: Castleton Church *1582*, Tideswell [1393] *1575*. ***Instruments***: Hope *1783* Bassoon, oboe [1759], Youlgreave *2064* Bassoon [1751], Bass viole [1742], Haddon Hall chapel *2366* instrument gallery. ***Organs***: Edensor [1857] *2569*, Hartington [1537] *1360*, Longnor Methodist [1850] *0865*, Warslow Methodist [1860s] *0858*. ***Psalters***: Castleton [1723] by priests *Robert* [1723-53] and *John Barber*. ***Singers*** Bakewell *2168* parish clerks father, *Samuel Roe* [1747-92], and son *Philip* [1815-?], Elkstone [1830] *0559*, Warslow [1820] *0858*, Youlgreave *2064* west end singers' loft. 'Performing arts'.

The vocal powers here let us mark
*Of *Philip our late parish clerk*
In church non ever a layman
With a clearer voice say 'Amen'
Who now with hallelujah's sound
Like him can make the roof resound?
The choir lament his choral tones
The town – so soon lie here his bones
Sleep undistrurbed within thy peaceful shrine
Till angels wake thee with such notes as thine.

Open air churches: See also 'Crosses' Cucklet *2176* evangelism: Gospel Hillock *1771*, 'Kirk' Dale *1868*, Lud's *9865*, River Bradford gorge *2164*.

Papal dispensation: [1538] Appointment of young *Richard Comberford* to Hartington *1360*

People: *'Albigensians'*: Cotterell. **Benefactors**: Sir William Avenel. **Bishop**: De Novant. **Chaplain:** Ricus dell Hilla [1375] Hartington *1360*, Shalcross Chapel semi-parish *0179*, Richard *Shalcross* [1307-27]. **Clergy**: Revds Leonard Slater, Thomas Stanley, William Mompesson. **Clergy place names**: Priestcliffe *1371*. **Curates:** examples *Ralph Rigby* Eyam 'Parish' Church [1718-40] *2176*, Taddington 'Chapelry *Anthony Mellor* [1679] *1471*. *'Dog whipper'*: Baslow *2572* Warslow *0858*, Youlgreave *2064*. **Friars:** Friar's Ridge *2583*, Converted dungeon for overnight stopover from Ecclesfield Priory *3594*. **Hermits**: St Bertram's Well *1351*, Cave *2262*. **Hospital chaplain:** Peak [1377] hospital for paupers endowed by *Edward III*. *'Lollards'*: *Walter de Ludank*. **Monastic orders:** 'Augustinian', 'Benedictine', 'Cistercian', 'Cluniac', 'Poor Clares', 'Pre-monstratentian'. **Part-timers:** [1725] *Mr Baines*, Baslow *2572* parson + Dronfield *3578* schoolmaster; [1653-55] *John Cantrell* Minister at Parwich *1854* + schoolmaster at Darley *2763*, Elton *2261*, Parwich *1854 and* Winster *2460*. *'Patrons'*: Bakewell *2168* [1534] *Brian Rowcliff*, hereditary chief patron, Derwent *2383* [1764] bought by *Dr Joseph Denman* from *Charles Balguy* other examples Baslow *2572* 'Duke' of Devonshire [1811], Elton *2260* vicar of Youlgreave *2064* until [1725] then freeholders for £200, Eyam *2176* [1317-84] *Furnival*, [1432-1569] *Talbot*, Hartington *1360* before [1534] Abbess of Minories then [1693] *Cavendish* Hartington Deanery *Sir Hugh Bateman* [1817]. **Preachers**: Franciscan' [Grey] Friar's Ridge *2583* from lands at Dronfield *3578* given by rector *Roger de Bangwell* [1366], 'Methodist' *John Wesley* [1703-91] Visits: [25/03/1766], Eyam *2176*, [11/08/1772] Grindleford Bridge *2478*, Longnor *0864*, Wensley *2661*. Presbyterian *William Bagshawe* [1628-1702] *James Clegg*. '*John Manners*', 'Recusants' 'Yeomen'. **Prebendary:** * [1327] *Robert Bernard* Bakewell *2168*, his Embezzlement and derilection of duty [1330-35], **Puritans:** Slab and trestle moveable communion table Haddon Hall *2366*, Alsop en le Dale *1655*. **Rectors:** *Eyam *2176*, Fenny Bentley *1750*, Thorpe [1536] *1550*, 'Tithes'. **Sacristan:** [1330] Bakewell *2168*. **Vicars:** * examples Castleton *1582*, Youlgreave *2164*, patron of Elton 'Chapelry' *2261*. Non resident [1536] *Edmund Eyre* of Tideswell *1575* living at Grindon *0854*. * Instead of distinguishing between them the word minister was frequently used in records.

Persecution: 'Covenanters', 'Recusants', Alport Castles Farm Dissidents [1662] *1391*, Alsop en le Dale *1655*, Bradwell *1781*, Chelmorton [15th century] 'font' carvings of sword hilts possibly represent martyrdom. *William Bagshawe, William Bott, FitzHerberts (Thomas died in the Tower of London [1591], Nicholas Garlick, Robert Ludlam, Arthur Meverell, Thomas Stanley, Richard Topcliffe*, 'Manors' and 'Parishes'.

Plurality: [1650] *Sherland Adams* Eyam *2176 and* Treeton *4387* (South-west of Rotherham).

'Praemunire': *Thomas Cockayne.*

Presbyterian Buildings: Ashford in the Water *1969*, Bradwell later Unitarian *1781*, Grindon [1696/7] *0854*, Malcoff *0782*, Stoney Middleton later Unitarian *2275*, *Bagshawe.*

Private chapels: Derwent Hall [1877] *2383*, Chatsworth House *2670*, Haddon Hall [12th century] *2366*, Hassop (Roman Catholic) [1816] *2272*, Lyme Hall *9682*, Rowtor Hall [1769] *2362*.

Public chapels: Derwent *2383*, Edale *1285*, Eyam *2176*, Foolow *1976*, Jenkin *9876*, Macclesfield Forest (Toot Hill – St Stephen) *9771*, Padley *2579*, Rowtor *2462*, Warslow [13th century] *0858* Winster *2460*.

'Quaker' Buildings: Bamford *2083*, Ford *0882*, Longnor [1723] *0864*, Monyash [1711] *1566*.

Recycling: [1110 & 1260] Sepulchral slabs used in rebuilding Bakewell *2168*; [1614] Stone from the demolished tower of Youlgreave church *2064* used to build Middleton Hall [1626] *1963*.

Roman Catholic: Pre-Reformation Buildings, subsequently Anglican. **Saxon;** Alstonefield [982] *1355*, Ilam *1351*, Parwich *1854*. **Norman;** Alsop en le Dale *1655*, Ashford in the Water *1969*, Bakewell rebuilt [1110] *2168*, Ballidon *2055*, Beeley *2667*, Birchover *2462*, Castleton *1583*, Parwich *1854*, Thorpe *1550*, Tideswell *1575*, Tissington *1752*, Youlgreave *2064*. **12th** century; Beeley [1150-60] *2667*, Grindon *0854*, Longnor *0864*, Monyash 1198] *1566*, Waterfall *0851*. **13th** century; Chelmorton *1169*, Eyam *2176*, Great Longstone *1971*, Hanbury *1728*, Hartington *1360*, Little Longstone *1871*, Longnor [1223] *0864*. **14th** century; Bradfield *2692*, Fenny Bentley *1750*, Hathersage [1381] *2381*, Hope *1783*, Taddington *1471*, Tideswell *1575*. **Grange chapels;** Grindlow *1877*, Meadow Place *2065*, One Ash *1665*.

Roman Catholic: Post-Reformation: Bakewell *2168*, Bamford *2083*, Hassop [1816] *2272*, Hathersage [1806] *2380*, North 'Lees' *2383* (built by permission of *James II* [1688] but destroyed by Protestants), Padley [1933] *2579*.

Routes: Friar's Ridge *2584*, Priests Way *0970*.

Shrines: *0275* St Bertram/Bertholin [13th century], *0074* St Joseph [1889] in memory of *Miss Dolores*, companion to *Mrs Grimshawe*, Errwood House *0175*.

Unitarian Buildings: Bradwell formerly Presbyterian *1781*, Great Hucklow [1696] *1777*, Stoney Middleton formerly Presbyterian *2275*.

Wesleyan Reform Buildings: Birchover *2462*, Curbar *2574*, Eyam *2176*, Foolow *1976*, Froggatt *2476*, Over Haddon [1861] *2066*, Stanton in the Peak *2464*, Stoney Middleton *2375*, Winster [1837] *2460*, Youlgreave *2064*. *George Scriven.*

Figure 6	Granges

Dark Peak

Derwent
Only
Harratt
Abney

Harley   Harewood
Benty
Hurdlow
Wincle Yewtree Cronkston   Meadow Place
Needham
Swythamley

Roche   Boosley Smerrill
Glutton
Biggin   Mouldridge
Gotham   Ivonbrook
Aldwark
Gateham   Roystone
Hoe
Stanshope New Hanson
Onecote
Hanson   Bostern
Newton
Musden

Not to scale

Figure 7a								Church Graphics
CHRISTIAN TOPIC				ILLUSTRATION				
	Beam	Chair	Cross	Font	Reredos	Typanum	Wall	Window
ANGELS	Padley		Eyam					
APOSTLES								Haddon
Paul				Bakewell				
Peter				Bakewell				
BIBLE			Eyam	Bakewell				
CHRIST								
Annunication								Haddon
Ascended				Bakewell				
Crucified				Wheston				Haddon
			Hope					
Lamb of God						Parwich		
Teaching				Bakewell				
CREATOR								
Farm animals			Bakewell			Parwich		
						Ashford		
Plants			Bakewell				Chelmorton	
			Castleton				Haddon	
			Hope					
Trees						Ashford		
Wild animals			Bakewell	Tissington		Ashford		

CHURCH TRIUMPHANT	STURDY BUILDINGS HIGH ABOVE SURROUNDING HOUSES LOFTY CHANCELS, SPIRES, PINNACLES, TOWERS

DIVINE ORDERLINESS			Taddington Bakewell					
HOLY FAMILY							Haddon	
JOHN THE BAPTIST				Bakewell				Haddon
KING DAVID				Bakewell				
OPPOSITION								
Demons				Thorpe				
Devil								Haddon
Dragon				Youlgreave				
Lion					Parwich			
SAINTS				Bakewell				
Anne								Haddon
Christopher								Blore
George								Haddon
John								Haddon
Michael								Haddon
SPIRIT'S SWORD			Bakewell					
Lily emblem								Blore
VIRGIN MARY		Eyam	Wheston	Winster	Youlgreave			Haddon

Benedictine   Cistercian   Dominican   Franciscan   Poor Claire

Religious Order Landowners

63

Figure 7b			Church Architecture Styles
STYLE	APPROXIMATE DATES		PEAK EXAMPLES
	Start	End	
Saxon	7th century	1066	Bakewell west wall
Norman	1066	1189	Bakewell west front, Beeley south doorway
Early English	1189	1280	Bakewell south transept
Decorated	1280	1377	Hope tower
Perpendicular	1377	1500	Chelmorton clerestory, Tideswell tower
Tudor	1500	1603	Haddon panels, ?Youlgreave clerestory
Jacobean	1603	1689	Haddon roof beams
Georgian	1689	1837	Elton, Winster tower
Victorian	1837	1900	Edensor, Winster

Contrasting Places of Worship

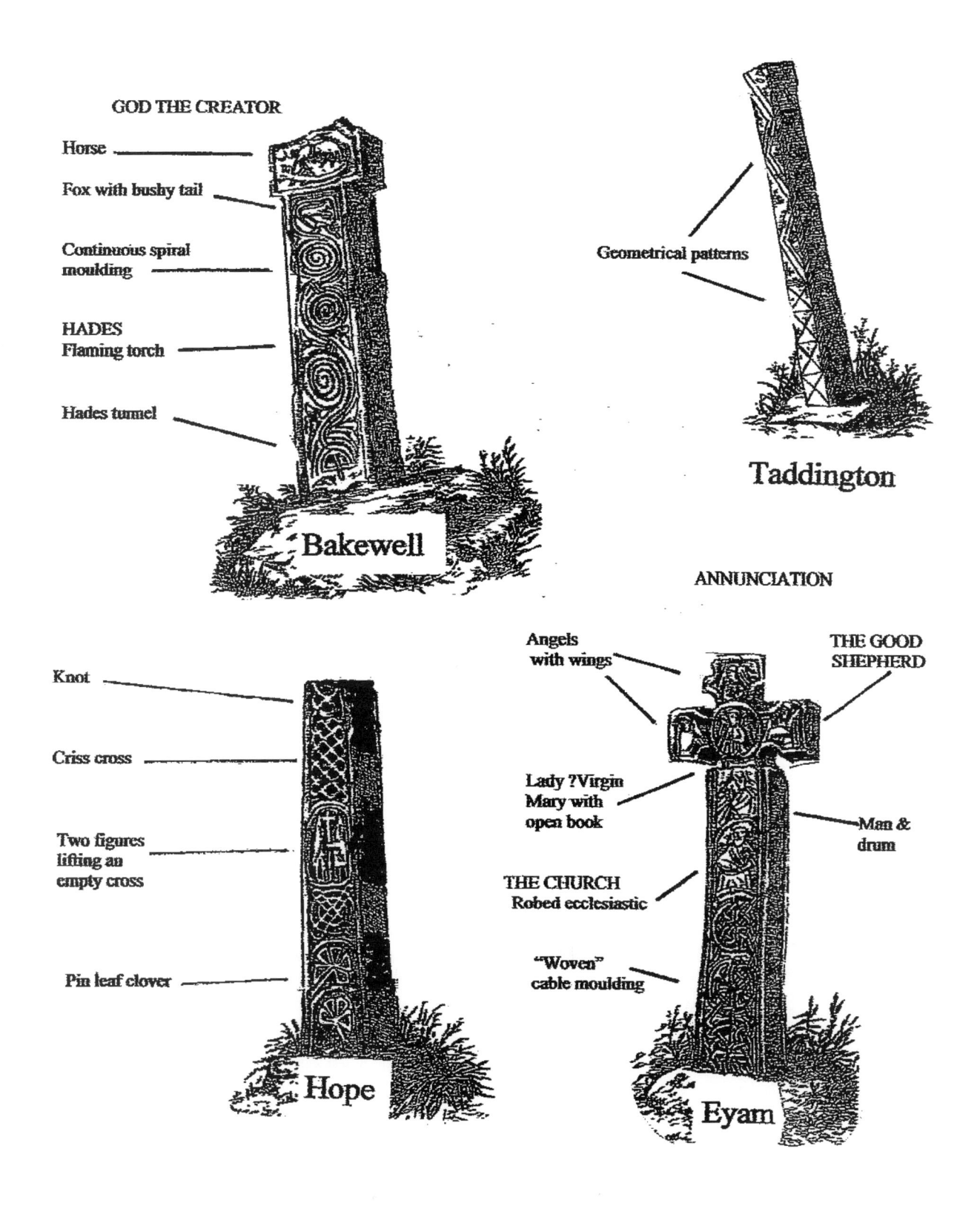

Stone Crosses with Carvings

Bakewell
- GOD THE CREATOR
- Horse
- Fox with bushy tail
- Continuous spiral moulding
- HADES Flaming torch
- Hades tunnel

Taddington
- Geometrical patterns

Hope
- Knot
- Criss cross
- Two figures lifting an empty cross
- Pin leaf clover

Eyam
- ANNUNCIATION
- Angels with wings
- THE GOOD SHEPHERD
- Lady ?Virgin Mary with open book
- Man & drum
- THE CHURCH Robed ecclesiastic
- "Woven" cable moulding

BAKEWELL
Plinth-mounted eight-sided font 14th century

- Ogee arches with leaf and branch carvings
- Hooded monk
- Sword of the Spirit which is the Word of God. *Ephesians 6 verse 17*
- Peter with a key [to heaven]

WINSTER
A floor standing 16th century (Post Reformation) font partly copied from an 11th century one

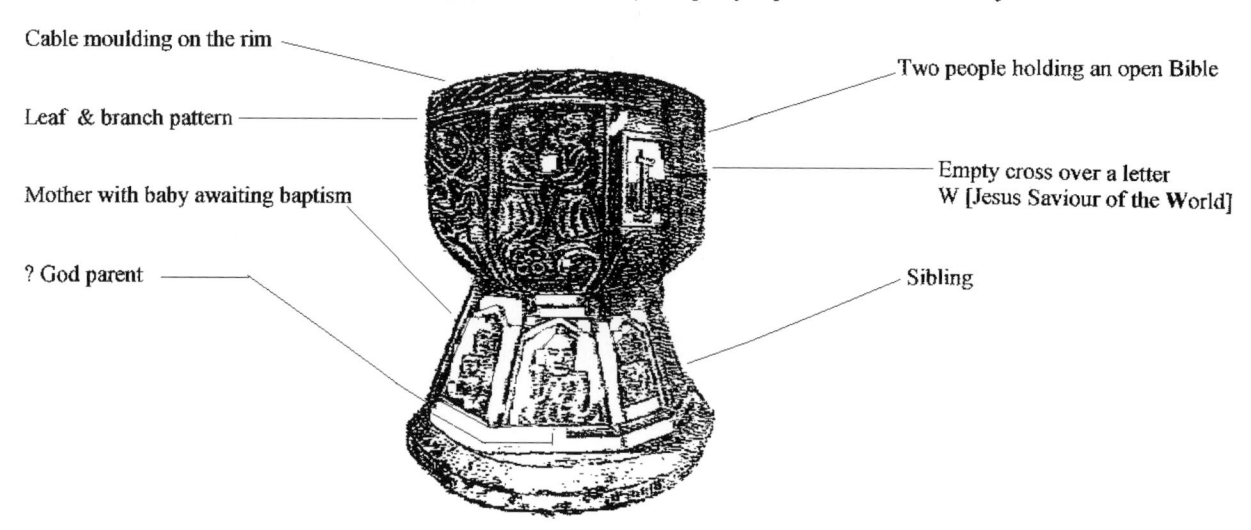

- Cable moulding on the rim
- Leaf & branch pattern
- Mother with baby awaiting baptism
- ? God parent
- Two people holding an open Bible
- Empty cross over a letter W [Jesus Saviour of the World]
- Sibling

YOULGREAVE
A circular pillar-mounted tub font. 1833 ownership dispute with Elton after being found in the King William IV public house garden

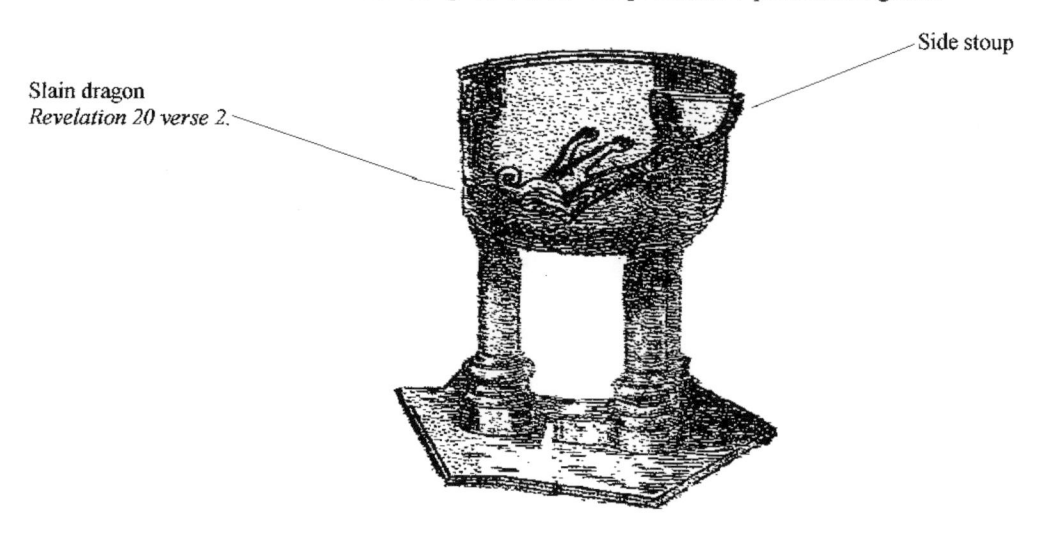

- Slain dragon *Revelation 20 verse 2.*
- Side stoup

Baptismal Fonts

Figure 8　　　　　　　　　　　　　　　　　　　　Economic History Web

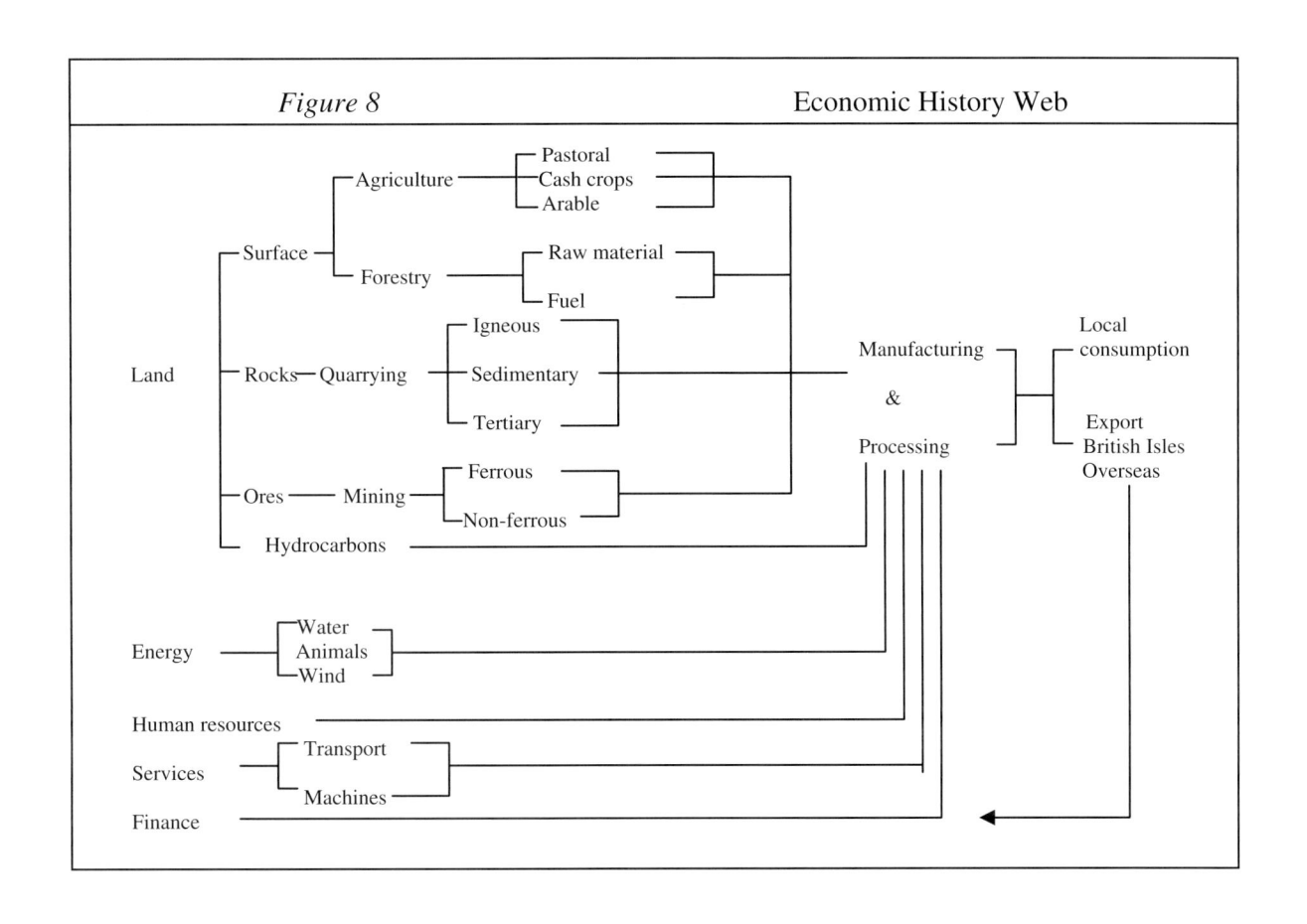

```
                    ┌─ Pastoral
         ┌─ Agriculture ─┼─ Cash crops ──┐
         │              └─ Arable        │
    ┌─ Surface                           │
    │    │          ┌─ Raw material ─────┤
    │    └─ Forestry ┤                   │
    │               └─ Fuel              │
    │          ┌─ Igneous ───┐           │                ┌─ Local
    │          │             │           ├── Manufacturing │   consumption
Land├─ Rocks ─ Quarrying ─┼─ Sedimentary ─┤       &       ─┤
    │          │             │           │   Processing    └─ Export
    │          └─ Tertiary ──┘           │                    British Isles
    │                 ┌─ Ferrous ────────┤                    Overseas
    ├─ Ores ─ Mining ─┤                  │
    │                 └─ Non-ferrous     │
    └─ Hydrocarbons ─────────────────────┘

              ┌─ Water
Energy ──────┼─ Animals
              └─ Wind

Human resources ──────────────────

           ┌─ Transport
Services ──┤
           └─ Machines

Finance ──────────────────────────
```

Flora	17%	
Uplands	14%	
Land characteristics	12%	
Named early owners	10%	Human activity
Fauna	9%	
Farmsteads 'ton	8%	Human activity
Water and Wetlands	7%	
Birds	6%	
Rocks	5%	
	4% **Clearings** 'ley'	Human activity
	3% Woodlands	
	3% **Livestock**	Human activity
	2% Weather	

Place Name Influences

WORKING and EARNING

Animal Feeds: *Fodder* Barley Thirkelow *0468*, Hay Little Hayfield *0288*, 'hobble', *holegn* = holly: Hollin Knowl *1285*, Hollinsclough *0666*, 'Quile' 'Johnson'. See Arable: Rye processing Caudwell Mill *2566*, 'Whin'.

Arable Farming: 'Lynchet' 'Fallinge' *2666*, **Bamboo** *bambusa vulgaris* [1875] Chatsworth *2670* for paper. **Barley** Barley Close, Abney *1979*, Barleyleighford *9464*, Eyam *2176*, 'berewick' 'maw'. **Beet** Beet Farm *0583*. **Cabbage** Close, Tissington *1752*, 'Flax' Dale *1863*, 'bun', 'harle'. **Herbs**: wild – *allium sativum* Parsley Hay *1463*, Garlick Close, Ashford in the Water *1969*, Garlic(k), Mustard Close, Tideswell *1575*. **Oats** Eyam *2176*, *Manners*. **Onion** Close, Great Hucklow *1777*. **Peas** and **beans** – 'swad' bean and *pise*: Banafurlong, Great Longstone *2071*, Bean Beatings, Hope *1783*, Bean Close, Stanton *2464*, Pease Bonges, Hope *1783*, Pease Furlong, Eyam *2176*, Potatoes Eyam *2176*, 'hill', 'wyzel'. **Rye** (unless wild *elymus* or *lolium perenne* grass for fodder) OE: *ryge* Rioth, Little Longstone *1871*, Roych *9784*, Rye Brook *0753*, Rye Croft *0558*, Rye Croft, Abney *1979*, Great Longstone *2071*. **Wheat** OE: *hwaete*, 'Arnfield', 'Brandreth', 'Flail', 'Geff', 'Hill', 'Hoppet', 'Wyzel', Wheat Croft, Kettelshulme *9879*, Wheatlands *2472*, 'Wad'. Heavy snow 16/01/1614-28/05/1614 delayed sowing. *Figure 8*, Farming, refers

Banking: *Henry Balguy, Ible Ibba*.

Bankruptcy and impecunity: Gradbach Mill (flax) [1837] *9965*, *Cotton/Cromwell, Cockayne, Downes*. 'Mills'. **Debt settlements** *Henry Cavendish* [1550-1616] sold the reversion of Chatsworth *2670* and much land to his younger brother *William*, 1st 'Earl' of Devonshire [1551-1626]; *William Cavendish*, 2nd 'Earl', sold land to discharge hospitality debts; *Sir William Vernon* inherited debts from his father *Sir Richard* [1451]. [1660-1760] many people trapped in **credit networks**. *Georgina*, Duchess of Devonshire died [30/03/1806] owing £5,000 + interest on a **loan** from *Richard Arkwright*. 'Brenner'.

Building: *End uses and raw materials* (animal, mineral, organic) Beams and 'Lintels'. 'Sessile oak' 'Millstone grit'. Floors *rushes*, 'Sandstone'. Glue Boiled animal *hooves* or *pitch* from 'Scots Pine'. Interiors 'Limestone' *plaster, bast mats, wainscoting* 'Oak' – Hill Top, Beeley *2667*, hearthstones. Roofs 'Sandstone' *slab* "slates" '*slate*' 'Flax' *thatching*. Walls Bricks, 'Limestone', 'Millstone grit' *stone*, 'Limestone' - *mortar, rubble* Sparrowpit *0980*. Waterproofing 'Scots pine' *pitch*, lead. **Equipment** '*sty*' = a ladder. **Personnel** Carpenter, '*Carver*', mason, plasterer, plumber.

Communications: **Bridges** Danebridge *9665*, Dunford Bridge *1502*, Packhorse: Conkesbury *2165* on Youlgreave → Bakewell route, St Bertram's, Ilam *1350*; Rivers Kinder and Sett confluence *0587*, Sheepwash: Ashford in the Water *1969*, Bakewell *2165*, Thornbridge *1971*, *Bridgeman*. **Fords** Ashford *1969*, Bamford *2083*, Barleighford *9464*, Beresford *1259*, Bradford *2064*, Dunford Bridge *1502*, Fernyford *0661*, Ford *0882*, Grindleford *2477*, Hazelford *2379*, Lumford *2169*, Salterford *9876*, *Clifford, Pickford, Stafford, Stratford*. **Lane** cut through woods Hacked Lane *9572*. **Path** Winding upland Sherrow *9578*, 'Green Lane' 'Packhorses', 'Portways', 'Railways', Saltways', 'Stagecoach', 'Turnpike'.

Dairying: 'Bower', 'Bowk', 'Brig', 'Bud', 'Carving', 'Kimnel', 'Kit', 'Ream', 'Stripping', Milking Close, Abney *1979*, Milking Hillock, Castleton *1583*, Milking Place, Hathersage *2380*. **Equipment** and Facilities 'Bawd', 'Carf', 'Daymath', 'Grass nail', 'Groop', 'Hack', 'Helm', 'Jag', 'Pele', 'Pinfold' 'Quile', 'Whin' Foolow *1976*, Grindon *0854*, Longnor *0864*, Warslow *0858*, Iron and wooden implements.

Economic activity indicated by names: '*Barn*': prefix Barnesley. **Boundary**: Pittle 'Mere' *1378*. **Clearing**: '*ley*' suffix Beeley *2667*, Bleakley *2163*, Hinkley Wood *1250*, Leam *2379*, Padley *2579*, Pilsley *2471*, Pott Shrigley *9479*, Rowsley *2566*, Swythamley *9764*, *Adderley, Barnesley, Brindley, De Derley, Lameley, Padley, Rollesley, Shirley, Stanley, Wendesley* **Copse**: '*scaega*' suffix = a copse or thicket *Bagshawe, Bradshawe, Grimshawe*. **Cote**: suffix = a 'shelter' Crowdecote *1065*, One Cote *0455*. **Court** *Shirley*. **Crops**: barley Barlow hay Clegg. **Cultivation**: '*fallinge*' *2666*, *Allen*. **Dung**: mixon = manure: Mixon *0457*, Old Mixon Hay *0257*. **Enclosure**: '*rhos*' = an enclosure on a moor *Rossington*: hay Cockey *1979*, Old Mixon Hay *0257*, Parsley Hay *1463* word (another possible meaning = open space) *Cavendish, Wentworth*. **Farm**: '*wich*' suffix = a common or a dairy farm Parwich *1854*, **Farmstead**: '*ton*' Bretton *2078*, Ecton *0958*, Elkstone *0559*, Middleton *1863*, Offerton *2181*, Snitterton *2760*, Stanton *2462*,

68

Taddington *1471, Ashopton, Brampton, Brereton, Buxton, Litton, Marchington, Middleton, Newton, Paunton, Plumpton, Rossington, Upton* 'Enclosures'. **Field**: *'feld'* Alstonefield *1355*, Bradfield *2692*, Brushfield *1672. Hatfield, Oldfield.* **'Ham'**: Broadham *0862*, Needham *1665*, Swythamley *9764*. **Haystack**: *'kleggi'* Clegg. **Home**: *'hulme'* Kettelshulme *9879*. **Homestead**: *'ham'* Gotham *1958*, Ringham *1666. Needham.* **Open space** 'worth' Chatsworth *2670*, Sugworth *2389*, *Wentworth*. **Pasture**: *'bedisc'* suffix = enclosed pasture 'outrake', *Cavendish*. **Processing**: *bones* in a kiln. Pyegreave *0477*. *milk* Butterton *0756*, Smerill *1962 Wentworth, Whyngates.*

Enclosures: Alstonefield *1355*, Cockey Farm *1979*, Gardom's (Bronze Age stock) *2773*, Edge Lawrence Field *2579, 2494, 2495, 2780,* Peppercorn [low rent] Hey. Tintwistle *0297*, Warslow *0858;* Three **Butts** [ends of open strips] Hope *1783*, Six Lands [**consolidation**], Brough *1882, 2462*, Three Roods, Curbar *2574*, Hope *1783*, Kingsterndale *0972*, Seven Castleton *1583*. Waste Warslow *0858*. *'thimble'*, OSca: *haga* Hagg *1687*, Hayes *0860*, Hayesgate *0859*, OE *loc* Locker Brook *1689*. **Commons** Hartington *1360* [*1798*]. **Complaint** by poor cottagers of Tideswell *1575* that the Earl of Shaftesbury's enclosures robbed them of pasture. **Consolidation** preliminaries by mutual exchange of 'selions' [1760] between *Daniel Taylor* of Tideswell *1575* and *Robert Freeman* of Wheston *1376* before [1807-21] enclosure. **Direct action** 68 Ashford in the Water villagers broke down the 'Earl' of Westmorland's fences at Churchdale Meadow enclosing 120 hectares (300 acres). **Landless inhabitants** [1658] Abney *1879* 73%, Bradwell 50%, Little Hucklow 76%, Wardlow 77%. **Pingel** = paddock, small enclosure The Pingle Castleton *1583*. Walled strips Tideswell *1575*, Wheston *1376*. **Pit** OE: *pightel* = a small enclosure Elmin *1587*, Raddle *2089,*' Tinkers' *0170, 0270*. 'Assarts' 'Hay', 'Ham', 'Holt', 'Housebote', 'Limestone', 'Smeuse', 'Smoot', 'Ton'.

Farm Buildings: *Field Barns*: *9763*, Helmesley *9867*, The 'Laithes' *9671*, Latham *1149*, Middlehill *1754*, Staden *1359*, 'Boosley' *0662*, 'Boskin', 'Laith'. **Shed** OE: *sceo* Sheen *1161*. **Shelters** The Cote *0587*, Heath 'Cote' *1460*, Onecote *0455*, Wolfscote *1358*, Sheepfolds: *0259, 0852, 0950, 1154, 2576, 9975* + *'Lees'*: Allstone *0477*, Birchinlee *1491*, Broad *0376*, Haylee *0378*, Long *0188*, Old Lees *2081*, Rowlee *1589*, Stanton *2563*, White 'Lee' Moor *2694*, Ewe Close *2169*. *Sty* Swine Sty *2775*. **Vaccary** (dairy) *0653*, 'Butterburs' 'Dur','Rake'.

Farm Labour: *Drover*: Edward Buxton of Bakewell *2168* [17th century]. **Farriers** Edale later a public house *1285*, Hammerton *1573*, Old Smithy *9763*, Smithy Hill *1781*. 'Tew', Farrar, *smidde* = smith *Smith* Blacksmith keys Emblem in the wall of Chelmorton Church *1170*. **Obligations** 'Boon', 'Cotter', 'Statute Fair', 'Villein'. **Payment** 'Tut work'. **Reapers** Dialect: group of reapers Binns *0802*. **Recruitment** 'Statute fair'. **Rights** 'Firebote, 'Hedgebote', 'Plowbote', 'Team', 'Toll'. **Work arrangement** Saturday Piece, Monyash *1566*. **Work content** in days: Three, Four, Five, Six , Edale *1285*, Hope *1285* 'Daymath'.

Farming Methods: 'Assarting', 'Bearda', 'Brand', 'Caggle', 'Carder' 'Casson/cazon', 'Ditches', 'Fallinge', 'Lees', 'Ley' suffix, 'Lynche', 'Poll', 'Reens', 'Slang', 'Sole'. **Clearing** Bramley *2473*, Boosley *0662*, Fallinge *2666*, Fawfieldhead [1308] *0763*, Greasley *9466*, Stanton *2462*, Swainsley *0957*, Swythamley *Brindley*. **'Enclosures'** Field systems. Medieval *2085, 2185, 2279, 2580, 2775, 2872, 'sceat'* Second Field, Castleton *1583*, Chelmorton *1169*, [Enclosure Acts 1760-1830] 'Pit', 'Tithes'. **Husbandry** 'Strunt'. **Irrigation** Iron Tors pump *1456*. **Liming** Lime Piece Derwent *2383*, Lime Field, Flagg *1368*, Great Hucklow *1777*, Kettleshume *9879*. **Manure** 'Dunge', 'Greaves', 'Mardo', Mixon *0457*, 'Shool' Allgreave *9767*, Birchover *2462*, Warslow *0858*, sock' Paring and burning Beaten Flat, Great Longstone *2017*. **Strips** Chelmorton *1169*, Ilam *1350* 'Poll', 'Ryding', 'Sole' The Riddings, Ashford in the Water *1969*. **Terraces** Snitterton [medieval] *2760*.

Farm services: *Lime kilns* Farms had their own in the limestone White Peak. **Machine storage** Engine Close, Wensley *2661*, Cales Dale, River Lathkill junction on One Ash Grange *1765*. 'Farriers', 'Pinfold'.

Farm Settlements: suffixes *'ham', 'ley, 'ton'.*

Farm Vehicles: 'Felloes','Kick', 'Rathes', 'Walt', 'Wain' Wainstones *0277*. 'Gait'.

'Granges': Abney *1979*, Aldwark *2357*, Benty *1564*, Biggin *1559*, Boosley *0662*, Bostern *1553*, Cronkston *1165*, Derwent *2383*, Ford *0653*, Gateham *1156*, Glutton *1960*, Gotham *1858*, Griff(e) *2456*, Hanson *1153*, Harewood *3168* (*Robert Eyre*), Harley *0868*, Harratt *0980*, Hoe *2155*, Hurdlow *1166*, Ivonbrook *2458*, Meadow Place *2065*, Mouldridge *2059*, Musden *1251*, Needham *1165*, New Hanson *1554*, Newton *1653*, Only *1484*, Roche *9963*, Roystone *2156*, Shallow *0970*, Smerrill *1962*, Stanshope *1254*, Sugworth *2389*, Swythamley *9764* Wincle *9665*, Yewtree *0865*. 'Cistercians'.

Heating: ***Bitumens and hydrocarbons:*** 'Carbonite' Mam Tor *1283*, Coal *'Adits'* Baslow *2572*, 'Chatsworth' 17th century. Alton seam near the surface; used for heating greenhouses during World War I [1914-18], *'Bell pits'*: [17th century] Wildboarclough *9868*, Old Pits *0487*, *Charles Eyre. Deeper* Berristall *9478* See 'stall' Axe Edge *0271*, Boothmans' Cottages *0267*, Dane Colliery *0069*, Derbyshire Bridge *0171*, Errwood *0175*, Fernilee *0178*, Harrop *9678*, Coal Pit Field, (Big Smut coal) Pott Shrigley *9479*, Goldsitch (poor quality) *0064*. *Thin seams*: Bakestonedale *9579*, Big Low *9577*, Billinge Hill *9577*, Errwood Hall *0175*, Goyts Moss (Yard coal) *0271*, Heathylee [15th century] *0763*, Quarnford [16th century] *0066*, Imports from Chesterfield via Coalpit/Conksbury Bridge *2165*, Old Coalpit Lane *1070*, NB Hearth stones: Hearthstone Field, Curbar *2574*. Cinder disposal: OE: *sinder*. Cinder Hill, Wildboarclough *9868*. 'Elaterite' Ecton *0958*, Windy Knoll *1383* (Used by miners for illumination). Gas Stoney Middleton *2375*. Oil Stoney Middleton *2375*, 'Olefinite': Windy Knoll *1383*. **Organic:** Bracken, 'Charcoal' Buckthorn Meadow, Ashford *1969*, Cow dung 'Casson' also known as 'cazon' Gorse/furze *ulex europeaus*. Peat Grindslow Knoll *0186* fuel for Edale inhabitants who carried it on sleds down Sled Road, Peat Pits *2793*. *John Harpur's* at Alstonefield *1355*, Turves Flagg *1368*, 'Turbary' OE: *turf* = peat. Wood for smelting and lime burning + gorse and peat. OE: *brand* = logs Brand *0468*, Forest depletion substituted coal. 'Firebote', 'Housebote' 'Lighting'. *Figure 27*, refers.

Imports: Cotton goods from Manchester firm *Mrs Bullock* – Bakewell *2168*, *Thomas Oliver*, Longnor *0864*. Pedlars' merchandise – handkerchiefs, jewellery, fancy leather goods.

Investors: ***Companies*** *William Cavendish,*1st 'Earl' of Devonshire [1551-1626] East India, North West Passage, Russia, Somers Island and Virginia Companies, *William Cavendish* 2nd 'Earl' [1590-1628] member of Somers Island and Virginia companies. ***Enclosures*** *'Lancaster'*. ***Financial services*** *Richard Arkwright* Interest bearing £5,000 loan to *Georgina*, Duchess of Devonshire died [30/03/1806]. ***Mines*** Magpie *1768*. ***Mill lessee*** *Thomas Gilbert*, Capital diverted from declining industries into cotton mills. *John Fairburn, Gell* family **Mine** lessees *W & L J Bowman*. 'Ecton'. ***Transport*** Infrastructure *Richard Arkwright* (a) Bakewell 'turnpike' *2168* (b) High Peak 'railway'. Vehicles *Harry Hulley* of Baslow *2572* Chauffeur, taxi owner, buses [1921], 'Bankruptcy', 'Land', 'Manors', 'Mill owners', 'Moities', 'Soughs', 'Yeomen'.

Inventors: *Richard Arkwright, Samuel Fox, Henry Watson, Sebastian Ferranti.*

Land *Area:* Acres; Six, Seven, Pott Shrigley *9479*, Ten, Flagg *1368*, Twenty, Pott Shrigley *9479*, Hyde; OE *higid* (24 – 48 hectares: 60 – 120 acres) *Hyde* Small; The Patch, Foolow *1976*, Wren Park, Edensor *2468*, Stoney Middleton *2375*, Scythe cuts wide; OE: *swaeo*: Ten, Castelton *1583*, Eighteen Swaths, Bamford *2083*. **Aspect:** Bleak; Cold Halfacres, Tideswell *1575*, Windy; Half Acre, Offerton *2181*, **Condition:** Boggy; ON: *kjarr*: Moss Carr *0765*, Clayey; OE: *claeme* Clemley Park, Little Longstone *1871*, Crumbly Dialect: *barm* = yeast Barmings *1800*, Dry; OE: *drygge* Dry Hills, Bakewell *2168*, Lumpy; ME: *clod*. Clod Hall Farm *2972*, Overgrown; [with rushes] OE: *risc* Rix Acre, Foolow *1976*. Poor; OE: *hungor*. Hungry Close, Bakewell *2168*, Pityful Meadow, Bakewell *2168*, Rich; Fat Close, Abney, *1979*, possibly Honey Spots, Hope *1783*, Sour; OE: *sur*; Sour Lands, Great Hucklow *1777*, Sticky; possibly Honey Spots, Hope *1783*, Pudding Field, Hope *1783*, Pudding Pie Field, Wheston *1376*, Soggy OE: *sugga* Sugworth *2389*, Stoney; Stannery *0766*, Stanton *2464*, Stanshope *1354*, Stoney Middleton *2275*, Sweet; OE: *swete*, Sweet Piece, Brough *1882*, Uncultivated; OE: *haeo*: Heathy Piece, Monyash *1566*, Unploughed; OE: *balca* The Balk, Hathersage *2380*, Unproductive; OE: *bere*: Bare Field, Elton *2260*, Barren Close, Abney *1979*, Bareholme *0601*, Unstable; Shifting Meadow, Little Longstone *1871*,Dialect: Sliddens *0503*. Wet; Wet Field, Kettelshume *9879*, Withered; Withered Low *1076*. **Location:** Far; OE: *feor*: Far Field, Hope *1783*, 'Garbroods', ME: *gardin* = strips in the gore of a common field 'Garbroods' Castleton *1583*, Middle [of other land]; OE: *middel*: Middle Acres, Great Hucklow *1777*. **Ownership:** Church: Church Croft, Great Longstone *2071*, ON: *kikja*. Kirk Acre, Bradwell *1781*, Common; ownership OE: *gemaene*: *1070*, Mean Field, Edale *1285*, Fenny *2197*, Upper *2096*; Copyhold; Copyhold Carr, Hope *1783*, Co-tenancy; Jointry, Wildboarclough *9868*, 'Geneat', 'Glebe': Glebe Farm *0079*, Lease; OE: *laes* Lease Lands, Flagg *1368* Priest; Priest Acre, Great Hucklow *1777*, Disputed: OE: *geflit*. Flitland, Rowland *2172*. **Price:** Five Penny, Little Longstone *1871*, Guinea (£1 05p) Pightle, Monyash *1566*. Nobility 'Duke', 'Earl', 'Marquis', 'Viscount', Baron'. **Shape:** Angled: OE: *elnboga*: Elbow Close, Great Longstone *2071*, Elaborate, Ginger Bread Close, Tideswell *1575*, Narrow ME: *shovel*. Shoe Broad, Ashford in the Water *1969*, Short; OE: *sceart*: Acre, Eyam *2176*, Brodds, Great Longstone *2071*, Butt, Monyash *1566*, Flatt, Foolow *1976*, Tricorne: Cockthat, Bradwell *1781*, Twisted OE: *wrio*: Wry neck, Hope *1783*, Wigleymeadow *2058*, and ME: *slang*: The Slang, Brough *1583*.

Terrain: Coloured, partly Pied Leys Piece, Edale *1285* Red Flatt, Hope *1783*, Flat: ON: *flat*: Flat Furlong, Bamford *2083*, Level; ON: *sletta* Sleigh, Loam; OE: *lam*: Loam Close, Wincle *9665*, Rough; The Craggs, Taddington *1471*, Steep; OE: *staeger*. Stair Field, Wincle *9665*, Swamp; Eyam *2176*, Water Meadow; ON: *holmr*. The Holme, Baslow *2572*.

Livery companies: *Robert Bateman* Grocers, *George Blackwell* Skinners, *Anthony Bradshawe* Goldsmiths, *Roger Columbell, John Taylor* from Youlgreave *2064* [1604] Merchant Tailors, *John Millward* Silkmen.

Livestock: ***Bees*** hunig = honey 'Colt' Bee Croft, Curbar *2574*, Honey Spots, Hope *1783*. **Bulls** Bull Clough *0554 & 1897*, Bull pit *1081*, Butterton *0756*. ***Calf*** Calves = *bovidae* family Calton *1050, 1171 & 2368*, Calver *2374*, Malcalf/Malcoff *0782*. ***Cows*** Cow Close, Offerton *2181*, Cow 'Hey' *1694*, Middleton *1963*, Mixon *0457*. ***Donkey*** 'cuddy'. ***Geese*** OE: *gos* Goose 'Pingle', Eyam *2176*. ***Goats*** = *capra hircus* Gateham Grange *1156*, Goats Cliff *2477*, Gotham *1858*, Hathersage *2380*. ***Horses*** Horsely Head *0609*, Horse Croft Meadow, Bakewell *2168*, Castleton *1583*, Horse Hayland *9862*. ***Ox*** bos taurus, Oxdale *2883*, Oxensitch *0268*, Ox 'Hey' *1694*, Ox Low *1280*, Oxstone *2783*, 'Choking rope'. ***Pigs*** OE: *swin* Swine Sty *2775*, Swint Clough *1291*, Swythamley *9764*, Kimber Court *2382* Dialect: *kimmel* = oval tub for scalding slaughtered pigs and salting bacon. ***Poultry***: 'Cletch', 'Wiggy' steor = Steer Croft, Monyash *1566*, 'Calk', 'Codder', 'Grin', 'Hack', 'Tallet', 'Temse'. 'Terret' Pigs: 'Bally', 'Chawbacon', 'Gilt', 'Hull', 'Trip' *Blith, Pickford.*

Manufacturing and Processing: Animal Inputs ***Bones***: Combs Strefield Mill *1782*, Handles for brushes and cutlery, Fertiliser ('greaves') 'Cupellation'. ***Fat***: Possibly soap with bracken *pteridium aquilinum* ash. English soap manufacture began in Devizes [1192], 'Tallow', 'grease' & 'Greaves' renderinge *9767*, The Greaves, Beeley *2667*, Monyash candles *1466*. ***Fur*** Bradwell beaver hat for miners, as well as men and women in general *1781*. ***Hides***: cattle, goats, sheep: leather, clothing, harness, footwear eg military knights' boots, shoes Calver *2472*, Eyam *2176*, Stoney Middleton *2275*, covering wood for painting triptychs, cups. 'Benty Grange *1467*', Tanning: Bakewell *2168*, Bradwell *1781*, Edale *1385*, Grindleford *2477*, Great Longstone *2071*, Little Hayfield *0387* 'Agriculture', 'Birch', 'Limestone', 'Oak', 'Saltways, Barker. ***Horns***: Saxon helmet Benty Grange *1564*, Hooves: Glue. ***Meat***: food, Coke, Hathersage, Hunter. 'Hunting', 'Saltways'. ***Milk***: Butter: Butterlands *9467*, Butterton *0756*, Smerrill *1962*, Cheese: Milk from ewes and cows. Fawfieldhead [1840s] *0763*, Glutton Bridge *0866*, Hartington *1360*, Hope *1255* - co-operative of 20 farmers [1847], Hopedale [1878-1930] *1255*, Parwich [1900] *1854*, Reapsmoor *0861*, Rewlach Farm [1881] *0961*. Herbs added [early 19th century] 'Groaning cake'. ***Silk*** Gradbach *9966*, Meerbrook *9860*, Wildboarclough *9869*, Wincle *9665*; Buttons Flash *0267*, Eyam *2176*, Clothing gowns, stockings. Footwear 'Hides', Scarves 'Tideswell' *1575*, 'Sericulture', 'Mills'. ***Tortoiseshell***: combs *Rowland Holmes* Ashford in the Water *1969*. ***Wool***: Bleaching Crowden *0799*, scouring fleeces in a stream *9971*, Clothing Felt hats Baslow *2572*, Bradwell *1781*, Outer garments and underwear, 'hodden', hosiery Great Longstone *2071* Framework knitting Low Bradfield *2692*, Weaving Tintwistle *0297*, 'Tenter'.'Agriculture'. 'Cistercians', 'Creative arts' and 'Granges'. ***Washing plant***: *1778*. *Figure 9*, Animal Raw Material Inputs, *16* Live Cattle Supply Chain and *17* Cattle Carcasses Supply Chain refer.

Manufacturing and Processing: Mineral Inputs ***Chemical***: salts (compounds from metals and ores): dyes and pigments, 'mordants': 'haematite'. ***Clay***: Bricks Longstone Hall *1781*, Friden fire brick refractories *1660*, Custard Fields, Hartington *1360*, Winster Market Hall [17th century] *2460* Tiles All Saints, Bakewell [15th century] *2168*, Reaps Moor [1850s] *0861*, 'jowl'. '***Rocks***': 'agricultural' and 'building' lime, construction of roads, creative arts, railways, reservoirs. 'Limestone' Cement Works *1783*, Lime Kilns *1373, 1473*, Kill Pingle, Bamford *2083*, Kiln Piece, Edale *1285*,Top of the Hay *2469*, *Hurlock*, Steep Low *1256* and 'Millstone Grit'. '***Silica sand***': Refractories. Bakestonedale *9579*, Friden *1660*, Bradwell telescopes, opera glasses, spectables [1862] *1781*, '***Metals***': *Farrar, Smith*, Wire products Hathersage *2281*. ***Ore***: Crushing Alport 'galena' *2264*, 'Lode' Mill *1455*, Milldale ('Haematite' 'ochre') *1354*, Smelting: copper Greenlowfield *1555*. Furnace Hill *2589*, Smelting Mill *2666*, iron William Clough [13th century] *0689*,'Bole'. Washing Buddles – sloping stone troughs Bonsall Moor *2559*. *Figure 13*, Rock Extraction, refers.

Manufacturing and Processing: Organic Inputs ***Cereal***: barley, oats (Derbyshire and Staffordshire oat cakes for farmers' and labourers' diet. Caudwell *2566*, Gradbach [1640] *9966* Hartington *1360*, Dialect: 'earn' 'groaning cake' ***Cotton***: Candle wicks, Kettelshume *9880*, Monyash *1566*, lace thread *1385*. Customers of Manchester cotton firm Bakewell – *Mrs Bullock*, Longnor – *Thomas Oliver*. Dyes and colours (mineral and vegetable) 'Alder' bark, copper salts. '***Flax***': *linum usitatissimum* for Linen, Bast matting. Ropes - mining 'Hemp' Rope Walk, Bakewell *2168*, Monyash *1566*, 'Lime trees'. Thatch, Lamp wicks. Gradbach Mill *9966*, Upper Hulme *0161*, Waste Pob Green *0106*, *Roper*. *Pob* = flax refuse Pobgreen *0106*. **Hemp**: *cannabis sativa* OE: *haenep* = rope. Bakewell *2267*, Elton *2260*, Hempen Butts, Eyam *2176*, Monyash *1466*, Peak Cavern *1482*, Taddington *1471*, Upper Hulme *0160*. ***Herbs***: peppermint Cressbrook *1772*, **Nettles**: *urtica doica* camouflage dye Nettlebeds *9565*, **Trees** Building – oak beams, containers: casks (*Cowper*), Farm equipment 'Batwell', 'Bowk', 'Brig', 'Hack', 'Heel rake','Kimnel', 'Kit'. enclosures – 'Fleck', 'Stoases', 'Raddle'; fasteners – pegs *Pegge*; Floor coverings – mats from lime tree fibres, rushes, Food and drink cups and plates 'Sole' Fuel 'Heating and Lighting', Interior decoration panelling, wainscot, Derwent Hall *2383*, 'Mordants': Oak galls and also mineral 'haematite' twigs - besom brooms, Monyash *1466*, Stoney Middleton *2275*, Thornhill *1983*, Winster *2260;* 'Hoppet', 'Whisket'; *Advent, Hunstone* and Tideswell Church *1575*, Paper Allgreave Mill *9767*, Rope, from 'lime' tree fibres Peak Cavern *1482*, *Roper*, Sealants pitch 'Scots Pine', Vehicles – 'Felloes', 'Rathes' wheel hubs Hubber Dale *1469*.

Merchandising: ***Factors and wholesalers***: Cheese: Alstonefield area, [1830s]. George Hambleton, Samuel Mellor, Anthony Massey, Bartholomew Massey, Buttons Flash *0267* James Wardle, Hollinsclough [1757] *0666*, William Wood, Corn 'Badger': Ore 'Brenners'. ***Purchasing agents***: for lead smelters and merchants to whom miners, the producers, were often indebted every week.
Fairs: Bradfield cattle [1714] founded by Joseph Swicket *2692*, Hope cattle [1770] founded by John Balguy [1683], 'Tideswell' *1575*. ***Financiers***: *Henry Balguy, Ibba'* **Markets**: * = Fair and market Alstonefield [1308] *1355*, *Bakewell [1254 also 1330] *2168*, Blore *1349*, Castleton [1222] *1582*, Hartington [1203] *1360*, Hope sheep and cattle [1715] *1783*, Monyash [1340] *1566*, *Tideswell [1250] *1575*, *Winster [1690] lead mining income *2460*. ***Market*** halls: Bakewell [17th century] *2168*, Longnor *0864*, Winster [1700] *2460*. ***Retailing***: 'Hawkers' and pedlars [1785] about 400 around Flash *0267*, Hollinsclough [1780s] *0666*, Micah Mellor, 'Badger', 'Huckster', 'Swailer', ***'Staple'***: Lead Calais *50°57'N 1°50'E*. '**Yeomen**' *Joseph Burke* sent 20 horseloads of meat and wheat flour to Manchester about [1758] from Tideswell 1575, For distribution see 'Packhorses', 'Portways, 'Saltways', 'Turnpikes' 'Beeston Tor 1054'.

Metals: ***Alloys***: with copper: '*Bronze*' (Copper + Lead + Zinc) Cooking utensils*, memorials, church furnishings Italian 'stoup' [1596] in Holy Trinity Church Stanton in the Peak *2464* and weapons; '*Latten*'/cullen plate for memorial brasses. 'Tinker' Tinker's Pit *0270, Fulwood*. 'Pewter' for plates and tankards. "Silver" coins Roman denarius of *Severus* [193-210AD] found at Brough *1882*. *Edward the Confessor*, [1042-46], mixed silver + zinc + copper for the coin edging Benty Grange Tumulus contents *1467*. ***Compounds***: Arsenic sulphide: King's yellow pigment. Trevise wrote of it as the 'colour of gold.' [1398]. It also improves the surface of lead fishing weights Copper salts: 'Mordanting', blue dyes, Iron oxide: 'haematite' for 'mordanting' and dyeing. ***Fabricated***: Copper: for coins,cooking utensils*, roofs, sheathing ship bottoms (copper bottomed.) Known since [4000BC]. Lead: In use since [3000BC] coffins, drains, pools - waterproof lining, roofs Waltham Abbey [1177-83] *3800*, stained glass window assembly – [12th century] onwards, Zinc: roofs - last 300 years. ***Ores***: 'Anglesite': lead sulphate Eyam *2176*, 'Arsenopyrite': arsenic sulphide Ecton *0958*, 'Azurite': copper carbonate Ecton *0958*, 'Bornite': a type of copper pyrites Ecton *0958*, Calamine See 'Smithsonite', 'Chalcanthite': copper sulphate Ecton *0958*, 'Chalcopyrite': copper pyrites Ecton *0958*, 'Cinnabar': mercury Sheldon *1768*, 'Cuprite': copper oxide Ecton *0958*, 'Galena': lead sulphide and other metals Castleton *1583*, Eyam *2176*, Grindon *0854*, Haddon *2366*, River Lathkill valley *1865*, Sheldon *1768*, Warslow *0858*, Youlgreave *2064*, 'Cupellation' Haematite': ferrous oxide [red ochre] Youlgreave *2064*, 'Heminorphite': hydrated zinc silicate Eyam *2176*, 'Limonite': iron oxides generic term [Yellow ochre] Eyam *2176*, Winster *2460*, 'Malachite': copper carbonate Beresford *1259*, Ecton *0958*, Grindon *0854*, Mercury: See 'cinnabar', Silver: in argentiferous lead. Odin Mine, Castleton *1583*, 'Smithsonite': zinc carbonate Eyam *2176*, 'Sphalerite': zinc sulphide Castleton *1583*, Sheldon *1768*, 'Wad': manganese oxide Elton *2260*. Forms of deposits 'Flat': Burnt Heath *2075*, 'Pipe [vein] Bradwell *1781*, 'Rakes' Coalpithole *0981*, Deep *2273*, Dirtlow *1481*, Dirty *1975*, Earl *1680*, High *2073*, Hollinsclough *0666*, Long *1764*, Magshaw *1867*, Mandale *1866*, Moss *1580*, Shuttle *1479*, Watersaw *1973*, White *1974*, 'Scrins': Sheldon *1768*, 'King's Field', 'Liberty', 'Quo Warranto'.

Mills: Alport *2264* 'galena' crushing, Ashford in the Water *2068* 'Marble' [1748-1905], Bakewell managed by *Robert Arkwright, Richard's* son [1814] *2168*, Bamford corn until fire [1780] then cotton following rebuilding by *Moores* of Manchester *2083*, Bradfield *2692*, Calver 3 storeys with Arkwright machinery *2475*, Cressbrook cotton [1783] by *Richard Arkwright* bought [1835] for Nottingham lace thread *1772.* Cotton (unnamed) *0388, 1385,* See 'roak' Dains *0161,* Diggle wool *0108,* River Dove ore *1455,* Eagle Tor *2362,* Edale lace thread [1792] *1285,* Edensor corn *2568,* Errwood Hall *0175,* Eyam cotton/silk# (*Ralph Wain*) 100 employees, #bought by Macclesfield Methodists Dainty, Ryle & Co *2176,* Fernilee gunpowder [1909-20] *0178,* Flewitt's corn *1969,* Folly paper *9766,* Ford corn *0653,* Ginclough silk *9576,* Glutton Bridge corn *0866,* Goytsclough paint *0078,* Gradbach flax [1785-1837], silk [?-1862], timber [1885-?] barn [?-1977] *9966,* Grangemill probably cereals *2457,* Greenlowfield copper *1555,* Green's House paper *2383,* Hartington corn *1360,* Hathersage Dale 5 mills needles, hooks, cotton 'Schools' *2380,* Highlow corn *2179,* Hodgkinson's corn *2572,* Holme wool weaving *1005,* Hope corn *1783,* Ible corn *2456,* Ivonbrook corn *2457,* Lamb Hole/Lumb cotton candlewick/linen *9880,* Lead corn *2380,* Litton cotton [1782-1960s]/nylon *1675,* 'Lode' ore crushing then [1814-1930] corn *1455,* Longnor timber *0864,* Low Bradfield *2691,* Ludburn corn *0962,* Lum(s)ford undershot water wheel cotton 300 employees [1778] *2168,* Lumbhole *9878,* Marle's corn/timber *2772,* Mill 'clough' *0078,* Mill Brook cotton *9475,* Milldale [1282] ochre crushing *1454,* Mill Hill [wind] *0590, 2176,* Onecote corn *0455,* Carters, One ash *1766,* Overheyes/Pott Mill corn *9479* Padley corn *2578,* Phoside wool spinning, weaving, fulling *0387,* Peak Forest corn *1178,* Primrose Vale tanning/ cotton or linen stiff buckram *0387,* Rowarth cotton *0189,* Saw *1869,* Sheldon bone/timber *1869,* Sour [1865] *2066,* Smelting *2666,* Stanton corn *2363,* Strefield bone combs *1782,* Thorpe corn *1450,* Tideswell cotton/velvet/fustian/calico/silk *1575;* Upper Hulme flax *0161,* Victoria corn *2168,* West Side [1584-1880] corn *1058,* Wetton corn [1577] *1055,* Wildboarclough silk/cotton/wool carpets *9868,* Wincle silk, cotton *9665,* Windmill *1677,* Winster cotton (Boulton & Watt steam engine) *2460,* Woodeaves [1784] cotton *1850,* Wormhill [1203] corn *1274,* 'Rivers' with weirs for **water power.** *Employee accommodation*: Manager Crag Hall *9968,* Cressbrook orphans *1772,* Forty Row Cottages, Fletchers Paper Mill *0202.* **Personnel**: Flemish weavers Great Longstone *2071, Sir Richard Arkwright, Thomas Cantrell* Brund *1061* and Hartington *1360,* German entrepreneur at Hathersage *2380, Milnes, Milward.* 'Coiners'. *Figure 12* Water and Wind Mills refers.

Mill Owners: * = bankruptcy **Thomas Oliver,* *Thomas White,* *James Oliver,* Alstonefield *1355;* *C Kirk,* Bamford [1783] *2083;* *T Cantrell & Sons,* Brund *1790;* **Barker, *Bossley & Co,* Cressbrook [1809-10] *1773;Gardom* (Bakewell hosier, Gardoms Edge *2773), Pares & Co,* Calver [1778] *2377;* *N Cresswell,* Edale [1790] *1285; J Gooddy,* Hartington *1360; Needham, Frith & Co,* Litton [1782] *1675; W Keeling,* Peak Forest [1792] *1179,* (a)**William Gibson,* (b) **Ellis* and **John Needham,* Tideswell *1575,* (a) **Benjamin Stone* and **Edward Harrison,* Winster [1791] (b) *Henry Wooley,* grocer, cotton Winster [1803] *2460.*

Mine owners: Dukes of Devonshire, *Thurstan de Bower, Henry Watson.* 'Barmaster', Great Longstone *2071,* Hathersage *2380,*'Bagging' 'Livery companies', 'Merchandising', 'Workers' accommodation'.

Mines: #Coal * Ore ^Rock or clay *Explosion*: [1932] 8 killed Mawstone *2163* 'firedamp'. **Locations**: *Bincliff *1154,* Bird *1581,* *^Blue John *1383,* *Coalpithole *0981,* #Bradfield *2590,* *Dale *0958,* *Clayton, Ecton (gunpowder used [1670]) *0958,* #Errwood Hall *0074,* *Fieldgrove *1769,* ^Glebe [until 1979] *2176,* *Highfields *1153,* *Hillocks *1467,* *Hubbadale *1369,* *Kirkdale *1868,* *Knotlow *1467,*^ *Ladywash *2176,* *Magpie *1768,* *Mandale *1866,* *Mawstone/Mosstone [closed 1932] *2064,* Maypitt *1768,* *Mill Dam *1778,* Mixon *0457,* *Mogshaw *1867,* *New Engine [until 1884] *2277,* *Odin [1230 -] *1383,* Old Edge *2176,* *Old Tor *1382,* *Oxpasture *2172,* *Pindale/Aston's *1682,* *Placket *2361,* * Portway *2361,* *Raper *2165,* *^Sallet Hole *2174,* *Silence *1878,* *Speedwell *1382,* *Tideswell *1575,* *Treak Cliff *1383,* *True Blue *1768,* ^Ughill *2590,* *Watergrove *1875,* ^Wheatshire *2590,* #Wildboarclough *9868,* Yatesstoop *2361. Methods*: Gunpowder introduced [1670], 'Cupellation'.'Gin', Leat', 'Sough', 'Wheal', Cornish Engine pump Sheldon *1768. Personnel*: Cornish immigrants, Dutch [1686] Ecton *0958,* 'barmaster', 'breene', 'caver', carrier, hewer, pickman, 'jagger', winder, *Cavendish, Eyre, Farrar, Fulwood, Ellis Needham* (Litton *1572), Smith, Talbot, Vernon.* See 'tut work'. Disputes Pay [1630] *John Manners* undercut Tideswell *1575* miners at Hazelbadge *1780* by employing Bradwell *1781* miners; Magpie versus Maypitt [19th century] *1768. Regulation* 'Barmote', 'Freeing', 'Meer', 'Nick'. **Waste**: 'Open', 'Shack', 'Brood', 'Cross' 'Transport' *Figures 10* Metal Ore Extraction, *11* Rock Extraction and *27* Fire and :Light refer.

Occupations and personal names: *Archer, Arkwright, Armiger, Barber, Barker, Bird, Bowman, Bridgeman, Carver, Clerke, Coke, Cowper, Degge, Farrar, Garlic, Greaves, Harpur, Hunter, Hurlock, Hyde, Kniveton, Leche, Lynford, Marbury, Marshall, Melland, Metcalf, Milnes, Milward, Pegge, Roper, Salt, Smith, Spencer, Thacker, Ward, Warren, Wright.*

Organised labour: *Box club*: miner's insurance fund Birchover [1777] *2462*. *Disputes* Hill Carr Sough *2261* [1777] first recorded strike and lock-out, Wincle *9665*[1851]; *'Manners'*. **Friendly society**: Eyam *2176* miners [1797]. 'Law'.

'Packhorses': *Bridges*: Coalpit, Conkesbury (coal from Chesterfield) *2065*, Crowdecote *1065*, Sheepwash (R Wye) *1969*, Viator *1455*, Washgate (R Dove) *0567*. *By pass*: Lumford *2169*. *Crossroads*: Alstonefield *1355*, Ashop Ridge *1289*, Hollins Cross *1384*, Jaggers' Clough *1487*, Stoke Ford *2179*, Three Shire Heads (Junction of five trails: Cumberland Brook valley; Dane Head; Dane Valley [north and south]; Dane Hollow;) *0068*. *Guidestone*: *2774*, Inn Crowdecote *1065*. *Places served*: Alstonefield (Route centre) *1355*, Ashford in the Water *1969*, Bakewell *2168*, Baslow *2572*, Biggin Dale *1457*, Curbar *2579*, Edale *1285*, Eyam *2176*, Great Longstone *2071*, Hartington *1360*, Hope *1783*, Milldale *1454*, Monyash *1566*, Taxal *0079*. *Inns*: Crowdecote *1065*, Monsal Head *1871*. *Routes*: Ashford in the Water *1969* → Eyam *2176*; Baslow *2572* → Curbar *2574* → Chesterfield; Chapel en le Frith *0580* → Sparrowpit *0980* → Bakewell *2168*; Derby → Monyash *1566* → Manchester; Derwent Valley *1397* → Cut Gate *1996* → Penistone *2402*; Edale *1285* → Barber Booth *1184* → Mam Tor *1283* → Winnats *1382* → Castleton *1582*; Flagg *1368* → Monyash *1566*, → Macclesfield Forest ('Ridgeway') *9671* → Hope *1783*; Ford *0882* → Malcoff *0782* → Shireoaks *0783*,Tideswell *1575* → Manchester. 'Portways', *Thomas Pickford*. *Figure 14*, Route Planning refers.

Pastoral Farming: *Disease*: 'Foul' Tideswell *1575* Cow [Insurance Club] founded [1838] *John Manners*. *Facilities*: for sheep *ovis aries*, Sheepwash Bank *2394*, Sheepwash Bridge *1969*, Washbrook *1651*. **Sheep Dog Trials**: Lantern Pike revived [1997] *0288*, Longshaw started [1898] *2679*. *Grazing*: 'Holm', 'Meadows', 'Ditches' - upland: Broad *1163*, *2488*, *9855*, Broadham *0862*, Soles Hill *0952*, Stock *9862*, Willow Meadow *0354*, **Groves**: Dun cow (brownish-grey) *0466*. *Pasture*: = grazing land Alstonefield *1355*, Shawfield *0661*, Butter Field, Great Hucklow *1777*, Eyam *2176*, Hayesgate *0959*, Cow <u>Pasture</u>, Hope *1783*, Little Hucklow *1678*, Ollset *0285*, The <u>Pasture</u>, Over Haddon *2066*, Stoney Middleton *2375*. <u>Pasture</u> Tops *1849*, Good quality Butterley *0901*, Stanshope *1354*, Thorpe *1551* + The 'Raikes' *1159* + <u>Ramsley</u> Moor *2875*, Summer track Lansett *2100* 'Swineherd'. *Emblem*: Wool stapler shears in the wall of Chelmorton Church *1170*, 15th century [Flock size: 250 common 400 not unusual]. 'Brand' 'Haematite'. 'Water Engineering: Troughs'.

Portways/oldways: *Marker stick* Brogging *2191*. *Routes* Ashford in the Water *1969* → Great Longstone *2071* → Eyam *2176* Derby → Monyash *1566* → Manchester; Nottingham → Bakewell *2168* → Hope *1783* Macclesfield Ridgeway: Shining Tor *9973* → Tors *9974* → Pym Chair (Goyt) *9976* → Windgatter Rocks *9978* → Taxal *0079*. 'Packhorses'.

Railways: *Ashbourne → Buxton*: Stations: Hurdlow *1266*, Parsley Hay (High Peak junction) *1463*, Hartington *1461*, Alsop en le Dale *1554*, Tissington *1752*, Fenny Bentley *1650*. Constructed [1890s]. Closed [1967]. *Chinley → Derby*: Stations: Millers Dale *1373*, Monsal Dale *1771*, Thornbridge Hall *1971*, Hassop *2170*, Bakewell *2269*, Rowsley *2665* Cowburn tunnel *0783*, Opened [1863]. Closed [1968]. *High Peak*: Cromford *2956* → Whaley Bridge *0181* – Cromford → Peak Forest Canals link) Friden shunting yard *1660*, Gotham *1858*, Minninglow *2057*, Parsley Hay (Ashbourne→ Buxton junction) *1463*. Lime works extension *0294*. Constructed [1830s] Cost: £200,000. Closed [1967]. *Dore → Chinley*: Sheffield → Manchester [1894]: Stations: Edale *1285*, Hope *1883*, Bamford *2082*, Hathersage *2381*, Grindleford *2578*. *Manifold Valley*: (Narrow gauge 2'6"): Stations: Sparrowlee *1059*, Beeston Tor *1054*, Thor's Cave *0954*, Wetton Mill *0956*, Swainsley *0957*, Ecton *0958*, Hulme End *1059*. Closed [1934]. *Manchester → Sheffield → Lincoln*: Woodhead tunnels (4.9km) *0900*, Stations: Crowden *0899*, Dunford Bridge *1502*. *Eyam Edge → Waterfall* both *2077* Fluorspar 2 ft gauge. *Figure 13*, Railways refers. 'Recreation'.

Rocks and minerals: *'Amethyst'*: Millers Dale *1373*. *'Barytes'*: 'Arbor' 'Low' *1663*, Coombs Dale *2274*, Friden *2476*. **Basalt**: Calton Hill [1906-69] *1171*, Ible *2556*, Tideswell Dale *1574*, ***Blue John'*:** Castleton *1583*, *'Calcite'*: Castleton caves (stalagmites) *1583* Ecton *0958*, Eyam *2176*, Monyash *1566*. *'Chalcedony'* Friden *2476*. *'Chert'*: Ashford in the Water 1969, Friden *2476*, Holme Bank *2169*, Little Longstone *1871*, Pretoria *2168*. *'Clay'*: Bakewell *2168*, *white sinks, tiles* Harrop *9678*, 'Bole' Hills, Clay Pits *2589*, Hope *1783*, Reaps Moor *0861*, Stoney Middleton *2376*, Ughill *2590*, *silica fire bricks* Friden *1660*. *'Derbyshire Diamonds'*: Cavedale *1482*, Priestcliffe *1371*. *'Derbyshire onyx'*: Barium sulphate from stalactites 'Arbor' 'Low' *1663*, Coombs Dale *2274*, Friden *2476*. *'Dolerite'/*diabase: Calton Hill *1171*, Wormhill *1274*. *'Fluorite'/*fluorspar: Eyam *2176*, Great Hucklow *1777*, Hazlebadge *1780*, Ricklow *1766*, Upper Cupola *2175*. *'Ganister'*: Loadfield *2594*, Royd Edge *0909*, **Gravel**: OE: *greosn* <u>Greasley</u>

9466. Gritstone/'Millstone Grit'/Namurian: Bamford *2085*, Beeley *2667*, Birchover *2462*, Bury Cliff *2161*, Danebower *0170*, Hathersage *2579*, Hope *1784*, Longnor *0865*, Macclesfield Forest *9671*, Nether Padley *2578*, Nether Tor *1287*, Reeve Edge *0169*, The Roaches *0062*, Runninghill *0107*, Sandmill Hollow *0390*, Sheen *1060*, Stanton Lees *2563*, Tintwistle *0499*. '*Jasper*': Friden *2476*. '*Limestone*': Beresford *1259*, Bradwell *1780*, Calver *2374*, Ecton *0958*, Eyam *2176*, Flagg *1269*, Harthill *2264*, Horseshoe Dale *0967*, Ilam Tops *1352*, Little Longstone *1871*, Litton *1675*, Monyash *1566*, Onecote *0455*, Pindale *1682*, Roystone Grange *2057*, Shiningbank *2365*, Stoney Middleton *2275*, Thorpe *1550*, Tideswell *1575*, Tissington *1753*, Windy Knoll *1283*. '*Marbles*': 'Anthraconite' Black Ashford in the Water until [1905] *1969*, 'Black Birds Eye' Netler Dale, Ashford in the Water *1969*, Sheldon *1768*, 'Derby Black' Ashford Dale *1969*, 'Duke's Red' Alport *2164*, 'Monyash'/grey Ricklow *1666*, 'Pink Birds Eye' Parsley Hay *1563*, 'Rosewood' Ashford in the Water *1969*, Sheldon *1768*. **Oakstone**: See Derbyshire onyx. '*Olivine /Olivineare*': Kirk Dale *1868*. '*Opal*': Bakewell *2168*, Eyam *2176*. '*Porphyry*': 'Arbor' 'Low' *1663* Middleton Mine *1963*. '*Quartz*': Calton Hill *1171*, Friden *2476*. '*Rottenstone*': Hazlebadge *1780*. **Sand**: Lowmorr *1956, 1656, 1857*. '*Sandstone*': roof "slates", Offerton *2181*, Ridge *0062*, Cleulow Cross *9664*, **Shale**: for cement, Edale *1285*, Mam Tor *1283*. **Slate**: OF: *escalate* Slate Pit Moss *0304*, Slate Lands, Bamford *2083*. **Silica**: Hartington *1562*, Middleton *1963*, **Slates**: *2783*. '*Toadstone*': Cavedale *1482*. Priestcliffe *1371*, '*Travertine*': Elder Bush Cave *0955*, Kinder Valley *0788*. '*Umber*': Smerrill *1961*. '*Whinstone*': Whinstone Lee 'Tor' *2087*. *Figure 11*, Rock Extraction refers.

Saltways: NB Salt Cellar *1989* is a land form feature. **Routes:** Altrincham → Tintwistle *0297* → Woodhead *0900;* Cheadle → Haddon *2366* → Bakewell *2168* → Chesterfield → Salter 'Sitch' → Sheffield. Cheshire → Taxal *0079* → Warslow *0858* → Hartington *1360* and Salter's Brook Bridge *1300* → Barnsley NB Fiddlers' (Time wasters') Green *1500*; Etherow Valley *0799* → Woodhead *0900;* Macclesfield → Saltersford *9876* → The Street (Roman) *0076* → Goyt Bridge *0171* → Buxton; Toot Hill *9771* → Macclesfield Forest *9772* → Bottom of the Oven *9872* → Torgate *9872* → Taxal *0079*. **Salter**: *George Salt* Methodist Dissenter at Longnor [1838] *0865*. **Uses:** preservation of fish and meat, tanning. *Figure 15*, Saltways refers.

Stagecoach: Places served from Bakewell [1830s] *2168*, Belper, Buxton, Chesterfield, Sheffield, Winster *2460*. York → Longendale *0397* → Chester.

Transport: 'Bawk', 'Bridges', 'Fords', 'Gate', 'Green Lane', Horse Stead ON: strahr = a place, 1471, 'Jags and Jaggers', 'Packhorses, 'Plowbote', 'Portways', 'Railways', 'Ridgeway', 'Roman roads', 'Saltways', 'Stagecoach', 'Turnpikes', 'Wagons'. *Figure 14*, refers.

Travellers' accommodation: Ashford in the Water [1840] *1969*, Rutland Arms Hotel, Bakewell *2168*, Bamford *2083*, Devonshire Arms, Beeley *2667*, Biggin *1559*, Birchover *2462*, Butterton *0756*, Cat and Fiddle built by *John Ryle*, Macclesfield Methodist banker [1823] *0071*, Chelmorton *1169*, Crowdecote *1065*, Edale *1285*, Flagg *1368*, Fox House *2482* named after farmer *George Fox*, Great Longstone *2071*, Hurdlow House [1730s] *1166*, Little Hucklow *1678*, Litton *1675*, Monsal head *1871*, Newhaven *1660*, Parwich *1854*, Peak Forest *1179*, Reaps Moor *0861*, Ringinglow *2883*, Nag's Head and Red Lion, Rowsley *2566*, Sheen *1161*, Snake Inn, (a snake is in the crest of the Dukes of Devonshire) originally the Lady Clough *1190*, Sparrowpit *0980*, Taddington *1471*, Anchor Inn, George Hotel, Tideswell *1575*, Upper Elkstone *0559*, Warslow *0858*, Wetton *1155*, Bull's Head, Youlgreave *2064*. 'Packhorse'.

'**Turnpikes**': **Guidestone**: *2274*. **Places served**: Bakewell *2168*, Butterton *0756*, Ecton *0958*, Edensor *2468*, Hulme End *1059*, Longnor *0864*, Onecote *0455*, Woodlands *1489* [1819] built by *Thomas Telford* [1757-1834]. **Routes**: Ashford in the Water *1969* → Edensor *2468*; Buxton → Cat and Fiddle *0071* → Macclesfield [1759]; Buxton *0673* → Ashford in the Water *1969* about [1810] [Wye Valley]; Grindleford *2477* → Newhaven *1660*; Hathersage *2381* → Bamford *2083* → Ashopton *1986* [1777]; [1757] Ringinglow *2883* → Houndkirk *2881* → Grindleford *2578* → Great Hucklow *1877* → Tideswell *1575* → Wormhill *1274* → Buxton [1757]; Loughborough → Grindelford [1738] *2477*, Manchester → Chapel en le Frith → Castleton *1582* → Hathersage *2381* → Sparrowpit *1582* [1757]; Newcastle under Lyme → Great Longstone *2071* → Hassop *2272* → Snake Pass *0892* [1820]. **Toll Booth**: Baslow Far End *2672*, Brierlow 'Bar' *0869*, Flash Bar *0267*, Grindleford Bridge *2477*, Longnor [1765] *0864*, Monyash *1466*, Ringinglow [1778] (3 routes) *2883*, Stoney Middleton [1840] *2375*, Stoney Ridge *2780* for beer, coal, flour, millstones [1816-84], Stony way *9972*, Waterhouses *0850*, *2070*, *2170*.

Wagons: Transport of lead to Southampton for export [16th century].

Water engineering: *Aqueducts*: Chatsworth Cyclopean, (millstone grit) *2670*, Lathkill Dale *1865*. ***Canal***: underground Ecton Mine *0958*. ***Dams***: ME: *damme* Bradfield *2692*, Derwent [1916] *1791*, Eyam [1354] *2176*, Howden [1916] *1793;* Rivelin *2786*. ***Dew ponds***: Hartington *1360, 1456*. *#**Ditches***: OE: dic = ditch/di(y)ke Delf Foulstone *2191*, Grey *1781*, Thornseat *2292*, OE Bar Dyke *2494*, Bleakley *2163*, Devil's Dike *0993*, Hobson Moss [drainage] *2194*, Rake Dike *1005*, 'Reen', Scalderditch *1159*, Dialects: (a) Gutter *0263*, (b) Strines Dike *2190*. ***Floods*** Dale Dike [11/03/1864] *2692*. ***Fountains***: Conduit Head, Youlgreave *2164*, Emperor *2670*. ***Irrigation*** Iron Tors Pump House *1456*. ***Mains drinking water***: Longnor [1877] *0864*, Conduit Head Fountain, Youlgreave [1829] *2164*, Borehole Grindslow Knoll *1086* → Edale *1285* 69,000 litres daily; River Noe tunnel *1686* → Ladybower *1687*; Springs Brocket Booth *1484* + Crookstone Hill *1488* →Castleton *1582*, 67,000 litres daily output*;* Roych *0784* + Shireoaks *0783* via Shireoaks reservoir → Chapel en le Frith 227,000 litres daily; Sponds coal 'adit' *9779* → Macclesfield 45,460 litres daily; Wall Cliff *1477* → Tideswell *1575* 90,920 litres daily. '***Meres***': *1052*, Heathcote [1482] *1460*, Monyash Fere *1566*. ***Mill Races***: Milldale *1454*, See 'Mills'. ***Pools***: Lumbhole *0661*, Potluck *1377*. Sparrowpit *0880*. ***Reservoirs***: Agden *2692*, Black Moss *0308*, Bottoms *0297*, Deaths of Longendale workers from cholerai, Broomhead *2695*, Butterley *0510*, Chew [1912] *0301*, Dale Dyke *2391*, Damflask *2790*, Derwent [1911] *1790*, Diggle *0207*, Digley *1007*, Dovestone [1967] *0103*, Errwood [1967] *0175*, Fernilee [1938] *0177*, Greenfield [1903] *0205*, Harden *1503*, Howden [1911] *1792*, Ladybower [1945] *1888*, Lamaload *9775*, More Hall *2795*, Ramsden *1105*, Rhodeswood *0598*, Riding Wood *1105*, Snailsden *1304*, Swellands *0309*, Torside *0698*, Valehouse *0397*, Wessenden *0508*, Windleden *1501*, Winscar *1501*, Woodhead *0899*, Yateholme *1104*, Yeoman Hey [1880] *0205*. Private: Hassop Hall Caves *2272*, Navvies Birchinlee *1691*. '***Soughs***': Calver *2374*, Mandale *1966*, Odin *1482*,Pindale *1482*. ***Troughs***: (for washing and drinking by animals and humans) Hall Hill and Wat Lane, Eyam [1588] *2176*. ***Weirs***: 1. Angling Rivers Dove *1451*, Goyt *0177*, Lathkill *1865*, Manifold *1152*. 2. Power Overshot and undershot water wheels, Derwent *2475* Wye *1772*. Underground water wheel-driven pump Ecton Mine *0958*, Water turbines Cressbrook [1890] *1773* 'Mills'. 'Limestone' 'Mills' 'Mines'. Dialect: 'Mole plough', 'Reen'. Ebbing and Flowing/Weeden Well *0879*. 'Literary Connections *Sir Aston Cockayne*'. # Saxons dug ditches as 'parish' boundaries.

Workers' accommodation: Bamford *2083*, Birchinlee *1691*, Boothmans *0271*, Crag Hall *9968*, Cressbrook *1773*, Lyme Hall "attic" *9682*, Lumford *2169*. Taxal *0079*. 'Granges'

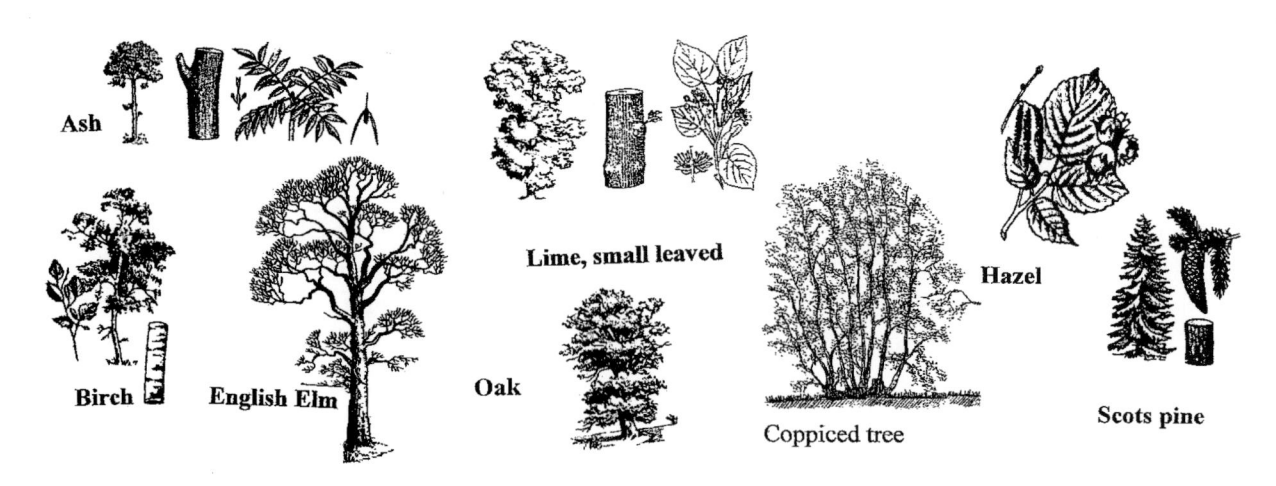

Useful Trees

Figure 9   Ubiquitous Farming

                                                    Sheepwash White Lee

                        Birchinlee [pastures and shelter]
                                      Rowlee
Long Lee [shelter]

               The Cote [shelter]

Ollset [pasture]

                               Castleton [farmstead]
       Malcoff [calf]
    Kettelshulme [wheat]
          Ox Low   Hathersage
                 Abney   Field System   Field System
Haylee [shelter]   Swine Sty
                         Eyam
                    Tideswell   Field System
                      Calver [calf]
Hammerton [farmstead]

                                              Field System
Laithes   Calton   [smithy and farmstead]
[field barn]   Chelmorton [farmstead]
        Oxensitch   Calton   Bakewell [market]
Allgreave [rendering]
                               Caudwell Mill
Barleyleigh   Fawfieldhead [vaccary]
Old Smithy   Broad Meadow Flax Dale
      Stock Meadow   Birchover   Stanton
Horse Hay   Rewlach [milk]
                      Heathcote
       Sheep fold   Staden   Raikes
                                    Gotham
         Mixon [dung]
             Butterton   Gateham [goat]   Hope [milk]
                                  Alstonfield [milk]
Broad   Onecote   Sheep fold
Meadow   Middlehill
              Soles Hill   Thorpe
                    Calton   Blore   Pasture Tops
                             [market]

77

Figure 10 Animal Raw Materials and Products

Strefield **Bo**, *Co* *Han*
Bradwell **Fu**, *Ha*
Eyam **Hi**, *Cl*, *Fo*, *Hs*
Si *Cl*, *Fo*, *Ho*
Stoney Middleton **Hi**, *Tr*
Great Longstone **Wo** *Ho*
Ashford **To** *Co*

Wildboarclough **Si**

Gradbach **Si**
Flash **Si** *Bn*
Butterlands **Mi** *Bu*   Allgreave **Fa** *Ta*   Monyash *Ta* *Ca*
Fawfieldhead **Mi** *Ch* Glutton Bridge **Mi** *Ch*
Benty Grange **Hi** *Cu* **Hn** *Saxon* **He**
Hartington   Smerril **Mi** *Bu*
Mi *Ch*

Reapsmoor and Rewlach **Mi** *Ch*
Butterton **Mi** *Bu*   Alstonefield Ewe **Mi** *Ch*
Hopedale **Mi** *Ch*
Parwich **Mi** *Ch*

Materials: **Bo**nes, **Fa**t, **Fl**ax, **Fu**r, **Hi**des, **Ho**oves, **Hn** Horn **Mi**lk, **Si**lk, **To**rtoiseshell, **Wo**ol.

Products: *B*eaver *H*ats, *Bn* Buttons, *B*utter, *C*andles, *Ch*eese, *C*lothing, *C*ombs, *Cu*ps, *F*ootwear, *G*lue, *Ha*ts, *Han*dles, *Hs* Harness *He*lmet, *Ho*siery, *Ta*llow **Triptych boards**

Weir   Input

Gravity fed output

<u>Grain Mill Driven by Undershot Wooden Water Wheel</u>

78

Figure 11a — Metal Ore Extraction Sites

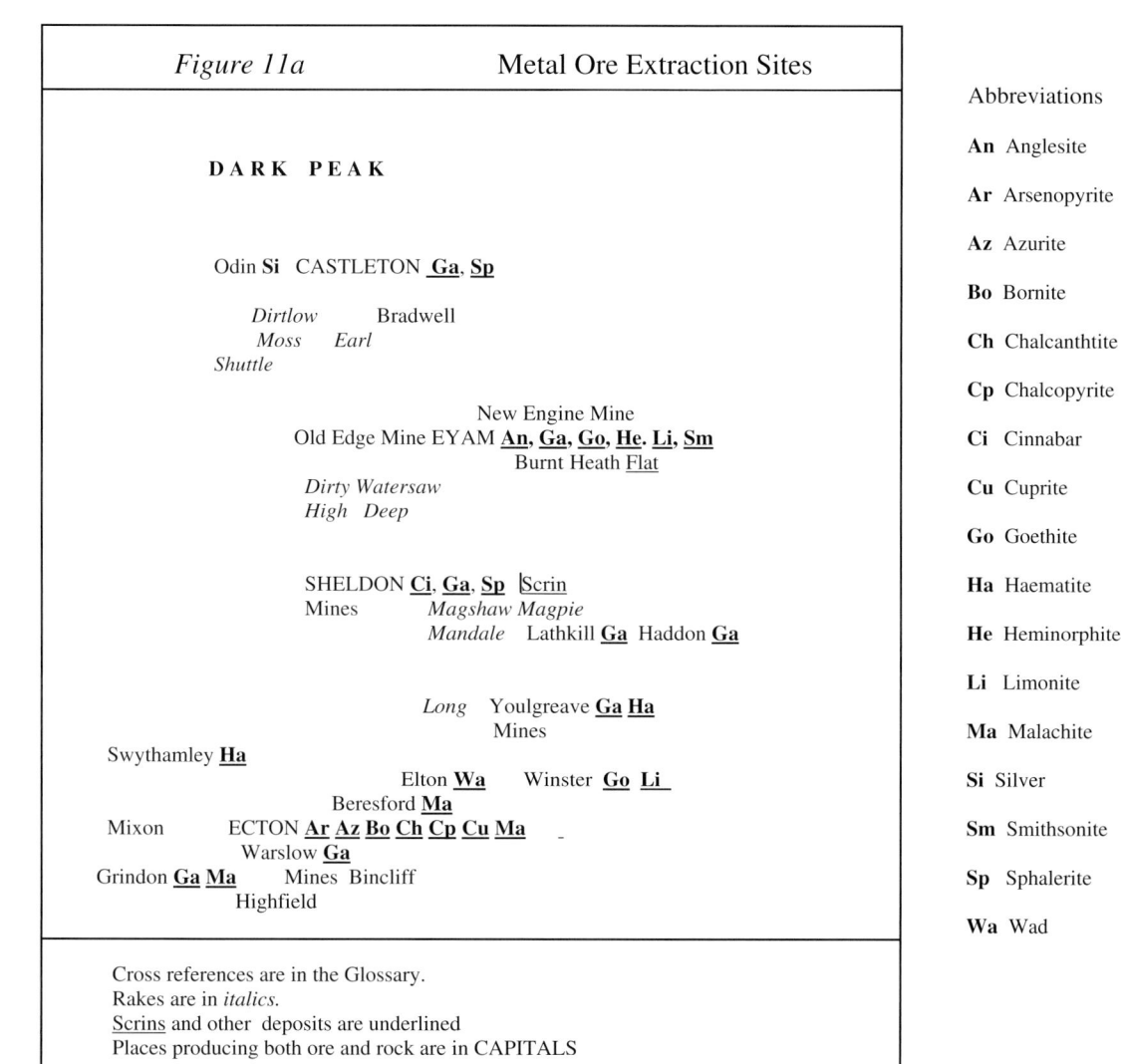

DARK PEAK

Odin **Si** CASTLETON **Ga**, **Sp**

Dirtlow Bradwell
Moss Earl
Shuttle

New Engine Mine
Old Edge Mine EYAM **An, Ga, Go, He. Li, Sm**
Burnt Heath <u>Flat</u>

Dirty Watersaw
High Deep

SHELDON **Ci, Ga, Sp** <u>Scrin</u>
Mines *Magshaw Magpie*
Mandale Lathkill **Ga** Haddon **Ga**

Long Youlgreave **Ga Ha**
Mines

Swythamley **Ha**

Elton **Wa** Winster **Go Li**
Beresford **Ma**
Mixon ECTON **Ar Az Bo Ch Cp Cu Ma**
Warslow **Ga**
Grindon **Ga Ma** Mines Bincliff
Highfield

Cross references are in the Glossary.
Rakes are in *italics*.
<u>Scrins</u> and other deposits are underlined
Places producing both ore and rock are in CAPITALS

Abbreviations

An	Anglesite
Ar	Arsenopyrite
Az	Azurite
Bo	Bornite
Ch	Chalcanthtite
Cp	Chalcopyrite
Ci	Cinnabar
Cu	Cuprite
Go	Goethite
Ha	Haematite
He	Heminorphite
Li	Limonite
Ma	Malachite
Si	Silver
Sm	Smithsonite
Sp	Sphalerite
Wa	Wad

Figure 11b — Economic Aspects of Metal Ore Extraction

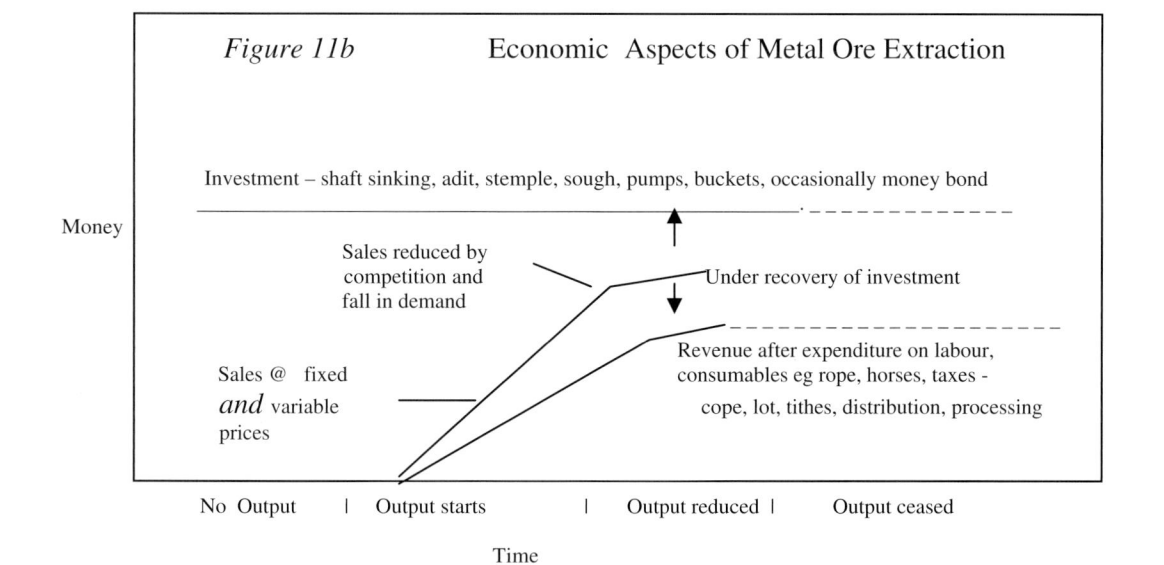

Money (y-axis)

Investment – shaft sinking, adit, stemple, sough, pumps, buckets, occasionally money bond

Sales reduced by competition and fall in demand

Under recovery of investment

Sales @ fixed *and* variable prices

Revenue after expenditure on labour, consumables eg rope, horses, taxes - cope, lot, tithes, distribution, processing

No Output | Output starts | Output reduced | Output ceased

Time

```
                    Figure 12                              Rock Extraction Sites.

        Royd Edge Ga
                                                              Loadfield Ga
                                                              Ughill Cl
                            DARK PEAK

            Moss Rake Ca                       Nether Padley Mi
                Gt Hucklow Fl
                    EYAM Ca, Fl, Li Op      St Middleton Cl, Li
                Litton Li
    Wormhill Do  Tideswell Ba, Li  Combes Dale B, Do   Calver Li
            Millers Dale Am
  Greasley Gr
            Calton Hill Ana Ba Do Q   L Longstone Che Li
                Priestcliffe DDb To
            Flagg Li                      Ashford An BBE DB R Che
                                          Holme Bank Che
            SHELDON BBE R  Kirkdale Ol    Pretoria Che  Bakewell Cl Op
                                                Beeley Mi
        Monyash Ca, DR, Li
                Ricklow Fl         Youlgreave Ca
                    Ridge Sa   Upper Cupola Fl  Shining Bank Li
                            Alport DR    Harthill Li
        Parsley Hay PBE  Middleton Op, Po, Si                Stanton Mi
        Arbor Low B Do Po
            Hartington Si      BERESFORD Li  Friden B Cha Che Do  Birchover Mi
            ECTON Ca                         J Q Si
        Smerrill Um                        Bury Cliff Mi
        Sheen Mi
        Pea Low Pi


                                        Royston Grange Li
        Lowmorr S                                   Ible Ba


                        Tissington Li
                        Ilam Li
                        Thorpe Li
```

Amethyst, **Ana**lcine **An**thraconite, **Ba**rytes, **Ba**salt, **B**lue **J**ohn, **Ca**lcite, **Cha**lcedony, **Che**rt, **Cl**ay, **D**erbyshire **D**iamonds, **D**erbyshire **O**nyx, **Do**lerite, **Fl**uorite, **Ga**nister, **Gr**avel, **J**asper, **Li**mestone **Mi**llstone grit, **Marbles** *in italics* – *An*thraconite, *B*lack *B*ird's *E*ye, *D*erby *B*lack, *D*uke's *R*ed, *M*onyash, *P*ink *B*ird's, *E*ye, *R*osewood, **O**livine, **Op**al, **Pi**solite, **Po**rphyry, **Pr**ez, **Q**uartz, **Rt** Rottenstone, **S**and, **S**andstone, **Sh**ale, **Si**lica, **Sl**ates, **To**adstone, **Tr**avertine, **Um**ber, **Wh**instone Places producing both ore and rock are in CAPITALS. Cross references are in the Glossary.

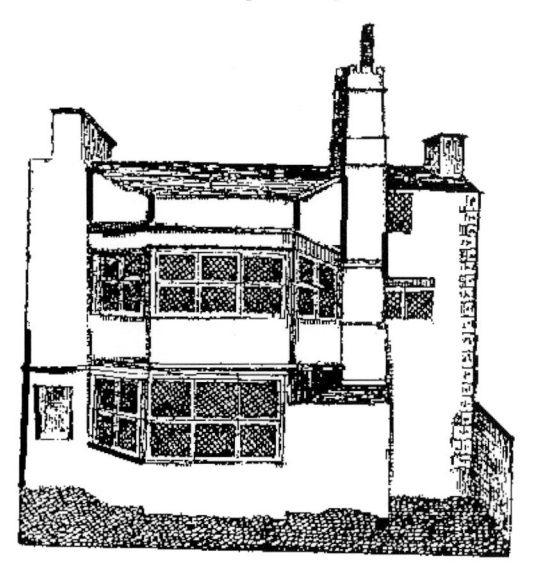

Foolow   Haddon

<u>Halls with Large Bay Windows and Small Panes</u>

Figure 13	Water and Wind Mills

Inputs for Processing	
Imported	Peak Area
Cotton	Animal: Bones, Fleeces, Hides Mineral: "Marble", Metal ore Vegetable: Barley, Flax, Oats, Trees, Wheat

```
              R Etherow  o  Langendale
Not                      o  Fletchers  Pa       R Holme-
Peak          R Kinder   o  Rowarth    Co       o  Holme  Wo
Park                     o  Phoside    Wo
                                                       R Rivelin
                              Wind                     o  Low Bradfield  Ce
                         o  Mill Hill
         R Goyt.        .o  Windmill                        R Derwent
      o  Lamb Hole  Ca, Li                             o  Bamford        Co
      o  Goytsclough  Pt        R Noe                  o  Greens House   Pa
      o  Errwood      Ce    o  Edale    LT             o  Strefield      Bo
      o  Goyt         Pt    *  Hope     Ce             o  Bradwell       Co
   ←R Dean  o Ginclough Si   o  Brough   Co            o  Hathersage     Wi
                                                       o  Lead           Ce
      R Bradford →       R Lathkill →    R Wye         o  Highlow        Ce
      o  Alport  Ga     o  Eagle Tor  o  Cresssbrook Pe Co   o  Padley   Ce
                       .o  Saw   Ti   o  Flewitts  Ce  o  Eyam       Co Si
                                     .o  Litton   Co   o  Hodgkinsons   Ce
                                     .o  Lumford  Co   o  Marles        Ce
                                     .o  Peak Forest Ce o  Edensor      Ce
                                     .*  Ashford  Ce M o  Ivonbrook     Ce
                                     .o  Sheldon  Bo Ti o  Grangemill   Ce
                                     .o  Tideswell Co Ve o  Ible        Ce
   ←R Dane  o Folly  Pa               *  Victoria  Ce
            o Gradbach  Li, Si, Ti         R Manifold          R Dove
                                       o  Longnor   Ti    o  Glutton Bridge  Ce
                  R Hamps →            o  Ludburn   Ce    o  Greenlowfield   Ore
                  o  Onecote  Ce       o  Brund     Ce    o  Hartington      Ce
      R Churnet   o  Ford     Ce       o  West Side Ce    o  Lode            Ce
     .o  Upper Hulme  Li                o  Wetton    Ce   o  Milldale        Ce
      o  Dains        Li                                  o  Thorpe          Ce
                                       *  Tissington
```

Bo Bone **Ca** Candlewick **Ce** Cereals **Co** Cotton **Li** Linen **Ga** Galena **LT** Lace Thread **M** Marble
Pa Paper **Pt** Paint **Pe** Peppermint **Si** Silk **Ti** Timber **Ve** Velvet **Wi** Wire **Wo** Wool
* In Domesday Book   River names cover main stream and tributaries.

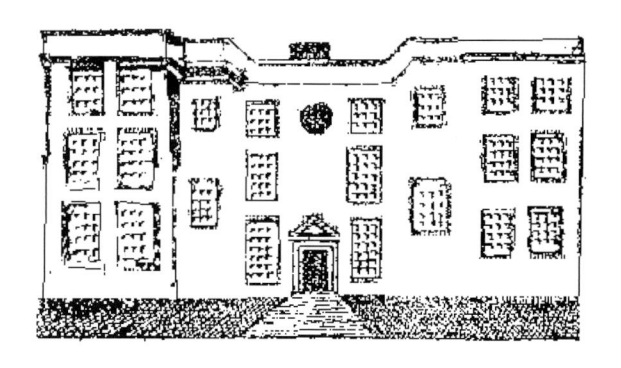

Wheston

Hassop

Holme

Three Storey Halls with Parapets and Curved Wall Openings

```
                    Figure 14                                              Railways.

            MANCHESTER ←            → SHEFFIELD  →   LINCOLN
                         Crowden   Woodhead  Dunford Bridge
                              o_____o
                         CHINLEY
                              Edale  Bamford    Grindleford
            WHALLEY           o-----o------o--------o-----o----------
            BRIDGE                      Hope   Hathersage
                                                     FLUOSPAR
                                                     # Eyam Edge
                         ↑                           # Waterfall
                      HIGH
                      PEAK    Lime    BUXTON
                              Works      o Hurdlow              o Millers
                                         o Parsley Hay o          Dale
                         ----------#-----                       o Monsal
                                         o Hartington             Dale
                      MANIFOLD                                  o Thornbridge
                       o  Hulme End                 Friden        Hall
                       o  Ecton                     o Gotham    o Hassop
                       o  Swainsley                 o Minnin-
                       o  Wetton Mill                 glow      o Bakewell
                       o  Thor's Cave                           o Rowsley
                       o  Beeston Tor
                       o  Sparrowlee                             DERBY
                                       ASHBOURNE   CROMFORD    LONDON

            Key:  o passenger station.   Passenger and Freight Lines = 6;   # Mineral Lines
```

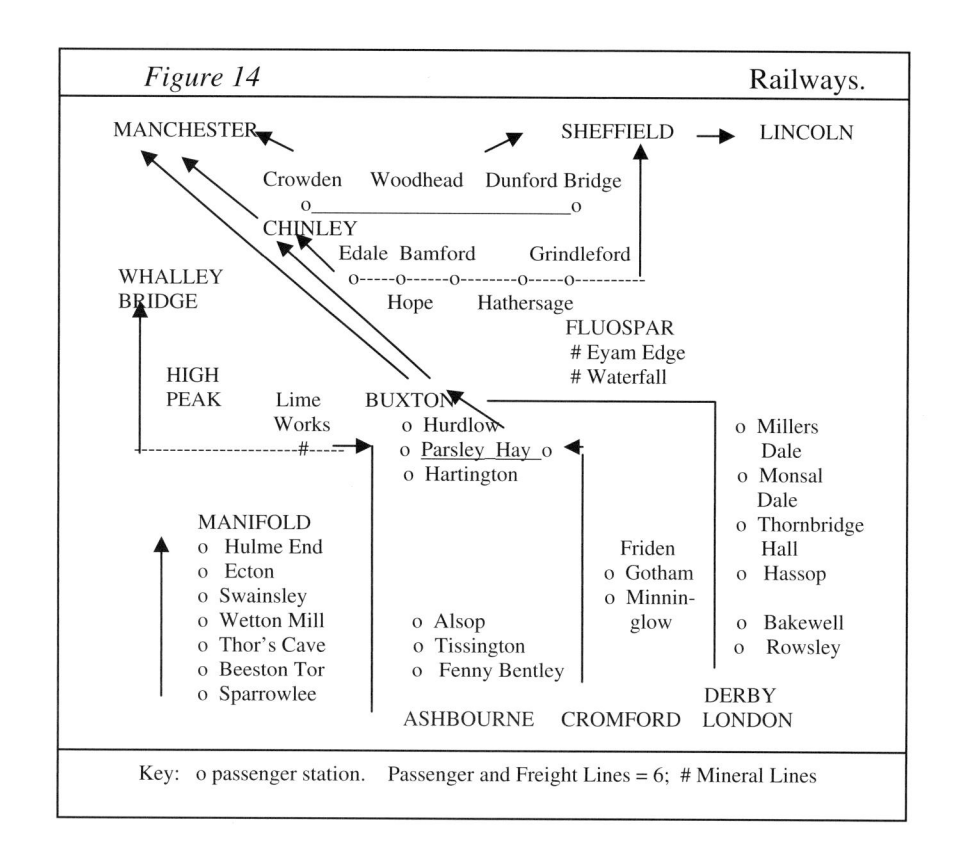

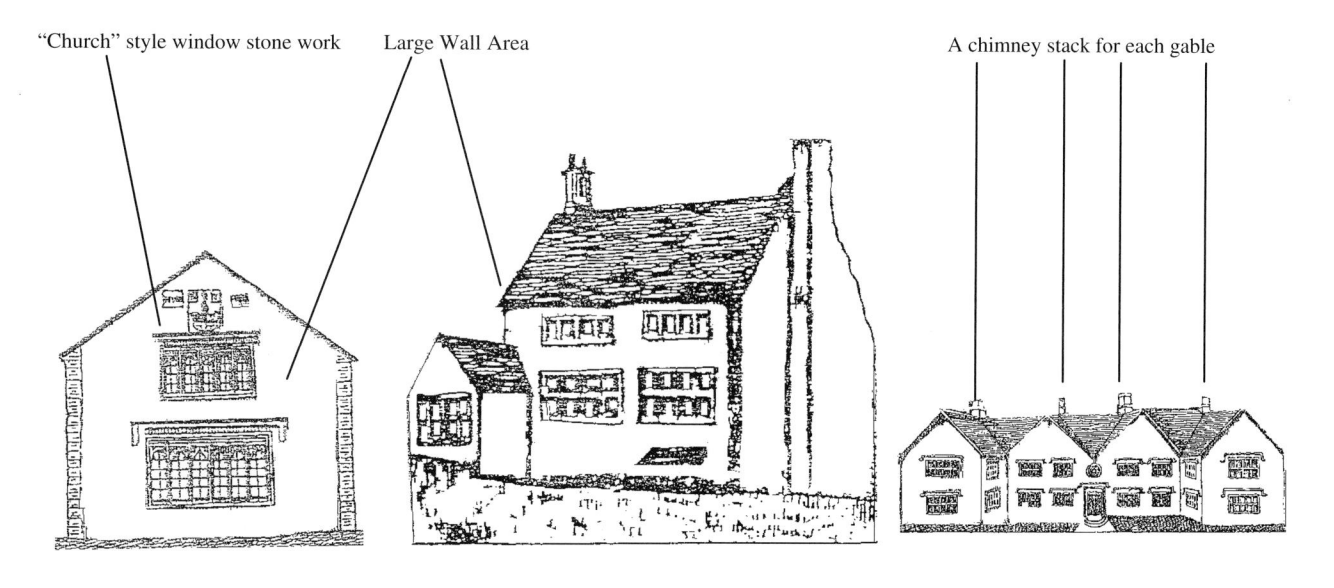

"Church" style window stone work | Large Wall Area   A chimney stack for each gable

Hazlebadge. Part of Dorothy   Beeley. Bought by the Duke of Devonshire 1747   Ford. Home of Colonel Bagshawe
Vernons' dowry when she married   who served Robert Clive in India.
John Manners in 1565

Two Storey Halls

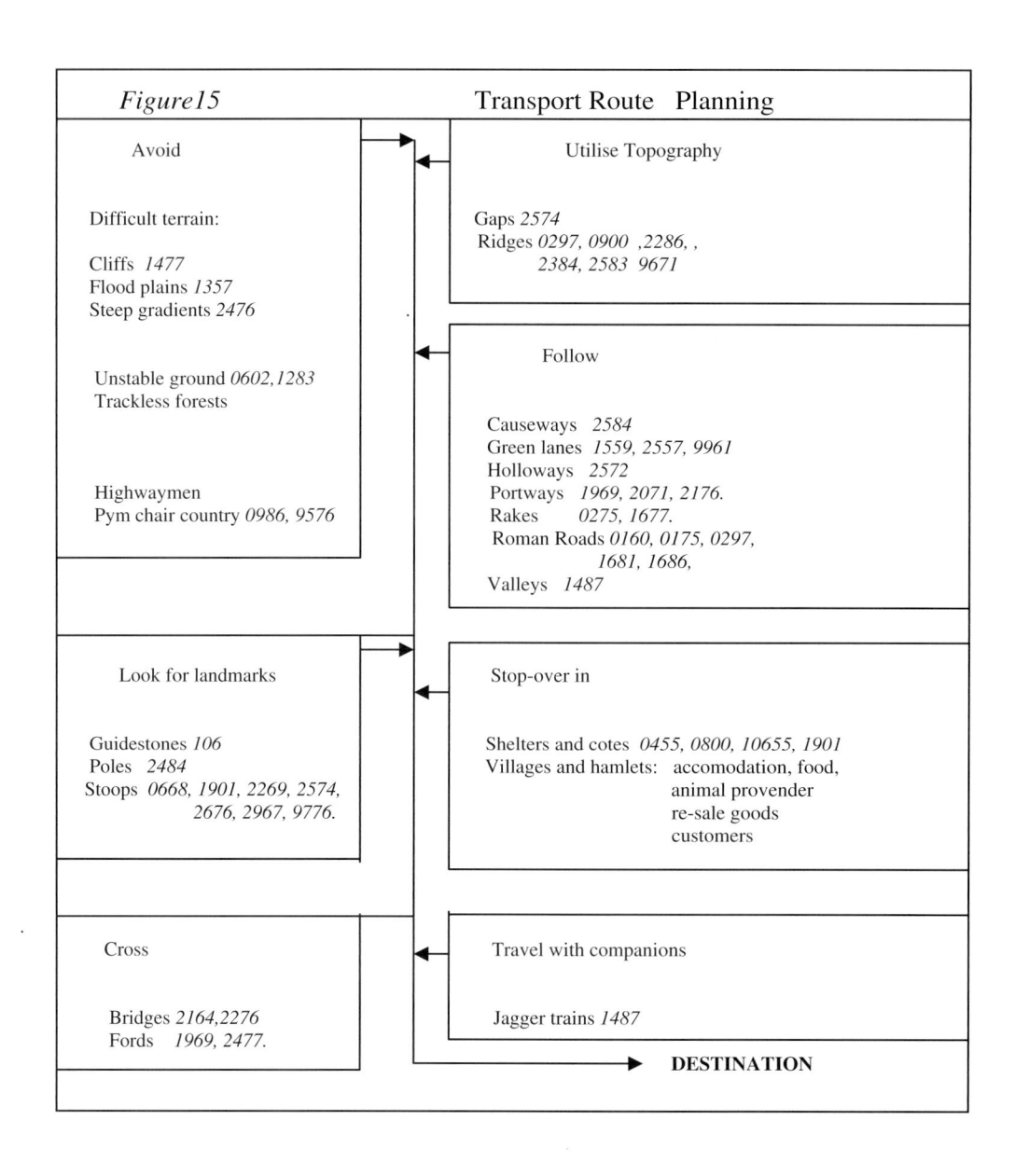

Figure 15	Transport Route Planning
Avoid Difficult terrain: Cliffs *1477* Flood plains *1357* Steep gradients *2476* Unstable ground *0602, 1283* Trackless forests Highwaymen Pym chair country *0986, 9576*	**Utilise Topography** Gaps *2574* Ridges *0297, 0900, 2286,,* *2384, 2583 9671*
	Follow Causeways *2584* Green lanes *1559, 2557, 9961* Holloways *2572* Portways *1969, 2071, 2176.* Rakes *0275, 1677.* Roman Roads *0160, 0175, 0297,* *1681, 1686,* Valleys *1487*

Look for landmarks
 	
Guidestones *106*
Poles *2484*
Stoops *0668, 1901, 2269, 2574,*
    2676, 2967, 9776.
	Stop-over in
	
	Shelters and cotes *0455, 0800, 10655, 1901*
	Villages and hamlets: accomodation, food,
	                animal provender
	                re-sale goods
	                customers

Cross Bridges *2164, 2276* Fords *1969, 2477.*	**Travel with companions** Jagger trains *1487* → **DESTINATION**

84

Little Longstone. Thomas Longsdon led Parliamentary troops near Sheffield 1658

Oriel window

Snitterton. John Dakyn, who called Robert FitzHerbert his brother, moved here when he married Dorothy Needham.

Foolow. People prayed and plotted behind the upper oriel window

Manor Houses

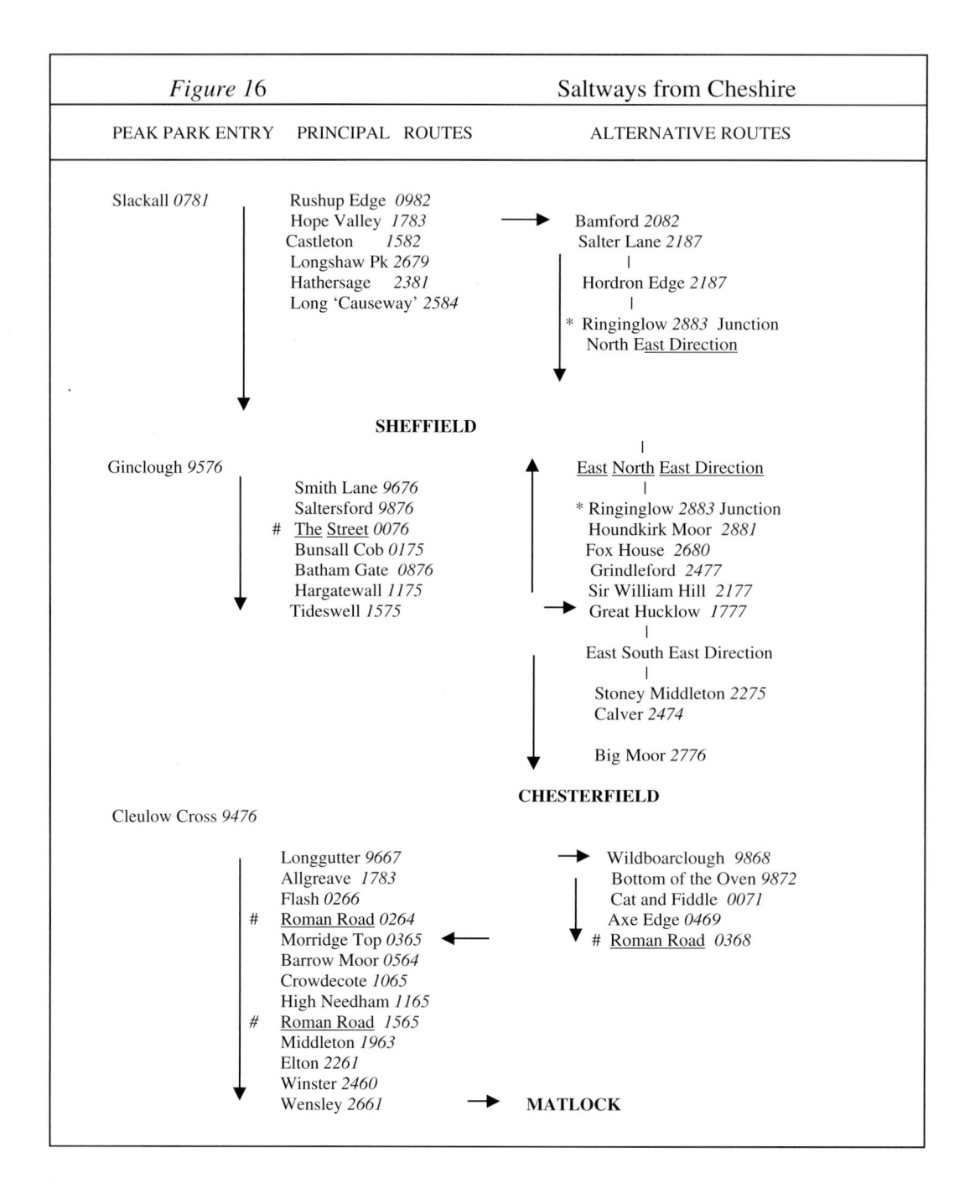

Figure 16		Saltways from Cheshire
PEAK PARK ENTRY	PRINCIPAL ROUTES	ALTERNATIVE ROUTES

Slackall *0781*

    ↓

              Rushup Edge *0982*
              Hope Valley *1783*   →   Bamford *2082*
              Castleton   *1582*   Salter Lane *2187*
              Longshaw Pk *2679* |
              Hathersage   *2381*   Hordron Edge *2187*
              Long 'Causeway' *2584* |
                                             * Ringinglow *2883* Junction
                                          North <u>E</u>ast <u>Direction</u>
                                          ↓

                              SHEFFIELD
                                                  |

Ginclough *9576*   ↑   <u>East</u> <u>North</u> <u>East</u> <u>Direction</u>

    ↓   Smith Lane *9676* |
              Saltersford *9876*   * Ringinglow *2883* Junction
       # <u>The</u> <u>Street</u> *0076*   Houndkirk Moor *2881*
              Bunsall Cob *0175*   Fox House *2680*
              Batham Gate *0876*   Grindleford *2477*
              Hargatewall *1175*   Sir William Hill *2177*
              Tideswell *1575*   → Great Hucklow *1777*
                                          |
                                East South East Direction
                                        |
                                Stoney Middleton *2275*
                                Calver *2474*
                         ↓
                                Big Moor *2776*

                           CHESTERFIELD

Cleulow Cross *9476*

            Longgutter *9667*   → Wildboarclough *9868*
            Allgreave *1783*   Bottom of the Oven *9872*
            Flash *0266*   Cat and Fiddle *0071*
    #   <u>Roman Road</u> *0264*   Axe Edge *0469*
            Morridge Top *0365* ←   # <u>Roman Road</u> *0368*
            Barrow Moor *0564*
            Crowdecote *1065*
            High Needham *1165*
    #   <u>Roman Road</u> *1565*
            Middleton *1963*
            Elton *2261*
            Winster *2460*
  ↓   Wensley *2661*   → **MATLOCK**

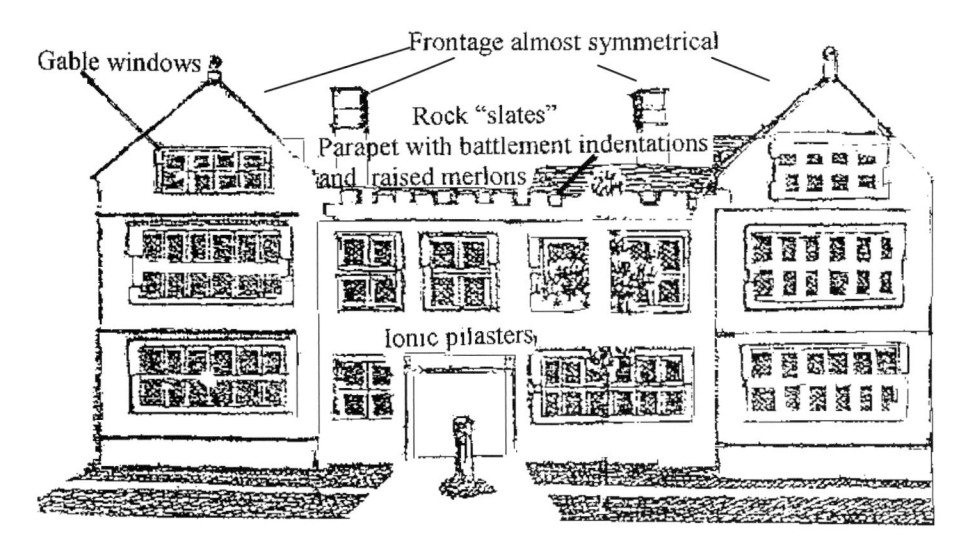

Snitterton

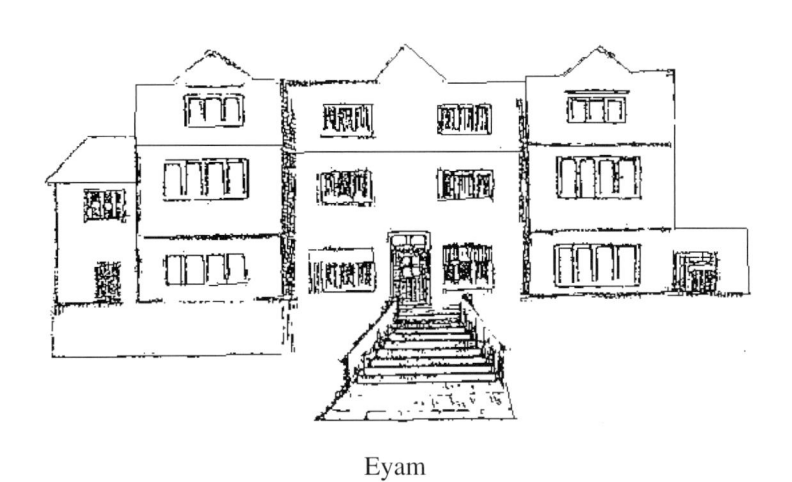

- Gable windows
- Frontage almost symmetrical
- Rock "slates"
- Parapet with battlement indentations and raised merlons
- Ionic pilasters

Eyam

Imposing Frontage Halls

Figure 17					Live Cattle Supply Chain
PRIMARY INPUTS →	ANIMALS	ANCILLARY + INPUTS →	PRIMARY OUTPUTS	PROCESSES →	END PRODUCTS
Grazing: 1	Bulls: 5 Calves : 6	Wooden pails: 10 Rennet: 6	Milk: 13	Breeding Curdling	Offspring Cheese: 16
	Cows: 7	Transport: 12 Salt: 13			Milk: 14
Fodder : 2 Ash		Butterwort 11	Milk: 14	Churning Wrapping	Butter: 17 "
Bracken Broom	Oxen: 8				Whey 18 Traction
Grass Gorse Hay	Steers 9				
Holly			Dung : 15		Fuel : 15 Manure : 15
Equipment : 3 Buildings: 4					

Cross references   See the Glossary for the meanings of *italicised* words below.

PRIMARY INPUTS

1. Grazing River valleys, Broad Meadow x2, Broadham, Willow *Bower, Ham, Gait, Haye, Raike, Sole*
2. Fodder Ashop, Monyash, Whin, Little Hayfield, Parsley Hay, Hollin Knowl, *Bose, Carf, Daymath, Elm, Hobble, Johnson, Quill, Tallet,*
3. Equipment *Choking Rope, Hack, Hazel*
4. Buildings *Booth, Elm, Helm, Helmesely, Pinfold*

ANIMALS

5. Bulls: Bull Clough x2
6. Calves Calton x 3, Calf Close, Great Hucklow, Calver, Malcoff *Bud* Rennett from the stomachs of calves
7. Cows: Cow Close, Offerton, Cow Low
8. Oxen: Ox Low x 2, Ox Stone
9. Steers: Steer Croft Monyash

ANCILLARY INPUTS

10. Wooden pails – *Ash, Bowk, Hazel*
11. Butterwort leaves *pinguicula vulgaris*
12. Transport *Jag, Kick, Packhorse, Pannier, Plowbote, Portway, Railways, Rathes, Rolley, Turnpike, Wain*
13. Saltways

PRIMARY OUTPUTS, ASSOCIATED PLACES and WORDS

14. Milking Close, Abney, Milking Hillock Castleton, Milking Place, Hathersage, Vaccary, *Brig, Groop, Stripping*
15. Dung Mixon, Dunge Clough, *Casson, Mardo, Shool, Sock.*

END PRODUCTS

16. Cheese: Hartington, Parwich
17. Butter: Butterton
18. Whey.   Pig feed Longnor

Figure 18				Cattle Carcasses Supply Chain	
PRIMARY INPUTS	ANCILLARY INPUTS	EQUIPMENT	PROCESSES	PRIMARY OUTPUTS	END PRODUCTS
Bones Butchered remains	Fuel Alum - - - Barytes Walnut oil -	Cauldron - - - - - - -	Rendering - - - - - - - -	Tallow - Hardened tallow Fatty oil - - - - - - -	Combs Candles + flax wick Lamps -Soap
Flesh		Knives, saws	Butchery	Cuts of beef and veal [14th] Rennet – calves 1.	Fresh meat Cheese
Hides	Salt - - - - Fuel *Fig 22* Bark Birch Oak Willow Alum Barytes	- - - - - - - Oven Vats	Preserving Cooking Tanning	Leather	Preserved meat Clothing Footwear Harness Buckets Bags
Horns		Tools	Cutting		Headwear

Cross references: Manufacturing and Processing Animal Inputs   Figure 9
             Heat *Figure 22*
             Glossary: Alum, Barytes, Saltways, Trees – birch, oak, walnut

Notes   Flesh : Rennet from the stomach of a calf for cheese making
                 Salt for preserving meat. *Figure 15*

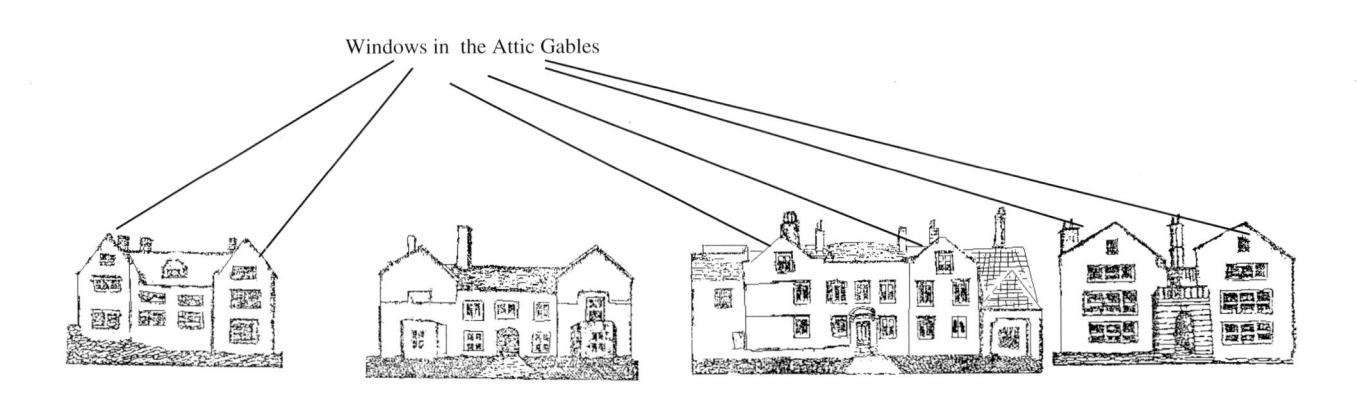

Windows in the Attic Gables

Offerton   Stoney Middleton   Wormhill   Fynney Cottage

Halls with Symmetrical Gable-ended Side Bays

Sough Mine Drainage

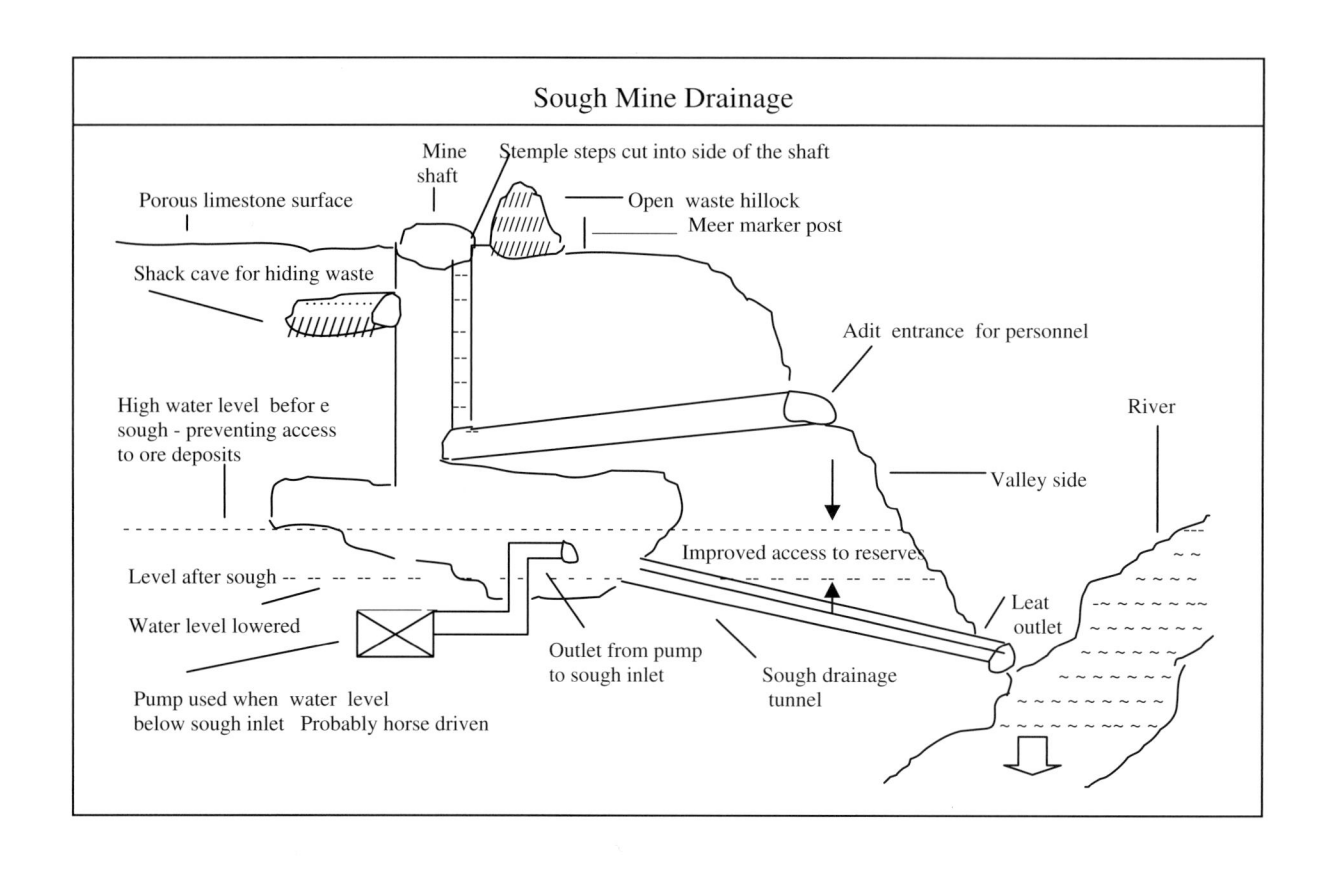

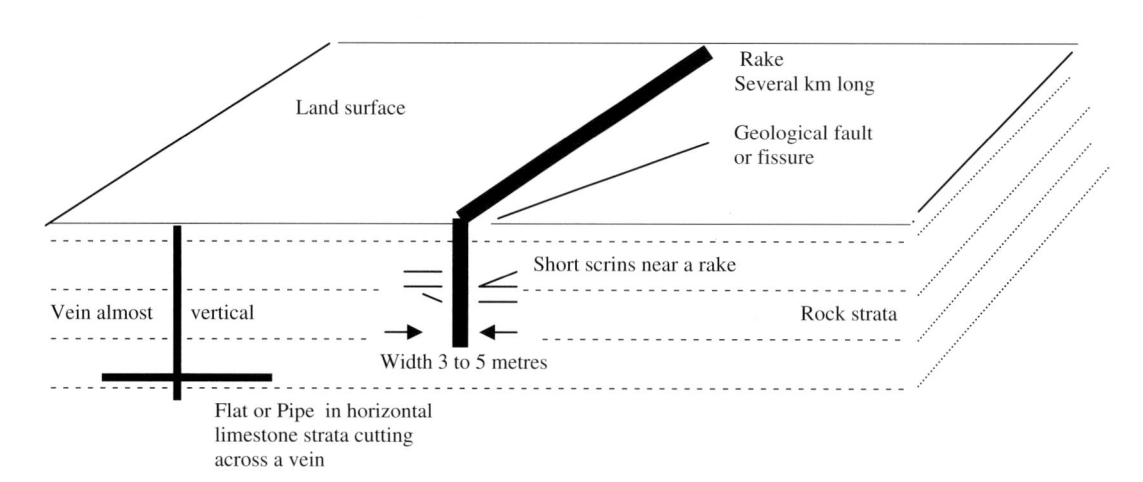

Ore Deposit Formations

Eating: A Microcosm of Past Local Products

Source	Crops	Food & Drink
Field	Barley	Beer
	Oats	Oat cake, porridge
	Peas, beans, potatoes	

	Livestock	Food & Drink	Raw material By products
Forest	Deer	Venison	
	Pheasant		Bones
	Pigs	Pork	
Meadow	Cattle	Beef	&
		Milk	
Moor	Grouse		
Pasture	Goats		Hides
	Sheep	Mutton	

	Raw materials	Intermediate product	End product or process
Field	Flax	Fibres	Floor mats
			Candle Wicks
Forest	Wood		Table
	Logs	Fuel	Cooking
Meadow	Bone	Cutlery handles	Knives
		Fertiliser	Recycled
	Hides	Leather	Cups
			Diners'
			Clothing
			Footwear
	Hooves	Glue	Furniture
	Milk	Whey	Butter, cheese
Pasture	Fleece	Wool	Diners'
			Clothing
			Hosiery
Mine	Copper		Cauldron
			Cup
	Copper + Lead	Pewter	Tankard
Quarry	Clay		Cup
			Plate
			'Porringer'
		Bricks	Oven
	Millstone grit		Fireplace

Stone fireplace

Copper Cauldron

Log fire in Stone Fireplace

Wooden table

Cups

Leather   Bronze

Earthen ware

Pewter tankard

Wooden plate

Bone handled knife

Oat cake

Cheese

Meat

Figure 19a   Military   History   Web

```
Recruitment           ┌── Copper cladding for wooden ships' keels
    │          ┌─Sea ─┼── Ratings
    │          │      └── Officers ──────────────┐
┌─Personnel ───┤      ┌── Crashes ───────────────┤
│   │          ├─Air ─┼── Aerodrome rocks        │
│   │          │      └── Weapon development   Memorials
│ Compassion   │      ┌── Fortifications and Decoy │
│   │          └─Land ├── Lead bullets ┌─ Britain ─┤
│ Desertion           └── Battles* ────┼─ Europe ──┤
│                                      └─ Peak ────┤
│              Civilians ──────────────────────────┘
└─ Prisoners of War
```

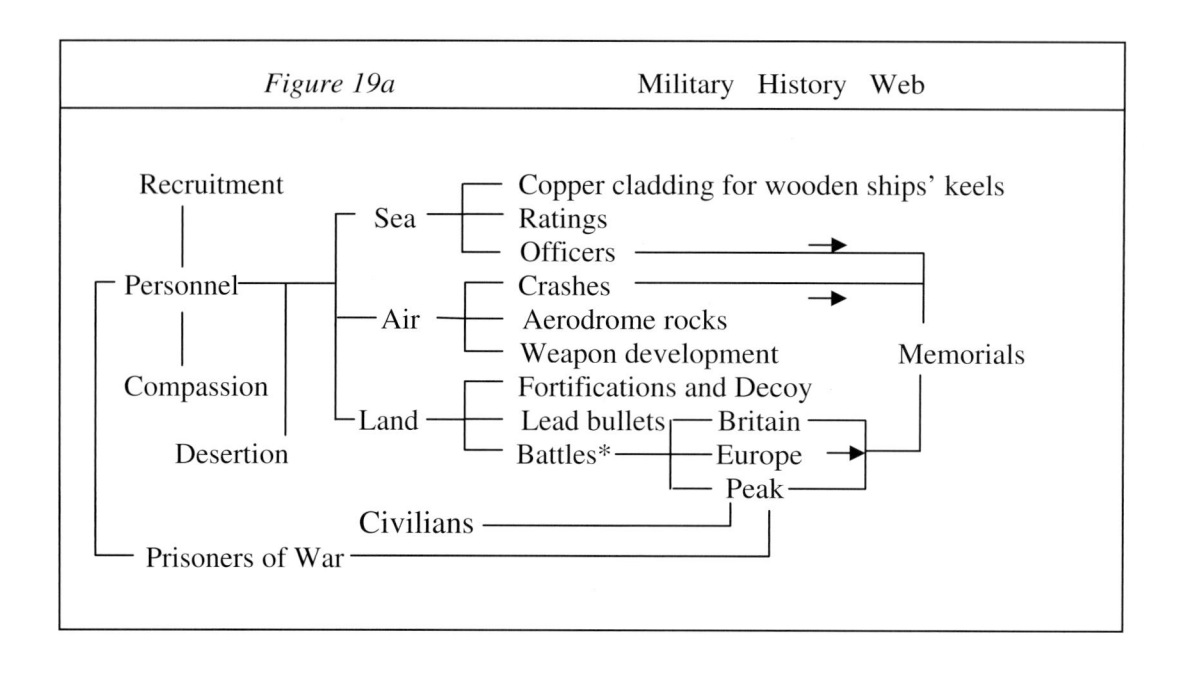

Figure 19b   Battles

Dark Ages	Danish Invaders	Norman Invaders	Anglo Scottish	Baronial War	100 Years War	Wars of the Roses	Civil War	Napoleonic Wars
Win Hill	Bakewell 924	Hastings 1066	Standard 1138	Chesterfield 1265 Evesham 1265	Crecy 1346 Poitiers 1356 Agincourt 1415 Patay 1429	Shrewsbury 1403 Stoke 1487	Hartington 1643 Newark 1643 Nantwich 1644	Albuera 1811

WARS and BATTLES

Aerodromes: 'Limestone' for aircraft runways. Heathcote *1460*.

Aircraft crashes: Dark Peak 'Memorials'.

Battles: ***Agincourt*** *50°26'N 2°6'E*. Artois, France *Sir Thomas Beresford* of Fenny Bentley *1750*, *Sir Thomas Danvers* of Lyme *9682*, the *Jodrell* family of Taxal *0079*, *Robert Eyre*, *Roger Padley* and *Sir Ralph Shirley*, *Cockaynes, Curzon, FitzHerbert, Strelley* horsemen were involved in the battle [1415]. English longbowmen, led by *Henry V* [1413-22], defeated vastly superior numbers of French soldiers. ***Albuera*** *38°41'N 6°47'W*. Spain [1811] Peninsular War against *Napoleon. Marshal Beresford;* ***Bakewell*** *2168* [924] against Danish invaders. ***Blore Heath*** *8445* [23/09/1459] *Downes* and *Legh* families on the losing Lancastrian side. ***Bosworth*** *6484* [1485] *John Cheney*. ***Chesterfield*** *3871* [1265] *Ferrars*. ***Crecy en Pontieu*** *50°15'N 1°51'E*. *Sir Thomas Shirley, Sir Thomas Danvers* of Lyme Hall *9682* and probably *Robert Lord Holand* involved in the battle [1346]. The first decisive battle of the Hundred Years' War in which the English, led by The Black Prince [1330-76], defeated the French. ***Evesham*** *0344* [1265] *Ralph Basset*. ***Hartington*** *1360* [1643]. ***Hastings*** *8009* [1066] *Godfrey Foljambe*. ***Losehill*** *1585* ['Dark Ages']. ***Nantwich*** [1644] *6552* Royalist *General Mon(c)k's* Road *0291*. ***Neuvilly*** *40°10'N 5°04'E*. [1918] *Joseph Pickford*. ***Newark*** [1643] *7953, Thomas Eyre*. ***Patay*** *48°15'N 1°20'E*. [1429] *Sir John Talbot* defeated by *Joan of Arc*. ***Poitiers*** *46°35'N 0°16'E* [1356] *Sir Thomas Shirley*. ***Shrewsbury*** *4912* [21/07/1403] *Henry IV* [1399-1413] was victorious and became the undisputed ruler after "Hotspur", *Henry Percy*, son of the powerful *Earl of Northumberland*, was killed together with many 'knights' and soldiers including *Edmund Cockayne* and *Sir Thomas Wendesley*. 'Rowland'. ***Standard*** (Northallerton *3793*) [1138] *Robert de Ferrars* helped *King Stephen* defeat *King David* of Scotland. ***Stoke*** *7549* [16/06/1487] *Sir Henry Vernon, Baron Shipbrook* [1445-1551] fought for *Henry VII* against the rebels in the last battle of the Wars of the Roses.

Bomb damage: Earl Sterndale Church *0967* destroyed by an incendiary bomb [World War II].

Bouncing bomb development: Ladybower reservoir *1886* [1943]. *Sir Barnes Wallis*.

Civil War: [1642-49] *John Bradshawe*, regicide. Broomhead Hall *2496* badly damaged by Parliamentary soldiers during 42 day seige [1642]. *Christopher Fulwood*, Cavalier, executed [1643]. *Rowland Eyre*, Cavalier. 'Tissington Hall' *1752*.

Compassion payments by Youlgreave *2064* constable. [1736] disabled soldier; [1745] sick soldier and his wife from Carlisle; [1745] former prisoners captured by the Turks; [1746] soldier and his wife whose son was ill.

Decoy: Emlin Ridge *2393* mock village failed to mislead German bombers on the way to Sheffield [1940].

Deserters: Youlgreave *2064* constable. [1710] search for soldiers. [1729] apprehension and detention.

Earthworks: Bar Dyke *2494* – length 411 metres (450 yards), rampart height above the ditch 3 metres (10 feet) above the surrounding ground 2 metres (6 feet) Grey Ditch *1781*, Tissington *1752*, Torside Castle *0796*. Unnamed *0699, 0810, 1261, 2268, 2396, 9772*. Castle Hill *2268, 2792*. 'Motte and baileys' *1163, 1261*, Bakewell built by *Edward the Elder* [924] *2268, 2692* – motte height 18 metres (60 feet), bailey area 0.3 hectare (0.75 acres).

Enclosed camps: Castle Ring *2262*, Camp Green (British or Danish) *2381*. Folly *1682*, Tideswell Moor *1479*, Tissington seigework *1752*.

Fortified manor houses: Brookfield *2382*, Haddon *2366*, Lyme Hall Cage [15th century] *9683*.

Forts, castles and houses: OE: *burg* and ON: *wark* = a fort Ald*wark* *2357*, Bakewell *2168*, Ball Cross *2269*, Bradfield *2792*,Brough *1882*, Burrs Mount *1778*, Burbage (Dialect: stream adjacent to a fortification ie Carlwark) *2782*, Burton *2067*, Carl*wark* *2681*, Conkes*bury* *2065*, Dids*bury* *0498*, Dinas 'Stitch' 'Tor' *1190*, Earl Sterndale (Saxon) *0967*, Fin Cop *1771*, Haddon *2366*, High Knot*bury* *0168*, Mam Tor *1283*, Peak/Peveril *1583*, Middleton *1863*, Pils*bury* *1163*, Ringham Low *1666*, Throwley Hall 'Pele' *1152* Tissington house demolished [1460] *1752*, Torside *0796*, Unnamed *0578, 2581*. Brad*bury*. Dialect: *whittle* = lower level fort (possibly below) Pilsbury Whittle *1064*.

Gunpowder manufacture: Fernilee [1909-20] *0178*.

Invasion fear: [1793-1815] Hollins Hill *0667*.

Lancastrians and Yorkists: *Cheney, FitzAlan-Howard, Plumpton.*

Map making: Soldiers' Lump on Black Hill *1704* Royal Engineers triangulation point.

Memorials: 'Battle Stone' *1250; William Billings* Longnor Church *0864* Gibraltar [1704] *36°10'N 5°22'W*, Ramillies [1706] *50°39'N 4°54'E,* Jacobite Rebellions [1715], [1745]; *Colonel Brockenhurst* of Swythamley Hall *9764* killed in Burma [1942] Hanging Stone plaque *9765;* Nelson [1758-1805] *2772* Battle of Trafalgar [21/10/1805] *36°10'N 6°05'W; Duke of Wellington* [1769-1852] *2676* Battle of Waterloo [18/06/1815] *50°42'N 4°23'E,* organised by *Dr E M Wrench* and erected by *John Brightman,* both from Baslow; Reform Stone *2080,* Grindon *0854* Eight RAF personnel who crashed in [1947] blizzard. Wildeboarclough *9868,* High Wheeldon *1066* Staffordshire and Derbyshire men killed in World War II, Middleton *1963* plaque for bomber crash at Smerrill *1862*.

Military policing by the Youlgreave *2064* constable. Searches. [1710] for soldiers; [1756] alehouses for sailors. 'Desertion'.

Pensions: for wounded soldiers. Youlgreave *2064* [1614] Church wardens, [1736] Constable.

Prisoners of War: French from Napoleonic Wars in Bakewell [1793-1815] *2168*. Italians in Dove Dale World War II [1939-45] landscaping *1452*.

Rebellion: Baslow *2572,* Castleton *1583,* Eyam *2176* and Longstone *1871* miners against the Supplementary Militia Act [1796]. Rebellion Knoll *1880*.

Recruiting: by the Youlgreave constable. [1706] warrant, [1772] down payment for militia recruits. Press gang [1744] soldiers, [1759] seafarers.

Target practice: Burbage Rocks *2682* for the RAF [World War II].

Fighting Men with their Arms and Armour

Peak Men in Conflicts

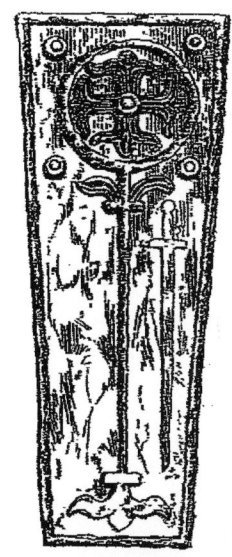

Not to scale

Map locations: Standard Northallerton, Losehill, Bosworth, Chesterfield, Newark, Shrewsbury, Stoke, Bakewell, Nantwich, Blore Heath, Evesham, Hastings

Chelmorton Stone Sepulchral Slabs

Four corners of the earth = a traveller with Jerusalem at the centre

Decorated crosses with vertical fluting

Knight's sword

Identification of deceased by carved symbols

The carpenter marks an outline with a compass
Isaiah 44 verse 13

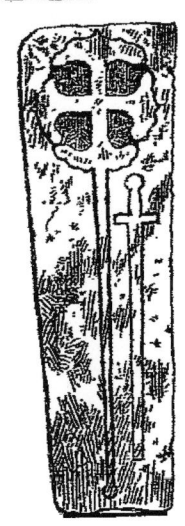

Deceased Person's Identity Indicators:
Encircled cross = a knight templar
Sword = a knight

THE NATURAL WORLD

Figure 20 — The Natural World Web

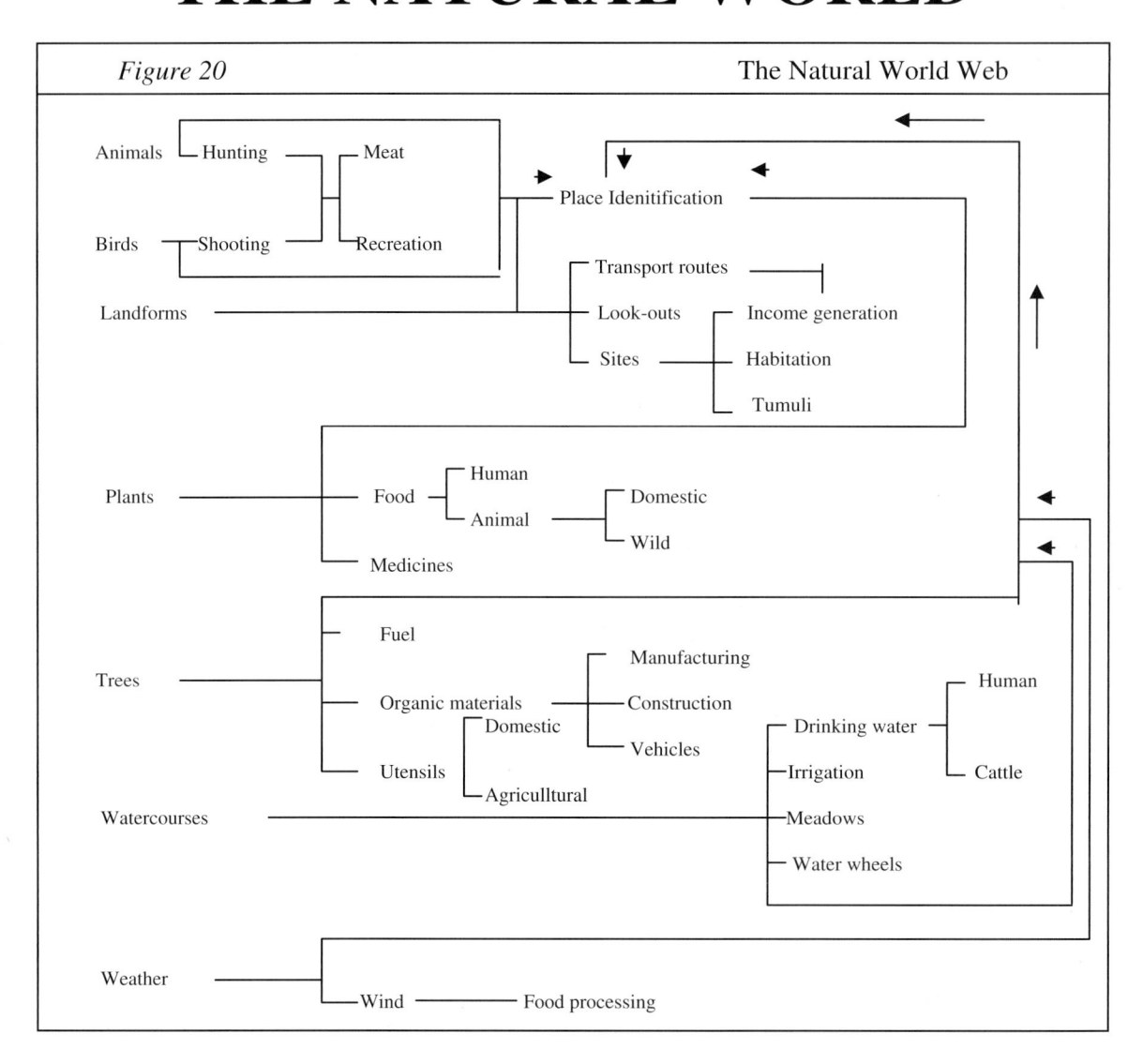

[Diagram: The Natural World Web showing hierarchical relationships:
- Animals → Hunting → Meat; Birds → Shooting → Recreation
- Landforms → Place Identification, Transport routes, Look-outs, Sites → Income generation, Habitation, Tumuli
- Plants → Food (Human/Animal → Domestic/Wild), Medicines
- Trees → Fuel, Organic materials → Manufacturing, Construction, Vehicles; Utensils → Domestic, Agricultural
- Watercourses → Drinking water (Human/Cattle), Irrigation, Meadows, Water wheels
- Weather → Wind → Food processing]

Bird population and dialect words: *Bob* = **Robin** *erithacus rubecula*. *Brand-tail* = **Redstart** *phoenicurus phoenicurus*. *Bush oven* = **Long tailed tit** *aegithalos caudatus*. *Butter-hump* = **Bittern** *botaurus stellaris*. *Char-bob* and *spink* = **Chaffinch** *fringilla coelebs*. *Chepster* = **Starling** *sturnus vulgaris*. *Churn owl* = **Nightjar** *caprimulgua europaeus*. *Culver* = **Dove** *columba oenas* or **woodpigeon** *columba palumbus*. *Happinch* = **Lapwing** *vanellus vanellus*. *Hud lark* = **Skylark** with a hood [crest] *alauda arvensis*. *Jenty* = **Wren** *troglodytes troglodytes*. *Neezen* = **Bird nesting**. *Philip* = **Sparrow** *passer domesticus*. *Pianet* = **Magpie** *pica pica*. *Proud tailor* = **Goldfinch** *carduelis carduelis*. *Throstle* = **Song thrush** *turdus philomelos*. *Yoldring* = **Yellow hammer** *emberiza citrinella*. See Birds and Place Names for additional members of the bird population.

Birds and place names: **Blackbird** *turdus merula* OE: *osle* Ouzelden *1590*. **Chaffinch** *fringilla coelebs* Spink *1261*. **Corncrake** *crex crex* ON: *kraka* Crake Low *1753*. **Crane** *grus grus* Conkesbury *2065*. **Crow** probably *corvus corone* Hill *0078*, Crowden *0799*. **Cuckoo** *cuculus canorus* Butts, Offerton *2181*, Stones *9971*, **Dove** *columba oenas 1451*. [sparrow] **Hawk** probably *accipiter nisus* Hawk's Nest *0167*, Hawkslee *9365*. **Heron** *ardea cineria* Dialect: *yarn* = heron Yarnshaw Brook *9870*. **Jackdaw/carder** *corvus monedula* Carder Low *1362*. **Lapwing/peewit** *vanellus vanellus* Field, Pott Shrigley *9479*, Pewit Hall *0453*. **Magpie** Mine *pica pica 1768* **Pheasant** *phasianus colchicus* 'Clough' *9962*, NB River Phasis (modern Rioni) in Colchis region *42°08'N 41°39'E*. **Raven** *corvus corax* 'Clough' *1294*, Cronkston (croaking of raven) Low *1166*, Ravensdale *1773*, Raven's Tor *0971*. **Robin** *erithacus rubecula* 'Clough' *0067*, Robin Croft, Derwent *2383*, **Shrike** *lanius collurio* Pott Shrigley *9479*, Pye 'Clough' *0464*. **Sparrow** probably *passer domesticus* Sparrowlee *0951*, Sparrowpit *0980*. **Swallow** *hirundo rustica* 'Dale'

96

9366. ***Water wagtail*** *motacilla lugubris* Ladywash *2277,* **Woodcock** *scolopax rustica* OE: cocc sccyte – land on which *woodcock* dart Farm *0594,* Cockshut Meadow, Pott Shrigley *9479.*

Caves and caverns: 'Blue John' *1383,* 'Elder Bush' *0995,* Hermit's *2262,* Peak *1482,* Reynards *1452,* Robin Hood *2483,* Speedwell *1382,* Thor's *0954,* Treak *1382.* Unnamed *0457, 0767, 0955, 0956, 0966, 0971, 1055, 1358, 1453, 1456, 1457, 1680, 1765, 1865, 1965.*

Colours: Brown 'Knoll' *0885,* Golden 'Clough' *1287,* Rud Hill *2784.*

Environment influencing personal names: *Agard, Ashton, Bache, Bagshawe, Barlow, Beresford, Birch, Blackwall, Bourne, Bowden, Bradbury, Bradshaw, Brampton, Brereton, Clifford, Denman, Eyre, Ferne, Ford, Fulwood, Greaves, Grimshawe, Hamilton, Hatfield, Holland, Hope, Howe, Hurlock, Kniveton, Litton, Longsdon, Middleton, Needham, Oldfield, Pickford, Pole, Rossington, Rowe, Sheldon, Shirley, Shore, Slack, Slingsby, Stanley, Stratford, Swynbourne, Thornhill, Upton.*

Fauna: *Adder* vipera berus Adders Green *0265.* **Badger** *meles meles,* Bagshaw *2168, Brittlebank.* **Bear** *ursidaea* Beresford *1259, Beresford.* **Beaver** *castor fiber* Bradwell (hats) *1781.* **Bees**: *apoidea* Bee Low *1964,* Bee Croft, Curbar *2574* OE: *hunig* = honey, Honey Spots, Hope *1783,* Dialect: *colt* = swarm of bees. **Boar** *sus scrofa* Boars Grove *0462.* **Cat** wild *felis sylvestris* Cat Clough *1101.* **Deer/hart/roe** *cervidae* Deer Hill *0710,* Deer Knowl *0998,* Harthill *0189, 2262,* 'Harrop' *9578.* Hartington *1360,* Hartle *2764,* Rowland *2172, Ward.* **Elk** *alces alces* Elkstone *0559,* Elton *2260.* NB Elk may also be a personal as well as an animal name. **Fox** *vulpes* Fox Holes *3232.* **Frog** *rana temporaria* Froggatt (near River Derwent) *2476.* **Glutton**/wolverene *gulo gulo* Glutton 'Grange' *0867.* **Hare** *lepus europaeus* OE: *hara* possibly Hare Cops *1158,* Harewood Grange *3168,* Dialect: *mawkin,* 'smoot', Mawking, Macclesfield Forest *9671.* **Hedgehog.** *urchins mier* Urchin Hole, Great Hucklow *1777* **Ladybird/cow[lady]** *coccinella septem-punctata* Cow Low *1059,1 482.* **Midge** *chironomidae* Midgley *9766,* Midgleygate (NB River Dane) *9966.* **Mouse** *muridae* Musden *1250.* **Otter** *luttra luttra* Otterbrook *1285.* **Rabbit** *orytilagus cuniculus* ME: *rabet*: Conies Farm *1280,* Rabbit 'Warren' *2768,* Rabbit Bana, Wincle *9665,* 'puss nets' **Reptiles** Adders' Green *0270,* Snake *0790, 0892,* Wormhill *1274.* **Snails** *helicidae* OE: *snegl* Snailsden *1303.* **Toad** *bufo bufo* Toadepoole *2477.* **Trout** *salmo trutta* River Dane *1451.* **Weasel**/wizzel/wizzle/weezle *mustela* or *putorus nivalis.* Ouzelden *1590,* Wigt Wizzle *2595.* **Wild boar** *sus scrofa* Boars Grove *0462,* Wildboarclough *9868,* 'Clough' *0897.* **Wolf** *canis lupus* Wolfscote *1358.* [1286] wolves trapped in Peak Forest. Dialect 'oobit' = "woolly bear". **Tiger moth** larva. Rearmouse = hrenemus = **Bat.** Scopperil = **Squirrel** *sciurus vulgaris.* **Water rat/vole** *larvico,a terrestris* Bones found in a tumulus *1552, Weasel.*

Flora: *Aniseed* pimpinella anisum Aniseed, Little Longstone *1871* [16th century]. '**Beech**' *fagus sylvatica bitch*: Thursbitch *9975.* '**Birch**' *betula)* Birchfield *1784,* Birchhill Bank *2271,* Birchin *Hat* (Dialect = a cluster) *1491.* **Bluebell** *scilla nutans* Bluebell Close, Calver *2374.* **Briar**: *erica arborea* Brierlow *0869, Brereton.* **Broom** *cystis* and *sarothamnus bromede* Bramley *2473,*Brampton *2970,* Broomhead Hall *2496,* Broom Hill *9465,* Brund *1061, Brampton.* '**Buckthorn**' *rhamnus catharticus* Buckthorn Meadow, Ashford in the Water *1969* **Butterbur** *petasites vulgaris* Batterdock, Parwich *1854.* The leaves were used for wrapping butter **Butterwort** *pinguicula vulgaris* yellow colour Butterley Moss *0801.* **Clover** *trifolium claefre*: Clover Sitch, Hope 1783. **Cress** *rorippa nasturtium – aquaticum* or *nasturtium officinale* Cressbrook *1772,* **Daisy** *bellis perennis* Bank *2056,* **Dame's violet** *hesperis matronalis* Siney Sitch *1980.* **Dyer's greenweed** *genista tinctoria* Green Gutter Head *0065.* **Fern** *filicino phyta fearn* Farnsley *2075,* Fernilee *0178,* Fernyford *0661.* **Hard** *blechnaceae spicant* Harden *1404, 1698,* Hardron *1799,* **Garlic,wild/ramsons** *allium sibiricum* Ramsden *1105.* **Globe** *flowertrollinus europaeus* Goldsitch Moss *0064.* **Gold**/**ox eye daisy** *chrysanthemum lencathemum* Gold Sitch *0064.* **Gorse** *ulex europeaus gors*: Gorsey Nook *1077,* **Grass** 'Bent/hare's tail *agrostis canina* Fenny Bentley 1750, *Allen,* Blue Moor *sesteria albicans* Blue Hills *0162,* Button *avena elatior* Pearls *9866,* Cotton *eriophorum* white colour in summer Featherbead *0400, 0892, 1198, 1498, 1994,* White Brow *0588,*Lee *0981,* Mare *0797* Wagging [tall] Waggon Low *1164.* **Hawthorn** *crataegus oxyacantha cwic* OE: haguthorn and MHG: hagendorn. = a hedge + thorn Hawthorn 'Clough' 1200.Thornhill 1893. **Heather** *calluna vulgaris* Haddon *2366,* Heathy 'Roods' *0857.* **Rough horseweed** *equisetum hyemale* Horsehill Tor *0984,* Horseley Head *0609,* **Jacob's Ladder** *polemonium caeruleum 1865, 0886,* **Lichen** *mycophyocophyta* 'Stannerie(y) *0766.* **Lady's smock/cuckoo flower** *cardamine pratensis* Lady Booth brook *1386.* **Madwort** *aspergo procumens* Madwoman Stones *1388,* **Marjoram** *origanum vulgare* Organ Ground *1766,* **Mayweed** *tripleurospermum indorum* OE: maegtha Magdalen Springs *0807.* **Moss/mouse**

Mouse Low *0853*, sliding Sliddens *0603*. **Moneywort** *lysimachia nummularia* Money Stones *1561*. **Monkshood** *aconitum napellus* Monk's Dale *1374*. **Nettles** *urtica dioica netele* Nettly Knowe *1456*, Nettlebeds *9565*. **Parsley** *petroselinum sativum* Parsley Hay *1463*, **Peat** Black Chew *0502*, Hill *0704*, Moor *0691*, Moss *1098*, Tor *0600* Brown Knoll *0306, 0885*. **Plantain/lamber** *plantago major* Lamber Low *0850*, Osier Hipper *3068*. **Primrose** *primula vulgaris primerole*: Primrose, Foolow 1976, **Reeds** *phragmitis communis* Bunsal *0175*, Bunster *1451*. **Rose** *rosa canina* Dialect: 'Nips' = fruit of the wild rose, red colour Rose 'Clough' *1299*. **Rush** *juncaeae* OE: *risc*: Rix Acre, Foolow *1976*, Rushley *1251* Rushy Field, Edale *1285*. Used for floor coverings. **Sedge** *cyperaceae family* OE: *secg*: Sedgy Spring, Bakewell *2168* - used for thatch, **Sphagnum moss** *rubellum* green colour Green Clough *1592*, Hill *0604*. **Thistle Faw** thistle or teasel. *labrum veneris* Fawfield *0763*, woolow = thistledown Woolow *0972*. **Thorns** *crataegus oxyacantha* Bostern *1553*, Castern *1252*, Thornbridge *1971*, Thornhill *1983*, Thorny Lee *0378*, Winster *2460*, **Tormentil** *potentilla erecta* yellow flower. Golden Clough *1287*, Yellow Stacks *0695* **Walder** Weed found in cornfields, Waldershaigh *2696*. **Whitethorn/bullace** probably *prunus insititia* Whitethorn Clough 0391. 'Medicines'.

Forests and Woods: Bagshaw *2168*, Bose (Bushy) Low *1652*, Ferriser *9770*, Harrop Wood *9678*, Hope Dale *1783*, Longshaw *2679*, Macclesfield *9671*, Peak *1179*, Seal Clough OE: *scaga* = wooded *1089*, Flats *1189*, Stones *1188*, Shawfield *0661*. **Clearance** East Moor *2970*. **Dark** Umberley *2969*. **Dense** Danebower *0170*, Dean Head *0606*. **Foul smelling** Smeekly *2976*. **Young** OE: *stor* Storth Field, Offerton *2181*, Bradshawe, Foljambe, Ford, Litton, Shirley, Ward, Woderofe.Dialect 'Holt, 'Hurst', 'Slive' and 'Agriculture clearings', 'Trees, 'Agister', 'Estover', 'Forester in Fee', 'Frith', 'Ginclough', 'Greave', 'Hedgebote', 'Heating and Lighting', 'Housebote', 'Law', 'Regard', 'Shaw', 'Trees', 'Verderer', 'Woodward', '*Vernon*'.

Fruits influencing place names: *Apple* OE: *aepell*: Appletree Close, Bakewell *2168*, Appletree Furlong, Hope *1783*, OE: *pippen* Pippen Field, Eyam *2176*. **Berries** Berristall *9478*, Cranberry *vaccinium oxycoccus* Cranberry Clough *1795*, Merry = wild cherry *prunus avium* Dialect. Merryton Low *0460*, #Crowberry *empetrium nigrum* Emlin *2393*, Raspberry wild *rubus idaeus* Hen Cloud *0061*,Strawberry Lee, Great Longstone *2071*, Wimberry/whimberry/whortleberry/bilberry/myrtleberry *vaccinium myrtillus* Wimberry Moss *0102*. **Crabtree**: *malus* ME: *crabbe*: Crabtree Butt, Derwent *2383*, Crabtree Piece, Hathersage *2380*. **Plum** OE: *plume*; Plum Cake, Parwich *1854*. # Origin: Late Glacial Ice Age 20,000-8,000BC.

'Lows': *With a tumulus*: Aleck *1759*, 'Arbor' *1663*, Bee *1964*, 'Blake' *2170*, 'Bose' *1652*, Brood *1279*, Carder ('Jackdaw') *1362*, Cart (cart-like tilt) *1051*, Cow *1059 1482*; 'Crake' *1753*, Cronkston *1166*, Cross *1655*, 'Grind' *2066*, Hawks (axe head shape) *1756*, 'Highlow' *2180*, Kenslow (conspicuous 'knoll' with cliffs) *1761*, 'Knot' *1467*, Lamber *greater plantain 0850*. 'Medicines', Letts *0859*, Mag (with finger spurs) *0781*, 'Mamtops' *1352* Merryton *0460*, Moat = tumulus *1554*, 'Ox' *1280*, 'Pea' *1356*, 'Pike' *2097*, Ringham (Ancient fort) *1666*, Sharp *1652*, Stand (like a barrel) *1553*, 'Steep' *1256*, 'Stone' *2871*, The Low *0862*, 'Tides' *1477*, 'Warslow' *0858*, 'Waterfall' *0852*, 'Wetton' *1154*, Wind *1175*, Withered (poor condition) *1076*, Yearns (demanding ascent) *9675*,+ Eldon Hill *1181*, 'Gautries' Hill *0980*.

'Lows': *Without a tumulus*: 'Abney' *2079*, 'Baslow' *2472*, 'Blackstones' *2055*, 'Bleak' *0996 & 2173*, Boothlow *0964*, Dirtlow *1481*, 'Foolow' *1976*, Glossop (in the Peak National Park) *0696*, Grinlow *1877*, Grislow *2573*, Haddock *0980*, 'High' *1568 & 1465*, 'Hucklow' *1878*, Hurdlow *0260 & 1166*, Martins (pairs of rivulets) *0752*, Mosey (easy walk) *1264*. Mouse (moss) *0853*, Rainowlow *9577*, Thirkelow (malted barley feedstuff) *0468*, 'Tintwistle' *0298*, Waggon *1164*, Wickenlow *0367*, Woolow (thistledown) *0972*, also Shutlingloe *9769*. 'Barrows.', 'Places and Sites', 'The Natural World'.

Lowlands: *Acoustics* Ringing Roger *1287*, Chelmorton. **Bottom** *1169*. **'Cloughs'** deep OE: hol Holinslough *0666*, Linch [steep sided separating Ox from Cow Hey] *1694*, elevated [like a noble ON: jarl Jarvis *2186*, muddy OF: brai Bray *0592*, narrow, like a fiddle neck, Fiddlers *1585*, oyster [shaped] *1191*, shut in Peep o'Day *0485* wobbly Wogden *1701*, dimpled Dimpus *0685*, Wildboarclough *9868*, **Cumb** Coomb *0378*, **'Dale'** Alsop en le Dale *1655*, Dowell (thin as a dowel pin) *0767*, Earl's Sterndale *0966*, Edale *1285*, Hassop *2272*, High *1571*, Hope *1783*, Howden *1597*, Ible *2457* King's Sterndale *0973*, Lin *1551*, Monsal *1871*, Narrow *1257*, pin [shape] Pin *1581*, Stanshope *1354*, OE: saelig = pitiable Silly *1876*, **Valleys** dean/dene (Abbey Brook) OE: denu = dene Howden *1892*, dinted/shallow Dingers Hollow *9870*, middle Midhope *2199*, round oven [shape] Bottom of the Oven *9872*, OE:slakki = shallow 'Slack' *0781*, 'Slack' Close Head, Hope *1783*.

River systems: ***Brooks*** Brook Houses *0389*, Cress<u>brook</u> *1771*, Grinds<u>brook</u> *1186*, Otter<u>brook</u> *1285*, <u>dawdling</u> Wyming *2685*. ***Burn*** Lud<u>burn</u> *0862*, *Swin<u>burne</u>*. ***Confluences*** Eyam *2176*, Shatton *1982*, Tintwistle *0297*, *Wicga's* fork Wigtwizzle *2495*. ***Noise of water*** 'Rouster' *9764*, Fagney (Dialect = garrulous) Clough *1492*, <u>Ludburn</u> *0862*, <u>Ludwell</u> *1262*. ***Peninsula*** between Rivers Ashop and Westend, Locker Brook *1689*. ***Rill*** Smer<u>rill</u> *1962*. ***Rivers*** Alport *1392*, *Bradford *2064*, *Dane [*1220 Henry III*] Dialect: slow flow (many meanders) *9564*, Dean Dialect: deep valley (middle reaches) *9575*, *Derwent *2475*, Little Don/Porter *1900*, Don Dialect: watery (many tributaries) *1302*,*Dove *1451*, Etherow *0511*, Goyt *0173*, Hamps *0953*, Kinder *0788*, *Lathkill *1865*, *Manifold *1059*, <u>waegs</u> = to wade *0954*, *Noe Latin: *nao* = to flow *1486*, Rivelin Dialect: energetic (steep upper reaches) *2786*, Sett Dialect: folded (interlocking spurs) *0585*, *Wye *2276*, * mill weirs. *Figure 22*. ***Rivulet*** pairs Dialect: <u>martin</u> = heffer twin of a bull calf) <u>Martins</u> Low *0752*, OE: *wella* = ***Spring*** OE: *wella* Bake<u>well</u> *2168*, Black<u>well</u> *1272*, Brad<u>well</u> *1781*, Lud<u>well</u> (loud) *1262*, Tides<u>well</u> *1575*, Blackwa(e)ll, Ayton *0189* 'fords' Woolow *0972*. ***Streams*** Bobus *0309*, Diggle *0207*, Bache, Bourne, 'Mill' Brook *1889* - inspiration for *Brian Asquith* of Youlgreave *2064* sculptor and designer, <u>cluster</u> Grains *0604,1094, 1202*, <u>dissected</u> by streams Chew *0502*, <u>nearby</u> OE: *hun-wella* Bradley Howel *0065*. ***Underground trickle*** Roger Rain, Peak Cavern *1482*, ***Watercourse*** OE: *lad* Lode 'Mill' *1455*. 'Rivers' by name.

Rocks and Stones: ***Angled*** Hern *0995*. '***Breccia***' Breck<u>tor</u> *1279*. ***Compact*** Hurkling Stones *2088*. ***Concealed*** Blindstones *0301*. ***Colour*** Blake Low *2170*, Blackstones (millstone grit) Low *2055*, Green Hill *0604*. ***Dark stack*** Laddow *0501*. ***Disorderly heap*** Cluther *0787*, Rollick *0898*. ***Gaping*** Grinan *1396*. ***Gravel*** Greasley *9466*. ***Knarre*** = a rough stone or knot in a tree *0067*. ***Shapes*** '<u>millstone grit outcrops</u>' Cakes of bread *2090*, Chimney Dialect: Lum Edge *0560*, Ram's genitals Tup Stones *0901*, Salt Cellar *1989*. ***Natural hole*** Thurlstone *1702*. ***Perched*** Chee *1273*. ***Rugged*** 'Knarr' *0290*. ***Stoney*** Stannery *0766*, <u>Stoney</u> Cliffe *0260*, <u>Stony</u> Middleton *2275*.

Trees and shrubs: $'***Alder***': *alma glutinosa* <u>Alder</u> Close, Great Longstone *2071* <u>Alders</u> Farm *1749*, Oller<u>brook</u> *1285*, Oll<u>erset</u> *0285*. '***Ash***': *fraxmimus excelsior* <u>Ashes</u> Farm *1749*, <u>Ash</u>ford in the Water *1969*, <u>Ash</u>op *1289*, <u>Ash</u>opton *1986*, 'Breech' *0558*, High <u>Ash</u> *0465*, Mony<u>ash</u> *1566*, One <u>Ash</u> *1665*. <u>Ash</u>ton. ***Aspen*** *populus tremula* <u>Aspen</u>shaw Hall *0188*, <u>Aspen</u> Butts, Hathersage *2380*. Coppiced for poles, *0188*. '***Beech***': *fagus sylvatica* <u>Beeches</u> Farm *2457*, Thursbitch *9975*. *#'***Birch***': *betula pendula* <u>Birch</u>encliff *9480*, <u>Birch</u>field *1884*, <u>Birch</u>in Hat *1491*,<u>Birch</u>inlee Pastures *1491*, <u>Birch</u>over *2462* Dialect: 'birk'. ***Chestnut***: Chestnut Centre *0782*, $. '***Elm***': *ulnus procera*, <u>Elm</u>in 'Pits' *1587*, Ridge *2393*, <u>Elm</u>ore *1882*. ***Hawthorn***: *crataegus oxycantha* Dialect: hay. <u>Quick</u>sets Saxon: *cwic*, Earl Sterndale *0967*, <u>Hawthorn</u> Clough *1200*, #. '***Hazel***': *corylus avellana* Elder Bush Cave *0995*, <u>Hazel</u>badge *1780*, <u>Hazel</u> Barrow *0163*, <u>Hazel</u>hurst *0377*, <u>Hazel</u>ford *2379*. ***Holly***: *ilex aquifolium* <u>Holly</u> Bush Farm *1959*. $'***Lime***': *tilia cordata* Hope *1783* <u>Lime</u> tree farm *1061*, <u>Lime</u>tree Wood *2767*, ***Montpelier maple*** *acer monspessulanum* Elder Bush cave *0995*, ***Mountain ash***/rowan/<u>wicken</u> *sorbus aucuparia* <u>Wicken</u> low *0367*, <u>Wicken</u> Walls *0167*. $'***Oak***': *quercus robur and petraea* OE <u>ac</u> = <u>oak</u> + *denu* = <u>valley</u>, Ag<u>den</u> *2692*, Chatsworth *2670*, River Derwent *2475*, <u>Oaks</u> Wood *2179* <u>Oak</u>enclough *0563*, Shire<u>oaks</u> *0783*, *quercus coccifera*, host for *kermes illices* insect, used to make red dye Grains *1202*, Cheney. *#'***Scots Pine***': *pinus sylvestris* Habitat: Rocky ground in the 'Dark Peak' before deforestation. Bleaklow *2173*. '***Sycamore***': *acer pseudoplatanus* Hope *1783*, <u>Sycamore</u> Lodge *0653*, '***Walnut***': *juglans regia* Probably introduced by the Romans. Stanton *2563*. '***Willow***': Probably crack willow *salix fragilis* OE: *widig*. Habitat Cold <u>wet</u> soil: <u>Wet</u> Withens *2376*, <u>Willow</u>meadow *0354*, <u>Willows</u>, Parwich *1854*; Withers, Bakewell *2168*, Withenstake *9864*. '***Yew***': *taxus baccata* Stanton *2563*, <u>Yew</u>tree 'Grange' *0865* 'Wiggy' * Stumps in the peat Lady Clough Moor *1092* and Tintwistle 'Knar' *0399*. # Origin: Late Glacial Ice Age 20,000-8,000BC when British Isles and continental Europe joined. $ Origin: Atlantic Period 8,000-6,000BC when separating from Europe.

Uplands: ***Banks***, edges, moors, ridges and cliffs: *banke* = land on or near a bank, Bin<u>cliff</u> *1154*, Birchen *1098*, Calver *2374*, Edensor *2468*, Hathersage *2380*, Higher Bongs *9966*, Nield *9367*, Priest<u>cliffe</u> *1371*, <u>steep</u> Wall Cliff *1377*, Banks, Clifford. ***Edges*** <u>brown</u> Brown *2879*, Froggatt *2576*, <u>cracked</u> Cracken *0383*, <u>gentle</u> Dialect: Flask *2878*, Holland. ***Heaths*** OE: *haesel* <u>Heath</u>cote *1460*. ***Hills***: ON: *ball* = rounded hill Gam<u>ball</u> *0367*, <u>bare</u> Dialect: Callow *2582*, *bent* like a stick Gib *0264*, *breost* = round breast [shape] <u>Breast</u> Lands, Castleton *1582*, Blore *1349*, *calu* = bare hill <u>Callow</u> *2582*, *cern* = churn [shape] Chinley <u>Churn</u> *0383*, '*castle*', *clud* = a hill Five <u>Clouds</u> *0062*, Thorpe <u>Cloud</u> *1550*, Bunsal 'Cob' *0175*, *cown* = rocky cliff <u>Cowns</u> *1290*, *0291*, <u>crooked</u> <u>Crook</u>stone *1488*, <u>dead</u>/unspectacular Upper Dead Edge *1301* (unlike Withens *1102*), <u>detached</u> Higger/Hu-gaer *2581*, *dun* = hill Balli<u>don</u> *2055*, Mus<u>den</u> *1250*, Shel<u>don</u> *1768*, Bow<u>den</u>, Longs<u>don</u>, <u>fragmented</u> OE: *bryttian* Brit<u>land</u> Edge *1002*, <u>empty</u> Owler *2580*, *gris/greece* =

staircase (compared with steep gristone edges) Groslow *2573*, <u>hey</u> = a hill Cow and Ox *1694,* <u>Hey</u> Ridge *1390,* The <u>Heys</u> *0485* <u>high</u> High Low *1465* & *1568* <u>ho</u> = spur Hoo Moor *0077,0687*. Pil<u>hough</u> *2564,*Upper <u>Ho</u> *0687, indentation* Bosley Minn *9366,* Wincle Minn *9466, jagged* Twizle Head *1003,* <u>knoll</u> Knowle *0861,* ME <u>knot</u> Knotbury *0168, lookout* Pym Chair *0886, 9976,* Tooley *0803,* '<u>low</u>'. Huck<u>low</u> *1777,* Langsett *1699,* Thorn<u>hill</u> *1983,* Thorpe *1550,* Bar<u>low</u> *'nab'* Lower *9668,* Shooters' *0610, 'neb'* High Neb *2285, needle-point* Nield *0367, ossom* = leaning [to the east) Ossom Hill *0955,*(compare Wessenden *0508).* OF: <u>graver</u> = parting Swain's Greave *1397, 'pike'* Pike Lowe *2097, rod shape* Rod *2788, reddish* (heather) colour <u>Rud</u> Hill *2784, round* Roundhill *0602, scars* Scaurs *9971, sharp* = sandy <u>Sharp</u> Low *1652, side* of Axe Edge Cheeks *0269, sideless truck* [shape] Dialect Rolley *1873, slope* OE: *lang* = long + *sett* = slope Langsett Moor *1699,* OF: *chaiere* = initial gentle slope Shay/Chez 'Knowl' *2566, standing out* Issue Edge *0805, steep* Steep Low *1256, 'tor'* Row<u>tor</u> *2261,* <u>Tor</u> side *9797, twisted* Throwley *1052,* Wincle *9665, wheel* [shape] High <u>Wheel</u>don *1066,* Howe, Field *sletta* = level Sleigh, *westerly* Wessenden *0508*.

Weather and climate: ON: *bleikr* = **Bleak** <u>Bleak</u>low *0996,* <u>Bleak</u> 'Knoll' *1879, 2173.* **Blustery** Roych *0883, calwe* = **Cold** Callow *2481, how* = **<u>Howling</u>** <u>How</u>den 'Dean' and Moor *1892.* **Icy** Dialect: Issue *0805, spon* = **Snow spindrift** Back [sheltered from north snow bearing winds] <u>Spon</u>ds *9779, Mr Baines,* Baslow *2572* parson and Dronfield *3578* schoolmaster died in snow storm on Froggatt Moss *22476* [31/12/1725]; *snideren* = biting blast. <u>Snid</u>dles *0065.* **Windy** Gates Winnats *1382,* Wind Low *1175.*

Wetlands: Water<u>slacks</u> *0856.* **Ditches, bogs, ponds** Aldery bog with 'alder' trees *0966,* The Swamp *1095, 'jarnett' 1469,* Moscar *2388,* OE: *lecc* The <u>Laches</u> *9673,* Dialect: *hollow with a deep pool* Potluck *1377,* Rew<u>lach</u> *0961,* Scalder<u>ditch</u> *1159,* Sparrow<u>pit</u> *0880,* Tinkers Pit *0270,* Wythen <u>Lache</u> *0277.* **Marker pole** Brogging Moss *2091.* **Marshes**: Fynney *1871,* Leash Fen *2973,* Gulshaw Hollow *9574* (surrounded by steep valley sides) *slaed* = marshy; <u>Slad</u> Piece, Abney *1979 mouldy* Moscar *2388, muddy* Howels Head *0503* Slack *2757* Denman, Eyre, Slack. **Meander** <u>cu</u>rve <u>Cu</u>rbar *2574,* enclosing land Carr *2083'naze'* Peak<u>naze</u> *0496.* **Meadow** ON: *hom* = water meadow The <u>Home</u>, Baslow *2572.* **Pool** Potluck *1377.* **Stream adjacent** OD: <u>hulme</u> Hulme *1059,* Kettles<u>hulme</u> *9879.* **Swamp** OE: *mos* = moss *0102, 0172, 0303, 0400, 0500, 0503, 0601, 0602, 0604, 0609, 0610, 0701* 2x, *0765, 0802, 0804, 0892, 0895, 0896, 0901, 0996, 1003, 1098,1194, 1198, 1300, 1498, 1994, 2191.*

Woods: *'frith'* Litton *1773.* OE: <u>fiergen</u> = wooded Ferriser *9770 dense* Dean Head *0606,* 'Clough' *0806, Fulwood, Greaves.* 'Lows' Saplings transplanted for 'assarts'.

Hare
Otter
Trout
Wild boar
Deer
Bear
Badger
Elk
Wolf
Pheasant
Mouse

Wildlife

INCOMERS

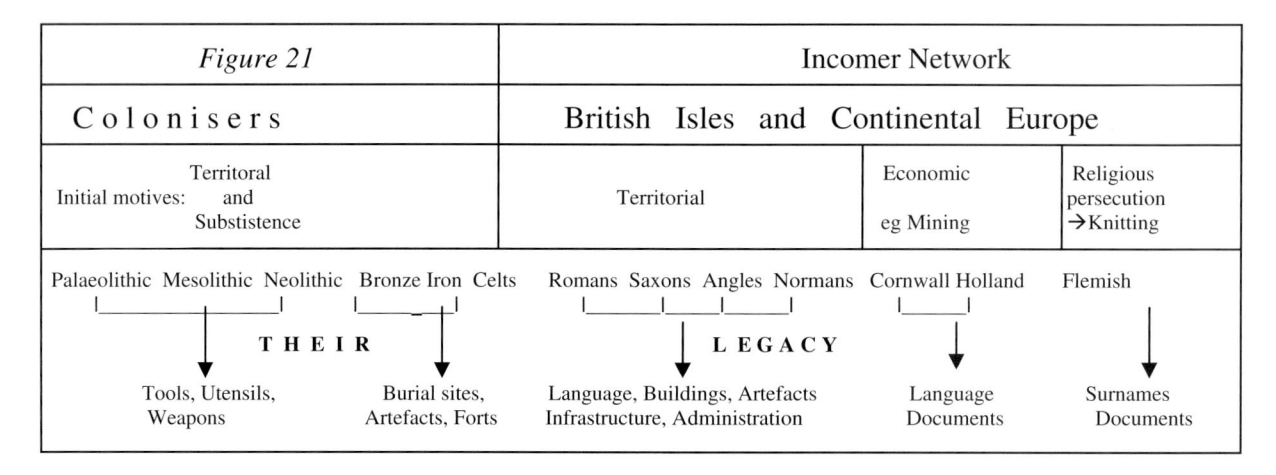

Figure 21	Incomer Network
Colonisers	British Isles and Continental Europe
Initial motives: Territorial and Substistence	Territorial	Economic eg Mining	Religious persecution →Knitting

Palaeolithic Mesolithic Neolithic Bronze Iron Celts   Romans Saxons Angles Normans   Cornwall Holland   Flemish

THEIR → Tools, Utensils, Weapons ; Burial sites, Artefacts, Forts   **LEGACY** → Language, Buildings, Artefacts, Infrastructure, Administration ; Language Documents ; Surnames Documents

Angle occupation: Bakewell *2168*.

British Isles Places and Family Names: ***Cambridgeshire:*** *Helyon;* ***Cheshire:*** *Ashton, Bradshawe, Marbury, Moore, Newton, Winnington, Upton.* ***Derbyshire:*** *(excluding Peak): Barlow, Brampton, Dale, Harpur, Kniveton, Longford, Morton, Rowland, Stanley.* ***Durham:*** *De Eston.* ***Lancashire:*** *Mellor, Plumpton.* ***Lincolnshire:*** *Bourne, Carrington, Morton.* ***Norfolk****: Howe, Morton, Needham.* ***Nottinghamshire:*** *Langford, Leake, Strelley, Sutton, Upton.* ***Scotland****: Eyre, Leslie.* ***Shropshire:*** *Morton, Newdigate, Peplow, Sutton.* ***Staffordshire:*** *Brereton, Cresswell, Ford, Leake, Longsdon, Marchington, Stafford, Stanley, Sutton.* ***Suffolk:*** *Cavendish.* ***Yorkshire:*** *Bradbury, Clifford, De Stokes, Fulwood, Gargrave, Gisbourne, Hatfield, Mulgrave, Nussey, Rossington, Rydale, Slack, Slingsby, Topcliffe, Wentworth.* These names indicate either migration from elsewhere to the Peak or absentee property ownership. 'Sheldon'.

Bronze Age: About [1800-550 BC] in the British Isles 'Arbor' 'Low' *1663*, Aston *1884*, Doll 'Tor' *2463*, Five Wells *1271*, Ilam *1350*, Letts Low *0859*, Lord's Seat burials *1183*, Mam Tor *1283*, Minninglow *2156*, Mouse Low *0853*, Nine Ladies *2563*, Tintwistle *0298*, Wardlow *1874*, Wet Withens *2376*, Wincle *9665*. ***Forest clearance*** East Moor *2970;* 'Round Barrows' *Figure 21*, bronze Age Sites refers.

'Cairns': ***Celtic*** *1069,1081, 1263,1271.* ***Chambered****, 1362, 2065, 2097, 2178* (ring), *2184, 2279, 0669,* (3 in the vicinity – Stanton Moor) *2463, 2675, 2873*.

Celtic Occupation: Bull *bwlch* Hill *9474*, Castleton *1583*, Chez Knoll *2566*, Mam Tor fortress *1283*, Sharp Low *1652*, Steep Low *1256*, Thor's Cave *0954*, Taddington Cross *1471*. 'Cairns'. Allen.

Danish occupation: *Fynney, Sotehill, Swain.*

Early man: Early settlers: Dates are approximate: [30,000 or earlier-12,000BC]. ***'Palaeolithic'*** (Old Stone Age); [13,000-3,000BC]. ***'Mesolithic'*** (Intermediate Stone Age); [3,000-1,800BC]. ***'Neolithic'*** (New Stone Age); [2,000-500BC]. ***'Bronze Age'***; [500BC-AD55]. ***'Iron Age'*** overlapping with ***'Celts'***; [AD49] ***'Romans'***; [495] Anglo - ***'Saxons'***; [850] Danes; [1066] ***'Normans'***. Undated human remains Hinkley Wood *1250,* 'Bronze Age', 'Iron Age' and 'Pecsaetan'.

European Places and Family Names: Berry – Berry, Bernay – Balguy, Finnes – Fynney, Quesnay – Cheney, Ferrieres – Ferrars, Gournay or Gourdon - Gernon, Lisle - (De) Lisle, Lude - (De) Lude, Mesnieres – Manners, Mesnil – Meynell, Mortagne – Morteyne, Mont Pincon – Mompesson, Neuville – Neville, Sau Cheverell – Sacheverell, Savil – Sainville, Vernon – Vernon. Map references are in the People chapter entries. *Figure 14*.

Iron Age: About [550BC-AD43] in the British Isles. ***Forest clearance*** East Moor *2970*. ***Forts*** possibly Bar Dike *2494*, Carlwark *2681*, Combs Moss *0578*, Fin Cop *1771*, Mam Tor *1283*, possibly Meltham *0810*. ***Tumuli****:* Kenslow *1761*, Steep 'Low' *1256*. 'Long barrows'.

'Languages' and Names: Links between people, places and languages may be tenuous

Breton: Old and Middle: People *Allyn.*
Celtic Gaelic: People *Leslie, Maxwell, McCreagh.* **Celtic Welsh:** Old and Middle: People *Allen, De Paunton, Evans, Wallesby.* Places Arrock *1869*, Derwent *2383*, Dove *1451*, Goyt *0173*, Hamps *0953*, Heathy Roods *0857*, Ilam *1350*, Kinder *0888*, Perryfoot *1081*.'Lows' for dialect. 'Flash' *0267*.
Dutch: Middle Places Raper Lodge, *2165*, 'Brink' *1785*.
Middle English: People *Arkwright, Bird, Carver, Cokayne, Cowper, Fox, Galliard, Garlick, Harpur, Hodgkinson, Hope, Howe, Hurt, Lowe, Metcalf, Pegge, Rocliffe, Rowe, Slack, Spencer, Stephenson, Twigge, Watt, Wells, Woderhope.* Places Shoe Broad, Ashford *1969*, Tentry Croft, Barthomley *9665*, Blore *1349*, The Slang, Brough *1882*, Garbroods, Castleton *1583*, Crabtree Butt, Derwent *2383*, Edale *1285*, **1.** Dam Close, **2.** Pippen Field, Eyam *2176*, Flagg *1368*, Crabtree Piece, Hathersage *2380*, Knotbury *0168*, The Pasture, Over Haddon *2066*, Sheldon *1768*, Warren Carr, Wensley *2661*, Rabbit Bana, Wincle *9665*.
Old English: People *Ashton, Bache, Barlow, Beresford, Barnesley, Blackwall, Birch, Bradshaw, Bowden, Bourne, Bowman, Bradbury, Brampton, Brereton, Brindley, Brittlebank, Brown, Bullock, Buxton, Clifford, Coke, Cotton, Dawkin, Eyre, Freeman, Fulwood, Gladwin, Greaves, Hamilton, Hatfield, Hunter, Hyde, Leche, Litton, Lamb, Langford, Longsdon, Lowe, Ludlam, Marchington, Middleton, Milne, Milward, Moore, Morton, Needham, Oldfield, Pole, Roper, Rossington, Savage, Shallcross, Sheldon, Shirley, Shore, Smith, Stafford, Stanley, Stanshope, Statham, Stratford, Sutton, Swynbourne, Thornhill, Upton, Ward, Wentworth, White, Whynyates, Woderhofe, Wright.* Places Rake Heads, Slad Piece, Abney *1979*, The Riddings, Walkmile Croft, Ashford *1969*, Dry Hills, Sedgy Spring, Withers, Bakewell *2168*, Ballidon *2055*, Bamford *2083*, Bradley Howel *0065*, Sweet Piece, Brough *1882*, Burton *2067*, Calton Hill *1050 & 1171*, Breast lands + Gawtree Thorn, Castleton *1583*, Chunal *0391*, Cockey *1979*, Dane River *9665*, Shutts, Derwent *2383*, Dove Rover *1451*, Quicksets, Earl Sterndale *0967*, Hollin Knowl, Mean Field, Edale *1285*, Elkstone *0559*, Goose Pringle, Hempen Butts, Wood Close, Eyam *2176*, Fallinge *2666*, Lease Lands, Flagg *1368*, Flash *0267*, Flatt, Rix Acre, Foolow *1976*, Butter Field, Sour Lands, Stonego Close, Greasley *9466*, Great Hucklow *1777*, Church Croft, Elbow Close. Short: Broods, Great Longstone *2071*, Haddon *2366*, Hare Butts, Hartington *1360*, Hawthorn Clough *1200*, Hayes *0860*, Hazelhurst *0377*, Helmesley *9867*, Hollinsclough *0666*, Clover Sitch, Honey Spots, Far Field, Pease Bonges, Wry Neck, Hope *1783*, Hurdlow *0260 & 1166*, Kill Pingle, Wheat Croft. Kettelshume *9879*, Knotbury *0168*, Rioth Clemley Park, Little Longstone *1871*, Litton *1675*, Ludwell *1262* Butt, Heathy Piece, Steer Croft, Monyash *1566*, Musden *1250*, Nettly Knowe *1456*, Cockshut Meadow, Cow Close, Offerton *2181*, Lows *1059 & 1482*, Otterbrook *1285*, Plum Cake, Parwich *1854*, Pilhough *2564*, Pittle Mere *1378*, Six Acres, Pott Shrigley *9479*, Quicksets, Reaps Moor *0861*, Rewlach *0961*, Flitland, Rowland *2172*, Rushley *1251*, Scalderditch *1159*, Smerrill *1962*, Smithy Hill *1781*, Thornhill *1983*, Thorpe *1550*, Thirsbitch *9975*, Tintwistle *0297*, Tunstead *1074*, Cinder Hill, Wildboarclough *9868*, Hawkesyard, Loam Close, Stair Field Wincle *9665*, Winter *2460*, Wye *2267*.
French: Norman and Old: People Appearance, character and occupation names *Barber, Basset, Bennett, Blount, Bouer, Bowles, Carver, Columbell, Cotterell, Farrar, Franceys, Francis, Gargrave, Gernon, Joliffe, Marbury, Meynell, Paunton, Peverell, Prime, Russell, Scriven, Senior, Spencer, Tyrell, Vavasour, Wallesby.* Places 'Greasley' *9466*, 'Motte and bailey' *1163, 2692*.
German: Old and Middle High, Middle Low: People *Avenell, Bardolf, Bunting, Chaworth, Gilbert, Greaves, Hibbertson.* Places Allgreave *9767*, Bradwell *1781*, Brecktor *1279*, Chatsworth *2670*, Hawthorn 'Clough' *1200*, Smerrill *1962*.
Irish: *Boyle.*
Latin: River Noe *1486*.
Scandinavian: *Norwegian*, Old (Norse): People *Clegg, Grimshawe, Slingsby, Thacker,Thorpe, Wake.* Places Blore *1349*, Crake Low *1753*, Flat Furlong, Bamford *2083*, Gamball *0367*, The Holme, Baslow *2572*, Kirk Acre, Bradwell *1781*, Lathkill *1865*, Litton Slack *1673*, Moss Carr *0765*, Storth Field, Offerton *2181*, Otterbrook *1285* and other 'booths, Sheen *1161*, Slack *0781*, Swainsley *0957*, Waterslacks *0856*. *Scandinavian*: Old and *Danish*: People *Agard, Banks, Barker,Norman, Slingsby, Thacker, Thorpe.* Places Biggin *1559*, Holme *2169*, Hulme *1059*, Kettleshulme *9879*, Latham *1149*, Odin *1383 & 1483*, Ravensdale *1773*, Rowland *2172*, Slaley *2757*, Swainsley *0957*, Taxal *0079*.

Medieval and Early Settlements: *1670, 2061, 2065, 2579.*

Neolithic Period: 'Arbor' 'Low' *1663*, Minninglow chambered tombs *2057* 'Long barrows'. Forest clearance East Moor *2970*.

Norman Occupation: *Domesday Book place names* Abney *1979*, Alsop en le Dale *1655*, Alston(e)field *1355*, Aldwark *2357*, Ashford *1969*, Aston *1884*, Bakewell *2168*, Ballidon *2055*, Bamford *2083*, Baslow

2572, Beeley *2667*, Birchover *2462*, Blackwell *1272*, Blore *1349*, Bradshaw *2176*, Bradwell *1781*, Bramley *2473*, Broadlowash *1549*, Bubnell *2472*, Burton *2076*, Calver *2374*, Castleton *1583*, Chatsworth *2670*, Chunal *0391*, Conk(e)sbury *2065*, Ecton *0958*, Edale *1285*, Edensor *2468*, Elton *2260*, Eyam *2176*, Fenny Bentley *1750*, Flagg *1368*, Ford *0882*, Gratton *1960*, Grindon *0864*, Haddon *2366*, Hanson Grange *1153*, Harthill *2262*, Hartington *1360*, Hassop *2272*, Hathersage *2380*, Hazelbadge *1780*, Highlow *2180*, Holme *2169*, Hope *1783*, Hucklow *1777*, Ible *2457*, Kinder *0888*, Litton *1675*, Longstone *1871*, Macclesfield Forest *9671*, Middleton *1963*, Monyash *1566*, Offerton *2181*, One Ash *1665*, Parwich *1854*, Pilsbury *1163*, Pilsley *2471*, Priestcliffe *1371*, Ravensdale *1773*, Rowland *2172*, Rowsley *2566*, Salterford *9876*, Shatton *1982*, Sheldon *1768*, Snitterton *2760*, Ston(e)y Middleton *2375*, Taddington *1471*, Thorpe *1550*, Tideswell *1575*, Tintwistle *0297*, Tissington *1752*, Tunstead *1074*, Warslow *0858*, Wensley *2661*, Winster *2460*, Wormhill *1274*, Youlgreave *2064*.

Ecclesiastical buildings and artefacts Ashford in the Water *1969*, Bakewell *2168*, Ballidon *2055*, Beeley *2667*, Castleton *1583*, Earl Sterndale *0966*, Eyam *2176*, Monyash *1566*, Parwich *1854*, Youlgreave *2064*. <u>Fonts</u> Eyam *2176*, Fenny Bentley *1750*, Haddon *2366*, Parwich *1854*, Thorpe *1550*, Tissington *1752*, Winster *2460*.

Personal names Cheney, Curzon, Ludank, Manners, Mompesson, Neville, Saville, Tibetot, Tracy, Turvill, Vernon. 'Languages' **Titles**: 'Baron', 'duke', 'viscount'. *Norman*. 'Honour'. *Figure 24*, Domesday Survey refers.

'Palaeolithic' Period: Beresford *1259*, Brown Edge *2784* – flint/'chert'arrow heads, blades, knives, scrapers, Fox Hole *0866*, Monyash *1566*, Swythamley *9764*, Thor's Cave *0954*, Tintwistle *0298*. Bull stones, arrow heads Longgutter Farm *9667*.

Roman Occupation: [AD43-410]. ***Altars*** Brough *1882*, Haddon *2366*. ***Artefacts*** <u>brass pins</u> Longstone Edge *2073*, <u>coins</u> Elton *2260*, Eyam *2176*, Fenny Bentley *1750*, Gib Hill *1563*, Hulme End *1059*, Longstone Edge *2073*, Minninglow *2156*, Parwich *1854*, Thirkel 'Low' *0469*, <u>enamelled dish</u> Benty Grange *1564*, <u>iron spade</u> Taddington *1471*, <u>jewellery</u> bracelets – copper + silver Carlswark *2681*, Thirkel 'Low' *0469*, Wincle – gold *9665*, Wormhill – necklace *1274*, <u>pottery</u> Arbor Low *1663*, Bakewell *2168*, Bank Top *1361*, Chelmorton *1169*, Coldeaton *1456*, Haddon *2366*, Hart Hill *2262*, Minninglow *2156*, Ringham 'Low' *1666*, 'Samian' <u>Urns</u> Fenny Bentley *1750*, Grindlow *1877*, Parwich *1854*, <u>weapon</u> Parwich *1854*, <u>wooden coffin</u> Brundcliffe *1661*. ***Additional Discovery Sites*** Figure in [ ] indicates number in a vicinity: Brough (west) [3] *1882* Hope [1] *1984*, Reynards Cave *1452*, Thor's Cave *0954*, Wetton *1055*. ***Bath*** Stoney Middleton *2275*. ***Flora*** introduced: 'Nettles' (for rubbing on soldiers' cold legs) 'Walnut'. ***Forts*** Brough *1882*. ***Lead pigs*** Bradwell *1781*. ***Persecution*** of Christians Bradwell *1781*. ***Roads*** *0160* → *0170*, *1686* → *1687* (Hope Cross), *0278* → *0376*, Doctor's Gate *0894* → *1190*, Stanage Edge (Ridgeway) *2286* → *2483*,, The Street *0175* – *9976*, Batham Gate *1681* →, Flagg *1368*, Stockport → Taxal *0079*, ***Tribes***: 'Brigantes', 'Cornovii'.***Valley*** and dale discovery ***corridors*** – River Bradford [4] *1565*, River Derwent [1] *2670*, Jumber Brook [5] *2177*, River Manifold [7], River Wye (upper reaches) [2] *1672*, Cressbrook Dale [1] *1773*, Hartington Dale [1] *1059*, Lathkill Dale [3] *1865*, *Figure 22*, Roman Occupation refers.

Saxon Occupation: About [500-1066]. ***Burials***: Steep Low *1256*. ***Ecclesiastical sites and artefacts*** Alstonefield *1355*, Bakewell *2168*, Blackwell *1272*, Beeston Tor *1054*, Crowdecote *1065*, Eyam *2176*, Gospel Hillock *1771*, Hindlow *0868*, Hitter Hill *0866*, Hope *1783*, Macclesfield Forest *9671*, Throwley *1152*, Wetton *1055*. ***Earthwork***: Town ditch at Castleton *1583*, 'Military History'. ***Farming*** Totley *2779* *Tota's* clearing. ***Fort*** Possibly Earl Sterndale *0967*. ***Manors and settlements***: Abney *1979*, Beeley *2667*, Castleton *1583*, Chatsworth *2670*, Edensor *2468*, Elton *2260*, Eyam *2176*, Hazlebadge *1780*, Hope *1783*,Hucklow *1777*, Stanton *2464*, Wormhill *1274*,Youlgreave *2064*. **'Portways'** to Ashford in the Water *1969*, Bakewell *2168* Eyam *2176*, Great Longstone *2071*, Hope *1783*,Winster *2460*. **'Thanes'** and lords of manors: *Cashin, Chetal. Colle,Colne, Ernvi, Godric, Gurneburn, Hundine, Levenot, Lewin, Raven, Siward, Swein, Uchtred, Wudia.* 'Crosses', 'Honour', 'Languages' *Figure 23* Saxon sttlements refers.

Sites often indicated by suffixes, prefixes and syllables in the names of people and places. ***High*** 'bury', 'cliffe', 'cote', 'don', 'ham', 'hill', 'hough', 'lee', 'low', 'stan/stone(y)', 'ton', 'High', 'Upper'. ***Low*** 'badge', 'bridge', 'brook', 'clough', 'dale', 'ford', 'hop(e)', 'well', 'Low'.

Stone Circles and Remains: *Named* Arbor 'Low' Bronze Age or Neolithic *1663*, Birchover 'Druid' *2462*, Castle *2262*, Doll Tor Bronze Age *2463*, Harthill *2262*, King Stone *2463*, Nine Ladies Bronze Age *2563*, Wet Withens Bronze Age *2376*. *Unnamed 2186, 2284, 2362, 2396.*

Tumuli: *9675, 9664, 9779, 0461, 0666, 0755, 0758, 0853, 0863, 0867, 0957, 0981, 1050, 1052, 1154, 1166, 1181, 1251, 1352, 1357, 1467, 1552, 1553, 1560, 1561, 1582* (more than one), *1652, 1660, 1663, 1664, 1666, 1669, 1767, 1778, 1861, 1867, 1873, 1960, 1962,* **2166***, 2180* (more than one) *2273, 2358, 2368, 2368, 2396, 2467.* 'Barrows', 'Cairns', 'Lows'.

Vikings/Norsemen: Eric of Norway, FitzWaltheof, Norman, Slingsby.

Wheat

Potatoes

Strawberries

Barley

Peas

Garlic

Raspberries

Rye

Oats

Apples

Cabbage

Bilberries

Parsley

105

Figure 22	Bronze Age Sites		Abbreviations

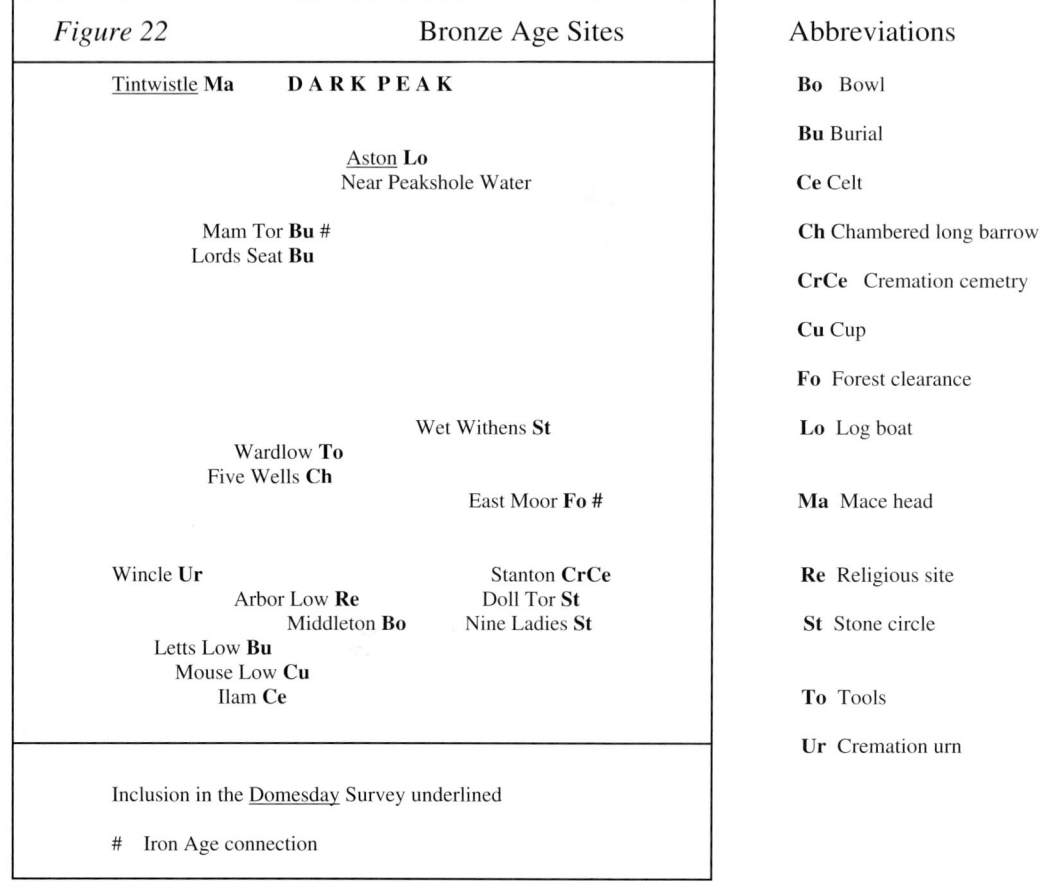

<u>Tintwistle</u> **Ma**   D A R K P E A K

<u>Aston</u> **Lo**
Near Peakshole Water

Mam Tor **Bu** #
Lords Seat **Bu**

Wet Withens **St**
Wardlow **To**
Five Wells **Ch**
East Moor **Fo** #

Wincle **Ur**   Stanton **CrCe**
Arbor Low **Re**   Doll Tor **St**
Middleton **Bo**   Nine Ladies **St**
Letts Low **Bu**
Mouse Low **Cu**
Ilam **Ce**

Bo Bowl
Bu Burial
Ce Celt
Ch Chambered long barrow
CrCe Cremation cemetry
Cu Cup
Fo Forest clearance
Lo Log boat
Ma Mace head
Re Religious site
St Stone circle
To Tools
Ur Cremation urn

Inclusion in the <u>Domesday</u> Survey underlined

\# Iron Age connection

[Map of Europe showing: Norsemen, SCHLESWIG, Angles, HOLSTEIN, Saxons, PEAK, FLANDERS Weavers, CORNWALL Miners, GERMANY, Pre-monstratensians, Normans, Cistercians, FRANCE, ? Bronze, Benedictines Franciscans, Albigensians, SPAIN, ? Celts, Dominicans, ITALY, Romans]

Note: Earlier names of constituent parts of countries differ from the modern ones used for ease of identificaton.

<u>Economic, Military and Religious Incomers</u>

Figure 23   Roman Occupation

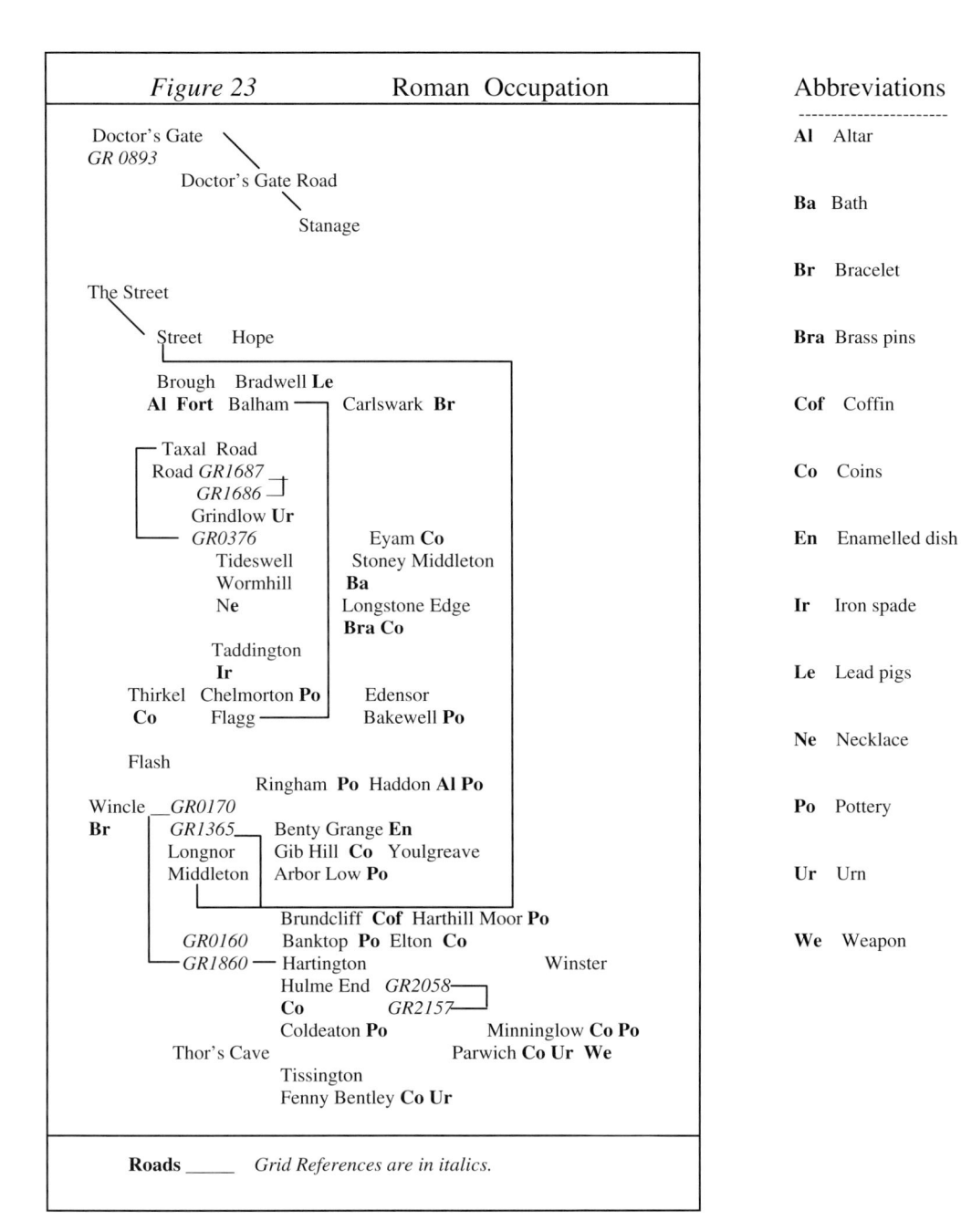

Doctor's Gate
GR 0893
　　　　Doctor's Gate Road
　　　　　　　　Stanage

The Street
　　Street　Hope
　　　Brough　Bradwell **Le**
　Al Fort　Balham　　Carlswark **Br**
　　Taxal　Road
　　Road *GR1687*
　　　　GR1686
　　　Grindlow **Ur**
　　　GR0376　　Eyam **Co**
　　　Tideswell　Stoney Middleton
　　　Wormhill　**Ba**
　　　Ne　Longstone Edge
　　　　　Bra Co
　　　Taddington
　　　Ir
　Thirkel　Chelmorton **Po**　Edensor
　Co　　Flagg　　Bakewell **Po**

　Flash
　　　　Ringham **Po**　Haddon **Al Po**
Wincle　*GR0170*
Br　*GR1365*　Benty Grange **En**
　　Longnor　Gib Hill **Co**　Youlgreave
　　Middleton　Arbor Low **Po**

　　　　Brundcliff **Cof**　Harthill Moor **Po**
　GR0160　Banktop **Po**　Elton **Co**
　　GR1860　Hartington　　　　Winster
　　　　Hulme End　*GR2058*
　　Co　　　　*GR2157*
　　　Coldeaton **Po**　　Minninglow **Co Po**
　Thor's Cave　　　　Parwich **Co Ur We**
　　　Tissington
　　　Fenny Bentley **Co Ur**

Roads _____ *Grid References are in italics.*

Abbreviations

Al　Altar

Ba　Bath

Br　Bracelet

Bra　Brass pins

Cof　Coffin

Co　Coins

En　Enamelled dish

Ir　Iron spade

Le　Lead pigs

Ne　Necklace

Po　Pottery

Ur　Urn

We　Weapon

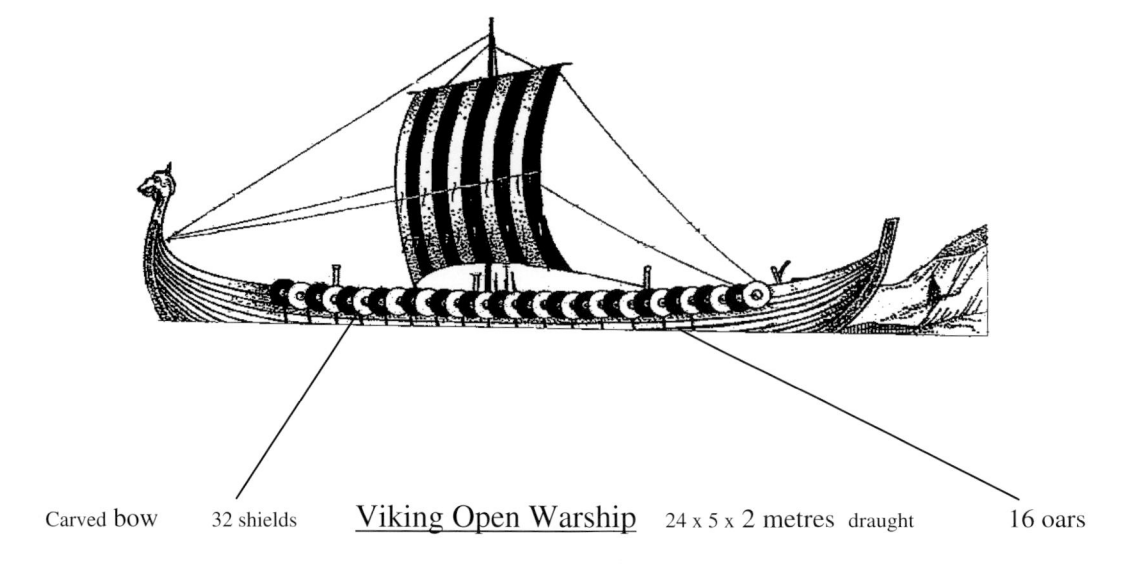

Figure 24 Saxon Settlement	Abbreviations
DARK PEAK Wigtwizzle **Pn** Rowlee **Pn** Ughill **Pn** Castleton **Ea Ma** Hope **Ma Po Re** Offerton **Pn** Kettelshulme **Pn** <u>Taxal</u> **Pn** Padley **Fa Pn** Pott Shrigley **Fa Pn** Hazelbadge **Ma** Abney **Ma Add** Tideswell **Pn** Foolow **Pn** Taddington **Pn** Hucklow **Ma** Foolow **Pn** <u>Eyam</u> **Cr Po Re** Wheston **Cr** <u>Wormhill</u> **Ma** Macclesfield Blackwell **Re** Great Forest **Re** Longstone **Po** Bubnell **Pn** Hindlow **Re** Gospel **Re** Hassop **Pn** Baslow **Pn** Hillock Chatsworth **Ma** Ashford **Po** <u>Bakewell</u> **Cr** <u>Edensor</u> **Ma** **Po Re** Beeley **Ma** Crowdecote **Re** Rowsley **Pn** Swainsley **Pn** Pilsbury **Pn** Youlgreave **Ma** Stanton **Ma** Winster**Pn** Elton **Ma** Wensley **Fa Pn** Warslow **Pn** Narrowdale Snitterton **Pn** <u>Tissington</u> **Pn** Steep Low **Bu** Alstonefield **Re** Ecton **Pn** <u>Alsop</u> **Pn** ***Wincle*** **Pn** Elkstone **Pn** Beeston Tor **Re** Wetton **Re** Throwley **Re** ***Ilam*** **Cr** Hinkley **Pn**	---------------------- **Bu** Burial **Cr** Cross **Ea** Earthwork **Fa** Farming **Ma** Manor **Pn** Person's Name **Po** Portway **Re** Religious Site Cross referencres ---------------------- Figure 21 ***Bold italics*** Bronze Age Figure 23 <u>Underlined</u> Romans

Carved bow   32 shields   <u>**Viking Open Warship**</u>   24 x 5 x 2 metres   draught   16 oars

| *Figure 25* Domesday Survey |

Tintwistle

Chunal

Harthill

Kinder **DARK PEAK**

Edale

Aston

Ford Castleton +

Hope * Shatton

Bradwell Offerton

Hazelbadge Hathersage

Abney Highlow

Salterford Hucklow

Eyam **Fo** Bradshaw Stoke

Tideswell Litton Burton Stoney Middleton

Tunstead Wormhill Ravensdale Calver

Rowland Bramley Bubnell

Macclesfield Hassop Baslow

Forest Blackwell Longstone Pilsley

Taddingston Priestcliff Chatsworth

Ashford + * Holme

Flagg Sheldon Bakewell +

Beeley +

Earl Sterndale + Monyash + Haddon **Fo** Rowsley

One Ash Conkesbury

Youlgreave **Fo**

Middleton

Pilsbury

Harthill

Wensley

Hartington Winster **Fo** Snitterton

Gratton Elton

Ecton

Warslow Aldwark

Ible

Alstonefield Alsop **Tfo Ty** Ballidon +

Grindon Parwich **Fo**

Hanson

Tissington + *

Thorpe **TFo** /l

Fenny Bentley +

Blore /l Broadlowash

Fo Norman Font in a church

TFo Norman tub font

Ty Typanum

Saxon connection Underlined

/l Old Norse Place Name

+ Christian building or artefect

* Water Mill

HOME and FAMILY LIFE

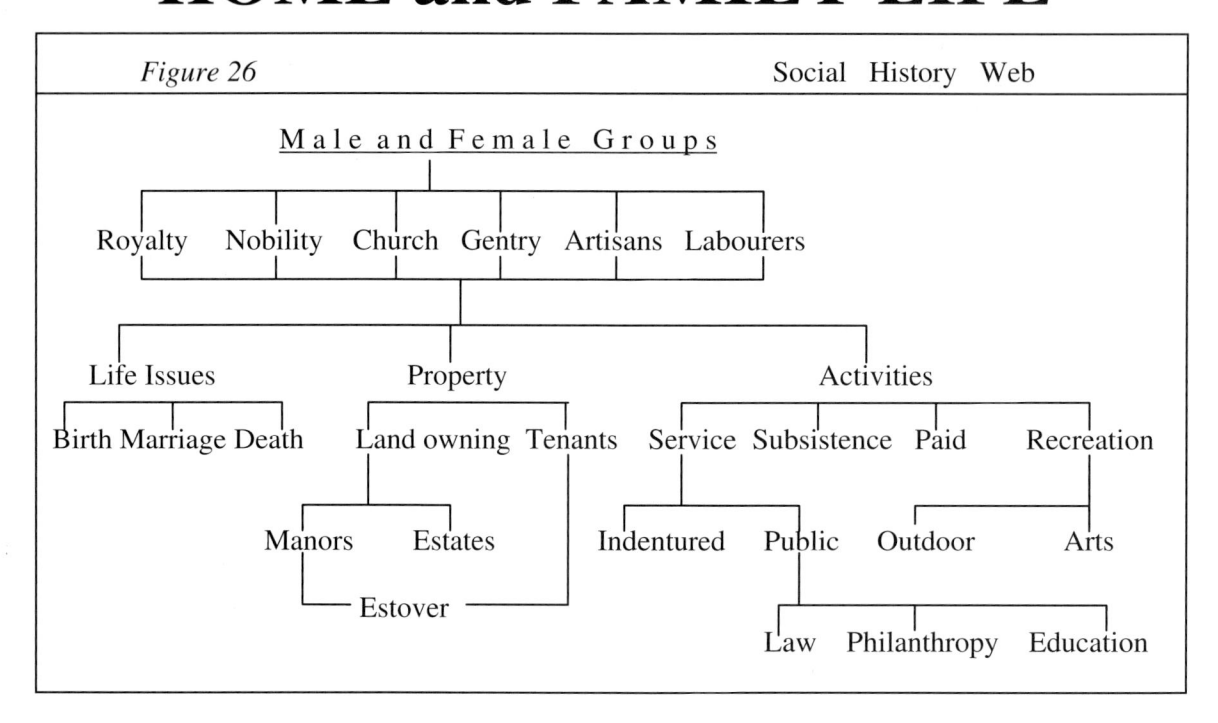

Figure 26   Social History Web

Male and Female Groups
- Royalty, Nobility, Church, Gentry, Artisans, Labourers
  - Life Issues: Birth, Marriage, Death
  - Property: Land owning (Manors, Estates, Estover), Tenants
  - Activities: Service (Indentured, Public [Law, Philanthropy, Education]), Subsistence, Paid (Outdoor), Recreation (Arts)

Burials: *'Barrows'*: <u>Kite</u> shaped Gateham *1156*, Gratton *1357*, <u>Long</u> (Neolithic [4000-2400BC) Specifically identified at Ordnance Survey Grid reference *0980* and Five Wells *1271*. Oval: Ecton *0957*, Narrowdale Hill *1257*, <u>Rectangular</u>: Lady *1449*, <u>Round</u> Bronze Age Beechenhill *1252*, Burton Moor *2067*, Chelmorton Lows *1069*, Cop Low *1780*, Dun *1149*, End Low *1560*, Gautries Hill *0980*, Gib Hill *1563*, Hay Cop *1773*, Grind *2067*, Hob Hurst *2969*, Ilam Tops *1352*, Liffs Low *1557*, Long Low, Lord's Seat *1183*, Minninglow Hill *2156*, Musden *1250*, Pea *1356*, Stanton Moor (Andle, Cork, Gorse, Heart Stones) *2463*, Stanshope *1354*, Tides *1578*, Wardlow *1874*, Wetton Low *1154*. **Grounds**: Baslow *2572*, Litton *1675*. Steep 'Low' *1256*, Tideswell *1575* [early death apprentices from Litton Mill *1573*, Warslow *9838* 'Barrows','Cairns', 'Lows', 'Tumuli'. *Figure 26*, Tumuli on Named Lows refers.

Child abuse: 'Litton Mill' *1675*.

Child care: *Barbara Wells (nee Marshal)*.

Commemoration: Bagshaw(e) Cavern *1680*, Butterton *0756* Plaque to *Rowland Cantrill, William Hambleton and Joseph Wood* who died attempting to rescue *Joseph Shenton* from disused mine shaft [1842]. Crossley's Plantation *1204*. Doctor's Gate *John Talbot 0992*. Eyam. *2176 Harry Bagshaw*, Derbyshire cricketer born Foolow *1976* [1859] died [1927]. Fox's Piece *1692*, Fox Stone *Tom Morton, Brian Toase 0203*. Gardom's (mill owner) Edge *2773*. Hollins Cross *Tom Hyett* of Long Eaton *1384*. *Ken Holloway*, walker [1915-80] Bretton Clough *2078*. Hook's Car *2483*. Johnson's Knoll *1557*. Lost Lad *W H Baxby 1991*, Manners Wood *2368*. Middleton *1963* BJ652 Wellington bomber crew crash [21/01/1944]. Mitchel Field (geologist [1923] Survey) *2481*. Mompesson's Well *2277*. Orme's (geologist) Moor *0201*. Parsons/Fox Tor *Rev R Lomas* of Monyash fatal accident [11/10/1776] *1765*. Queen Mary's Bower *2570*. Riley Graves, Eyam *2276*. Thomason's Hollow *0992*. Twelve Apostles *1451*. Ward's Piece *1585*. William Hill [1687] *2178* after *Sir William Hill*, 2nd 'Marquis' of Halifax. Wood's Cabin *0592*. 'Church History', 'Military History'.

Cremation: Brown Edge *2879*, 'Doll Tor' *2463*, Ecton 'Low' *0957*, Stanton Moor *2463*.

Creative arts: *Carvings* Derwent <u>Chapel</u> *2383* eagles, fish, harps, seal, turtle [1584]; '<u>Fonts</u>' [13th century] Bakewell *2168*, Winster *2460*, <u>Sedilia</u> tracery Monyash *1566*, Tideswell *1575*, <u>Sepulchral slabs</u> Bakewell *2168*, Chelmorton *1169*, <u>Stone crosses</u> Bakewell [Saxon] *2168*, Eyam *2176*, Hope *1783*, Taddington *1471* '<u>Typanum</u>' Parwich *1854*. **Materials** <u>Glue</u> from hooves, <u>Leather</u> from hides: covering wood before painting triptychs, <u>Linen</u>: Glued over cracks and irregularities in wooden sculptures, Flax Dale *1863*, Gradbach *9966*, Upper Hulme *0161*. <u>Metals</u>: 'Brass', 'Bronze', Iron, 'Latten', Lead 'pewter' *Farrar* '<u>Ochres</u>' pigments and dyes: blue – copper compounds, 'Pyrite', gold – 'Arsenopyrite', green –

'Buckthorn', red – 'Haematite', yellow – 'Limonite' Eyam *2176*, Iron Pits *0652*, Winster *2460*, vermilion – 'cinnabar', white – 'Barytes', 'Umber'. Plants pigments and dyes, green –'buckthorn', Porcelain: 'Chert' Great Longstone *2071*. Stone: Blue John, 'Marbles', 'millstone grit', Wood: 'Oak' Derwent Hall *2383* carvings. **Paintings** Haddon Hall chapel walls *2366*. **Personnel** Brian Asquith [23/02/1930-16/03/2008] sculptor and designer resident of Youlgreave [1963-] *Jane Goodwin* painter Alstonefield *1355*. **Preparation** of surfaces: 'Gesso' – limestone. 'Literary connections'. **Products**: Ink stands, memorials, obelisks, pictures, statues, tables, vases. **Sculpture** Brian Asquith Mill Brook *1889*; **'Well dressing'**: Ashford in the Water *1969*, Bakewell *2168*, Bamford *2083*, Bradwell *1781*, Cressbrook *1773*, Eyam *2176*, Foolow *1976*, Great Hucklow *1777*, Grindon *0854*, Hartington *1360*, Hathersage *2380*, Hope *1783*, Little Longstone *1871*, Litton *1675*, Longnor *0864*, Middleton by Youlgreave *1963*, Monyash *1566*, Peak Forest *1179*, Pilsley *2471*, Rowsley *2566*, Stoney Middleton *2275*, Taddington *1471*, Tideswell *1575*, Tintwistle *0297*, 'Tissington' resumed by *Mary Twigg* after [1615] drought *1752*, Wardlow *1874*, Wormhill *1274*, Youlgreave *2064*. *Figure 7*, Church Graphics refers.

Crimes: *Abduction*: Pott Shrigley *9479*. **Bigamy**: *Meverell*. **Body snatching**: look-out on High Bradfield Church *2792*. **Breach of promise** To marry [1690s] *Joseph Hunt*, rector of Eyam *2176* sued by Derby ex-fiancee when he married so he lived in the church vestry. **'Felon', Kidnapping**: *Rowland*, **Murder**: Cutthroat Bridge *2187*, Henry and Clara Winnats [1758] *1382*, 'Performing Arts: Ballads', Macclesfield Forest *9671*→ Pott Shrigley *9479*, *John Gould*, **Poaching**: Ford *0653* keeping sheep worrying dogs [1758], Longnor about [1087] *0864*, Overton Hall *0078*, *Savage*, **Regicide**: *John Bradbury*, **Robbery**: 'Pym Chair' Highwaymen's look-out *0986*, *9976*, **'Sake** and **soke'**: (Ine's Law) *Allen, Beorn, Boden, Cokayne, Dering, FitzWaltheof, Freeman, Gould, Meverell, Rowland, Savage, Thornhill, Uchtred, Wensley*. **Theft** Stained glass [1828] Haddon Hall Chapel *2366*, **Treachery**: Sir Richard Vernon 'Law'.

Deserted villages: *2061, 2065* Lawrence Field *2579*, Lea Hall [16th century] land converted from arable to sheep pasture *1951*, Settlements *1273, 1771*.

Education: *Schools* Boarding [1560] *Henry Cavendish* [1550-1616] at Eton 'Tutors'; Dame Hartington [19th century] *1360*, Parwich [1861] *1854*, Tissington [1837] *1752*, Elementary Bakewell *Mary Hague's* will [1715] *2168*, Bamford* *2083*, Baslow [1777] share of *Humphrey Chapman's* legacy rent on Hartington land *1360*, Ford School [1797] *2572*, Birchinlee *1691*, Brand Top [1776] built by *Thomas Taylor 1360*, Bradwell *1781*. Castleton *Edward Bennett's* will [1720] *1583*, Derwent * *2383*, Edale* *1285*; bequests and gifts [1722] *John Ashton*, [1768] *Joseph Tyon*, Elton [1862] *2260*, Eyam *Thomas Middleton* [1745] *2176* + *Honorable Rev Edward Finch*, former rector + voluntary refurbishing contributions [1826], [1784] *Joseph Champion* Flash [1760] *0267*. Great Longstone [1787] + Inclosure Commissioners allocation of building land, *2071*, Hartington *Thomas Taylor*, builder, + *Abraham Naden* [1807] *1360*, Hathersage *Moores* family owners of cotton mill *2381*, Hollinsclough Frank Weldon [19th century] *0666*, Hope [1655] *Thomas Stevenson 1783*. Lower Bradfield [1706] *Thomas Marriott 2692*, Monyash [1749] *Edward Cheney* gave land *1566*, Priestcliffe *1371* with Taddington *1471 Revd Roger Wilkson* of Wormhill *1274*, bequest of Biggin lands *1559*. Stanton in the Peak [1871] *2462*, Stoney Middleton* *2275*, Taddington, White's School *1471*, *Michael White* bequest [1798], Tissington [1837] *1752*, Winster *2460*, *Thomas Eyre* bequest, Youlgreave [1752] *2164*. Fieldwork Losehill Hall [1972] *1583*, Grammar Ashford in the Water *1969* Sir John Coke gave Tharnley Croft for a school building [1631] also *William Harris* [1680], Bakewell *Lady Manners* [1636] *2168*, Fernilee *0178*, estates of *Thomas Ouff* in Kettelshulme *9879*, bequest to pay school master, Tideswell [1558-1927] *1575*, Warslow [1640] *0858*, Wetton *1055*. Hall: Errwood (30 pupils) *0074*, Methodist Sunday Schools: Alstonefield [1851] *1355*, Bradwell [1844] *1781*, Flash [1814] *0267*, Hartington [1851] *1360*, Hazelbarrow [1818] *0163*, Hollinsclough joined to the church [1840] *0666*, Rewlach [1920s] *0961*, Wetton [1851] *1055*. Sunday Schools taught secular and Christian subjects. Outdoor pursuits White Hall [1950] *0376*. Roman Catholic: Derwent Hall combined with chapel [1883] *2383*, Hathersage [1825] *2380*. 'Poverty and Philanthropy'. **Tutors** [1567] for *Henry Cavendish* [1550-1616] 'boarding schools'; *Thomas Hobbes*, political philosopher [1588-1679] at Chatsworth for *William Cavendish*, 2nd 'Earl' of Devonshire [1590-1628] and then his son *William Cavendish* 3rd 'Earl' [1617-84]. * [1720] Share of legacy from *Robert Turie*, curate of Eccleshall *3282*. *Figure 29* Schools and Colleges refers.

Evacuation: *Mompesson*.

Family and place name links: Abney *1979* - *Abba*, Alsop en le Dale *1655* – *Aelle*, Alstonefield *1355* - *Aelfstan*, Bakewell *2168* - *Baedace*, Baley *1454* – *Balle*, Bartomley – *Beorhtwynn 9665*, Baslow *2372* – *Bassa*, Beeley *2667* - *Beage*, Bostern *1553* – *Bota*, Brushfield *1672* – *Beohtric*, Castern *1252* – *Catt*,

Chatsworth *2670 – Chetal*, Chunal *0391 – Ceola*, Didsbury *0498 – Dydda*, Dunsa *2470 – Dynne*, Ecton *0958 – Ecca*, Edensor *2468 – Eden*, Elkstone *0559 – Eanlac*, Emin *2493 – Eama*, Fynney *1871 – De Finnes*, Gamball *0367 – Gamall*, Gautries Hill *0980 – Goutri*, Hassop *2272 – Haett*, Hinkley Wood *1250 – Hynca*, Hucklow *1777 - Hucca*, Ible *2457 – Ibba*, Kettelshume *9879 – Ketil*, Macclesfield Forest *9671 – Macca*, Offerton *2181 – Offere*, Padley *2579 – Padda*, Parwich *1854 –* possibly *Pever*, Pilsbury *1163 – Pil*, Pilsley *2471 – Pil*, Pittle Mere *1378 – Pyttel*, Pott Shrigley *9379 – Pott*, Rowsley *2566 – Hrowulf*, Snitterton *2760 – Snytra*, Sugworth *2389 – Sucga*, Taddington *1471 – Tada*, Taxal *0079 – Tatuc*, Tideswell *1575 – Tidi*, Tissington *1752 – Tidsige*, Toothill *2482 – Tota*, Ughill *2389* & *2590 – Ugga*, Warslow *9858 – Waer*, Wensley *2661 – Wendel*, Wincle *9665 – Wineca*, Winster *2460 – Wine*, Wormhill *1274 – Wyrma*. 'Grimston hybrids'.

Family size: Bradfield Dale Dike *2692* flood [1864] killed family of ten, *Beresford, Blackwall, Eyre, Gilbert, Hancock, Marshall.* 'Bounty', 'Memorials'.

Feminism: *Heiresses and property* Abney *1979*, Ashford in the Water *1969*, Bakewell *2168*, Baslow *2572*, Beeley *2667*, Birchover *2462*, Bubnell *2472*, Edensor *2468*, Elton *2260*, Eyam *2176*, Gratton *1960*, Grindlow *1877*, Hartle *2764*, Hassop *2272*, Hathersage *2380*, Hazelbadge *1780*, Highlow *2180*, Little Longstone *1871*, Lyme *9682, Middleton 1963*, Monyash *1566*, Nether Haddon *2266*, One Ash *1665*, Over Haddon *2066*, Padley *2579*, Rowland *2172*, Snitterton *2760*, Stanton *2563*, Stoke *2376*, Tideswell *1575*, Winster *2460*, Wormhill *1274*, Youlgreave *2064.k* 'Inheritance'. **Opponents** of 'free' mining in Hazelbadge *1780 Anne Daniel* and *Mary Bradwell* [1630]. 'Literary connections'.

Feuding families: *Sir Nicholas Longford + William Vernon* versus *Walter Blount + Shirleys* (their relations) [1454] regarding land ownership. *Vernons* versus *Gresleys* [1461].

Film and TV Locations: Calver Mill *1274 - **Colditz**;* Haddon Hall *2366 - **Chronicles of Narnia, Elizabeth, Inspector Linley Mysteries, Jane Eyre, Lady Jane Grey, Moll of Flanders, The Prince and the Pauper, The Princess Bride,*** Lyme Park *9682* = Pemberley home of D'Arcy in BBC's ***Pride and Prejudice***; Macclesfield Forest Chapel *9671 - **Jewel in the Crown***; Raper Lodge *2165 - **The Virgin and the Gypsy***; Thor's Cave *0954 - **The Lair of the White Worm*** directed by *Ken Russell* [1927 -] based on a story by *Bram Stoker* [1847-1912] and set in Derbyshire; Shutlingsloe *9769 - **One Man and His Dog**.* **TV Mast:** Holme Moss [1951] *0904*.

Halls and houses: *Uncertain date*: Berristall *9478*, Dam *1179*, Gig *9564*, Hargate *1175*, Hurdlow *1166*, Lomberdale *1963*, Middleton *1963*, Moorseats *2288*, Pott *9479*, Priestcliffe *1372*, Rudyard *9659*, Stanshope *1354*, Swythamley *9764*, Thornbridge *1971*, Warslow *0959*. **Saxon**: Possibly Beresford (demolished [1858]) See also 16th century *1259*. **12th** century: Haddon *2366*, Peak /Peveril *1583*. **13th** century: Hartle *2764*, See also 18th century. **14th** century: Hartington *1360*. **15th** century: Blore (demolished) *1349*, North 'Lees' *2383*. **16th** century: Alsop en le Dale *1655*, Alstonefield *1355*, Ashford Rookery *1969*, Aston *1884*, Beresford *1259*, Chatsworth (demolished) *2670*, Flagg *1368*, Fynney *1871*, Hazlebadge *1780*, Highlow *2180*, Lyme *9682*, Monks *2163*, North Lees lease owned by non resident *Jessops* [16th century] *2383*, Offerton *2181*, Ollerset *0285*, Padley *2563*, Snitterton *2760*, Stanton in the Peak *2464*, Stoney Middleton *2375*, Throwley *1052*. **17th** century: Bagshaw *2168*, Beeley *2667*, Bradshaw *2176*, Broomhead *2496* (rebuilt [1831], Bubnell *2472*,Chatsworth *2670*, Derwent *2383*, Elton [1668] *2260*, Eyam *2176*, Fenny Bentley *1750*, Foolow *1876*, Ford *0882*,Gradbach *9966*, Hazelford *2379*, Hassop *2272*, Holme *2169*, Leam *2379*, Long Lee *0188*, Overton *0078*, Stanshope *1354*, Stanton in the Peak *2564*, Wheston *1376*, Winster *2460*, Wormhill *1274*, Youlgreave *2064*. **18th** century: Biggin *1559*, Castern *1252*, Hartle *2764*, Longstone [1747] *1972*, Overton *0078*, Parwich *1854*, Salterford *9876* Slack *0781*, Stoke *2376*, Sugworth (*Hurt* family) *2389*, Tissington *1752*, Wheston *1376*. **19th** century: Broomhead [1831] *2496*, Crag *9968*, Cressbrook [1835] *1773*,Er(r)wood [submerged 1839] *0074*, Ilam *1350*, Losehill (Study Centre) *1583*, Park *0388*, Shrigley [1824] *9479*, Warslow *0959*. NB Mock Beggars' is a rock mass with two projections resembling chimneys *2262*.

Homelessness: 20,000 after Bradfield Dale Dike *2692* flood [1864].

Hunting and shooting: *Accidental* death by shooting [13/12/1827] *Revd Bache Thornhill*, perpetual curate of Ashford in the Water *1969*, Longstone *1971* and Winster *2460*, 'Literary Connections'. **Ballads** The Driving of the Deer [William Peverell Hunt], Squire [George] Vernon's Fox-Chace. **Birds**: Red grouse *lagopus scoticus*, Broomhead *2295* and Longshaw *2679* Moors [mid 19th century] Partridge *perdix perdix*, Pheasant *phasiananus colchius*, snipe *gallinago gallinago*, wild duck *anas platyrhynchos*, woodcock *scolopax rustica*. **Books**: 'Hunting' [1591] by *Thomas Cokayne*. **Mammals**: *Deer *cervidae*

Place names beginning 'Hart', Hares *lepus timidus* Flagg *1368*, Dialect: '*bawd*', Rabbits *oryctakagus cuniculus*, *Wild boar *sus scrofa* Wildboarclough *9868*, Dialect: *grin* = a snare Grinan Stones *1396* 'Law' Gamekeeper's lodges [1850s] Fawfieldhead *0763*, Longnor *0864*, 'Squire' *Bagshaw, Hunter, Manners, Strelley, Dukes of Rutland*. **Sites, Cabins and Lodges**: Bleaklow *0896*, Chatsworth Tower [1527] *2570*, Dunford Bridge *1502*, Hallam Moors *2684*, Harrop Wood *9678*, Hazlebadge *1780*, Kinder *0883*, Longshaw [1827] *2581*, Longstone Hall for *Henry VIII 1871* Lyme Cage [1520] *9682*, North Longendale *0498*, Macclesfield Forest *9671*, Peak Forest *1179, 2188*, Shooter's 'Clough' *0175*, Shooters 'Nab' *0610*, Snipe *9662*, Stanton Woodhouse *2564, 1186, 1187*, Swythamley Medieval. **Lodge** *9764*, Warslow *0858*, Woodcock farm *0594, 0491, 0602, 0990, 1187, 1189, 1191, 2088, 2285*. 'Assarts', 'Forests', 'Overton Hall *0078*', 'Warren'. *Figure 19*. The Natural World Network refers. * Hunted for eating.

'Knights': Men returned to Parliament [1294-1831]. NB First Reform Bill [1832]. *Adderley, Blackwell, Blount, Bradshawe, Cavendish, Chaworth, Cokayne, Foljambe, Gilbert, Kniveton, Leche, Longford, Manners, Padley.*

Law: *Accusation* against *Robert Legh* (Lyme Hall *9682*) for assault, forced entry and theft when pursuing *John Cade's* rebels from Blackheath [1450]. *Complaint* by the Earl of Rutland to the House of Commons that miners invaded his estates [1649]. *Courts*: 'Barmote', Monyash *1467*, 'Baron' [13th century] free tenants who decided the fate of other free tenants. Chancery Highlow *2180*, Tideswell *1575 Birch*, [1578] Calver 'manor' *2374* lord v lead miners re free mining in the King's Field. Duchy of Lancaster ruled in favour of Leicester Abbey in cattle grazing dispute with Over Haddon *2066* inhabitants; free mining rights guaranteed at Great Hucklow *1777*, Little Hucklow *1678*, Winster *2460*, Youlgreave *2064* [1619-32] Ore sales in Snitterton *2760* and Wensley *2661* areas [1528]; Ecclesiastical/consistory (Lichfield Diocese), Canon *John Manners*. 'Forest'. 1. Attachment met every 40 days without power to convict. 2. Regard without power to convict. 3. Swainmote, the effective court of the forest, its name is connected with pig feeding. 4. Justice Seat met every 3 years ie 4 forest courts. Exchequer *Raphe Oldfield's* lead tithe dispute [1615, 1625, 1632]. Hall Moot OE: *heal gemot* ('Baron', Folk, 'Hundred', 'Manor', 'Shire'), 'Court leet' 'Frankpledge', 'Honour' *Peverill*, Sat at least once a month. Alstonefield *1355*, Hayesgate *0959*, Longnor *0864*, *Shirley*, Warslow *0858*, [theft of fern in Bubnell Dale *2472* resolved at Baslow Manor court *Katherine Eyre* 4d (2p) [1504]. King's Bench Earl of Rutland prosecuted *William Heaward* for riot and trespass at Nether Haddon *2266* [1648]; Star Chamber Disputes [1613] about free mining and enclosures *Raphe Oldfield* at Litton *1675* and Tideswell *1575* ' Sake and Soke', 'Team' **Costs** Wormhill *1274*. *Custody*: Dungeon: High Bradfield Church *2692*, Lock up. Curbar *2574*, One Ash 'grange' *1665*, Longnor [18th] and [19th] centuries *0864*, Lyme Cage *9682* overnight en route to Chester assizes, **Order** obtained by the Earl of Rutland from the House of Lords preventing miners entering Nether Haddon *2266* [1648]. *Personnel*: Constable – Alstonefield [1377] *1355*, Youlgreave *2164*, Bailiff of Forest *Thomas Foljambe* 'Justices in Eyre', Justices of the Forest, 'Justices of the Peace', Landlords, 'Peelers', 'Sheriffs', 'Squires', Wardens, 'Verdurers' Lord Chief Justice of England *Thomas Denman* of Stoney Middleton *2275*. *Punishments*: 'Gin', 'Borh', 'Bot' Burning village for poaching Longnor about [1087] *0864*, Fines: Tideswell Ringers' Rhyme, 'Recusancy' *Fitzherberts* [16th century] Negligent churchgoing [1630]. (Letter from *John Manners* to *Francis Bradshaw*, High Sheriff). Gallows, Gawtree Thorn, Castleton *1583*, Peter's Stone *1775* [01/01/1815] 211 year old *Anthony Lingard* of Tideswell for murder hung in chains Gibbeting; 'Steep Low' *1256*, Forbidden by the *Duke of Devonshire* after hearing the screams of a vagabond who murdered a kitchen maid when stealing food [18th century] *2870*, Overton Hall *Downes 0078*, Taxal *0079*, *Gould*; Maiming, Destruction in the forest of boars, deer and wolves. *William I* [?1027-87] loss of eyesight; *William Rufus* [?1056-1100] death, *Henry II* [1133-89] loss of a limb *Richard I, the Lion Heart* [1157-99] torture. Outlawing Salters' Brook Inn *1300*, Three Shires Head *0068*, Stocks Eyam *2176*, Longnor [17th century] *0864*, Tideswell *1575* (Ringers' Rhyme) Warslow *0858*, Wormhill *1274*, Youlgreave – renewed [1707] & [1780] *2064*, 'wergild'. Whipping *David Wright* a man paid by the Youlgreave [1713] constable *2164*. *Rights* 'Sake and soke', 'Toll', Team', 'Infangenetheof'. 'Forests and Forestry'. *Ford*.

Life expectancy: Cressbrook Mill *1773*, Hartington *1360*, Longnor *0864*, Taddington *1471*, *Badaly, Bagshawe, Goodwin, Fidler, Foljambe, Leake, Marshall, Mellor, Newton, Sutton.*

Lighting *Candles*: Beeswax Expensive and clean Curbar *2574* Tallow from slaughtered animals. Monyash Factory *1467*, 'Alum', 'Granges', 'Names' Wicks Cotton 'mills'. 'Flax'. 'Elaterite'. *Electricity*: Alstonefield [1939] *1355*, Hollinsclough [1960] *0666*, Lamb Hole Mill (water wheel generated) *9880*, Longnor [1940] *0864*. Wind turbines Royd *0909*. *Gas* produced on the premises replacing oil. Lamb Hole Mill *9880*. *Oil* Lamb Hole Mill *9880*. **Rush lights**: Rush pith dipped in tallow. Rushley *1251*.

Literary connections: *Arabic literature*: *John Greaves of Beeley 2667*. *Fiction and plays*: *Jane Austen* Pride and Prejudice [1813] Bakewell *2168* = Lambton; *Charlotte Bronte* Jane Eyre [1847] possibly North Lees *2383*, *Ellen Nussey*, Hathersage *2380* = Morton; '*Baron*' *Edward George Earle Lytton Bulwer-Lytton* [1803-1873] Paul Clifford, 6th Duke of Devonshire [1790-1858] = Bachelor Bill; *William Congreve* [1670-1729] Old Batchelor play [1692], Ilam *1350*; *Georgina Duchess of Devonshire* married 5th Duke [1 June 1774] The Sylph, *Berlie Doherty* White Peak Farm [1994], Dark Secret [2004], Ladybower Reservoir *1886*; *George Eliot* [1819-80] Adam Bede [1859], Dovedale *1451* = Eagledale; *Richard Greaves* Spiritual Quixote, Tissington *1752* references, *William Horwood* Duncton novels, Willows in Winter [1993] based around Ilam *1351*, *Lady Caroline Lamb* [1785-1828] Glenarvon [1816], Duke of Altamonte = 6th Duke of Devonshire [1790-1858]; *D H Lawrence* [1885-1930] Wintry Peacock – Mrs Goyte, Griffe Grange *2456*, Ible *2457*, Via Gelia *2556*; *W Massie* Sydenham or Memoirs of a Man of the World [1830], 5th Duke of Devonshire [1748 - 1811] = Duke of Claverdon; *Nancy Mitford* [1904-73], sister of *Deborah* who married the 11th Duke in 1941, The Pursuit of Love [1945], Linda Radlett = Duchess of Devonshire, Love in a Cold Climate [1949], Linda Radlett = Duchess of Devonshire, Don't Tell Alfred [1960], Northey Mackintosh = Duchess of Devonshire; *Lawrence Du Garde Peach* [born 1890] Wind o' the Moors *Sir Walter Scott* [1771-1832] Peveril of the Peak [1823], Haddon Hall *2366* = Martindale Castle; *Anthony Trollope* [1815-82] Phineas Finn [1869], Lord Chiltern = 8th Duke of Devonshire [1833-1908], *Mrs Humphry Ward* [1851-1920] The History of David Grieve [1892], Needham = surname of a person living at Snitterton [1541] *2760*. *Journals*: '*William Bradbury*', *Gage Earle Freeman*, curate of Forest Chapel *9771*, wrote falconry column for The Field based on Staffordshire Peak moors. *Non fiction*: H H Arnold-Bemrose [1875-1939] Geology Arbor Low [1904]*1663*, Tideswell *1575*, 'Toadstones' [1907] *William Bagshaw* [1628-1702] Sermons, *E A Baker* Moors, Crags and Caves of the High Peak [1904], *Thomas Bateman* Vestiges of the Antiquities of Derbyshire [1850], *Thomas Becon*, religious refugee at Alsop en le Dale [1542] Jewel of Joy Religious Dialogue, *Walter Blith* The Merits of Pig Keeping [1652], *William Cambden* [1551-1623] Britannia [1586], *George Cavendish* Life of Wolsey, *Thomas Cockayne* A Short Treatise on Hunting [1591] Harthill *2262*; *Charles Cotton* [1630-87] Compleat Gamester [1674], Fruit tree Planters' Manual [1675], Wonders of the Peak [1683], *Revd Peter Cunningham*, vicar of Chertsey, Sermon preached at Eyam [23/04/1789] Thanksgiving for recovery of George III, *Georgina* Duchess of Devonshire Passage of the Saint Gothard [1816], *Francis Eyre* [1732-1804] A Short Essay on the Christian Religion [1795]; *Judge FitzHerbert* Natura Brevium [1458], *Amanda Foreman* Georgina Duchess of Devonshire [2008], *Llewellyn Frederick William Jewitt* Beauties of the Peak [1828], Ballads and Songs of Derbyshire [1867]. Mitchel [1923] Geological Survey *Mitchel Field 2481*, *Lawrence Du Garde Peach* Great Hucklow Village Players [1927-52], *Ebenezer Rhodes* [1762-1839] See Further Information, Cucklet *2176*, Ilam *1351*, *John Ruskin* [1819-1900] Fors Clavigera (opposition to Millers Dale railway 1573), *Thompson, Francis* History of Chatsworth [1949], *Francis Cornish Warre* born Bakewell [1839-1916] Jane Austen [1913]. 'Robin Hood'. **Poetry** *Anonymous* [1360] Middle English epic poem Sir Gawain and the Green Knight, Dove Valley *1132*, Swythamley = ?Castle of Hautdesert *9764*, Lud's "Church" = ? Green Chapel *9865*, The Roaches = ?'knorned stones' *0063*; *W H Auden* [1907-73] In praise of limestone (Castleton); *Rev W R Bell*, curate of Bakewell *2168*, The Parson's Tor [1864] – discovery of *Rev Robert Thomas* of Monyash' death [12/10/1776], *William Blake* Jerusalem [1807] Dovedale *1452*, Mam Tor *1283*, *John Brimlow* of Winster *2460*, Rev Bache Thornhill 'Hunting and Shooting', *Sir Aston Cockayne* A Journey into the Peak, Ebbing and Flowing Well *0879*. Milward Sonnets, [1658] Snitterton *2760*; *Eliza Cook* [1812-99] Monsal *1871*, Derbyshire Dales, *Charles Cotton* The Confinement [1679], A Journey in the Peak [1715], *Georgina Duchess of Devonshire* The Duchess of Devonshire's Cow, *Michael Drayton* Poly-olbion [1612] Dove and Manifold *1361*; *John Furness* Edale *1285* Rag Bag, *Rev Arthur George Jewitt* [1794-1828] Rhapsody On the Peak of Derbyshire, *William Newton* [1750-1830] Cockey Farm *1979*, Cressbrook Mill *1772*, *Ebenezer Rhodes* Cucklet *2176* Anna *Seward* born Eyam *2176* [1747-1809] The Swan of Lichfield, *William Wordsworth* [1770-1850] Chatsworth [1830] *2670*. **Short story**: Charles Edward Montague [1867-1928] Assistant Editor Manchester Guardian In Hanging Garden Galley (Water cum Jolly *1772*). **Translations**: *Charles Balguy* born Derwent Hall *2383* [1708] Boccaccio - The Decameron, Dante - Inferno; *Charles Cotton* French P Corneille [1606-84] Horace; G Du Vair [1555-1621] Bishop of Lisieux; G Girard died [1663] - The History of the Life of the Duke of Epernon [1554-1642], B de Lasseran-Massencome - The Commentaries of Marechal Blaise de Montluc [1502-77]; Lucian, M de Montaigne [1533-92] published

[1670]; L de Pontis [1583-1670] - Memoirs of the Sieur de Pontis; Tunis The Fair One of Tunis; Latin P Virgilius Maro (Virgil) - Aeneid, *Thomas Eyre* Gobinet died [1833] – Christian Piety. **Libraries** 1,000 volumes St Edmund's, Castleton *1583* founded by vicar *Rev Frederick Farrar* died [1817]; Chatsworth *2670* 45,000 books.

'Manors': ***Bought and sold***: Abney *1979*, Ashford in the Water *1969*, Bakewell *2168*, Beeley *2667*, Birchover *2462*, Brushfield *1672*, Calver *2374*, Chatsworth *2670*, Eyam *2176*, Gratton *1960*, Hartle *2764*, Hassop *2272*, Hathersage *2380*, Hazelbadge *1780*, Highlow *2180*, Hollinsclough *0666*, Little Longstone *1871*, Litton *1675*, Longendale *0297*, Middleton *1963*, Monyash *1566*, Narrowdale *1257*, One Ash *1665*, Padley *2579*, Parwich *1854*, Stanshope *1354*, Stanton *2563*, Snitterton *2760*, Stoke *2376*, Thornhill *1983*, Thorpe *1550*, Tideswell *1575*, Winster *2460*, Wormhill *1274*, Youlgreave *2064*. ***Compulsory sale***: Blackwell *1272*, Highlow *2180*, Tideswell *1575*. ***Confiscated***: Baslow *2572*, Castleton *1583*, Longendale *0397*, Sheldon *1768*, Youlgreave *2064 Birch, Bradshawe, Ferrars*. ***Consolidation***: Baslow *2572* + Bubnell *2472* about [1378]; Eyam *2176* + Stoney Middleton *2375* about [1383], Bradwell *1781* + Castleton *1583*, Calver *2374* + Rowland *2172*, Great Rowsley *2566* + Nether Haddon *2266*, 'Moiety' manors consolidated: Hathersage *2380*, Tideswell *1575*. ***Donated***: Ashopton *1986*, Baslow *2572*, Blackwell *1272*, Castleton *1583*, Chelmorton *1169*, Eyam *2176*, Grindlow *1877*, Hope *1783*, Little Longstone *1871*, Longendale *0397*, One Ash *1665*, Tideswell *1575*. *De Novant*. ***Inherited***: Elton *2260*, Rowland *2172*, Stanton *2563*, Thornhill *1983*, ***Leased***: Chelmorton *1169*, Hassop [1478] for 12 years *2272*, Hope *1783*, Swythamley [1534] for 7 years *9764*, Wensley *2661* by *Wensleys* to *Foljambes, Harpurs*. ***Managed by agents***: Tideswell *1575*. ***Non resident owners***: Alstonefield *1355, Lancaster,* Ashford *1969 Edmund Plantagenet* in [1319], *John Neville*, Earl of Westmoreland [1408], Beeley *2667 Gilberts* of Locko *4038* in [1734], Birchover *2462*, Castleton *1583 Warrenne* Earl of Surrey, Edensor *2468*, Elton *2260,* Eyam *2176 Thomas Lord Furnival* [1307], *Thomas Neville*, Earl of Westmoreland [1383], *Richard Boyle*, Earl of Burlington [1700], Gratton *1960*, Hartle *2764*, Little Longstone *1871*, Monyash *1566 Talbots* Earls of Shrewsbury [1460], ⅓rd moieties [1616] *Herbert* Earl of Pembroke *and* Montgomery, *De Eston,* [1638] *Earls of Arundel, Kent, Pembroke*, Oneceote *0455*, Over Haddon 'mesne' *2066 Cokes* of Trusley *2535*, Snitterton *2760 Shirley, Turner* of Derby, Stanton *2563*, Stoke *2376 Bridgemans* Earls of Bradford, Tideswell *1575 Curzons* Earls of Scarsdale, *Thomas Armiger* of Lameley, *Thomas* Lord *Cromwell* of Ardglass (County Down, Ireland) [1625-49]. Tissington *1752*, Winster *2460*, Wormhill *1274*, Youlgreave *Henry De Ferrars* [1087], *Shirley* [1272-1307]. ***Owned by Religious houses***: Blackwell *1272*, Priory of Lenton *5539* ('Cluniac') [1100-35], Brushfield *1672*, Abbey of Rufford *6464*, Conkesbury *2065* Leicester Abbey ('Augustinian') [1189-1199], Grindlow *1877* Monastery of Lilleshall *7315* ('Augustinian') [1199], Mixon *0457*, Musden *1259* both Abbey of Burton upon Trent ('Benedictine'). ***Sub divided*** into moieties and smaller lots Bamford *2083*, Beeley *2667*, Edensor *2468*, Hathersage *2380*, Monyash *1566*, Snitterton *2760*. ***Temporary possession***: Padley *2579*, Winster *2460*. 'Heiresses and property' and 'Royal involvement'. *Figure 28,* Manors refers.

Marriage: ***Arranged***: *Eyre, Foljambe, Plumpton*. ***Divorce*** *Manners.* ***Elopement*** *Anne Morton.* ***Forbidden***: *Garlick, Morton, Stanshope, Wells*. ***Forced*** [1690] *Joseph Hunt*, rector of Eyam *2176* compelled by bishop following a drunken mock ceremony. ***Foreign***: *Gisborne*. ***Parental consent*** Age difference 66 years Sheldon *1768* [1776] for 14 year old boy to 80 year old widow. ***Secret***: Peak Forest *1179*, Pott Shrigley *9479*. ***Re-marriage***: *Balguy, Cavendish, Cromwell, Talbot*. ***Teenage***: *Cavendish, Foljambe*.

Medicines: *Abbreviations of ailments and treatments*
Aa asthma, **Ab** after birth, **Ac** abcess, **Ad** anti depressant, **Ag** aching, **Ah** aphrodisiac, **An** analgesic, **Ap** appetite stimulant, **As** astringent, **At** anti toxin. **Ba** back, **Bal** baldness, **Bl** bladder, **Be** bile, **Bg** bleeding, **Bi** bites, **Bl** blood, **Bn** brain and memory, **Bo** bowels, **Br** bruises, **Bs** blisters, **Bt** breasts, **Bu** Burns. **Ca** catarrh, **Cc** colic, **Ch** chest, **Ci** counter irritant, **Cn** conception, **Co** cough, **Cr** cramp, **Ct** Constipation, **Cv** convulsions. **Dc** diuretic, **De** depression, **Df** deafness, **Dn** discoloration, **Do** dog, **Dr** diarrhoea, **Ds** discharge, **Dt** decongestant, **Dy** dropsy, **Dys** dysentery. **Ea** ear, **El** epilepsy, **Em** emetic, **En** enemas, **Ep** expectorant, **Ex** external, **Ey** eyes and sight. **Fc** flatulence, **Fe** feet, **Fh** freshener, **Fl** fleas and flies, **Fr** fever, **Ga** gangrene, **Gi** giddiness, **Go** gout, **Gr** gripe. **Ha** headache, **Hb** heartburn, **Hd** haemorrhoids, **Hg** haemorrhage, **Hn** hangover, **Hr** hair. **Ic** incontinence, **Id** indigestion, **If** inflammation, **Il** internal, **It** itches, **Ja** jaundice, **Jt** joints. **Ky** kidney. **Le** leprosy, **Li** liniment, **Lr** liver, **Lt** lactation, **Lu** lung, **Lx** laxative. **Mc** miscarriage, **Mn** menstruation, **Mt** mouth, **Mu** muscle. **Na** nausea, **Ns** nose, **Nv** nerves. **Ob** obesity. **Pa** palpitations, **Pe** pestilence, **Pl** plague, **Pr** pain relief, **Ps** paralysis, **Pu** purgative, **Py** pleurisy. **Qu** quinsy. **Re** reaper's wound, **Ru** rupture, **Rw** ring worm. **Sa** sciatica, **Sb** still birth, **Sc** scalds, **Sd** side, **Se**

sedative, Sg shingles, Sh stomach, Si skin Sl sleep, Sn snake, So stones, Sp spleen, Sr sore(s), St spots, Sta stab, Su sunburn, Sw swelling, Sy scurvy. **Ta** toothache, Tb tuberculosis, Th thorns, Tr throat, Tt tartar, Tu tumours. **Ul** ulcers, Ur urine. **Vg** vagina, VD venereal disease, Ve vertigo, Vo vomiting. **Wa** warts, Wd wounds, Wh wheezing, Wi wind, Wm worms, Wr wrinkles, Ww Whitlow, Wy Watery. Mineral: 'Alum' – astringent. *Peak Plants*: prescribed by herbal writers, used medicinally by early settlers and later residents. Plants believed to originate from mainland Europe in **bold**. 'The Natural World: Flora'. **A** Adder's tongue [SrEy VgDs Ul Wd – Br & Bo] *ophiglossum vulgatum*, **agrimony** [Dy FeFh Lr Sp Ur] *bidens tripartita*, 'alder' [Bu If] *alnus glutinosa*, anenome [Ep EyIf Ha If Le Ul], arssmart, hot [Fl] *polygonum hydropiper*, arssmart, mild [EaWm Ta Ul] *polygonum persicara*, 'ash' [Df Ob Pr Sc SnBi] *fraximus excelsior*, asperula/woodruffe [Ap Lr Sp Tb] *gallium odoratum*. **B** barley [Ac Fr] *hordeum vulgare*, '**birch**' [BdSo Ky SrMt] *betula pendula*, **bistort**/Dragon-wort/English serpentary/ osterick/passions/snakeroot [Br IlBg Mc Ul] *polygonum bistorta*, **black horehound** [DoBi Ep Ul Wm] *ballota nigra*, black poplar [El Go] *populus niger*, **borage** [Ad Ap EyIf Fr Lt Sr] *borago officinalis*, 'bracken' [Wd Wm Ul] *pteridinum aquililium*, briar *erica arborea*, **brook lime** [If Sb So Tu] *veronica becca bunga*, '**buckthorn**' [WA Wd] *rhamnus catharticus*, bugle [Bl Ga Hn IlWd Sr StaWd Ul] *ajunga reptans*, **butterbur** [At Fr Mn Pl St Wh Wm] *petasites vulgare*. **C** calamint [Ja Mn Ru] *calamintha ascendens*, **carrot** [Cn Dc Fc Mn Pr So] *daucus carota*, celandine [It Ja Lt ShPr Ul WyEy} *chelidomium majus*, cheese rennet [Bg - Il&Ns Bu Dc Sc] *galium verum*, chervil [Ab Ap Fc ShWi Tb Ul] *myrrhis odorata*, cinquefoil [El Fr Go Ja Pr Sg SoMt] *potentilla reptans*, clary [Ah Bl Ey Id Sh] *salvia verbenaca*, clown's wound wort [MuSw Ru Ul Wd] *stachys palustris*, **colt's foot** [Co Hd] *tussilago farfara*, **cowslip** [Pr Su Wd Wr] *primula veris*, crow's foot [Bs WyEy] *ranunculus auricomus*, cuckoo flower [Ap Dc Id Sh Sy] *caramine pratensis*, cudweed [As – Mn&Mt Br Wm] *gnaphalium ulinosum*. **D** Daisy [Bl Py] *bellis perennis*, **dandelion** [Dc Fr Sr] *taracum officinalis*, dock [Bl Lr Si] *rumex obtusiflorus*, dove's foot [Bl Br IlWd Ky So] *geranium molle*. **E** eglantine [Bi Wm] elder [Bal Dc EyIf Go] *sambucus nigra*, **eyebright** [Bn Ey] *euphrasis officinalis*. **F** figwort [Br Hd Tb Wd] *scrophularia nodosa*, **flax** [Aa Co If Py Tb Tu] *linum usisatissium*, fleabane [Dys Fl] *pulicara dysenterica*, fluellin [NsBg Ul WyEy] *veronica officinalis*, **foxglove** [Sr Wd] *digitalis purpurea*. **G** goat's beard [Ap Hb So] *trapopogon pratensis*, **golden rod** [Dc Mn MtUl VD] *solidago virgaurea*, good king henry/all-good mercury/goosefoot/Margery 1895 [Dc En Sy] *chemipodium bonus henricus*, groundsel [Br Dc Gr If Wm] *senecio vulgaris*. **H** hairy willowherb [Dr IlBg] *epilobium hirsutum*, hawthorn [Br Bt Dr IlPr Lx ShPr So SwEy Th] *crataegus oxycantha*,'hazel' [Co Ct Mn] *corylus avellana*, hemloc [An EySw Of Ul] *conium maculatim*, herb robert [Ky Ul Ur Wd] *geranium robertianum*, herb truelove [CoPr If Sr Ul] *paris quadrifolia*, holly [Cc Il] *ilex aquifolium*, honeysuckle [Co SrTr] *lonicera pericyclmenum*, hops [Dc Lr SiDn Sp] *humuls pupulus*, horsetail [Ab Co Dt Ep Lr Sp SrEy Wm] *equisetum arvense fluviatile*, hound's tongue [Bu Ca DoBi Hg Hr Sc VD] *cynoglossum officinale*. **I** ivy [Bl Bu Dc Mn Pl Sc Ul] *hedera helix*. **K** kidney wort [Go Hd If Sa Sh Wd] *cotyledon umbilicus*, knapweed [Bg – Mt&Ns Wd] *centauria scabiosa*. **L** laurel [Pu VD Wm] *daphne laureola*, lettuce, wild [Ha Id Lt ShPr Sl] *lactuca scariola*, lily of the valley [El EyIf Ps Se] *convallaria majalis*, lily, water [Fr Se SiPr Wd] *nymphaea alba*, 'lime' [El Ps Ve] *tilia vulgaris*, loosetrife [Wd] *lysimachia sylvestris*, **M** maidenhair spleenwort [Aa Dc Ja KySo Py] *asplenium trichomanes*, **mallow** [Ah Co Dc Lx Ta UrPr] *malva sylvestris*, marguerite/ox eye daisy [Br Lr Ul Wd Wy Ey] *chrysanthrmum leucanthemum*, meadowsweet [EyIf Fr Wd] *filipendula ulmaria*, mezereon spurge [Li Ul VD] *daphne mezereum*, mistletoe [El Gi Tu] *viscum album*, moneywort [IlBg Mn Ul Wd] *lysimachia nummularia*, **mugwort** [Ep Wd] *artemesia vulgaris*, mullein [Co Cr Cv Hd Pr – Bo & Ch&Sd Ta Wa] *verbascum thrapsus/densiflorum*. **N** narcissus/wild daffodil [AgJt BtSw Pu Wd] *pseudo narcissus*, '**nettle**' [At Ci Ep Ga It Pr Wm] *urtica dioica*. **O** oats [It PrSd Wi] *avena sativa*, orpine [Br Bu Fl Lr Lu Qu Sc] *sedum telephinum*. **P parsley** [Br Bt Lx ShPr SwEy Ur] *petroselium sativum*, parsnip [BtTu Fr Hd Hg SrEy SrMt] *sium augustifolium*, peppermint [Gr Lt Na] *mentha piperita*, '**pine**' [Ur] *pinus sylvestris*, **plantain** [Ca Dr Ey Go It Ja Ky Lr Pr – Bo&Hd Sg So Ul Wd Wm] *plantago major*, polypody [Pu] *polypodium vulgare*, primrose [Em Nv] *primula vulgaris*, **R ragwort** [Qu Sa Ul] *senecio jacobea*, raspberry [Tt Vo] *rubus idaeus*, rattle grass [Co Ey] *rhianthus minor*, rosebay willow herb [Dr IlHg] *chamaenerion*. **S** sage, wood [Cn Dc Mn Nv VD] *teurerium scordonia*, **sanicle** [BoPr Mn Ul Wd] *sanicula europeae*, **saxifrage** [Dc Fc HaWd Pe Sy] *pimpinella major*, self heal [Sr Ul Wd – Ex & Il] *prunella vulgaris*, shepherd's rod [Ap] *dispacus pilosus*, solomon's seal [Sr Wd] *polyganatum*, sorrel, common [Fr If IlUl Ja Rw] *rumex acetosa*, sorrel, wood [Bl Vo] *oxalis acetosa*, **St John's wort** [BdSo Br Dc De El Fr Ic Ps Vo Wd] *hypericum perforatum*, **strawberry** [Dc If – Bd&Ky Ja Lr Pa SrMt] *fragaria vesca*, 'sycamore' [Wd] *acer pseudoplanatus*. **T** thistle, sow [Df] *sonchus arvensis*. **V violet** [Be El EyIf Pr – Ba & Bd Py Qu Se] *viola odorata*, **W willow** [Bg Dc Hr Mn SiDn Vo] *salix alba*, wintergreen [Hg

Mn Wd – Ex & Il Ul – Bd & Ky] *pyrola minor*, woolly faverel [Sa Ww] *draba incana*. **Y yarrow/ wormwood** [Bg Hd Ul VgDs] *achillea millefolium*, **yew** [Lr] *taxus baccata*. **Mining hazards**: Drowning *John Daniel* and *Robert Berry* in Middleton Dale *1963* [1690], *Frances Gregory* of Eyam *2176* [1698]; Poisoning Dialect: *bellanding*; Psychosis 'mercury' in lead ore. **Pioneer**: in obstretrics *Thomas Denman* born Bakewell [1733] *2168* 'Economic History: Water Engineering – Eyam'.

Names of places and people: Many names had more than one syllable because they had more than one association. For example Ashton was connected with first with ash trees and secondly with a farmstead. *Allegiance personal*: names: *Allyn, Armine, Bateman, Daniel, Gilbert, Olivier, Rowland, Rowlandson, Stevenson. Appearance and characteristics*: personal names: *Basset, Blount, Bouer, Bowles, Brown, Bullock, Bunting, Columbell, Dakeyne, Foljambe, Galliard, Gladwin, Hibberson, Hodgkinson, Hurt, Joliffe, Lamb, Ludlam, McCreagh, Morton, Peverll, Prime, Russell, Savage, Senior, Twigge, Tyrell, Wake, White, Woderofe. British Isles place and identical personal names*: Boyle, Gisborne, Leake, Newdigate, Nussey, Ridel, Shuttleworth, Strelley, Topcliffe, Wentworth, Winnington.

Performing arts: *Harpur*. **Ballads**: Devonshire's Noble Duel [1687], The Ashopton Garland *1986*, The Drunken Butcher of Tideswell *1575*, Little John's End, The Taylor's Ramble (Ashford *1969* and Bakewell *2168*), Henry and Clara – Winnats *1382* Murder [1768] 'Hunting'. **Psalm singers**: Elkstone [1830] *0559*, Warslow [1820] *0858*. **Church organs**: Longnor Methodist [1850] *0865*, Warslow [1860s] *0858*. **Folk Music** Winster *2460*. **Hymn tunes** by *Revd Brian Hoare* [1935-] with Peak names – Chatsworth *2570*, Curbar Edge *2575*, Ridgeway *2384*. **Theatre** Great Hucklow [1921-71] *1778* 'Film and TV'.

Poverty and Philanthropy: *"Adoption"*: *Marshall*, **Begging**: Beggar's Bridge *0965*, Beggar Croft, Eyam *2176*. **Care** of the poor Meadow Place 'Grange' *2065*. **Children**: Education Bakewell, Hague's School *2168 Mary Hague* gave her house, garden and stables for teaching poor children [1715], Castleton *1583 Edward Bennett* made provision for educating the poor to the age of 14 years [1720], Pott Shrigley *9665 John Barlow* £6 for educating 10 poor boys [1684], *Thomas Bateman* Hartington *1360, Edward Downes* £1 [1747]; *William Lunt* £1 for 2 poor children [1688]; *Elizabeth Downes* £20 [1764]; *John & Eleanor Downes* £100; [1764], *Richard Edensor*. Warslow *0858 Thomas Gould* legacy for educating 6 poor children [1734], later *J W Russell* provision for free teaching of poor children [1819].
Complaint: Bradwell *1781* disagreed with Hope *1683* about relative contributions [1683].
Disabled soldiers: [1614] Youlgreave church wardens *2064*.
Donations: for the poor: In kind Beeley *2667, William Savile* [1676] St Mary's Hospital *1583, William Peveral* gave the warden pasture for a mare + foals, 8 oxen, sow + litter [1394]; Ilam *1350 John Port* gave wool to pay for maintenance of poor; Taddington *1471* [1771] *Charles Hayward* 5 shillings (25p) to be distributed as bread every 4th January' Wormhill *1274* [1714] *Roger Wilkson* 12d (5p) worth of white every Sunday to Taddington 'chapelry' poor *1471* provided they attended church. Money Baslow *2572* will of *Humphrey Chapman* a share in the rent from land at Hartington *1360*, Calver *2374*, Hassop *2272*, Longstone *1972* and Rowland *2172* annual Christmas and Easter gifts to each by *Gertrude & Rowland Eyre* 22 shillings (£1.10) Ford *0882, Dales* of Flagg *1368* to Parwich Wensley *2661*.
Hospitals for the infirm poor: Bakewell (*Sir John Manners* [17th century]) *2168*, Peak [1377] *Edward III* endowed a chaplain, £3 per annum + 4 bushels of oatmeal for certain paupers.
Job creation: *Charles Boot*, Sheffield builder, built Sugworth *2389* folly tower [1920s].
Legacy: Alstonefield *1355 German Pole* left £20 [1727]. *Partnership*: *William Newton*.
Poor relief: Accommodation St Mary in the Peak Hospital for the infirm poor [1338-1547] *1683*, Wetton *1055 Elizabeth Mellor* gave a cottage [1770], *Sir George Crewe* made more cottages available [1820], *Robert Pursglove* Almshouses, Tideswell *1575*, Bakewell Almshouses *2168*. Route to chapel *9772* used by alms appplicants. Charity Lane *9672*. 'Chawbacon', 'Hartington', 'Parish'.
Prisoners: King's Bench by Youlgreave church wardens *2064*. 'Workhouse'.

Public officers: 'Dymoke', 'Ealdorman', 'Justices of the Peace', 'Justices in Eyre', 'Knights', 'Lords Lieutenant' (*William Cavendish*), Members of Parliament (*Cavendish family*), Prime Minister: (*William Cavendish*), 'Sheriffs'.

Recreation: *Angling*: Trout (*salmo trutta*) Streams and rivers Bradford *2064*, Dove *1132*, Lathkill *1865*, Manifold *1059*, Wye ([1415-85] cull/bullhead/millers thumb *cottus gobio*,eel *anguilla anguilla*, grayling *thymallus thymallus*, pinks (small salmon), salmon *salmo salar*, [1884] rainbow trout *salmo gairdneri 2267, Bentley Brook 1850* 'full of trout and grayling' according to The Compleat Angler, Millers Dale – trout and grayling *1373, Charles Cotton* Charles Cotton Hotel, Hartington *1360*, Izaak Walton Hotel,

Dove Dale *1451*. River Dove Day tickets 12.5p from the Izaak Walton Hotel [1874]. Reservoirs: Errwood *0175,* Fernilee *0177,* Lamaload *9775,* Clegg 'Beyt'. **Archery:** ME: *butte* = land for archery Crabtree Butt, Derwent *2383,* Flax Butts, Eyam *2176,* Cuckoo Butts, Offerton *2181*. **'*Bog trotting':*** Dark Peak *0802*. **Bowling:** Beresford *1259,* Tidewsell *1575,* Winster green [1653] *2460*. **Bull ring:** Bull Pit *1081,* Foolow *1976,* Snitterton *2760*. **Cock fighting**: Alsop en le Dale churchyward *1655*. **Coursing**: *Clegg*. **Cricket:** Longstone *2071,* Pott Shrigley [1919] *9479,* Youlgreave *2064*. **Excursions:** *Thomas Cook* trips for train loads of workers to Chatsworth [1848], from Sheffield, Ashopton [1874] *1986,* Redmires Reservoir *2685*. **Falconry:** OE: *hafoc* Brough *1882,* Hawkesyord, Wincle *9665*. **Fell racing:** Bamford *2083,* Chelemorton *1169,* Lantern Pike *0288*. **Football**: Field, Bamford *2083*. ***Galloway pony races*:** [1728] Bakewell *2168,* Tideswell *1575,* Winster *2460* See 'jaggers'. **Gliding:** Hucklow [1934] onwards *1878*. **Golf**: Bakewell [1899] *2168,* Bamford (Sicklehome) [1897] *2083,* Izaak Walton Hotel [1899] *1450*. **Horse racing**: Bakewell *2168,* Point-to-point Flagg *1368,* Tideswell *1575,* Winster *2460 William John Legh* [1828-98], 'Baron' *Newton* [1892] member of Lyme Park *9682* jockey club. ***Morris Dancing***: Winster *2460 'Cecil James Sharpe'*. **Pancake Races:** Shrove Tuesday Winster *2460*. **Ploughing:** Bamford *2083*. **Prize fighting:** Three Shires Head *0068*. **Rifle shooting:** Bakewell *2168,* Edale *1285*. **Rock climbing:** *J W Puttrell's* Climbers' Club [1898] Cratcliffe Rocks *2261,* Dove Dale *1452,* Laddow Rocks *0501,* The Roaches *0062*. **Sailing:** Errwood Reservoir *0175*. **Skiing:** Edale *1285*. **Walking:** Boundary *1600,* Dane Valley Way *9665,* Gritstone Way *9363,* High Peak Trail [1972] (Midshires Way) *1463,* Limestone Way *2063,* Pennine Way [1965] *1284,* Snake Pass *0892* → Hayfield [1897] *0386,* Staffordshire Moorlands *9961,* Tissington Trail [1972] *1461,* Trans Pennine Trail *1802,* Mass Trespass [1932]. 'Hunting'.

Robin Hood: Brook *2382,* Cave *2483,* Cross *1880,* Stoop *2180,* Stride/Graned Tor/Mock Beggars' Hall *2262,* Well *2679* **Little John**: probably buried in St Michaels' Churchyard, Hathersage *2380*. **Picking Rods**/Maidenstones *0091,* at the meeting point of 4 'townships'- Chisworth, Ludwortjh, Mellor, New Mills - probably marked the land boundaries of an anonymous monastery

Royal involvement: ***Ceremony***: *'Dymoke', 'Garlands'*. **Command**: *Charles I,* via *John Manners* and *Francis Bagshaw,*ordered overplus grain to be taken to Bakewell *2168* and Tideswell markets [1630-31] *1575*. **Confiscation** of manors: Bakewell *2168,* Castleton *1583,* Longendale *0397*. **Descendants**: *Bagshawe family*. **Dissolution** of the monasteries: about [1534] Blackwell *1272,* Brushfield *1672,* Grindlow *1877,* One Ash *1665*. **Employment:** 'Ecton', *Devonshire, Leche, Lynford, Shirley, Strelley, Woderhofe* Taxal *0079,* Edensor *2569*. **Expulsion**: *Bradshaw.* **Fine** *'Christopher Wilson'*. **Forests**: for obtaining meat supplies by hunting Macclesfield [1237] *9671,* Peak *1179* and recreation. Kings owned the animals but not always the land. **Gifts:** Hereditary titles *Arundel, Bridgeman, Cathcart, Cavendish, Cowper, Cromwell, Curzon, De Blundevil, Eyre, De Ferrars, Furnival, FitzAlan-Howard, Furnival, Gaunt, Gilbey, Herbert, Hugh, Kent, Lancaster, Manners, Mulgrave, Neville, Plantagenet, Somerset, Talbot, Vavasour, Vernon, Warren, Wenunwyn*. 'Baron', 'Duke', 'Earl', 'Marquis', Hospital Of the Peak [1377] by *Edward III 1583*; Land *Henry I* [1100-35] Eyam 'Manor' *2176* to *William Peverell, King John* [1199-1216] Bakewell 'Manor' *2168* to *Ralph De Gernon,* Grindlow 'Manor' *1877* to Lilleshall Abbey *7315,* (in reality given by *Matthew De Stokes* and confirmed by *King John*), *Edward II* [1307-27] Castleton 'Manor' *1583* to *Piers Gaveston* then Earl *Warrenne, Henry VIII* [1509-47] Brushfield 'Manor' *1672* to *Talbot* Earl of Shrewsbury, *Edward VI* [1547-1553] Blackwell 'Manor' *1272* to *Sir William Cavendish*. **Hospital** Peak [1377] *1583* endowed by *Edward III* 'Poverty and Philanthropy'. **Royal Demesne**: **Manors**: [1086] Abney *1979,* Ashford *1969,* Baslow *2572,* Blackwell *1272,* Calver *2374,* Chelmorton *1169,* Eyam *2176,* Grindlow *1877,* Hassop *2272,* Monyash *1566,* Nether Haddon *2266,* Rowland *2172,* Sheldon *1768,* Snitterton *2760,* Stanshope *1354,* Stoke *2376,* Taddington *1471,* Tideswell *1575*. **Submission**: [917] *Edward the Elder* [899-925] received the submission of the King of the Scots, the Norse ruler of York and the Northumbrian people at Bakewell *2168*.

Wardship: *Foljambe infant – Leake – Plumpton.*

```
┌─────────────────────────────────────────────────────┐
│   Figure 27            Tumuli on Named Lows         │
├─────────────────────────────────────────────────────┤
│                                    Pike             │
│                                                     │
│              Mag       Ox                           │
│                                                     │
│                     Brood           High            │
│                  Withered   Tides                   │
│     Yearns          Wind                            │
│                                                     │
│                                       Blake   Stone │
│                          Knot                       │
│                    Cronkston   Ringham   Grind      │
│                                                     │
│                            Bee                      │
│                The Low   Carder    Arbor            │
│        Merryton                       Kenslow       │
│                                                     │
│                   Letts           Aleck             │
│                   Warslow                           │
│                   Waterfall  Steep                  │
│                                  Pea  Hawks         │
│                      Wetton   Moat  Cross           │
│                                                     │
│                         Stand      Crake            │
│                       Mamtops   Bose                │
│                                    Sharp            │
│                  Lamber                             │
│                      Cart                           │
│                                                     │
└─────────────────────────────────────────────────────┘
```

Figure 28	Fire and Light

Peat Pits
Bradfield **Co**

Grindslow **Pe**, **Tu**
Coalpithole
Aston **Tub**

Mam Tor **Ca**   Thornhill **Pt Tu**
Windy Knoll **El Ol**
Bakestonedale **Co**   Bradwell *Miners' Beaver Hats*
Pott Shrigley **Co**   Tideswell **Pt** 'turbary'
Berristall **Co**   Fernilee **Co**
Harrop **Co**   Derbyshire Bridge **Co**
Buxter Stoops **Co**
Big Low **Co**   Hucklow **Tu**
Billinge **Co**

Errwood **Co**   Tideswell **Tu**   Stoney Middleton **Ga Oi**

Goyt Valley **Co**
Curbar *Hearth Stones*
Baslow **Co**
Brand **Wo Es** Flagg **Pe**
Axe Edge Boothman's **Co**
Brund **Wo Es**
Dane Colliery **Co**   Ashford **Ch**
Wildboarclough **Co**
+ *Cinder Hill*
Quarnford **Co**

Goldsitch **Co**
Mixon **Du**
Heathylee **Co**

Products   **Ca**rbonite, **Ch**arcoal, **Co**al, **Du**ng, **El**aterite,
Gas, **Oi**l, **Ol**efinite, **Pe**at, **Wo**od.

Concessions **Es**tova, Housebote, **Tu**rbary   Cross reference for definitions: Glossary

```
    Figure 29                              Spread of Manors

         Longendale                    Langsett
                                                      Hallam
                    DARK PEAK
                                      Ashopton

                         Castleton #
                 Hope #   Thornhill
                      Brookfield
                            Bradwell
                        Hazelbadge #      Hathersage
                      Abney #   Highlow   Padley #

                       Grindlow    Hucklow #
                                     Eyam
                     Tideswell #     Stoke    Stoney Middleton
              Wormhill #  Litton               Calver
                      Rowland
         Macclesfield #            Blackwell  Brushfield Hassop   Baslow #
                           Longstone           Bubnell #
                                                         Chatsworth #
                                      Chelmorton    Ashford
                                       Sheldon        Bakewell #
                                                         Beeley
            Gradbach                Monyash  Nether   Great
                                    One Ash  Haddon   Rowsley
                                      Youlgreave  Hartle
                                      Middleton        Stanton #
                                                      Birchover
                       Upper Elkstone     Gratton    Winster #    Snitterton #
                              Alstonefield #
                         Narrowdale  Stanshope        Parwich


    #    Saxon  Owner  or  Place Name indicative of ownership
```

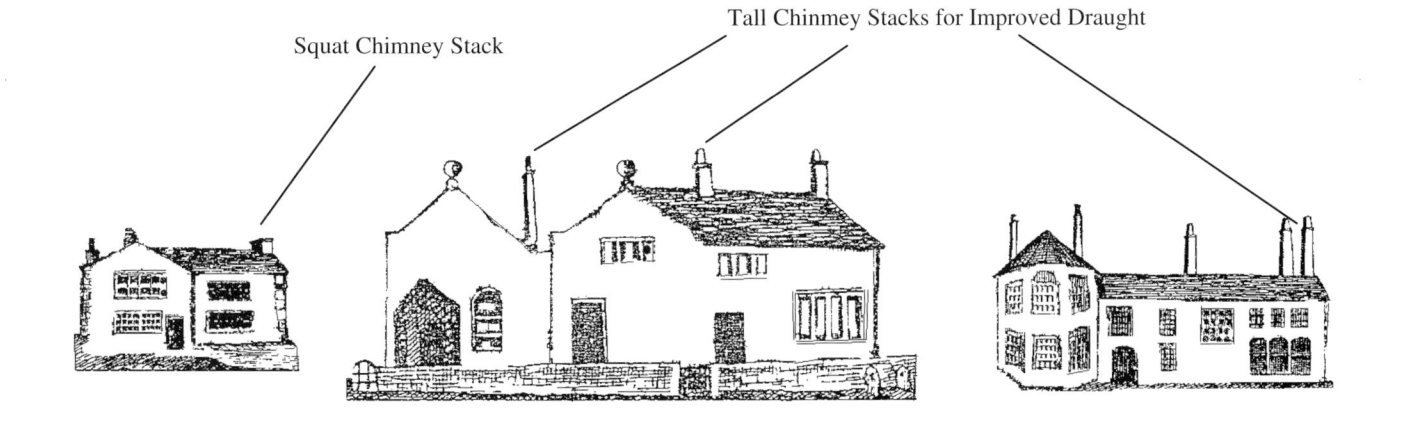

Squat Chimney Stack
Tall Chinmey Stacks for Improved Draught

Ollerset   Flagg   Ashford

<u>One Gable-End Bay Halls</u>

121

Figure 30 — Schools and Colleges

                  <u>Lower</u>
                  <u>Bradfield</u> **El**

    Edale **El**
             Derwent **El**
       <u>Hope</u> **El**
        <u>Castleton</u> **El**
<u>Ferniee</u> **Gr**   Bradwell **El Su** <u>Hathersage</u> **El**
Shrigley **Ch**
                    Stoney Middleton **El**

  Errwood **Es**   <u>Tideswell</u> **Gr** <u>Eyam</u> **El**
  Hollinsclough **El** <u>Taddington</u> **El**
       <u>Priestcliff</u> **El**   Cliff College **Ch**
                     <u>Baslow</u> **El**
          <u>Great</u> <u>Longstone</u> **El**
      <u>Flash</u> **El Su**   Monyash **El**

                      <u>Ashford</u> **Gr**
                      <u>Bakewell</u> **El Gr**
          Youlgreave **El**   <u>Stanton</u>
                      <u>in the Peak</u> **El**
Hazelbarrow **Su**
    Rewlach <u>Brand</u> <u>Top</u> **El** <u>Elton</u> **El**
    Su   <u>Hartington</u> **D El** <u>Winster</u> **El**
               Su
    Warslow **Gr**

        Alstonfield **Su**
     Wetton **Gr Su** Parwich **D**

        Tissington **D El**

Types: **Ch**ristian College, **D**ame, **El**ementary, **Es**tate
Grammar, **Su**nday   <u>Identified funding</u> underlined

GLOSSARY OF PEAK TERMS

Connections are made between natural resources, products, places and people so as to relate to the natural world, political, religious, social and economic history webs. Additional dialect words are found in 'The Natural World'. Entries for rocks and minerals include only basic geology.

Abaci: The top of an architectureal column. Duke's Red 'marble' from Alport *2164* in St John's College, Cambridge.

Adit: A coal or clay mine shaft entered by walking down a gentle gradient. [17th century word] *1153, 1262, 1461, 9579,* Ughill *2590.*

Advowson: OF. The inherited or purchased right of a person, under ecclesiastical law, to present a man to a vacant benefice/living. and the obligation to defend the man's rights. Derwent *2383* [1876] 'Duke' of Devonshire.

After damp: The lethal carbon dioxide CO_2 gas resulting from 'fire damp' explosions.

Agate: [16th century word]. See 'Chalcedony'.

Agister: OF: A forest official in charge of collecting money and pasturing livestock. *Litton.*

Alabaster: Greek *alabastros* $CaSO_4$ $2H_2O$ A pinkish white, easily worked and polished rock, used for monuments, found at Chellaston *3830,* Hanbury *1727* and Tutbury *2129. Sir Godfrey Foljambe* [1376], *Sir Thomas Wendesley* [1403] Bakewell *2168*; A knight and lady [1440] Tideswell *1575, Sir Thomas Cockayne* [1488] Youlgreave *2064,*

Albigenses: A Christian reform group flourishing in Southern France [11th-13th centuries]. They protested against clergy corruption but were suppressed by the Roman Catholic Church. *Cotterell.*

<u>Alder</u>/aller/<u>owler</u>: *alma glutinosa* OE: *alor* **Habitat** – banks of brooks and rivers. **Uses**: Clogs*, red dye, gunpowder charcoal - guns used at the Battle of Crecy [1346], cabinet making, cups, mus, platters,'medicine' <u>Alder</u> Close, Great Longstone *2071.* Dialect: Howler, Owler. Howler Knoll *9876,* Ollerbrook *1285,* Ollset *0285,* Over <u>Owler</u> *2580.* * Staffordshire Moorlands *0854* term: sparrow bits = nails for clogs and shoes.

<u>Alum</u>: OF. $K_2SO_4.Al_2(SO_4)3.24H_2O$ A colourless, soluble, hydrated double sulphate of aluminium and potassium **Uses** Manufacture of 'mordants', leather, for hardening tallow and as a medical astringent. Manufacture was perfected at Whitby by *Sir T Challoner.* <u>Alum</u> Field, Wincle *9665. Figure 18,* Cattle Carcasses Supply Chain, refers.

Amethyst: SiO_2 Latin: *amethystus.* A type of quartz. Calton Hill *1171,* Millers Dale *1373.*

Analcime/analcite: $NaAlSi_2O_6.H_2O.$ Greek: *analkimos* = weak. A pinkish white, grey or colourless zeolite (secondary minerals consisting of hydrated aluminium silicates of calcium, sodium or potassium) formed by volcanic activity. Calton Hill *1171. Figure 12,* Rocks, refers.

Andle: Dialect. Blacksmith's anvil. 'Andle Stone' *2462.* 'Tew'.

Anglesite/lead vitriol: $PbSO_4$ A secondary mineral formed by the oxidation of 'galena' into lead sulphate. Named after Anglesey. Eyam *2176. Figure 11,* Metal Ores, refers.

Angles: Settlers from Schleswig *55°N 0°8'W* who established the kingdom of Mercia about [550].

Annates/first fruits: ML: *annata.* A tax on a minor church benefice. It was based on the income of a newly appointed incumbent in his first year. Originally patrons benefitted but in [1306] Pope *Clement V*'s apostolic chambers began collecting it. *Sir Godfrey Foljambe* joined the opposition to annates in the House of Commons. [1536] *Henry VIII* took over this tax. [1704] Parliament devised a method of using it to supplement the incomes of poorer clergy.

Anthraconite/Ashford marble/stinkstone: Limestone impregnated with a bitumen. Stinkstone smells when fractured. Ashford in the Water *1969. Figure 12,* Rock Extraction, refers.

Anticline: Strata folded upwards in the form of an arch. Ecton Hill *0958.*

Antimony/black lead/stibium: SbS_2 Antimony sulphide. ML: *antinomia*. It may occur with deposits of 'sphalerite' and is not easy to distinguish* from 'arsenopyrite'. Arabs are said to have used it to stain eyelids. *Daniel Defoe's* reference to it at Birchover *2462* is suspect*.

Arbor/arbour/herber: OF: *herbier*. 1. A plot of ground covered with grass or turf or shrubs. 2. A bower with climbing plants and trellises. Arbor Low *1663*.

Arnfield: Broad, level, 7 or more metres wide strips in a ploughed field. Arnfield Flats *0200*.

Arretine ware: Pottery from Arretium (modern Arezzo *43°28'N 11°52'E*) which dominated the Roman market [30BC-AD70] 'Samian'.

Arsenopyrite/mispickel: FeAsS. Greek: *arsenikos* Known since [400BC]. Green arsenic pigments were used in Georgian and Victorian times to dye clothes and to colour wallpaper. Ecton *0958*. *Figure 11*, Metal Ore Extraction, refers.

Ash: *fraximus excelsior* OE: *aesc*. **Habitat**: Moist, cool atmosphere. *Uses*: Leaves for horse and cattle feed, (although eating them adversely affects butter quality), milk pails, because ash was supposedly a witch deterrent, fencing poles, after coppicing, corn theshing flail handles, joined by a middle band to holly or yew strikers, 'medicine' Dialect: *wicken* = mountain ash *sorbus aucuparia*. Ashop *1884*, Ashes Farm *1749*, Ash House Farm *1979*, Ashway *0204*, Monyash *1566*, One Ash *1665*. 'Breech'. Dove Dale plantations *1452*.

A(e)ssarting: Clearing land for cultivation; a process which began in the Peak in the 6th century. In [AD586] ⅓rd of England was wooded. Hedges from cleared wood land saplings marked boundaries; on *Richard I's* [1189-99] orders maximum hedge height 1.3 metres to avoid interfering with hunting. In the [13th century] 'copyholders' paid the Crown for their assarts in Macclesfield Forest *9671*. 'Names' ending in 'ley'.

Augustinian: A monastic order (Austin Canons) who followed the Rule of *Augustine*, Bishop of Hippo [395-430] and Augustine, the Benedictine monk sent by *Pope Gregory* to convert the English [597]. Austin Friars followed the monastic life while teaching and preaching but as canons living in the community not segregated monks in a monstery. As they required less land than 'Benedictines' their endowments were more numerous. Grindlow *1877* to Lilleshall Abbey *7315* and Hathersage *2380* to Launde *7904*.

Azurite/chessylite/blue malachite: $Cu_3(CO_3)_2Cu(OH)_2$ OF: *azur* = blue Copper carbonate. Resembles 'malachite'. Ecton *0958*. *Figure 11*, Metal Ore Extraction, refers.

Backspittle: Dialect: A wooden spatula for turning oatcakes while cooking. Youlgreave *2064* church accounts [1746].

Badger: Dialect. A licensed itinerant dealer in corn and oatmeal. Badgers' 'Croft' *0463*, Flash *0267*. *John Buxton* of Chelmorton *1169*. [July 1748] A badger elected at Bakewell Quarter Sessions topped a list of 318.

Bagging: Dialect. Packed lunch. Onecote *0555*.

Ball: ON A rounded hill. Ball Cross *2269*, Gamball *0367*.

Bally: Dialect. A litter of rabbits or pigs.

Banesters: See 'Panniers'.

Bar: 1. A settlement site near the bottom of steep slopes. Flash *0267*. 2. Abbreviation for 'toll bar'. Brierlow *0869*

Barmaster: Dialect. A local judge amongst miners, usually a member of the nobility or gentry. In Derbyshire he had charge of the standard dish (a large rectangular box) for measuring lead ore.

Barmote/Berghmote **Court**: A court for controlling lead mining comprising 24 miners, stewards and 'barmasters'. Established [1288]. Monyash *1466* for High Peak – met 6 monthly. 'Mines'.

Baron: A title introduced by the Normans meaning a king's tenant-in-chief. The lowest rank of nobility. Carlisle *(Carleuil) (Curzon))*, Dovedale *(Denman)*, Somerset *Botecourt)*, Vaux *(Gilbey)*, Wych Malbanc *(De Malbanc)*.

Baronet: An order instituted in [1611] giving a hereditary title to a commoner. *Bridgeman*.

Barrow: OE: *beorg* A long, round or oval mound of earth or stones erected over a grave usually on a hill ('low'). Long barrows are 'Neolithic', round ones - bowl, bell and disc - are 'Bronze Age'. Chelmorton *1170*, Hazel *0163*. Looting destroyed some in the [18th] & [19th] centuries.

Barytes/caulk/cawk/Derbyshire onyx/oakstone: $BaSO_4$. Greek: *barys* = heavy. Barium sulphate a 'gangue' vein mineral. *Uses*: 1. In the leather industry and enamels, (May have begun about [1800BC] in Egypt) 2. Barium "meal" because it is opaque to X rays and 3. A 'lithopone' for paint. 4. White barytes and lime as a pigment and dye Goytsclough paint mill *0078*. 5. Decorative artefacts 6. Nuclear shield 7. Oil well drilling. 8. Plastics 9. Rubber. 10. Paper. *Varieties*: Caulk (heavy spar), rose pink, 'Derbyshire onyx (oakstone), blue and reddish brown. 'Derbyshire onyx' takes a high polish. 'Arbor' 'Low' *1663*, Coombs Dale *2274*, Friden *2476*. *Figure 12*, Rock Extraction, refers.

Bast: OE: *baest*; MHG: *bast*. The fibrous material obtained from flax, lime trees and other vegetation. *Uses*: matting and rope making.

Batwell: Dialect. A wicker strainer.

Bawk/balk: Dialect: A raised strip of land between ploughed furrows with two uses. It was either a path with a right of way or boundary.

Beaker people: A tribe which originated in [2000BC] in Iberia, arrived in England about [1850BC] and lived on limestone uplands eg the White Peak. They made metal tools and always buried a beaker with the dead person. They may have been Celts from Russia and Spain arriving in the Peak via countries now known as Germany and The Netherlands. Grindon *0854*, Liffs Low *1557*, Sheldon *1768*.

Beard: Dialect: A low hedge of bushes and branches for stabilising sloping ground Bearda *9664*.

Beech *fagus sylvatica*: OE: *bece*. **Habitat**: uplands in woods. Beeches Farm *2457*, Thursbitch *9975*. *Uses*: Nuts eaten by deer and swine, handles for tools, manganese oxide found in the ashes for removing green colour from molten glass 'Swineherd'.

Bell pit/day hole: A shaft was sunk around a central axis. The coal was worked outwards from the central shaft. Wildboarclough *9868*. *Figure 28*, Fire and Light, refers.

Benedictine: A religious order founded by St Benedict [?480-?547] at Monte Cassino in Italy *41°30'N 13°47'E*. By the [8th century] monks were increasingly from noble families so manual work was replaced by cultural activities. Burton upon Trent Abbey *2423* held lands at Mixon *0457* (and also a mill), Musden *1250* and Onecote *0455*, 'St Mary de Pratis', '*Bennett*'. *Figure 3* Overseas Connections refers.

Bent grass: There are seven types. Brown bent grass *agrostis canina* grows in damp places. Bents *2289*, Benty Grange *1564*, Fenny Bentley *1750*, Good Bent *0806*.

Berewick: OE: *bere* = barley + *wic* = farmland. They were 'townships' of a 'manor'. At Domesday Ashford in the Water* *1969* embraced Baslow *2572*, Little Longstone *1871*, Bubnell *2472*, Hope - Aston *1884*, Edale *1285*, half of Offerton *2181*, Shatton *1982*, Stoke *2376* and Tideswell *1575*, Matlock *3060* - Snitterton *2760*. Bradfield *2692*, Midhope *2199*, Wightwizzle *2495*. *Alternatively may have been a berewick of Bakewell 'manor' *2168*.

Beyt/bait: ON: *beit* and OE: *bat* = bait. Beytonsdale *1179*.

Bierlow: A sub division of a 'parish' with facilities for funeral biers. Bradfield *2692 and* Walderhaigh *2696* were bierlows of Ecclesfield parish '*3694*'.

Birch/tree *betula pendula*: Dialect: *birk* and OE: *bierce*. **Habitat**: adjusts to different environments. *Uses*: 'Medicine' and bark for tanning leather The peculiar odour of "Russian leather" is attributable to birch bark tanning. *Barker* and *Birch*. Birchen Bank *1098*, Birchin Hat (small clump) *1491*.

Black Jack: See 'Sphalerite'.

Black lead: 'Antimony'. This is not the black lead formerly used on cooking ranges.

Blaze: MLG: *bles* = a path indicated by marks eg on trees Blaze Hill *9577*.

Blende: See 'Sphalerite'.

Blue John: CaF_2. French: *bleu* = blue + *jaune* = yellow. A 'gangue' mineral; a type calcium fluoride, coloured by films of oil deposited on the rock crystal faces. Colours vary: blue-black, light blue, purple, white, yellow *Uses*: Ornaments and decoration. Two Blue John vases were found at Pompeii *40°44'N 14°27'E*. Extraction rate 10 – 12 tons per annum in [1874]. Castleton *1582*. *Mulgrave*. *Figure 12*, Rock Extraction, refers.

Bog Iron ore: See 'Limonite'.

Bog trotting: A recreational activity begun in the Dark Peak about [1952]. Participants walk, trot (jog) or run across the bogs eg from Marsden (Not in the Peak National Park) *0411* → Black Hill *0704* → Bleaklow *1196* → Kinder Scout *0888* → Edale *1285*. *Thomas, Eustace.*

Bole: Greek *bolus* 1. Fine, compact clay, coloured brown, red or yellow by iron oxide ('haematite'). *Uses*: Treating wooden boards and effigies by medieval artists and possibly low-fired to make terra cotta vessels. 2. A smelting method until the [1570s]. A wall on an exposed hill, facing the prevailing south westerly wind. Ore and firewood were a layer stacked against the wall to melt ore. Beneath them was a lower layer, a shankard, for sampling molten metal before it it was tapped into a channel. Bole Hills *0584, 1075, 1867, 2177, 2291, 2479,* Calver *2374,* Hassop [15th century] *2272,* Smelting Hill *2080,* Smelting Mill *2666*.

Boon: ON: *bon* = a gift. The service given by a tenant farmer to a landlord at harvest time.

Boose: Dialect. A cow stall. Boosley *0662.*

Booth: ON: *buth* = a temporary structure for shelter initally for herdsmen. Barber/Whitemoorley *1084,* Farlands *0587,* Green *9877,* Grindsbrook *1186,* Hathersage *2380,* Nether *1485,* Ollerbrook *1285,* Sperrow *9576,* Upper *1085.*

Bordar: Probably a peasant of lower economic status than a villein.

Borh: A sum of money, under Anglo Saxon law, deposited as surety by guarantors of someone who had to pay a fine.

Bornite/'Peacock Ore': Cu_5FeS_4. Named after the Austrian, *Ignaz von Born* [1742-91]. A variety of 'chalcopyrite' showing all the colours of a peacock's multi-coloured plumage. Ecton *0958*. *Figure 11,* Metal Ore Extraction, refers.

Bose: Dialect. 1. Clump of shrubs 2. Coarse, long hay Bose Low *1652* – near Newton Grange.

Boskin: Dialect A partition of a cow house.

Bot: A sum of money paid, under Anglo-Saxon law, to an injured man. The sum varied in accordance with the part of the body concerned.

Bounty, Queen Anne's: The outcome of a long running series of investigations into transferring ecclesiastical income to augment the paltry income of 'parish' and 'chapelry' clergy. First payments were made [1714]. Clergy who served more than one place of worship were unable to benefit from the bounty. Application made [1746] by the Vicar of Bakewell *2168* and 'chaplain' of Monyash *1566,* father of 20 children, refused.

Bovate/oxgate/oxgang: 3 hectares (8 acres), a half 'yardland'. *Griffin* gave two bovates for Great Longstone 'chantry' *2071.*

Bower: A tenant who rents a herd of animals along with their pasture and fodder from a proprietor. He makes his profit from sales of their produce. An alternative arrangement is one whereby the tenant donates his labour free of charge and divides any resulting profits from sales with the proprietor. Bower Clough *9578,* Danebower *0170,* Ladybower (before the reservoir) *1888,* Bowers Hall *2364. Bower.*

Bowk: Dialect. A dairy pail.

Bracken *pteridium aquilinum* S: *braken*. *Uses*: Animal bedding, brick making and industrial fuel, ashes, which contain potassium carbonate, for glass and soap manufacture, a detergent and 'medicine'.

Bradder beaver: A basin-shaped hat manufactured in Bradwell *1781* and worn by miners.

Brandreth: Dialect A frame for supporting a stack of barley, oats, rye or wheat.

Brass: OE: *braes*. Copper + zinc alloys Known since [1000BC]. *Uses*: by the Romans for coins, in medieval memorials eg Tideswell *1575,* in miners' lamps invented by *Sir Humphrey Davy* [1778-1829] and, more recently engineering components.

Breccia: OHG: *brecha* A rock containing cemented coarse, angular fragments OHG: Brecktor *1279,* Rud Hill *2684.*

Breech/britch/breeck/break: OE: *brec*. 1. A fungus covering ash tree branches. 2. A temporary enclosure. Breech *0558.*

Brenner: Wealthy ore buyers acting for smelters and lead merchants to whom miners were indebted for loans and working capital. 'Yeomen'.

Brig: Dialect. An oak frame used in a dairy.

Brigantes: A powerful tribe living north of the River Trent and inhabiting the Pennine chain. Their revolt against the Romans led to the building, or rebuilding, of Brough (Anavia) *1882* in [AD158] by *Caesar Julius Verus*.

Brink: MD: *brinc*. The edge of a steep precipice. Hope *1785*, Thornhill *1785*.

Bronze Age: In England [2100-750BC] following the 'Neolithic' Period. Arbor Low *1663*, Doll Tor *2463*, Five Wells *1271*, Ilam *1350*, Letts Low *0859*, Minninglow *2156*. Mouse Low *0853*; the transitional period is known as the Chalcolithic. *Figure 22*, Bronze Age Sites, refers. The Bronze and Iron Ages overlapped.

Bronze: Italian: *bronzo*. The most likely alloy specifications based on Peak ores:– copper + lead + zinc and zinc + silver + lead for coins. *Uses*: Weapons, utensils, ornaments.

Brood: Dialect: Impurities in ore. Brood Low *1279*.

Buckthorn: *rhamnus catharticus*. *Uses*: charcoal, green dye, 'medicine' Buckthorn Meadow, Ashford in the Water *1869*. *Figure 28*, Fire and Light.

Bud: Dialect. A yearling calf.

Bun: Dialect. Dry stalks of flax. Bunster Hill *1451*. 'Bune'.

Bune: OE = a reed Bunsall *0175*, Bunster *1451*.

Buttie: 1. A small coal mine worked by farmers or contractors before the railway age. 2. A gangmaster.

Caggle: Dialect. To harrow the surface of rough ground.

Cairn: Gaelic: *carn*.1. A heap of rough stones often erected as a memorial on a summit *0191, 0786, 1081,1204, 1488, 1991* (Lost Lad memorial to boy shepherd *W H Baxter* [1901-77]), Pike Low (Pre-historic) *1998, 2080, 2180, 2184, 2185, 2279. 2285, 2868, 2872*, Edale Moor *2278* 'encircled cairns' according to *Sir Gardner Wilkinson*, a cover for a 'cist'. 2. Stones removed when clearing land.

Calamine: ML: *calamina* A reduction process by which zinc carbonate, or zinc oxide, is added to copper ore and melted with charcoal. Eyam *2176* *Uses* brass manufacture 'Smithsonite'.

Calcite/Iceland Spar: (a very clear variety) $CaCO_3$. Crystalline calcium carbonate, the Predominant mineral in limestones. Rare blue calcite has been found near Castleton *1583* and Monyash *1566*. *Uses*: White calcite for architectural stucco (weather resistant coating for outside walls), sculpture, cosmetics, chippings for flat roofs, white lines on roads, filler for plastics. Moss Rake *1480*, Youlgreave *2064*. *Figure 12*, Rock Extraction, refers.

Cale: Dialect. A turn in rotation. Cales Dale *1764*.

Calk Dialect. The turned over edge of a horseshoe.

Camp meetings: Open air, lengthy Primitive Methodist meetings for prayer and preaching Coatestown *0666*, Reapsmoor *0861*, Wilshaw Bottom *0566*, Wilshaw Hill *0566*.

Carbonite/Natural Coke: Coal which has been carbonised by the heat of an igneous rock intrusion Mam Tor *1283*. *Figure 28*, Fire and Light, refers.

Carf: Dialect. A section of a haystack cut for fodder.

Carr: Dialect: Low lying. Carr Bottom *2083*.

Carucate: The land unit of assessment, for Domesday purposes in the former Danish areas; as much land as could be tilled by 8 oxen and 1 plough. The area varies between 32 and 40 hectares (80 and 100 acres) according to soil condition and texture. The Domesday survey linked Bakewell *2168*, which had 8 'berewicks', with Ashford in the Water *1969* and Hope *1783* to for 50 carucates and 8 'towsnhips'/vills. 'Bovate' = 1/8th carucate.

Carving: Dialect. The thickening of milk as it curdles in butter making.

Casson/Cazon: Dialect. Cow dung dried for fuel. 'Mardo'.

Castle: 1. A large piece of rock shaped by weathering along fault lines, to resemble a castle turret. Moss *1691*, Dove Castle *1451*. 2. Land slip, attributable to the weathering of soft underlying shales and limestone, together with gravitational forces caused pieces of overlying millstone grit to become detached and move down slopes. *0602,* Alport Castles *1491.* Mam Tor *1283,* Moss *0791.* 3. A fortification Castleton *1582.*

Castellan/Chatelain: Latin: *castellum.* A keeper, constable or governor of a castle. Peak *1583.*

Caulk/cawk: See 'Barytes'.

Causey: Dialect. One or two lines of flagstones, usually 'millstone grit' used to repair surfaces damagede by the wheels of carts. Long Causeway *2484.* 'Holloway'.

Caver/purcasers: Dialect. Men and women who recovered small amounts of ore from abandoned mines.

Cegel: The prefix means a boundary. Chelmorton *1169.*

Celt: Late Latin: *celtes.* A stone or metal instrument with a bevelled edge like an axe. Ilam *1350.*

Celts: They were not a homogeneous race. The Gael branch settled in Scotland, the southern branch in Wales and western England, It is possible that 'Beaker' and 'Iron Age' people were Celts and groups from Europe were in the Peak before the 'Romans'. Bull *bwlch* Hill *9474,* Chez Knoll *2566,* Sharp Low *1652,* Steep Low *1256.* Subsequently Anglo Saxon invaders called them 'wealas' foreigners.

Ceorl: OE: *churl.* The lowest class of Anglo Saxon freeman.

Chalcanthite/bluestone: $CuSO_4.5H_2O$ Greek: *chalkos* = copper. Hydrous copper sulphate Ecton *0958. Figure 11,* Metal Ore Extraction, refers.

Chalcedony: SiO_2. Different coloured, compact varieties of fine grained quartz named after Chalcedon, modern Kadikoy, $40°59'N\ 29°04'E.$ **Uses** Gemstones and ornaments, Bakewell *2168,* Friden *2476. Figure 12,* Rock Extraction, refers.

Chalcopyrite/fools gold/copper or yellow pyrite: $CuFeS_2$. Greek: *chalkos* = copper. Copper pyrites (34% copper – high yield). Ecton *0958. Figure 11,* Metal ore Extraction, refers.

Chalybeate: Late Latin: *chalybeatus* Water impregnated with iron salts. Bakewell *2168.*

Chantry: OF: *chanterie.* An endowment for maintaining one or more priests to say mass daily, after their death, for the souls of the founders and their accomplices*, [pious laymen, not clerics] or alternatively a body of endowed priests eg Monyash *1566* Church of St Leonard south transept [1384] and Beresford *1259* [1511] *Warners* at Snitterton *2760* [1531] sold to *Richard Wendesley,* Ashford in the Water *1969,* Bakewell *2168,* Castleton Hospital *1583,* Haddon *2366,* Youlgreave *2064.* *[1492] at Pott Shrigley *9479* paid up members of the Fraternity, who had paid either a lump sum or by instalments, were included.

Chapel of ease: A church built for those living some distance from the 'parish' church or a 'chapelry'. Jenkin Chapel *9876,* Sheldon *1768,* Toot Hill *9771.*

Chapelry: A chapel, serving a smaller community, answerable to a larger 'parish' which might eventually be upgraded to a parish church in its own right. Bradfield *2692,* Wormhill *1274.* 'Tithing'. The man in charge was the chaplain. [1831] Bakewell *2168* 'parish' had 9.

Chapter: CL: *capitulum.* A governing body whose members are canons of a cathedral with the Dean as its head. Lichfield 'Diocese' [1530] Canon *Edmund de Strethay* applied corporal punishment to *Robert Ellot* for his offence in punching *Edmund Ellot's* nose before the altar of St Nicholas, Hope *1783.*

Charcoal: A fuel made by heating white wood, bones, buckthorn or other combustible materials in the absence of air. Before the advent of coke, it was used for smelting metal ores and was a reason for deforestation in the Peak National Park area. Buckthorn Meadow, Ashford in the Water *1969. Figure 28,* Fire and Light refers.

Chawbacon: Dialect. A pejorative name for people too poor buy any meat except bacon.

Chert/hornstone: SiO_2 Wedgelike flints or nodules of fine, microcrystalline 'quartz' found in 'limestone'. *Uses*: 'Mesolithic' tools and weapons; after [1760] for making porcelain in North Staffordshire and Yorkshire; in building; as an abrasive. Ashford in the Water *1969* with marble, Great Longstone *2071. Figure 12,* Rock Extraction, refers.

Choking rope: Dialect. A tube for extracting obstructions from windpipes of cattle.

Chrysolite: $(Mg,Fe)_2\ SiO_4$. A name formerly applied to peridot (transparent 'olivine').

Cinnabar: HgS. Greek *kinnabari.* Mercury sulphide. Mercury was obtained by distillation *Uses*: Vermillion pigment, Sheldon *1768.*

Cist: Latin *cista*. A box-shaped burial chamber made from stone slabs or a hollow tree trunk. Gib Hill *1566*, Ballidon *2055*. 'Cairn'.

Cistercian/white monks: A monastic order connected with Cluny *46°30'N 4°39'E* and Citeaux *47°08'N 4°57'E* in the Duchy of Burgundy. They arrived in England [1129] and created the 'grange' farming system. Sheep farming made it a wealthy monastic order, the capitalists of the Middle Ages. Gradually manual work was transferred to 'lay brothers' usually illiterate men who were not offered full membership of the order. *Gifts*: Manors: One Ash *1665* by *Sir William Avenell* to Roche Abbey *5489*, Brushfield *1672* to Rufford Abbey *6464 William De Malbanc* Alstonefield *1355*, 'Granges': Wincle *9665* gift to Combermere Abbey *5844*. *Figure 6*, Granges, refers.

Clapper bridge: An early type of bridge in which slabs of stone, or planks of wood, were placed across supporting piles of stones on banks. River Bradford *2164*, Slab Bridge over Bar Brook *2777*.

Clay: OE: *claeg*. Fine grained soft material consisting of hydrated aluminium silicate and quartz. When wet, it is malleable but when heated it becomes hard and rigid. *Uses*: Bricks*, tiles, chimney pots and ceramics. *'I instruct my steward to have the floor of my bedchamber to be made from either clay or plaster.'* Bess of Hardwick [1556] Bakestonedale *9579*, Bakewell *2168* 'Bole' Hills, Stoney Middleton *2375*, fireclay Bakestonedale *9579*, Ughill *2590*. * Before [1700] farm labourers lived in stone cottages.

Cletch: Dialect. A clutch of eggs or chicks.

Clod maul: Dialect. A heavy mallet for breaking clods of earth.

Cloud: OE: *clud* = a rock or hill. Five Clouds *0062*, Hen *0661*, Thorpe *1450*.

Clough: OE: *cloh* A narrow valley. Ginclough *9576*, Goytsclough *0173*, Hollinsclough *0666*, Jaggers Clough *1487*, Wildboarclough *9868* and Dark Peak examples.

Cluniac Monks: A monastic order founded in Cluny *46°30'N 4°39'E*. about [909]. The task of the monks was primarily to perform a daily cycle of worship with elaborate ritual. *Gifts*: Blackwell Manor *1272* to Lenton Priory *5238* by *Henry I* [1100-35].

Cob: 1. A rounded heap. Bunsal Cob *0175*. 2. Wall material made from straw and unbaked clay.

Codder: Dialect. A harness maker, worker in leather.

Coe: Dialect: 1. A miner's cottage. 2. Lead miner's toolbox.

Coffin route: The route taken by bearers of a coffin to the nearest church. Hollins Cross *1384*.

Coiner A maker of counterfeit coins. They squatted on waste land at Flash *0267*.

Collegiate church: One which has an endowed chapter of canons and prebendaries but is not a cathedral. Bakewell *2168*, given by Duke of Mortain, later *King John* [1199-1216] to the chapter provided for three priests and a prebendary (endowed priest) to say mass for him.

Colt: Dialect. The 3rd swarm of bees from a hive.

Compurgator: ML: *compurgatio*. One of several persons swearing oaths supporting litigants in Saxon times. The number of compurgators varied in accordance with the status of litigants.

Cope: 1. The tax paid by buyers of metal ores. 2. To get ore at a fixed sum per dish or measure.

Coping: A stone eg 'millstone grit' topping or cap at the top of a wall.

Copyholder: Together with leaseholders and tenants at will, copyholders replaced villeins as holders of parcels of manorial land by [1558]. In Macclesfield Forest *9671*, copyholders made payments for 'assarts' to the Crown, as lord of the forest. [13th century]. The relevant legal document was a copy of a manorial roll. Under the Stuarts [1603-1714] copyholders and leaseholders were often called 'yeomen'.

Cornovii: A Roman tribe based on Wroxeter *5608* who may have occupied the Peak.

Cote: OE: = a shelter. Dyson *1901*, One Cote *0455, 0587*. Ancote lonely shelter *0800* 'Agriculture'.

Cotter/Cottier/Cottar/Bordar: ML: *cottarius*. In late Anglo-Saxon, a cotsetle, and in Norman times, a 'villein', or a younger son of one, occupying a cottage and land in return for feudal services, payment in kind. *James Brindley* [1716-62], the canal engineer, was a cottier's son born in Tunstead *1075*.

Court leet: A manorial court, with criminal jurisdiction, which some lords were allowed to hold. Beeley *2667* was sold by the *Greaves* to the *Manners*. *William Heaward*, a 'free' miner of Ashford in the Water *1969* sat on the court [1649]. 'Frankpledge'.

Covenanters: People upholding the National Covenant [1638] and Anglo-Scottish Covenant [1643] to defend Presbyterianism. They were persecuted after the Act of Uniformity [1662] and met in isolated places. Alport Castles *1491*.

Cover/converse: Lay brothers from monasteries, usually 'Cistercian', who, unlike choir monks, worked on 'granges'.

Cow: OE: *cu* = cow. Cow Low *1059, 1482*.

Croft: Dialect. A plot of wasteland. Badgers Croft *0463*.

Crosses: Latin *crux*. 1. To mark a meeting place eg Eyam [Celtic] *2176* when no church existed either because one had never been built or had been destroyed eg in the Danelaw. 2. To mark a boundary or market eg Litton *1675*, Longnor *0864*. 3. To commemorate a dead person *James Platt* Liberal Member of Parliament for Oldham accidentally killed by a gun [27/08/1857] *0304*. 4. To indicate where roads crossed Hope [1737] *1783*. 5. To indicate where a miner was prospecting Cross Low *1655*.

Crozel/crozzill: Dialect. Slag and half burnt cinders inside a lime kiln. *1373*.

Cuddy: Scottish dialect: Probably introduced by immigrant miners = a donkey.

Cupellation: A process, dating from antiquity, for separating metals eg silver from lead in argentiferous ore. The crushed ore is melted on a bed of bone ash; silver is left as pellets. The lead bearing bone ash is smelted again to recover the lead. 'Bole' Hills, Cupola Field, Eyam *2176*, Smelting Hill *2080*, Upper Cupola *2175*. 'Charcoal'.

Cuprite: $Cu O_2$ Latin: *cuprum* = copper. Found in the weathered parts of 'veins'. Ecton *0958*.

Curate ML: *curatus*. A man charged with curing souls by officiating at baptisms and burials at a place of worhsip subsidiary to a 'parish' church. [19th century] onwards an assistant to an incumbent. Beeley *2667*. Pay was erratic. [1645] The parliamentary committee used Lichfield income to augment the income of the 9 Bakewell *2168* chapels but not all curates were paid.

Currencies: Conversion of currencies used in the past into £ sterling and pence is approximate. Moreover conversion rates in England were local. The abbreviation 'd' for penny, used until [1971], was derived from the first letter of denarius, a Roman coin. Silver pennies, of various designs, were struck by moneyers at numerous local mints during Anglo-Saxon, Danish, Norman and Plantagenet reigns. Mints nearest the Peak were at Derby and Lichfield. **Roman** coins: Denarius, silver and gold: **Saxon** coins in Mercia: shillings and thrymass (thrimsa) 1 shilling = 4d (pence) later 12d; 266 thrymass = 200 shillings so 1 thrymass = 1.3 shillings or 5 pence. From [1503] until decimalisation in [1971] the value of the shilling changed. 1 shilling = 12d (pence), 20 shillings = £1 = 240d. From 1971 £1 = 100p (pence) 1 mark = 66p *Ibba*. After [1717] 1 guinea = 21shillings = £1-1s-0d = £1 05p. *Mr Bagshaw* wrote a letter advising that the proposed recoinage could lead to insurrection among miners if their clipped coins were refused when they had no others [1696].

Custos rotulorum The principal 'Justice of the Peace' in a county appointed by the Lord Chancellor. He had custody of the rolls and records. *John Manners* [1580], *Sir William Cavendish* [1615].

Cut: Norwegian: *kuti*. A path across moors avoiding streams Cut Gate *1997* used by drovers from Hope *1783*, Derwent *2083* and Woodlands *1489* valleys going to Penistone market.

Dale: O Frisian: *del*, ON: *dalr*. OHG: *tal*. A valley in low hills. A term used by *King Alfred* in [893]. Beresford *1259*, Cressbrook *1772*, Dove *1451*, Silly/humble/mini *1876*, Tideswell *1575*.

Danelaw/Danelagh OE: *dena lagu* Territory, in the English Midlands (including the Peak) and North, occupied by Danish invaders in which Danish law and customs were observed. Ratified at the Treaty of Wedmore or Chippenham [878] by *King Alfred* [849-901]. 'Languages'.

Dark Ages: The period from the late 5th century, after the departure of the Romans, until the [11th century] before the 'Normans' arrived. Win Hill *1885* and Lose Hill *1585* are reputedly the camp sites of the winners and losers in a Dark Age battle.

Dark Peak: The presence of peat makes it dark in appearance. The principal rock is impervious millstone grit. Average annual rainfall is 125cm (50 inches). The area was originally forested by 'birch' *betula pendula*, 'oak' *quercus robur* and 'lime' *tilia cordata*. Grazing sheep prevent natural reforestation because saplings are eaten. 'Groughs', 'Hags'.

Daymath: Dialect. The area which could be mowed by one man in one day.

Delf: Dialect. A man-made ditch. Foulstone *2191*, Thornseat *2292*.

Delta 32: The mutant gene largely responsible for 433 people surviving the Eyam Plague [1665-66]. The gene prevents bacteria invading cells in the immune system of the human body.

Demesne: OF: *demeine*. The central portion of a 'manor'.for the lord's use. Land not granted out but possessed by an owner who is not subordinate to anyone. 'Royal involvement'.

"Derbyshire diamonds": SiO_2. Quartz crystals found in loose earth after weathering of 'toadstone'. Cavedale *1482*, Priestcliffe *1371*. *Figure 12*, Rock Extraction, refers.

Derbyshire onyx/oakstone: $BaSO_4$. A rare, hard type of 'barytes' which takes a high polish and has cream bands in it. Arbor Low *1663*, Coombs Dale *2274*, Friden *2476*. *Figure 12*.

Diocese: Gk: *dioikesis*. A geographical area comprising, Anglican and Roman Catholic churches, 'chapelries', 'chapels of ease', and 'chantries', but not cathedrals, under the control of a bishop. Lichfield.

Doccan: Dialect. A vessel for mixing oatcake dough. Youlgreave *2064* church accounts [1746].

Dog whipper: A remunerated person responsible for whipping dogs out of a church before a service Baslow *2572*, Warslow [1720s] *0858*, Youlgreave [1716] *2064*.

Dolerite/diabase/'toadstone': Greek: *doleros*. Dolerite was the name formerly given to medium grained diabase igneous sills of Tertiary or later origin, chemically similar to 'analcime' basalt, usually horizontal, formed by magma intruding and cooling between layers of carboniferous limestone *Uses*: Roads. Calton Hill *1171*, Ible *2457*, Peak Forest *1179*, Water Swallows *0875*.

Domesday Book: The record of the survey carried out by the commissioners of *William I* [1086] 'Norman Occupation'.

Dominican: A preaching order founded in [1215] by *Dominic de Guzman* [1170-1221] "Blackfriar" Ashopton *1986*.

Drabber: Dialect: A harlot. Drabbers' Tor *1357*.

Druids: Male members of a powerful Celtic tribe, who acted as judges, priests and teachers in the British Isles and Gaul (France) between [100BC] and [AD100]. Their power was broken by the Romans. Many of their ceremonies were connected with the worship of 'oak' trees although not exclusively with them. Birchover *2462*.

Duke: The name originated in France where they became the greatest nobles. *William I*, The Conqueror, was Duke of Normandy. Dukes were introduced into England by *Edward III* [1327-77] but only for royalty. *Richard II* [1377-99] created dukes from outside the royal family. Ducal property owners in the Peak park area: Devonshire (*Cavendish*), Lancaster *(Gaunt)*, Newcastle (*Cavendish)*, Norfolk (*FitzAlan-Howard*), Rutland (*Manners*). The hereditary peerage rank order is: prince 'Ecton', duke, 'marquis', 'earl', 'viscount', 'baron', 'baronet'.

Dun/don/den: OE A suffix: = a hill or fort. Balli<u>don</u> *2055*, Had<u>don</u> *2366*, Mus<u>den</u> *1250*, Shel<u>don</u> *1768*.

Dunge: ON: *dyngia* = manure heap. 1. Manured ground. 2. A valley area. <u>Dunge</u> Clough *9878*.

Dur: Dialect. A yearling sheep.

Dymoke: The hereditary champion of the sovereign. When a monarch was crowned an armour clad dymoke, accompanied by noblemen and heralds, rode into Westminster Hall to support the king. *Robert Dymoke* died [13/04/1526], soldier son of the beheaded Lancastrian *Sir Thomas Dymoke* [1428-71], sheriff of Lincolnshire in [1484], [1502] and [1509], attended the coronations of *Richard III* [1483], *Henry VII* [1485] and *Henry VIII* [1509], father of *Catherine* who married *Stephen Eyre* [1498].

Ealdorman/alderman: A title which may have originated as a hereditary title for a male born into noble ancient Germanic families. In Britain it was a person, often of royal descent, a chief man in a shire exercising authority under the king about [750]. He was responsible for shire levies, president of folk moots and executor of the king's commands. A high 'wergild' was payable if an ealdorman was killed. After the reign of *Cnut* [1017-35], a Dane, they were often called eorls and later 'earls'. *Edric Streona*, ealdorman of Mercia about [990]. 'Earl'.

Earl: A nobleman ranking, under *Ethelbert* [858-66], below an atheling, a member of the royal family. Later an earl was an under-king looking after one of divisions of England. Cheshire Peak, *Hugh* Mercia, *Beorn*. Comital forest belonging to an earl before [1066]. Featherbed Moss *0892*. The Normans created additional earls. Earl property owners in Peak Park area: Ardglass (*Cromwell*) Arundel *(Montgomery)*, Bradford (*Bridgeman*), Burlington (*Boyle*), Carlisle *(Carleuil)*, Chester *(De Blundevil)*, Cowper, Devonshire (*Cavendish*), Kent *(Plantagenet)*, Lancaster *(Gaunt)*, Newburgh (*Eyre*) Newcastle, Pembroke and Montgomery *(Herbert)*, Westmoreland *(Neville)*. Earl Rake *1680*, Earl Sterndale *0967*. 'Earldorman'.

Earn: Dialect. To curdle with rennit when making cheese.

Earthwork: Concentric circular, protective ditches around camps and forts in pre-historic times. The ditches were often filled with sharpened stakes and water. 'Military History'.

Elaterite: A dark brown, sticky carbon, resembling rubber, *Uses* Mine illumination. Ecton *0958*, Odin *1383*, Windy Knoll *1383*. *Figure 28*, Fire and Light, refers.

Elm: *ulnus procera*. OE: *elm* Elm trees have grown at 500 metres (1,500 feet) altitude. Probably introduced to England by the 'Romans' but decimated by Dutch elm disease, caused by the fungus *ophiostoma ulni* in the [1970s]. *Uses*: Coffins, farm buildings and boats, leaves browsed by cattle and deer, printing paper. St Anne's Churchyard, Baslow *2572*, Elmore *1882*, Stanton *2563*.

Embrasure: An indentation on a crenellated embattlement St Michael's Hathersage *2381*.

Erratics: Latin: *errare* = to wander. Boulders and stones transported from the Lake District and deposited by glaciation in the Peak District during the Quaternary/Pleistocene Ice Ages [600,000 years] ago. Stones: Barrow *1396*, Bleaklow *1096*, Cuckoo *9971*, Hern *0994*, Higher Shelf *0994*, Madwoman *1388*, Rocking *0708, 1797*, Seal *1188*, Wain *0995*.

Estova: Latin: *est opus* = there is a need. The medieval right to take wood from manorial woodland or waste. Firewood Brand *0468*, Brund *0264*. *Figure 28*, Fire and Light, refers.

Fallinge: OE: *fallinge* = newly cultivated land. Fallinge *2666*.

Felloes: Dialect. The segments of the rim of a wheel, morticed for spokes.

Felon: ML: *fello*. A person committing a serious crime eg murder Longnor *0864* association for their prosecution formed [1840s]. *Downes* of Taxal *0079* claimed the right to try, hang, draw and quarter felons without interference from anyone.

Fen: OE: *fenn*; OHG: *fenna*; ON: *fen* A marshy flat area. Leash Fen *2973*

Field of the Cloth of Gold: The ineffective, pompous meeting, near Calais *50°57'N 1°50'E*, between *Henry VIII* and *Francis I*; lasted from [7 - 24 June 1520]. *Foljambe, Sacheverell*.

Firebote: The medieval right to gather wood from the forest for fuel. 'Estova'.

Fire damp: A gas often found in mines, 97% methane CH_4. It is formed by decaying carbonaceous* matter. Explosions occur when it is ignited by a spark#. 'After damp' gas replaces fire damp after explosions eg [1833] Magpie after rivals working same 'vein' lit a fire# to drive them away. [1932] Mawstone/Mosstone* Mine explosion killed 5 miners and 3 rescuers.

Flash men: Itinerant men, 'coiners', 'badgers', hawkers with uncouth manners, and brutal pastimes. They camped on moors near Flash *0267* and travelled from fair to fair.

Flat: ON: *flatr*. Strata or bedding plane controlled ore deposits. Burnt Heath *2075*.

Flax: *linum usitatissimum*. OE: *fleax*. A plant, grown initially for its fibrous stems and later for seeds, from which oil is extracted. It probably grew wild in western Asia before becoming one of the first cultivated plants. Egyptian mummies were wrapped in flax fibres. Retting in water loosens the fibres. *Uses*: Linen, printing, 'medical', thatching, thread for book binding, wicks. Flax Butts, Eyam *2176*, Flax Dale *1863*, Flax Piece, Kingsterndale *0972*, Thatch Marsh *0270*. 'Bun', 'Harle'.

Fluorite/fluorspar: CaF_2. Latin: *fluere* = to flow (it flows easily when heated) Calcium fluoride, a 'gangue' vein mineral. The name, fluorite, refers to the fact that some types fluoresce (emit coloured light) when exposed to some wavelengths of ultra violet light. Fourteen types are known. 'Blue John' is one type. Another type is still quarried extensively for use as flux in steel making and as a source of fluorine. In [1886] *Henri Moisson* developed a process for isolating fluorine from fluorspar. Until the [1960s], fluorspar was the only practical source of fluorine. *Uses* 1. In the recent past, for toothpaste. 2. Refrigerators, in aerosols as a propellant until CFCs (chlorofluorocarbons) were banned. 3. PTFE (polytetrafluoroethylene) for electrical insulators, non-stick saucepans and fibre optics for telecommunications, enamels. Castleton *1583*, Eyam *2176*, Upper Cupola *2175*. *Figure 12,* Rock Extraction, refers.

Font: ML: *fons* A large bowl containing the water for infant baptism in a church or chapel. Norman: Eyam *2176*, Haddon *2366*, Parwich *1854*, Thorpe *1550*, Winster *2460*, Youlgreave *2064*; [13th century] Early English: Aston *1884*; [1300-50] Decorated: Bakewell *2168*; [1350-1530] Perpendicular: Chelmorton *1169*, Great Longstone *2071*. *Figure 7* refers.

Forest: ML: *forestis*. Usually an unfenced area of naturally propagated and distributed trees, not a plantation. *Uses*: 1. Meat (hence the creation of royal forests by the 'Normans' for hunting [1184] deer so numerous that dogs and people were trampled to death when they bolted. Macclesfield *9671* and Peak (*1179*). 2. Feed for pigs. 3. Timber for building. 4. Firewood. 5.Fencing. Dialect: *fluke* = a hurdle Alstonefield forest, which was also called Mauban and Malbank after the *Malbanc* family, included Fawfieldhead *0763*, Heathylee Moors *0363*, Hollinsclough *0666* and Quarnford *0066*. Peak forest from River Goyt *0173* to River Etherow *1299* and River Derwent *2475*.'Crosses','Purprestre', 'Stoases'. *Offences* subject to harsh laws and cruel punishments. Backbear: being caught with a dead animal. Bloody hand: seen with blood stains on clothing. Dog draw: following a wounded animal with a dog. Stable stand: seen drawing a bow. *Officials* [13th century]. Master forester/high steward (honorary) eg *Sir Richard Vernon* [1421], 'agister', 'woodmaster', bailiff of forest eg *Benedict Shalcross* [1307-1327], 'forester in fee', 'verderer', 'regard'.

Forester in fee: An officer having a heritable right to an office of profit granted by a supeior on condition of feudal service. *Bagshawe, Foljambe, Meverell, Needham, Shirley* and *Woderofe* families at various times. 'Verderer', 'Woodward'.

Foul: Dialect. Foot rot in cattle.

Franciscans: An order of grey friars based on the teaching of Francis of Assisi [1182-1226] integrated in communities as preachers, social workers and teachers. Friars' Ridge *2583* 'Poor Clares'.

Frankpledge: OF: *franc* = free + *plege* = pledge. The responsibility of each member of a 'tithing', in the Medieval times, for the good behaviour of each other. Every man of 24 years was compelled to find a bond for good behaviour or go to prison. Ten householders formed one security unit so obtaining a bond caused few problems. Where they existed 'courts leet' were vested with the criminal jurisdiction of frankpledge offences. 'Sheriffs' visited every six months to check that no one in a settlement was not covered. Three manorial lords of Alstonefield *1355* [1270s].

Freeing: Dialect. The procedure to be followed by someone discovering an ore deposit. Application had to be made to the 'barmaster' for permission to work the deposit. *William Heaward* [1656] of Ashford in the Water and *Francis Staley* [1656] were free miners on the 'Earl' of Rutland's land.

Freeman: A man who, unlike cotters and villeins, had no obligations to a feudal lord**.** Free tenants comprised more than 60% of village populations about [1279]. Often they were younger sons of knights, cotters and villeins who had escaped. *Robert Pykenase* paid 100 marks (£66) to *William le Wyne* and his wife of Baslow *2572* so that he and his offspring would be freed from service for ever. By the [13th century], they and 'knights' played an increasing part in local government. '*Wilson*'.

Frith: OE: *fyrhp* = woodland. Litton Frith *1773*.

Furlong/wong: = 220 yards in an open field. Knowtridge Furlong, Tideswell *1575*.

Gag: A bit for breaking in young horses Gag Lane *1552*.

Gait: Dialect. A [nineteenth century] unit indicating the number and type of animals permitted to graze on privately owned pastures, or common land, in accordance with a tariff.eg full grown horse = 2 gaits, 5 sheep = 1 gait, 1 cow = 1 gait. Thorpe Pasture *1551*.

Galena: PbS The name used by *Pliny* about [AD113] for a cosmetic named after the Greek Galen. Galena is a composite mineral ore for antimony, arsenic, lead and silver sulphides. [2000-1000BC] lead and silver were produced from galena by smelting and 'cupellation' Copper and zinc are also often found with galena. Castleton *1583*, Eyam *2176*. *Figure 11,* Metal Ore Extraction, refers.

Gangue minerals: F: *gangue*. The part of ore deposits from which metal is not extracted. 'Barytes', 'Blue John', 'Fluorite'.

Gan(n)ister: A sedimentary siliceous rock. Loadfield *2594*. *Uses* Furnace refractories.

Garbroods: Dialect. Strips of land in the triangular gore of a common field. Castleton *1583*.

Garlands: OF: *garlande* 1. An annual ceremony, held at Castleton *1583* on 29 May, to commemorate the restoration of *Charles II* in [1660]. A garland of flowers is hoisted to the top of St Edmund's church tower. 2. Funeral garlands at Ashford in the Water *1969*.

Gate(a): On: *gata* = a road. Har<u>gate</u>wall *1175*, Harvey *0256*, Hayes<u>gate</u> *0959*.

Gebur: Free peasants, some former slaves, economically dependent on the lord of the manor.

Geff: Dialect. Empty ears of cereals.

Geneat/gesette: In Saxon times, land let to tenants, originally a lord's companion or retainer.

Gesso: Italian. A mixture of lime plaster and glue size, used by Medieval artists to prepare canvas and wooden panels for painting.

Gilt: Dialect. A castrated boar. NB A gilt is usually a young female pig.

Gin/windlass: OF abbreviation: *en<u>gin</u>* An rudimentary beam arrangement pulled by horses or pushed by men, or women, for lifting miners, coal, ore and waste. 'Open', 'Shack' 'Wheal'. **Punishment** In the [14th century] ore thieves' hands were pinned to the upright of a gin.

Glebe: Latin: *glaeba*. Land granted to a clergyman as part of his benefice. <u>Glebe</u> Farm *0079*.

Glutton/wolverine: Latin: *glutto*. A large weasel like animal *gulo gulo* usally associated with North America and Eurasia. <u>Glutton</u> Grange *0867*.

Goethite: Fe2O3 80% when pure. Named after *Johann Wolfgang von Goethe* [1749-1832] well known poet, philosopher but also an amatuer mineralogist. A form of 'limonite' which when heated becomes 'haematite' Eyam *2176*, Winster *2460*. *Figure 11, Metal Ore Extraction, refers.*

Grange: ML: *granica*. A largely independent, usually 'Cistercian' farm settlement, often some distance from the monastery eg Roche Abbey *5489* and One Ash <u>Grange</u> *1665*, started by *Abbot Alberic* of Citeaux *47°08'N 4°57'E* [1099-1109]. At times inhabitants were ejected from villages to establish granges to be worked by 'covers' on short term assignment sent from the abbey, monastery or Priory. 'Covers' worked alongside locally hired labour. Accommodation was very basic. Wool was the main product from the more than 30 Peak granges but grain was milled at Grangemill *2457*. 1. Biggin *1559*, Grindlow *1877* given to 'Augustinian' Lilleshall *7315*. 2. Derwent *2383* to 'Pre-monstratensian' Welbeck *5674*. *Figure 1.*

Grass nail: Dialect. A rigid wire fixed between the blade of a scythe and the handle to prevent snagging at the joint.

Grease: The fat derived from hunted animals - badgers, boars, foxes, martens, rabbits and wolves. Bevy grease was from roebuck deer.

<u>Greasley</u>: OF: *craisee* = <u>thick</u> ie a clearing in a dense wood. <u>Greasley</u> *9466*.

Greave: OLG: *greven*. 1. The residue left after rendering tallow. LG: *greven*. All<u>greave</u> *9767*, The <u>Greaves</u>, Beeley *2667*, Con<u>greave</u> *2465*, <u>Greave</u> Piece *2977*, <u>Greaves</u> Lane, Ashford in the Water *1969*, Pye<u>greave</u> *0577*, Youl<u>greave</u>, *2064*, <u>Greaves</u> 2. Hill parting Swain's <u>Greave</u> *1397*. 3. OE: *graefe* = a thicket.

Green Lane: OE: *grene*. A wheeled vehicle route covered with green vegetation such as Grass, sometimes based on soil dug for 'parish' boundary ditches. *1559, 2557, 9961*.

Grimston hybrid: A technical term for place names in which the first part is a Scandinavian personal name + a second part indicative of a settlement. Offerton *218* = *Offa's* + *'ton'*.

Grin Dialect. A snare of horse hair or wire for catching small birds, mammals and trout.

<u>Grindle</u>/rindle: 1. A narrow ditch or stream 2. Flows only in wet weather. <u>Grindle</u>ford *2477*.

Grist: OE. The action of grinding sometimes with 'millstone grit' wheels.

Gritstone: See 'Millstone grit'.

Groaning/God cake: A special cake or piece of cheese offered, as a bringer of good fortune, to the first person of the opposite sex encountered after an infant baptism.

Groop: Dialect. The drain at the back of the stalls in a milking parlour.

Grough: Dialect. A natural channel on a peat moor. Bleaklow *0996* and Kinder Scout *0888*.

Grouse: *lagopus scoticus*. A game bird found on moors. Dunford Bridge *1502*.

Guild: ON: *gildi* An association of men sharing a common interest formed for mutual assistance, protection and maintenance of standards of workmanship. Alstonefield *1355*.

Hack: Dialect. A rack or manger for feeding horses or cattle.

Haematite/raddle/specular ore: Fe_2O_3. The Greek *Theophrastos* called it bloodstone* Ferrous oxide. The first ore to be smelted. From the [6th century] onwards iron was produced by melting iron ore + flux ('fluorite') + charcoal. Bowl/'bole' furnaces were used either with natural wind or bellows. The end product was 5kg (10lb) blooms. [1695] Birmingham merchants were interested in a petition to make the River Derwent navigable; they obtained iron, probably from Youlgreave *2064* with Rivers Bradford and Lathkill flood plain paths to the River Derwent. *Uses*: Red* 'ochre' was important for mordanting, marking sheep and metal components. Flash *0267*, Iron Pits *0652*, Iron Tors *1456*, Raddlepit *2089*, Swythamley *9764*, Youlgreave *2064*. *Figure 11*.

Hag: Dialect. An island of peat in the Dark Peak. 'Groughs'.

Hall Moot: OE: *heall* + S: *mot*. A manorial court.

Ham: OE *ham(m)*. A pasture or meadow surrounded by a ditch. Broad<u>ham</u> *0862*, Need<u>ham</u> *1665*, Swyth<u>am</u>ley *9764*.

Harle: Dialect. Stem or filament of flax.

Harrop: Dialect. A place where deer are hunted. *9578*, <u>Harrop</u> Moss *0896* <u>Harrop</u> Wood *9678*.

Hawker: MLG [16th century] *hoker* a person, often between sowing and harvesting, who travelled from place to place selling/peddling goods. [1696-7] purchase of a licence was compulsory. 'Alstonefield *1355*, 'Flash' *0267*, 'Hollinsclough' *0666*. Some goods were bought in bulk at fairs from Manchester [middle-] Men who criss-crossed the country with their mules and horses laden with cheap fabrics, clothes, ironmongery and cutlery [1685]. Steward of Haddon Hall *2366* bought from local hawker [1549].

Hay(e): 1. OE: *hege* = an enclosure <u>Hay</u> Dale *1276*, <u>Hayes</u> *0860*, <u>Hayes</u>gatewall *1175*, Nether *0060*, New Mixon *0357*, Ox<u>hay</u> *2479*, Parsley <u>Hay</u> *1463*, Wardlow *1874* and possibly. 2. *haigh*. Waldershaigh *2696*.

Hazel/cob: *corylus avellana*. ON: *hasl*. **Habitat**: requires good soil but it is almost ubiquitous. *Uses*: Fibres for making rope and matting for floor coverings, hoops for barrels and casks, stiffer branches for cattle prods and walking sticks, thinner branches for weaving into osiers, thatching and 'medicine'. Dialect: *flecks* = sticks used for hurdle making. <u>Hazel</u>badge *1780*, <u>Hazel</u> Barrow *0163*, <u>Hazel</u>hurst *0377*.

Hedgebote: The medieval right of a person to take wood for gates or fencing.

Heel rake: Dialect. A large, heavy rake for cleaning harvest straw ie barley and oats.

Helm: OE = a <u>roofed</u> <u>shelter</u> for cattle or OD = a barn. <u>Helm</u>esley *9867*.

Heminorphite: $Zn_4Si_2O_7.(OH)_2.H_2O$. Greek: *hemi* = half + *morph* = shape [crystals]. Hydrated zinc silicate. New Engine Mine, Eyam *2176*. *Figure 11*, Metal Ore Extraction, refers.

Henge: A Neolithic or Bronze Age circular area, similar to Stonehenge, made from stones or wooden posts. Arbor Low *1663*. *Figure 22*, Bronze Age Sites, refers.

Hide/<u>hyde</u>: OE: *higid* 1. The amount of land necessary to support one extended free family. 2. About [AD848] as much land as could be tilled by one plough by a team of 8 oxen. 3. A basis for taxation. The area of a hide, depending on the heaviness or lightness of the soil varied between 24-48 hectares (60-120 acres). Sometimes 1 hide = 4 yardlands. *Hyde*.

Hill: Dialect and OE: *helan*. To cover potatoes or celery with earth.

Hobble: Staffordshire Moorlands *0854* dialect. A pile of hay about 1.5 metres high.

Hodden: Dialect. Coarse grey, homespun woollen cloth.

Hold: ON. An intermediate class of noblemen between a 'thane'/thegn and an 'ealdorman'.

Holloway: A track made lower than the banks on either side as a result of heavy use. Holweyrode, Baslow [1359] 'portway' *2572*. 'Causey'.

Holm: S: *holm* = a hill and ON: *holmr* = an island. An island (Crowden Great Brook and Crowden Little Brook) Bare<u>holme</u> *0601*; (River Wye) <u>Holme</u> *2169*.

Holt: ON:*holt* = a copse or wood [trees enclosed by a fence] <u>Holt</u> *0069*.

Honour: A term, originating in 'Saxon' times and surviving into the 'Norman' era, applied to large areas of lands forming a lord's endowment, the king's greater tenants. The honours of several lords intermingled with one another because lands were scattered as a precaution against consolidated territorial holdings being used to raise private armies. Peak Castle *1582* was in the honour of *Peverill* along with 127 settlements in Northamptonshire, 120 in Derbyshire and a few in Leicestershire and Yorkshire. The last meeting of the honour court before abolition was in Nottingham on 31/12/1849.

Hoo: OE: *hoh* = a spur. Hoo Moor *0077*, Compare Pilhough *2564*.

Hoppet: Dialect. A small basket with a lid for for seed, fruit or packed lunch.

Hough: OE: *hoh* = spur of a hill, Pilhough *2564*. See 'Hoo'.

Housebote: The medieval right to take wood for a repairing a tenement as well as toppings and clippings for fuel. The right was curtailed when enclosures took place. *Figure 28*. Fire and Light.

Huckster: A licensed street seller of fruit and small articles.

Hull: Dialect. Pig sty.

Hulme: Danish. A small piece of land by a stream, brook or river. Hulme End (River Manifold *1059*), Kettelshulme *9879* near Todd Brook.

Hundred: ON: *hundrath*. A subdivision of a shire. Hundred boundaries extended outside Peak Park boundaries. ***High Peak***: Hundred of Derbyshire, known as Bakewell until [end 12th century] (Ashbourne ecclesiastical 'parish' covered: Alsop en le Dale *1655*, Parwich *1854*, + Bakewell *2168* 'parish' incorporated: Ashford in the Water *1969*, Baslow *2572*, Beeley *2667*, Chelmorton *1169*, Haddon *2366*, Harthill *2262*, Longstone *1871*, Monyash *1566*, Sheldon *1768*, Taddington *1471*, + Bradbourne: Tissington *1752* + Castleton *1583*: Edale *1285*, + Hartington *1260*: Earl Sterndale *0967* + Hathersage *2380*: Derwent *2383*, North Lees *2383*, Padley *2579*, Stoney Middleton *2275*, + Tideswell *1575*: Wormhill *1274* + Youlgreave *2064*: Elton *2260*, Rowtor *2261*, Winster *2460*). ***Macclesfield***: Hundred (Domesday Hamestan) of Cheshire. ***Totmonflow***: Hundred of Staffordshire (Alstonefield *1355*, Blore *1349*, Grindon *0854*, Ilam *1350*, Longnor *0864*, Sheen *1161*, Wetton *1055*). ***Wirksworth***: Hundred of Derbyshire (Bradbourne 'parish': Fenny Bentley *1750*. Hundreds may be derived from Germanic tribal units; in the Kingdom of the Franks [5th to 8th centuries] a hundred supplied 100 warriors. In England under *Edmund* [939-946] it was a financial, judicial and police unit. About [AD1000] it meant 100 'hides' of land or 100 households. In the Danelaw 'wapentake' tended to replace 'hundred' as an administrative unit. *Charles I* levied 3 shillings (15p) to pay the expenses of the High Peak hundred's 4,495 trained soldiers [1634]. The term 'hundred' was still in use in [1874] when *J Charles Cox* and in [1892] when *Joseph Tilley* were writing. Hundred courts were part of the legal system. Manywere in private hands by [1110].

Hurst: OE: *hyrst* OHG = a thicket on a hill. Hazelhurst *0377*, Nether Hurst *2182*, *0692*.

Husbandman: OE: *husbanda*. A small farmer who often worked for wages at harvest time, next in the social hierarchy to a 'yeoman'.

Iceland spar: See 'Calcite'.

Impropriator: ML A lay person owning church property. [1650] Edensor living/benefice *2569* given by the 'Earl' of Devonshire. 'Advowson'.

Infangenetheof: The right of an Anglo-Saxon landlord to do justice to a thief taken with stolen property on an estate.

Inheritance: *Henry III's* [1217-72] laws of inheritance allowed daughters to inherit if no sons were surviving when a testator died.

Iron Age: In England from [800BC] until about [AD55] (Roman conquest). Carlwark *2681*, Fin Cop *1771*, Kenslow *1761*, Mam Tor *1283*, Steep Low *1256*. 'Bronze Age', 'Celts'.

Jag: 1. A small load of hay. 2. A train of trucks from a mine. 3. A packhorse train. 4. A goad for horses. Jaggers Clough *1487*, Jaggers Lane, Hathersage *2380*.

Jagger: 1. A pedlar who carried a leather wallet jag. 2. A carrier/carter who used small, strong horses of 13-14 hands originally from Galloway in south west Scotland *4867* to "export" metal ore from the mines and return with coal. Jaggers Clough *1487*, Stanage Pole [landmark] *2484*. 'Packhorses'.

Jarnett: Dialect. A place so wet as to resemble a marsh. *1469*.

Jasper: SiO_2. Latin: *jaspis.* A red variety of 'chalcedony' or 'chert' containing 'haematite'. Friden *2476. Figure 12,* Rock Extraction, refers.

Johnson: A perennial grass *sorghum halepense,* used for feed and fodder, named after *William Johnson* [died 1859] USA agriculturist. Johnson's Knoll *1557.*

Jowl: Dialect. Earthenware vessel.

Justice in eyre: OF: *erre* = to wander. An itinerant, circuit judge travelling the counties on behalf of the king. The system lasted from about [1170] until the [late 13th century]. [1195] *Simon Bassett, Roger de Gernon, William de Vernon* [1210].

Justice of the Peace: An office instituted in [1327] Petty justice was largely in JPs' hands by [1603]. Appointments were made by the Crown on the advice of the 'Lord Lieutenant' [1641], 'Earl' of Rutland JP used his appointment against Harthill *2262* lead miners. *William Savile* JP, Earl of Rutland's steward, read out the House of Lords petition against Haddonfields *2165* lead miners. *Sir Henry Vernon* [1445-1515] a JP in Derbyshire and six more counties. *Walter Blount* for Staffordshire [1380], for Derbyshire [1388], *William Blount, Lord Mountjoy* for Derbyshire, Hertfordshire and Staffordshire [1532]. Issuers of licences to 'badgers', drovers', hucksters', swailers'; [07/7/1746] Bakewell *2168,* 5 licences, Taddington *1471* 6, Tideswell *1575,* 3. Inspection visit to Eyam silk mill [1807] *2176,* 'Derwent'. 'Custos rotulorum'.

Kibble: OHG: *kubel.* A horse load of copper ore.

Kick: Dialect. A tipping cart.

Kimnel: Dialect. A large, shallow, wooden vessel used in a dairy.

King's Field: The large lead mining area, in the Duchy of Lancaster's Peak estates, a result of the petition to *Edward I* in [1288] the Ashbourne Inquisition and Quo Warranto proceedings. The High Peak section comprised Bradwell *1781,* Castleton *1582,* Monyash *1566,* Taddington *1471* and Winster *2460.* 'Law'.

Kirk: ON: *kirkja.* The alternative name for a church used as far south as Norfolk. Kirksteads *0856,* Kirk Dale *1868.*

Kit: Dialect. A wooden milking pail.

Knarr: LG *knarre* Rough stone Knarrs 'Nook' *0290, 0067.*

Knight: OE: *cniht.* A non-hereditary title, originally a military servant of the king who may or may not enjoy a grant of land. Later knights were feudal tenants holding land on condition of service before becoming land owners with their own estates. *William Avenell* Nether Haddon *2266,* Wormhill forest *Eyres 1274.* In the [12th century] scutage, in lieu of military service, was allowed to be delegated in return for a payment to the knight. By the [13th century] knights and freeholders were increasingly involved in local government. Knights had to take part in the shire moot, formerly the folkmoot, presided over by itinerant 'justices in eyre' together with archbishops, bishops, abbots, freeholders, priors, earls, sheriffs and burghers. Daily wages: [1154-89] 3p; [1199-1216] 10p. About [1349] *Edward III* established the Order of the Garter as the premier order of knighthood.

Knoll: OE: *cnoll,* ON: *knollr* = hill top. Paddock *9677,* Thorpe Cloud *1550.* A small rounded hill.

Knowl: LG: *knull* = a hump. Knowles *0161,* Cheshire *0170,* Wilson *0266*

La(e)ch(e): OE: *lecc* = wet ditch or bog The Laches *9673,* Rewlach *0861,* Wythen *0277.*

Laith: Dialect. Field barn *9671.*

Languages: 'Family Names', 'Place Names', 'The Natural World' and the 'Glossary' show that a mixture of words, brought by incomers from overseas and other parts of the British Isles, together with local dialects, were used. Many words have survived to the present day and may be linked with their origins. Language evolution and fusing of one language with another was a feature. 'Knoll' may have its origins in either Old English or Old Norse or both. Activities, especially in agriculture and mining, gave rise to local dialect words, which, if used at all in other parts of the British Isles, often had different meanings. However establishing the origins of some words is beset by problems. Oral usually preceded written use. When committed to writing, by the minority able to do so, words could be abbreviated and letters misread by clerks and copyists; Devonshire was probably a misreading of Derbyshire. The quality of hand writing was affected by a writer's ability, contemporary styles, writing materials and implements. *Dr Samuel Johnson's* Dictionary, which contributed to the standardisation of spellings and definitions, was not published until [1755].

Medieval Latin: evolved from the Classical Latin of the Romans to become the language of the institutions of the Roman Catholic Church, officialdom and scholarship. (Taxonomic Latin names, for classifying fauna and flora taxonomy, devised by the Swedish botanist *Linnaeus* [1707-78] are still used). The Mercian dialect of **Old English,** was spoken and written from the [6th to the 12th centuries]. Anglo Saxon. miners', language was based on Saxon. There were also local words in the shires of Cheshire, Derbyshire and Staffordshire. Old English was later influenced by 'Danish' invaders and settlers from the [9th to the 11th centuries] especially in the 'Danelaw'.

Norman French: was spoken by 11th century Norman invaders.

Middle English: came into being when the effects of the Norman Conquest were absorbed between about [1150 and 1450].

Danish: had similar speech patterns to Old Frisian and Old Dutch. 'Old Norse' and Old English were mutually intelligible and widely used [1016- 42]. ***Old Norse***: was sometimes called 'Scandinavian' together with Old Danish. It was not spoken after [1200]. ***Norman French***, often referred to as Anglo-Norman, was the language of aristocrats and their retainers. 'Manors' 'Royal involvement'. Old High ***German*** from [750], Middle High German from [1150] and Early New German from [1350] also exerted some influence on these languages. A few words probably had **Cornish**, **Scottish** and **Celtic Welsh** origins.

Latten/cullen plate: OF: *laton*. A material for engraving 'monumental brasses', 65% copper + 32% zinc + 1% lead + 1% tin. It was imported from Cologne *50°54'N 6°57'E* until an inferior English product was substituted about [1550]. 'Metals'.

Lead mine personnel: 'Barmaster', 'brenner', 'caver', investor, pickman/hewer, carrier/'jagger', winder.

Lead vitriol: 'Anglesite'.

Leat: OE abbreviation: *watergeleat*. A ditch which directs water to a 'mill' wheel or takes it away from the end of a 'sough'. Mandale *1966*.

Lee: OE: *hleow*. A shelter for sheep to stand under. Allstone *0477*, Birchinlee *1691*, Broad *9860, 1185*, Hawks *9365*, Hay *0378*, Long *0188*, White *2694*, 'Whinstone' 'Tor' *2087*.

Lees: Plural of OE: *leah/ley* = clearings. Hucklow *1490*, North *2383*, Priestcliffe *1473*, Stanton *2563*. 'Leam'.

Levellers: A radical group, which in the [1640s] advocated republicanism and freedom of worship. Their journal, 'The Moderate', reported in [1649] that High Peak miners, who claimed free mining rights from their lord, *Earl of Rutland*, were being misrepresented by him.

Ley: OE: *leah* = a clearing. Bartomley *9665*, Beeley *2667*, Chinley *0484*, Helmsley *9866*, Hinkley *1150*, Houseley *1975*, Midgley *9765*, Ramsley *2875*, Rushley *1251*, Stanley *1776*, Swythamley *9764*.

Liberty: An area where the mineral rights belonged to the landowner or lord of the manor not the Crown. Ashford in the Water *1969* and Haddon *2366* were large estates outside the 'King's Field'; Taddington *1771*.

Lime: tree/pry. OE: *lim* Small leaved *tilia cordata*, the commonest tree in England [3000BC]. *Uses*: fibrous material for making ropes (*cord* in the botanical name), printing paper, 'bast' mats, carvings Lyme Hall *9682*, 'medicine'. Hope *1783*, Lime Tree Farm *1061*, Wood *2767*. Dialect: *bont* = rope.

Limestone, carboniferous/mountain: $CaCO_3$. A sedimentary rock formed from marine animal deposits. *Origin*: It comprises mainly calcareous remains (bones incorporating calcium carbonate) of marine animals deposited in internal seas. The so-called 'marbles' of the Peak are actually types of limestone with natural additives, not limestone metamorphosed into marble. Crinoidal limestone, slabs of which may be polished, incorporates lily-shaped echinoderms (marine invertebrates) fossils. Sheldon [1647] *1768*. *Formations*: Sometimes basin limestone deposits are stratified and tilted like those covering the Alton coal seam near Baslow *2572* and Chatsworth *2670*. At other times deposits are large reef masses. Examples of both can be seen in Dovedale *1451*. In the faults and joints, single and multiple, metal bearing ores were precipitated as 'Veins', 'Rakes', 'Scrins' and 'Flats','Chert'. Ornamental limestones with attractive "impurities" were in demand for making "marble" objets d'art and decoration Knoll reef limestone from Foolow *1976*. The lower millstone grit, horseshoe-shaped deposits of the Peak have been exposed where erosion has removed the limestone cover. *Uses*: 1. Aerodrome World War II runways. 2. Agriculture lime dressing for fields. 3. Lime (a) mortar, (b) plaster with hair North Lees Hall *2383*, (c) quick lime. Chee Dale [1880-1944] *1273*. 4. Enclosure walls. Shining Bank *2365*. 5. Flue gas desulphurisation: Coal-fired electricity generating stations. 6. Manufacturing: Lime for hardening glass, slagging flux for iron and steel smelting especially after the discoveries of the Gilchrists [1878], leather tanning *Barker*. 7. Weirs: Wolfscote Dale has adjacent small, grassed-over quarry excavations in the river banks alongside the all-weather path. *1456* 8. Buildings: Litton cottages *1675*, Bakewell houses *2168* + 'millstone grit' sills and cornerstones, St Thomas Church Biggin [1848] *1559*, Tideswell *1575*, Wormhill Church of St Margaret *1274*. ***Processing***: in 'lime kilns' Stoney Middleton *2375* and cement works Hope *1783; James Smeaton*, when building Eddystone lighthouse, found that he could make cement by burning limestone with clay [1756]. *Figure 12,* Rock Extraction, refers.

Limonite/xanthasiderate: Approximately $FeO(OH).nH_2O$. Latin: *limus* = a bog. Bog iron ore (yellow ochre). A generic term for iron oxides the most common being 'goethite'. The first iron to be smelted. Eyam *2176*, Winster *2460*. *Figure 11,* Metal Ore Extraction, refers.

Lin/flax: Lin Dale *1551*.

Lintel: A horizontal beam above a doorway usually from sessile 'oak' or stone.

Lithopone: Greek: *lithikos* = stony + *ponos* = work A white pigment for paint made from ground 'barytes'. Arbor Low *1663*, Coombs Dale *2274*, Friden *2476*.

Lode: OE: *lad* A fissure, usually in carboniferous 'limestone, filled with ore, often together with quartz. Lode Mill *1455*.

Lollards: Followers of the Protestant reformer, *John Wycliffe* [1324-84] from Lutterworth *5484*. OG: *lollo* = to shout. They were active from the [14th to the 16th centuries] and were persecuted by *Richard II* [1377-99]. *Walter De Ludank* and Lud's "Church" *9865*.

Lord lieutenant: *Henry VIII* [1509-47] may have created the office and given the military functions of sheriffs to lords lieutenant. On the other hand the office may have been created earler in [1453]. Lords lieutenant were usually peers or large landowners. *Cavendish.*

Lot: ON: *hlutr* = to share. The duty levied on lead miners' production at rates, typically 1/13th (7.7%), but varied by landowners. 'Cope'.

Love Feast: Greek: *agape* A practice dating from the time when the first Christians ate an agape meal together as a sign of their fellowship (Bible: 2 Peter 3 verse 13b, Jude verse 12) and later resumed by the Moravians - a Protestant missionary Church [1722] *49°30'N 17°30'E*. An annual Methodist event at Alport Castles Farm *1391* on the 1st Sunday in July since about [1745].

Low: The word has connections with hills and also burial sites. Distinguishing between the two uses is difficult because burial mounds, 'tumuli', were normally on hills. (a) In ME '*low*' = a ***hill*** from OE: *hlaw, hlaew*. Wardlow *1874*. (b) In Gothic, Germanic languages *hlais* = '*low*' = a ***grave***. Warslow *0858*. The majority of lows are 'Bronze Age'. Dismantling sepulchral lows, to obtain stone for enclosure walls, has made some indistinguishable from topographical lows. *Figure 27,* Tumuli on Named Lows, refers.

Lychgate: Dialect: *light gate* and OE: *lic* = a corpse. An open-sided, roofed shelter for a funeral at the start of a path to a church. Baslow *2572*, Taddington *1471*. Chelmorton [1668] later removed *1169*.

Lydgate: OE: *hlidgeat* A swing gate. Lydgate Graves *2276; George & Mary Darby,* victims of Eyam Plague [1666].

Lynchet/landshare/lantchett/lawchers/lynche: OE: *hlinc* = a ridge. A narrow cultivation terrace formed by ploughing a valley side. River Manifold valley *1152*, Crosslow *1656*, Priestcliffe *1371*.

Malachite: $Cu_2CO_3(OH)_2$ Greek: *malache*. Bright green copper carbonate (57% copper). Ecton *0958*. *Figure 11,* Metal Ore Extraction, refers.

Manganite: $MnO(OH)$. Italian: *manganese*. Discovery of manganese [1774] May be a constituent of 'wad'. *Figure 11,* Metal Ore Extraction, refers.

Manor: OF: *manoir* An imprecise, divisible unit of territorial organisation, acquired, wholly or partly, either by allocation, inheritance or purchase. 'Moiety'; 'Mesne'. It was possibly a lordship dating from Saxon times. 'Normans' comprehensively formalised the arrangement. **Saxon**: lords: *Chetal, Colle, Ernvi, Godric, Gurneburn, Hundine, Levenot, Lewin, Raven, Siward, Swain, Uchtred.* **Norman**: Numbers between [ ] refer to the number of Peak manors allocated to individuals. *King William I* Royal 'demesne' [17], *William Avenell* [1], *Chaworth,* [1], *Henry De Ferrars* [9], *Ralph Fitzhubert* [2], *Robert Fitz-Waltheof* [1], *William Peverell* [12]. Lords of manors were not always members of the nobility. Manors were divided and amalgamated. A 'parish' could include a number of manors'; Bakewell parish included

4 manors. Size meant there was a hierarchy of manors. Bakewell *2168* was a principal one. *Figure 29,* Spread of Manors.

Marble: Latin: *marmor.* In the Peak meaning of the word - any limestone taking a polish. Real marble is limestone which has been metamorphosed by heat and/or pressure. ***Ashford:*** *1969* 'Anthraconite'. Impregnated with bitumen. <u>Uses</u>**:** Exported to Rome for the manufacture of ink stands, obelisks and vases. ***Bird's eye:*** The colour is usually medium grey with crinoidal (marine invertebrate) fragments which resemble birds' eyes. Netler Dale, Ashford in the Water *1969* 20cm thick beds with 'chert'. ***Black birds' eye*** has small round coral "eyes" of fossilised entrochi. <u>Use</u>*:* Prince Arthur's tomb in Worcester Cathedral *8555*. Sheldon *1768.* ***Derby black:*** Ashford in the Water *1969* ***Derby fossil**/grey/ crinoidal/figured/Monyash*: Encrinite (marine invertebrate) fossil stems interspersed at different angles. It is usually medium grey in colour but can be blue with purple markings. Brecks *1467,* Ricklow *1656.* <u>Use</u>*.* Walls of the Royal Festival Hall, London [1951]. ***Dukes' red:*** Coloured blood red by ferric oxide in 'haematite'. <u>Use</u>*:* St John's College Chapel Cambridge 'abaci', Church of St Peter, Edensor *2468*, font, St Giles, Great Longstone *2071* pulpit pillar Alport *2174.* ***Pink birds' eye:*** is marble streaked with pink. Parsley Hay *1563.* ***Rosewood:*** the hardest marble has fine streaked reddish veins of bitumen in stratified limestone. When polished it resembles rosewood. Ashford in the Water *1969,* Sheldon *1768 Marbury. Figure 12,* Rock Extraction, refers.

Marcasite: FeS$_2$. See 'Pyrite'.

Mardo: Dialect. Manure. 'Casson'.

Marquis/Marquess: OF: *marchis.* A title introduced at the end of the [14th century] to indicate a nobility rank between a 'duke' and an 'earl'. When a 'duke' is also a marquis the title of marquis is passed, as a courtesy, to an eldest son. *Cavendish* family male member. <u>Marquis</u> of Hartington *0967,* [18/01/1702] Captain of the Yeomen of the Guard, [1687] *Sir William Savile* 2nd of Halifax.

Maw: Dialect 1. A place where hay or corn is heaped up. <u>Maw</u>stone *2163.* 2. Castleton *1583* mineralogist. 3. OE: *maga* = the mouth of a greedy person.

Meadow: OE: *maedwe.* Grassland that was good enough to be mown for hay. Willow <u>Meadow</u> *0354.*

Meer/meare: A boundary. Dialect. The distance between mining concessions 25-30 metres. Each meer had its own shaft. Compare 'mere'.

Mercia: A loosely organised kingdom in the Midlands, one of the seven [8th century] 'Saxon' kingdoms. The Peak National Park covers part of the kingdom. Its zenith was under *King Offa* [759-796]. Bakewell *2168* was in Danish Mercia. The kingdom was reduced in size by *Edward the Confessor* [1041-66] to an earldom [ealdormanry] under *Beorn 'Cearl', 'Edric', 'Streona'.*

Mercury: Hg. Latin: *Mercurius.* A liquid metal, known since [100BC], and occurring mainly in 'cinnabar'. <u>Uses</u>: Recovery and refining of various metals Sheldon *1768.* 'Medicine'. *Figure 11.*

Mere: OE. 1. *gemaere* = a boundary mark. Pittle <u>Mere</u> *1378.* 2. *mere* = an artificially or naturally clay lined pond to collect water often from a spring Heathcote *1460,* Monyash *1566.* 3. OE: *mere* = a small natural lake formed when ice blocks heavy with glacial drift melted. Blake [black] <u>Mere</u> *0361, 2558.*

Merlon: Italian: *merlone.* The raised "tooth" on crenelated embattlements. Snitterton Hall *2760.*

Mesne manor: OE: *meien* = middle. A manor held from a superior. <u>Mesne</u> Close, Abney *1979. Blackwell* and Blackwell *1272.*

Mesolithic Period: The middle Stone Age [8000-3000BC] between the Pre-Boreal and Atlantic climate periods. People possibly immigrated from Europe, living by hunting. 'Chert'.

Messuage: Property comprising a dwelling, outbuildings and adjacent land. 'Gifts'.

Methodism: A Christian movement which began while *Charles* and *John Wesley* were at the University of Oxford. They were nick-named Methodists because they were so methodical. The movement expanded after the 'heart warming experience' of John [24 May 1738] in Aldersgate, London. There was a close association between Methodism and mining communities in the Peak; their financial resources were sufficient only for the building of simple chapels, serviced by unpaid Local Preachers and exhorters, with only a few full time Ministers. Magistrates exempted preachers from toll payment at Waterhouses *0850* toll bar. By the 19th century there were four branches – Primitive (which had some women ministers), United, Wesleyan (closer to the Church of England) and Wesleyan Reform. Each branch had its own ethos. The Primitive, United and Wesleyan branches united in [1932] but many societies retained their buildings and held separate services long afterwards. 'Christian activity'.

Millstone grit/gritstone: of several types. *Origin*: A type of sandstone deposited in the delta of a river flowing 320 million years ago south from the north of England towards the Peak and associated with the many edges. Formations are either massive or slim lamellar sheets. The original vegetation on lower millstone grit slopes was mainly 'sessile oaks'. <u>Uses</u>: 1. <u>Bakestones</u> for oat cakes. 2. <u>Building</u> 'quoins', copings, steps and walls. Houses Eyam *2176*, Froggatt *2476*, Sparrowpit *0980*, Stanton in the Peak *2464*, Taxal *0079*, Wincle *9665*, Durability: 3,000 years. The Bath House in Bakewell *2168* is said to have been built from brownstone; a type of sandstone. Cladding of the central tower and steps and "slates" for the stable blocks at Haddon Hall, *2366*, "Slates" – sandstone flags Hollinsclough Church + School [1840] *0666*, from Kerridge *9474* for Jenkin Chapel *9876*, from Offerton *2181* for Castleton *1583*, Glossop Low quarry *0696* + paving slabs, Church of St Saviour, Wildboarclough *9868*, Winster *2460*, Fortification walls Carlwark *2681*. Checkered sandstone with 'limestone' Alstonefield Church *1355*. 3. <u>Construction</u> projects 'reservoirs', 'Roman roads' Field enclosure walls. 4. <u>Fireplaces</u> Light blue from Watts Cliff *2262*. 5. <u>Grindstones</u> for size reduction of metal, ores and grain ['grist', coarse], glass bevelling, paper pulping Bury Cliff *2161*, Ann Twyford, Stanton *2462*. Tool sharpening Whetstone Ridge *0170*. 6. <u>Monuments</u> Nine Ladies Stone Circle *2563*. 7. <u>Pavements</u> (a) Flagstones for London. Goytsclough *0173*, Plainsteads (paved track) *0290*, (b) 'Hollways'. 8. Pye/pot stones for heating tilt hammer workpeices. 9. <u>Recreation</u>: Edges, which are attractive to rock climbers and wear out their boots! Curbar *2575*, Frogatt *2576*. 10. 'Stoops'. *Quarries*: examples Beeley *2667* for Chatsworth House, Reeve Edge *0169* in the west, Stanton *2563* in the east. *Figure 12*, Rock Extraction, refers.

Millwright: The person responsible for the machinery in a mill.

Mire: ME: *myre* and *myer* = a <u>bog</u>. Great Longstone *2071*, Red *0484*, The <u>Mires</u> *2362*, Wardlow *1875*.

Moiety manor: ME Half a divided 'manor'. At a later date it meant any part of a whole manor. *Melland, Prime, Wallesby, Shuttleworth* and *Robinson* at Bamford *2083*, *De Salocia* and *De Eston* at Monyash *1566*, *Sacheverells* at Snitterton *2760*, *De Hockele* and *De Hamilton* at Taddington *1471*.

Mole plough: Dialect. A drainage plough with a missile shaped iron nose for making a tunnel below the surface of the ground.

Monyash marble: See 'Derby Fossil marble'.

Moot Court: S: *mot* + Latin: *cohors*. A 'Saxon' assembly, usually of a 'hundred', 'manor' or 'shire', dealing with legal and administrative affairs. 'Law'.

Mordant: Latin: *mordere* = to bite [into the cloth]. A primer used before the application of a dye such as 'haematite'. Youlgreave *2064*, or organic oak galls from Shireoaks *0783*. 'Alum'.

Motte and bailey: OF: *motte* = an artificial mound within the walls of a castle. + *baille* = bailey, the outermost wall of a castle or enclosed court, a fortified enclosure within the outer walls of an ancient or medieval castle. *1163, 1261, 2692*.

Mundic: See 'Pyrite'.

Nab: Dialect. A projecting part of a hill. Shooters' <u>Nab</u> *0610*, Lower <u>Nabbs</u> *9668*, Whiteley NB OE: *with* = curved *0292*.

Narlow: Dialect. A knot [of roads] <u>Narlow</u> *1650*.

Natural coke: See 'Carbonite'.

Naze: OE: *naes*(s) = marshy land. Castle *0578*, Dewhill *1001*, Peak<u>naze</u> *0496*, Torside *0797*.

Neb: OE: *nebb* = a peak High <u>Neb</u> *2285*.

Neolithic period: New Stone Age [3500-2000BC] As well as using flints and polished stone tools they engaged in arable farming.

Net sinker: An ancient British flint with a single perforation. Swythamley Grange *9764*.

Nettles: *urtica dioica*. OE: *netele*. Probably introduced by the Romans for use as textile fibres, in soups and porridge, as manure and as 'medicine'. World War II [1939-45] medicine and camouflage dye. <u>Nettlebeds</u> *9565*, <u>Nettly</u> Knowe *1456*.

Nick: 1. The mark in the barrel of a windlass made by the 'barmaster' to check whether a claimant to a lead mine was working it. If, after three nicks were cut, the original owner had not started to rework the mine a new claimant was allowed possession. 2. The gap in a range of hills. Oldgate *9976*, Winyards Nick *2581*.

Nook: A narrow access Knarrs Nook *0290*.

Normans/Men of the north/Norsemen: The collective name given to the invaders of England [1066] who originated from Scandinavia. They invaded Russia and Turkey about [850]. *Rollo* the 1st Duke of Normandy was a Dane. After much plundering of France, *Charles III, the Simple,* King of France [898-923] negotiated the Treaty of St Clair sur Epte [911], by which *Rollo* gained Neustra, part of which was renamed Normandy. *Charles the Simple* gave his daughter *Giselle* to *Rollo* to become his wife provided the Normans embraced Christianity. Not all members of the army which invaded England were from Normandy. Brittany, Burgundy, Champagne, Flanders, Picardy all provided personnel. Norman overlords patronisingly referred to the mass of the people as Saxons, irrespective of their ethnic origins. *Berry, Cheney, Curzon, Ferrars, Foljambe, Manners, Morteyne, Mountjoy, Neville, Savile, Tracey, Vernon. Figure 25.*

Oak: OE: *ac* 1. Common *quercus robur.* 2. Sessile *quercus petraea.* **Habitats**: clay soil and also sandy loam. Originally lower millstone grit edges were covered by woodlands comprising mainly sesssile oaks. Chatsworth *2670*, Oakenclough Hall *0563*, Oaks Farm *2179*, Shireoaks *0783*. **Uses**: 1. Acorns for pig feed. 'Agister' and 'Swineherd'. 2. Bark for tanning. 3. Beams Sessile [flexible] oak for construction of churches, religious houses, noblemen's houses, eg two massive beams in the west wing of Offerton Hall *2181*. 4. Galls for 'mordanting'. 5. Wood for coffins, panels Hartington Hall [1611] *1360*, monuments and 'whiskets', pews St Edmund's Church, Castleton *1582*. 6. Chests High Bradfield church *2692*. 7. Leaves Printing paper. A large proportion of oak wainscot was imported, not made locally. With the Restoration of the *Charles II* in [1660] 'walnut' began to supersede oak.

Oakstone: See 'Derbyshire onyx'.

Ochre: Greek: *okra* = a permanent colour eg 'haematite' (red), 'limonite' (yellow). Coloured clay was extracted from ochre pits. Iron Pits *0652*. Crushing Milldale Mill *1354*.

Olefinite/alkene: C_nH_{2n}. A form of carbon, rods of which burn like candles and were used by miners. Windy Knoll *1383*. *Figure 28,* Fire and Light refers.

Olivine/olevineare: $(Mg,Fe)_2SiO_4$. Olive coloured magnesium iron silicate; a variety of chrysolite. Green crystals found in a basalt vein. **Uses**: Gemstones. Earl Sterndale *0966*, Kirk Dale *1868*.

Opal: $SiO_2.nH_2O$ Sanskrit: *upala*. Hydrated silicon oxide. Not the gemstone variety. Bakewell *2168*, Eyam *2176*. *Figure 12,* Rock Extraction, refers.

Open: S: *opan.* 1. A surface site for depositing mining waste. Little Hucklow *1678* surrounded by mining waste hillocks. 2. A field shared by two 'parishes'.

Oriel: OF: *oriol* = a gallery. A window on an upper floor behind which priests in hiding used to say mass in the [16th, 17th and 18th centuries]. 'Recusant'.

Outrake: Dialect. Free passage of sheep from enclosed to open grounds Outrake *1871*.

Oxgate/oxgang: [1620] gift of 2 (= 1 'yardland/virgate) by 'Earl' of Devonshire to Longstone 'chapelry' *2071*. 'Bovate'.

Packhorse: From medieval times, until about [1750], the usual means of freight 'transport.' Often packhorse trains comprised 50 Galloway horses (under 14 hands*). Each animal carried two 'panniers'. The routes followed by packhorse trains were usually 'portways' dating from Saxon times. *1 hand = 10cm (4 inches) measured from the hoof to the horse's back. *Figure 15.*

Palaeolithic period: The Old Stone Age covering various culture periods [probably15,000-3,000BC]. Late Glacial Period 20,000-8,000BC People may have wandered during milder inter-glacial phases. Melting ice caused Britain to separate from mainland Europe about [9500BC]. Fox Hole *0866*. 'Home and Family Life: Medicine – Plants'.

Panniers/banesters: CL: *panarium* = a basket. Wicker containers on packhorses. Panniers' Pool *0068* 'Withen' Panniers were often carried for great distances on horses.

Parishes: Latin: *paroichia*. Parishes are thought to have originated in the [7th century] as ecclesiastical jurisdiction divisions centred on a local church. Boundary disputes sometimes occurred when two parishes shared one open field system. 'Crosses' and ditches may have marked boundaries. 'Chapelries' could be upgraded to parishes where populations increased. Large tracts of land were extra-parochial.

Parishes declined in importance until the Norman occupation because Saxon [parish] churches in the Danelaw were ravaged by Danes. Some parishes included a number of 'manors'. Bakewell *2168*. Not all the 'manors' had churches, or chapels, nor are dates available for all 'manors' which did have them.: Alstonefield [892] *1355*, Ashford [1870] *1969*, Bakewell [1192] *2168*, Baslow [1850s] *2572*, Beeley [1182] *2667*, Blackwell [1826] *1272*, Brushfield *1672*, Bubnell *2472*, Calver *2374*, Chelmorton [1200] *1169*, Hartle *2764*, Hassop [1816] *2272*, Little Longstone *1871*, Monyash [1198] *1566*, Nether Haddon *2266*, One Ash *1665*, Over Haddon *2066*, Rowland *2172*, Sheldon *1768*, Taddington *1471* Manors [14th century]. 'Crosses'. ***Alstonefield*** parish: included Alstonefield 'township' *1355*, Elkstone *0559*, Fawfieldhead *0763*, Heathy Lee *0363*, Hollinsclough *0666*, Longnor *0864*, Quarnford *0066*, Warslow *0858*. ***Bakewell*** parish: totalled 20 'townships', including Ashford in the Water *1969*, Bakewell 'township' *2168*, Baslow *2572*, Beeley *2667*, Blackwell *1272*, Brushfield *1672*, Bubnell *2472*, Calver *2374*, Chelmorton *1169*, Hartle *2764*, Hassop *2272*, Little Longstone *1871*, Monyash *1566*, Nether Haddon *2266*, One Ash *1665*, Over Haddon *2066*, Rowland *2172*, Sheldon *1768*, Taddington *1471* where parish priests were called seculars [1392] 'chantry' charter, 4 Domesday 'manors' and 7 'chapels'. ***Ecclesfield*** *3694*: included Bradfield *2692 and* Waldershaigh *2696*. ***Hope***: included Abney *1979*, Bradwell *1781*, Grindlow *1877*, Hazelbadge *1780*, Hope 'township' *1783*, Little Hucklow *1678*, Highlow *2180*, Stoke *2376*, Thornhill *1983*. ***Youlgreave***: included Birchover *2462*, Elton *2260*, Gratton *1960*, Middleton *1983*, Stanton *2563*, Winster *2460*, Youlgreave 'township' *2064*. ***Personnel:*** Under the 'Normans', several manors within one parish were under the control of a resident clergyman based on a parish church. His 'patron' was often a wealthy layman. ***Responsibilities:*** When monasteries, which had provided social services, were dissolved [1534-6] *Henry VIII* made parishes responsible for the care of the poor. The ecclesiastical parish became a unit of civil administration. Other civil responsibilities followed. 'Workhouse'. Parish registers were instituted in [1538]. Urban growth in the [19th century] necessitated civil administrative reforms. Civil and ecclesiatical parishes were separated. 'Hundred'. In urban areas the role of civil parishes, as instruments of government disappeared, but continued, on a reduced scale, in country areas, such as as those in the Peak, after [1868]. The Local Government Act [1974] introduced more changes. 'Church Music'. 'Tithing'.

Patron: CL: *patronus*. A person or group having a purchased, or hereditary right, to appoint a clergyman to assume responsibility for an Anglican or Roman Catholic place of worship. Castleton *1582* [1553] *George Wylmesley* through lease to him of the rectory by the Bishop of Chester. [1574] *Helen Wylmesley*, on the death of *George*. [1627] Bishop of Coventry and Lichfield after a lapse. [1631] Bishop of Chester.

Pea: Small concretions, pisolites in limestone similar in size to peas. Pea Low *1356*.

Peacock ore: See 'Bornite'.

Peak National Park: An area of 1,404 square kilometres, (542 square miles) created in [1950] comprising parts of the counties of Cheshire, Derbyshire, Staffordshire and Yorkshire originally populated by the Pecsaetan. In addition to Peak, Pecaetna, Pee and Pech have also been used as well as Peacloud [924], Pec [1130 *Henry I*]. In OE *peac* means a hill or peak.

> *Nine Things at the Peak we see*
> *A cave, a den, a hole the wonder be;*
> *Lead, sheep and pasture, are the useful Three*
> *Chatsworth, the Castle, and the Bath delight;*
> *Much more you see; all little worth the sight.*
>
> Britannia [1586] *William Cambden*

Pecsaetan: People of the Peak**,** early inhabitants of the Staffordshire Moorlands and Peak uplands, probably of 'Celtic' origin or descendants of an 'Iron Age' community. OE: *peac*.

Peeler: A nickname for a policeman named after *Sir Robert Peel*, British prime minister [1841-46] who reformed the police. Longnor [1847] *0864*. Their work was territorially restricted so outlaws moved across 'shire' boundaries to avoid arrest. Three Shires Head *0068*.

Pele tower: A look-out tower, often enclosed by a pale fence, with a ground floor for cattle, upper storeys for people being only accessible by a removable ladder. Fenny Bentley Hall *1750*, Throwley Hall *1152*.

Perry: W: *pefr* = bright Perryfoot *1081*

Peter: Star shaped Peter stone fossils, astroites. Peter Dale *1276*, Peter's Stone *1775*.

Pewter: OF: *peaultre*. Various alloys of tin (80-90%) + lead (10-20%) + possibly other metals eg copper. *Uses:* Tankards and plates. Flagon in Baslow Church *2572*. SiO_2, silica, in the horsetail plant *equisetum arvense* made it useful for polishing pewter.

Pig: Metal, eg lead, cast into a simple shape for ease of storing or transport. 'Lutudarum'.

Pike: OE: *pic* = pointed or conical hill, Lantern [shaped] *0288*, Pikehall *1959*, Topley *1072, 2097*.

Pinfold: OE *pundfald* = a walled, open-air, pound, for impounding stray cattle, horse and other animals. Abney Grange *1978*, Ashford in the Water *1969*, Bakewell *2168*, Baslow *2572*, Biggin *1559*, Bradfield *2692*, Bradwell *1781*, Butterton *0756*, Castleton *1582*, Chelmorton *1169*, Pinfold Hill, Curbar *2574*, Elton *2160*, Foolow *1976*, Great Longstone *1971*, Grindon about [1800] *0854*, Harthill *2264*, Hartington *1360*, Hassop *2272*, Hathersage *2381*, Pindale Road, Hope *1783*, Ilam *1352*, Little Hucklow *1678*, Longnor [19th century] *0864*, Monyash *1466*, Over Haddon *2066*, Quarnford *0066*, Sheldon *1768*, Taddington *1471*, Thorpe *1550*, Tideswell *1575*, Wardlow *1874*, Warslow *0858*, Waterfall *0851*, Wincle *9566*,Youlgreave *2064*. ***Pinder/pinner***: the manorial or parochial officer in charge of a pinfold.

Pipe: [vein] OE. Mineral and ore bearing deposits parallel to, and controlled by, the strata, not faults. Pipes are almost horizontal and cut across the main vein system eg Bradwell *1781* under the 'millstone grit' cover and 'fluorite' near Hazlebadge Hall *1780*. Volcanic lava may have flowed from the pipes before they became choked with debris. Fullwood *2063*, Moorfurlong *1482*, Speedwell *1482*.

Plantagenets: Kings *Henry II, Richard I, John, Henry III, Edward I, Edward II, Edward III, Richard II, Henry IV, Henry V, Henry VI, Edward IV, Edward V* and *Richard III*.

Plowbote: The medieval right to take wood to repair carts, ploughs and implements.

Poll: Dialect. Cattle with horns cut.

Poor Clares: A 'Franciscan' order of nuns founded in [1212]. *Clare*, an heiress of Assisi *43°7'N, 12°35'E* escaped by night from angry parents to follow Francis of Assisi. 'Gifts' 'Hartington [1291] & [1375] to Minorities/ Minoresses (Minor friars) convent in Aldgate, London [1291].

Porphyry: There are several versions. The Romans, prospecting for decorative stones in Egypt found *lapis pophyrites*, a type of granite which they used for columns, vases and slabs. Porphyry from the Middleton Mine *1963* resembles concrete because it has 'calcite' inclusions. Possible *Uses* by the Romans: road making as in the Mediterranean area near Frejus [Forum Julii]. 'Arbor' 'Low' *1663*. *Figure 12*, Rock Extraction, refers.

Porringer: ME: *potinger*. A bowl, often with a handle, for porridge and soup possibly made from 'pewter'.

'Portway': Latin: *portare* = to carry + OE: *weg* = way. Routes, possibly prehistoric, which were developed into throughways by the Anglo Saxons. Ashford in the Water *1969*, Great Longstone *2071*, Eyam *2176*, Winster *2460*. *Figure 15*, Route Planning, refers.

Praemunire Statute: A law of *Richard II* [1367-1400] against resorting to a foreign power or person [the Pope], for determination of what could be settled in a royal court. *Thomas Cokayne*.

Pre monstratensians: A monastic order of canons originated by *Norbert* in Magdeburg *52°6'N 11°35'E* founded about [1120] at Premontre *49°34'N 3°37'E* in Northern France and then by *Gilbert of Sempringham 1132*, Lincolnshire [1143]. They followed the Rule of Augustine but added to the Cara Caritatis (Charter of Affection) which the 'Cistercians' followed. Gift Derwent Chapel *2383* to Welbeck Abbey *5674*. 'Gilbert'.

Prez/praze/prase: SiO_2. Greek: *prasios*. Pale green, transparent quartz found in Roman jewellery. Bartomley *9665*. *Figure 12*, Rock Extraction, refers.

Priory: ML: *prioria*. A religious house governed by a prior and usually subordinate to an abbey. Lenton Priory *5238* [Blackwell 'Manor' *1272*], Tutbury *2129* [Tissington 'tithes' *1752*].

Pulp: Latin: *pulpa*. Pulverised material, eg ore or wood, mixed with water.

Pulpstone: Latin: *pulpa* + OE: *stan*. Large diameter eg 1.5 metres circular pieces of 'sandstone' similar to a millstone for grinding wood into 'pulp' for paper making. Export to Norway and Sweden from Stokehall *2376*.

Purprestre: A form of encroachment on forests involving building houses.

Puss nets: Staffordshire Moorlands *0854* word. Nets for catching rabbits *oryctolagus cuniculus*.

Pyrite/marcasite/mundic: FeS$_2$. Greek *pyr* and Arabic: *markasita* = fire because it sparks when rubbed with stone. *Uses*: Copperas (the common name for ferrous sulphate), tanning, dyeing and ink manufacture and also for Prussian Blue pigment when treated with K$_4$Fe(CN)$_6$ potassium ferrocyanide. Castleton *1583*.

Quakers/Society of Friends: A Christian group founded by *George Fox* in [1650]. Any member may speak at their meetings in which there are no formal ministers, sacraments or ritual. Bamford *2083*, Ford *0882*, Monyash *1566*.

Quartz: SiO$_2$. German: *quarz*. Silicon dioxide. There are variants - 'Amethyst', 'Chalcedony', 'Derbyshire Diamonds', 'Prez', 'Toadstone'- made by impurities. Friden *2476*. *Figure 12*.

Quill: Dialect. A haycock, a small conical pile of hay left in a field until dry.

Quoin: A dressed stone, eg 'Millstone grit', at the angle of a building.

Quo warranto/Ashbourne Inquisition: The law code allowing landless newcomers and residents to dig for lead on many manors irrespective of their ownership [1288]; a source of conflict between landowners and would-be free miners.

Raddle: 1. See 'Haematite' 2. OF: *redalle*. Green sticks used for hurdles.

Rake: 1. Originally a narrow hill path. OE: *hraca*. High Rake *1677*, Rake End *0275*, Rakes Moss *0500* and Dialect = a steep path on a hillside made by sheep. 2. Later a major ore bearing fissure fault [in limestone], usually at right angles to the parent rock strata, 3-5 metres wide and several kilometres long.

Raike: ME: *raik* = a space where animals pasture. The Raikes *1159*.

Rainolow: Dialect. A strip of uncultivated land in an arable field. Rainolow *9577*.

Ranger: An official responsible in the [fourteenth century] for ensuring forest law was kept.

Rascality: Rabble. Stanton manor *2563*. *Sir William Plumpton* disposed of the governance and marriage of his two fatherless granddaughters to *Henry Sotehill and Brian Rocliffe*.

Rathes: Dialect. Frames fixed to the sides of a wagon to increase its capacity.

Ream: Dialect. Cream .

Reaps: OE: *ripel* = a strip of land. Reaps Moor *0861*.

Recusants: Roman Catholics who refused to recognise and attend Church of England services after the Reformation [16th & 17th centuries). Fines, imprisonment and martydom were punishments. *Eyres, Richard Fenton* (North Lees) *2383*, *FitzHerberts, Garlick, Ludlam*.

Reen: Dialect. A drainage ditch.

Reeve: OE: *gereva*. An administrative officer in charge of an estate from which 'sheriff' was derived [tenth century].

Regard: OF = look at. The triennial inspection of forests.

Rew: OE: *lach* = a bog, Rewlach *0961*.

Ridgeway: Roads or tracks on high ridges used since pre-historic times to travel between hill forts. Macclesfield Forest *9671*, Stanage *2384*, Tintwistle *0297* → Woodhead *0900* → Sheffield. *Figure 15*, Route Planning, refers.

Rill: OLG: *rille* = a rivulet Headwaters of River Bradford, Smerrill *1962*.

Rind(le): A stream flowing only in wet weather. Blackdon *1188*, Grindleford *2477* possibly.

Roak: Dialect. A foggy mist. NB Humidity for cotton mills. See 'Mills'.

Rolley: Dialect. A low wagon without sides used for carrying heavy loads. The shape of Rolley 'Low' *1873* with its 1km west-east flat topped plateau and gently sloping flanks resembles one.

Romans: Conquest of England [55 BC]. Sack of Rome and departure [AD410].

Roos: OW = where heather grows. Heathy Roods *0857*.

Rottenstone: Soft decomposed limestone. *Uses*: Powdered to polish metal. Hazlebadge *1780*.

Rouster: Dialect. A great noise [water]. Rouster *9764*

Saddleman: Carriers of lead using the track through Rowsley *2566* → Chesterfield *3871*.

Sake and soke/sacu and socn: OE: *sacu* = a lawsuit + *socn* = seeking. Royal justice was delegated to private landlords in the 'hundreds'. Private courts were a familiar institution before [871]. The landlord had fiscal rights (fines) while the king retained judicial rights. Sake and soke may date from Ine's law in the [7th century]. Under Ine's laws a nobleman was expected to keep members of his household from wrongdoing.

Samian pottery/arretine ware: Reddish brown or black pottery, found on Roman sites, resembling pottery from Samos *37°45'N 27°45'E*. Wetton *1055*.

Sandstone: See 'Millstone Grit'.

Saxons: Settlers from West Holstein and the North German coast, west of the mouth of the River Elbe *53°14'N 10°50'E*. They first arrived in England under *Cerdic* in [AD495]. *Figure 24*.

Scaga: OE: *scaga/scaega* = a copse.

Sceat: OE: *sceat* = a block of strips or 'selions' constituting the main division of an open field system. Shutts, Derwent *2383*.

Scots pine *pinus sylvestris*: **Habitat**: In the past widespread distribution. Dark Peak. **Uses**: Distillation to obtain pitch for roofing and glueing, resin (burnt as incense), turpentine and 'medicine'.

Scrin: Dialect. Small ore bearing fissures a few metres long often in clusters near rakes. Scrins generally have a south east – north west orientation. Henry Barber *1482*, Quick *1482*, Sheldon Magpie Mine area *1768*.

Scrivener: OF: *escrivain*. A clerical expert, with legal training, employed in drawing up contracts, wills, bill bonds and mortgages and also in handling large amounts of money. *George Scriven* of Alport *2264* Wesleyan Reform preacher and Royal Engineers soldier in World War I Palestine, a companion of the author's father.

Selion: The smallest unit in an open field. The area varied between 1,000 and 3,000 square metres (¼ and ¾ acre). Strips were curved suitably for ox ploughing. Tideswell *1575*, Wheston *1376*.

Sericulture: The raising of silk worms *bombyx mori* on a diet of white mulberry leaves *morus alba*. Dates from [3000BC] in Japan. The silk industry probably employed many people about [1700]. Flash *0267*, Gradbach [late 18th century] *9966*, Wildboarclough *9868*, Wincle *9665*. *John Milward*.

Sester: OF *sestier* A jar of pitcher. [DB] measure of honey at Aston *1884*, Edale *1285*, Hope *1783*, Shatton *1881*

Shack: Dialect. A hidden cave used for depositing mining waste. 'Open'.

Shaw: OE: *sceaga*. A strip of woodland forming the border of a field. Bag<u>shaw</u> *2168*, Long<u>shaw</u> *2679*, Ram<u>shaw</u> *0262*, <u>Shaw</u>field *0661*.

Sheriff: OE: *scirgerefa*. The shire-reeve originated in the mid [10th century]. The shire was toured twice every year. The name sheriff was first used under *Cnut* [1017-35]. They presided over the 'shire' 'moot', often had the custody of 'royal demense' manors and were responsible for criminal, military and civil jurisdiction [before 1066] and, after [1066] tax assessment and until [1376] certification of 'knights'. When 'ealdormen' began to devote attention to more than one shire, sheriffs replaced them. Usually laymen such as barons, royal administrators and local gentry, they were at the height of their power under the Normans and approximated to vicomtes. However *Henry I* [1100-1135] discontinued the appointment of powerful barons. *Henry II* [1154-89] kept a close watch on their accounting; the office of sheriff was lucrative. High prices were paid for it. *Henry VIII* [1509-47] transferred their military functions to 'lords lieutenant'. The office continues in the 21st century, albeit with reduced responsibilities. **Personnel:** Sheriffs from the Peak Park appointed [1423-1888]: *Abney, Agard, Bagshawe, Balguy, Basset, Bateman, Blount, Bradshawe, Bullock, Carver, Cavendish, Chaworth, Cheney, Cokayne, Dale, Eyre, FitzHerbert, Foljambe, Fulwood, Fynney, Greaves, Hurt, Kniveton, Manners, Milward, Sacheverell, Saville, Shallcross, Shirtley, Statham, Sutton, Thornhill, Turner* Pott Shrigley [1826], *Vernon*.

Shire: S:*scire*; OE: *scir*. An administrative district consisting of a number of 'hundreds' or 'wapentakes' ruled jointly be any ealdorman and a sheriff who presided over the shire including its court. The Peak National Park comprises parts of four shires – Che<u>shire</u>, Derby<u>shire</u>, Stafford<u>shire</u> and York<u>shire</u>. The former Hallam<u>shire</u> probably included Bradfield *2692*, Midhope *2199* and Wigtwizzle *2595*.

Shivering mountain: As shale is soft, and relatively easily weathered, by frost and rain, shale hills are therefore unstable; slipping over underlying rocks and shivering occur. Mam Tor *1283*.

Shool: Dialect. Dung spade.

Sick/sike: Dialect. A small stream or spring which forms a marshy area. Hartland *2968*, Hipper *3068*, Millstone *3067*, Umberley *2969*. There are many examples in the Beeley Moor area.

Sieve: OE: *sife*. An implement used by 'cavers' after about [1568] to sift waste recovered from abandoned mines. Elton *2261*, Tideswell *1575*.

Silica sand: Latin *silex* + ON *sandr*. A mixture of sand, clay and pebbles deposited in pockets in the limestone. Friden *1660*, Green Lane *1662*, Heathcote *1460*, Kenslow *1861*, Washmere *1660*.

Sill: OE. *syll* An igneous intrusion usually injected along a bedding plane. Lava Tideswell *1575*.

Sitch: 1. OE: *sec*, A boundary. 2. ME: *siche* = a stream forming a marshy area. Felty<u>sitch</u> *039598*, Gold<u>sitch</u> *0064*, Green <u>Sitches</u> *1890*, Odin *1483* (in Norse mythology the supreme creator god), Oxen<u>sitch</u> *0268*, Salter <u>Sitch</u> *2878*, Scalder<u>sitch</u> *1159*, Siney *1980*. The term is used, in its second meaning, extensively in the western Peak area.

Slack: ON: *slakki* = a <u>shallow</u> <u>valley</u> or dell. Golden *9467*, Litton *1673*, <u>Slack</u> *0781*, Water<u>slacks</u> *0856*, Yellow *0695*.

Slang: ME. A narrow strip of land. The <u>Slang</u>, Castleton *1583*.

Slive: Dialect. The rough edge of a tree stump left by fracturing when it fell.

Slotch: Dialect. A plug made from lime and water used to seal lime kilns at weekends.

Smeuse: Dialect. A hole in a fence or wall for small animals. Allsop en le Dale *1655*.

Smithsonite/calamine: $ZnCO_3$. Zinc carbonate. It may also contain iron, calcium and cobalt. *Uses:* brass making. Smithsonite is named after *James Smithson* [1765-1829]. Eyam *2176*.

Smoot: Dialect. A hole in a hedge or fence for a hare.

Sniddles: ME dialect; *sniteren* = biting blast. <u>Snidders</u> *0065*.

Sock: Staffordshire Moorlands *0854* dialect and OE: *socian*. A liquid manure.

Sole: 1. Latin: *solea* [sandal shaped] animals' wallowing place. <u>Soles</u> Hill *0952*. 2. Dialect: a rope, chain or wooden collar fastening for cattle in a stall.

Sough: 1. Dialect. A drainage tunnel for lowering the water table in a mine. Deeper mining was made possible after [1630s] when *Sir Cornelius Vermuyden* designed the first one and gradually replaced rag and chain pumps. Calver *2374*, Hill Carr [1783] *2263*, Magpie constructed [1873-81] 176 metres depth in the mine x 2 miles to its tail *1768*, Moorwood *2275*. 2. OE: *swogan* = a soft, continuous murmuring sound Sough Top *1371*.

Specular ore: See 'Haematite'

Sphalerite/blende/Black Jack: ZnS Greek: *sphaleros* = treacherous [difficult to distinguish] Zinc sulphide. Castleton *1583*, Sheldon *1768*. *Figure 11*, Metal ore Extraction, refers.

Squint: A narrow hole in a church wall which enables an unseen person to look into the interior. Southwest corner of the Haddon Hall chapel chancel *2366*.

Squire: OF: *esquier* Originally a novice nobleman who attended a 'knight'. Later became the main landowner in a rural community. Some squires had a reputation for heavy handedness when punishing offences involving the killing of game in the [19th century]. *Thomas Bagshaw, John Manners, Fynney, Trafford* of Swythamley *9764*.

Stall: OE. *stall* 1. The working area in a coal mine between the support pillars. Berri<u>stall</u> *9478*. 2. A pool. NB 'Harrop' Brook *9478*.

Stainerie(y): A lichen used in dyeing *2095*. Compare Stannery *0766* = stoney.

Staple: MD: *stapel* = a warehouse. A town designated an exclusive market for a major export eg lead and Calais *50°58'N 1°50'E*. Wool stapler emblem, a pair of shears, is in the wall of the Chelmorton Church *1170*.

Statute Fair: A statutory annual fair for hiring farm labourers and domestic servants Low Bradfield *2691*. New Year's Day = Gorby Day Longnor *0864*.

Stibium: Sb_2S_3. 'Antimony'.

Stiddy/sthy: Dialect An anvil. 'Andle'.

Stinkstone: See 'Anthraconite'.

Stoase: Dialect. A stake for marking out the 'meers' which miners were allowed to work.

Stoop: 1. Dialect. Vertical blocks of 'millstone grit' erected as signposts on tracks. Ball Cross [1709] *2269*, Beeley Moor *2967*, Big Moor *2676*, Buxter *9776*, Curbar *2574*, Dyson Cote [1734] *1901*, Longshaw Park *2679, 0668*. 2. OE: *steac* A vessel for holy water. Stanton in the Peak *2464*.

Stoup: ON: *staup* = a beaker. A holy water vessel probably made from bronze and usually positioned near a church door. All Saints, Youlgreave *2064*. 'Stoop'.

Stripping: Dialect. The last of the milk taken from a cow at milking.

Strunt: Dialect. To dock the tail of an animal.

Stucco: OHG: *stukki* = a crust. White 'calcite' coating on exterior walls. Youlgreave *2064*.

Sty: Dialect. A ladder.

Swad: Dialect. Pod of peas or beans.

Swailer: Dialect: A dealer licensed to sell the small articles listed on his licence.

Swallet: OE: *swelgan*. A stream flowing underground, usually in a limestone area, after disappearing down a swallow hole. Stanton in the Peak *2464, 2077*.

Swineherd: OE: *swin + hirde*. The person who, with dogs, looked after the pigs in the forests and woods. After the Great Charter (Magna Carta) [1215], one of the three annual swainmote meetings, which regulated the use of forests and woods, dealt with pasturing pigs on the king's acorns.

Sycamore: *cer pseudoplatanus* Latin *sycomorus*. **Uses**: tables, flooring, bedsteads, 'medicine' and fuel. Sycamore Lodge *0653*, Stanton *2563*.

Tallet: Dialect. A hay loft over a stable.

Tallow: OE: *taelg*. A fatty substance extracted from sheep and cattle by rendering. Long horned cattle of Derbyshire, Lancashire, Staffordshire and Yorkshire produced good tallow, hides and horn and, being good milkers, were popular [1500-1649]. **Uses**: Candles and soap 'Greaves'.

Team: The right of an Anglo Saxon lord to hold a court in which men accused of wrongful possession of cattle, or goods, could prove their honesty.

Temse: Dialect. A sieve made from horse hair. OE: *temesian*; MD and MLG: *temesen*.

Tenant at will: A tenant at the will of the lessor [lacking security of tenure]. Together with leasholders and copy holders they replaced villeins by [1558]. Hassop Manor [1432], *Lord Furnival, Sir Roger Leech, Thomas Foljambe, Thomas Wild.*

Tenter: CL: *tendere* = to stretch A frame on which cloth is stretched so that its shape is not distorted while drying Holme Mill *1005,* Tenter Hill *0467,* Tentry Croft, Barthomley *1783* NB. On tenter hooks.

Terrace: OF: *terrasse*. Long, wide strips of farmland in staircase form; probably of Saxon origin Priestcliffe *1471, 2168*. 'Lynchnet'.

Terret: OF: *toret*. A decorative metal ring on a harness saddle for reins or a ring on a dog collar. The Terret of land *0371* between the present A53 from the Roman road to Buxton (Aqvae Arnemetiae) and the present A54 is almost a closed ring.

Tew: Dialect. Long handled pincers used by farriers for holding hot iron horseshoes.

Thane/thegn: OE: *thegn* OHG: *thegan*. 'Manors' In Anglo Saxon England a hereditary member of the aristocratic class below the rank of ealdorman. King's thanes were king's men, median thanes were not. *Ethelred the Unready* published the Wantage Ordinance to the effect that a court should be held in every hundred (wapentake) where 12 thanes and the reeve ['sheriff'] should be under oath to give information about criminals about [997].

Thatcher: Derbyshire roof thatchers preferred flax to rye straw. Flax Dale *1863*.

Thimble: Dialect. The iron ring of a gate post which acts as a hinge.

Throstle: S: *thrusla* ON: *throstr* = a song thrush *muscipidae*. Throstles Nest *0961*.

Tinker: 1. A travelling repairer of pots and pans ('copper') [13th century]. 2. A vagrant/itinerant trader/performer. Tinkers 'Pit' *0170, 0270*. The pit = a small enclosure.

Tithe: A comprehensive, 10% ecclesiastical tax, payable in kind* or money for the maintenance of a priest. Rectors received the great and small tithe, a vicar only the small tithe. Tithes were transferable. Bakewell *2168* tithes were appropriated to the Dean and Chapter of Lichfield. Some were treated like financial instruments, commodity tithes payable in kind* being leased to individuals for a yearly rent. Peak Forest *1179* corn, hay and lamb to *Sir Edward Leech* [1640]. Tithes were resented by lead miners, Roman Catholics and non-conformists. 'Lenton' ('Cluniac') *5238*, *Bradbury*, *Wilson*. **Tithe files** Chapelry' Bradfield *2692*, Derwent *2383*, Longnor *0864*, Warslow *0858*; Extra Parochial Place Griff Grange *2476*, Peak Forest *1179*. 'Parish' Castleton *1583*, Hartington *1360*, Parwich *1854*, Thorpe *1550*, Tissington *1752*. 'Townships' Abney *1979*, Abney 'Grange', Alwark *2357*, Alsop en le Dale *1655*, Ashford in the Water *1969*, Aston *1844*, Bakewell *2168*, Bamford *2083*, Ballidon *2055*, Baslow *2572*, Beeley *2667*, Biggin *1559*, Blackwell *1272*, Blore *1349*, Bradwell *1781*, Bubnell *2472*, Butterton *0756*, Calton *1050*, Calver *2374*, Chatsworth *2670*, Chelmorton *1169* + Flagg *1368*, Curbar *2574*, *Edale 1285*, Edensor *2569*, Elton *2260* + Winster *2460*, Eyam *2176*, Fenny Bentley *1759*, Fernilee *0178*, Foolow *1976*, Fraggatt *2476*, Gratton *1960*, Grindlow *1877*, Nether Haddon *2266*, Harthill *2262*, Hassop *2272*, Hathersage *2380*, Hazelbache *1780*, Highlow *2180*, Hope *1783*, Little Hucklow *1678*, Great Hucklow *1777*, Ible *2457*, Ilam *1350*, Litton *1675*, Great Longstone *2071*, Little Longstone *1871*, Lyme Handley *9862*, Macclesfield Forest *9671*, Monyash *1566*, Nether Padley *2579*, Offerton *2181*, Sheldon *1768*, Smerrill *1962*, Stanton *2463* + Birchover *2462*, Great Rowsley *2566*, Stoney Middleton *2275*, Taddington *1471* + Priestcliffe *1371*, Tideswell *1575*, Tintwhistle *1752*, Wensley *2261* + Snitterton *2760*, Wildboar-clough *9868*, Wincle *9665*, Winster *2460*, Wormhill *1274*, Youlgreave *2064*; Tithe Barn* for receipt and storage, long and short term, of payments in kind - fleeces, fruit, grain, hay, herbage, honey, milk (white tithe). Pigeons, rabbits, wax. Tithe Meadow, Aston *1884*, Tutbury Priory ('Benedictine') and Tissington *1752*. Winster *2460* benefice augmented [1702] by *Mrs Ann Phenney and Mr Henry Fenshaw* gave 25% of hay and corn tithes to the minister. 'Enclosures' often extinguished tithes before the enactment of the Tithe Commutation Act 1836].

Tithing: 1. A small adminstrative group of ten householders in a 'frankpledge' group. eg Alstonefield *1355* in [1270s]. 2. 10% of a 'hundred'.

Toadstone: The name given by Derbyshire lead miners to irregular igneous basaltic intrusions in carboniferous limestone. The basalt has bubbles of gas that have become filled with a light coloured material such as quartz. *Amygdaloidal basalt. Ible *2457*, Peak Forest *1179*, Tideswell Dale *1573*. *rounded aggregates of secondary material. *Figure 12*, Rock Extraction, refers.

Togs: Dialect. The hand grips of a scythe.

Toll: OE: *toln*. Originally the right of an Anglo Saxon lord to take a payment for the sale of cattle and other goods by a free peasant on his estate which became the fee for using a road or path. Lathkill *1966*. 'Turnpikes'.

Ton: OE: *tun/ton* = a fence; later a farmstead. Taddington *1471*. Tunstead *1075*.

Tor: OE *torr* = a high hill especialy a bare rocky one. Bach *1485*, Beeston *1054*, Broadlee Bank *1185*, Chee (limestone) *1273*, Eagle *2362*, Great *2084*, Higger *2582*, Ladybower *2086*, Laughman *1078*, Mam *1283*, Nether *1287*, Roych *0883*, Peak *2565*, Torrs *9974*, Upper *1187*.

Township: OE: *tun + scipe*./CL: *vill* A small town in a large 'parish'. Alstonefield *1355*, Bakewell *2168*, Hope *1783**, Youlgreave *2164*. *became a 'parish' with 20 townships. Pb in Places and Sites indicates a township in a lead mining area. 'Berewick'.

Travertine/calc – sinter: CaCO$_3$. A porous calcium carbonate deposited at the mouth of a hot spring. The name derives from Tivoli nar Rome where there are large deopists. *Uses*: Building. Finding travertine in 'millstone grit' as in the River Kinder valley *0788* is unusual. Elder Bush Cave *0959* with leaf impressions. *Figure 12*, Rock Extraction, refers.

Trip: Dialect. A litter of animals.

Tudors: *Henry VII, Henry VIII, Edward VI, Mary I* and *Elizabeth I*.

Tufa: CaCO$_3$. Italian: *tufa* A calcium carbonate solution subsequently deposited, sometimes enclosing fragments such as algae, moss and other minerals. River Lathkill valley dam *1865*.

Tun: See 'Ton'.

Turbary: ML: *turba = turf*. The medieval right to cut peat turves for fuel .Grindslow Knoll *0186* for Edale *1285*. Aston *1884*, Hucklow *1777*, Thornhill *1983* and Tideswell *1575* did not need a licence.

Turf: OE: *torfa*. The top grass and root layer of a field. *Uses* Fuel, Flagg *1368*

Turnpike: Originally a spiked barrier across a road to prevent attacks by horsemen. From about [1745] it was a road for which users had to pay a toll. Journey times became quicker but costs remained the same as before. Magistrates exempted Methodist preachers at Waterhouses *0850*.

Tut work: Dialect. Piece work. Possibly in mining or farming.

Tympanum: Greek: *tympanon*. The space between a doorway lintel and the space above it. Parwich *1854* Norman features a goose, a lamb holding a cross*, a stag, a pig and a lion. * 'He was led like to lamb to the slaughter'. Isaiah chapter 53 verse 7. *Figure 7,* Church Graphics, refers.

Umber: Latin: *umbra*. Earth made brown by insoluble FE2O2 (ferric oxide). *Uses* Pigment. *1861*

Vavasour: OF. A feudal tenant, a vassal, below the rank of baron and also a surname. Vavasours.

Vein: OF: *veine*. An almost vertical ore deposit Hucklow Edge *1878*, Old Edge *2176*, Hassop area *2275* Brandy Bottle, Cackle Mackle, Harry Bruce, Old Ralph, Strawberry 'Lees'. The highest metal yielding deposits were near the shale cover. 'Pipe', 'Rake' and 'Scrin'.

Verderer: OF: *verdier*. A forest official elected by freeholders, often a 'knight', below chief foresters and wardens, sworn to protect vert and venison. Their chief duty was to attend the forest court every 6 weeks. 'Woodward'.

Village: OF: *ville*. The lowest unit of political life in an area whose boundaries did not always coincide with a 'manor'. Some were independent while others were without freeholders because its inhabitants were obligated to a feudal lord. 'Townships' and villages were not clearly demarcated.

Villein: OF: *vilein* = a serf. A peasant who was personally bound to one or more feudal lords to whom he paid dues and rendered services. Their unpaid services were sometimes commuted to money rents in the Peak and elsewhere. Baslow *2572* manorial court ruled that no villeins should leave without permission [1391]. Villeinage was extinct by [1558]. The Black Death, caused by the *xenopsylla cheopsis* flea, reached the Peak by [June 1349] and reduced the pool of workers. Copyholders', leaseholders and 'tenants at will' replaced villeins. 'Geneat' similar to a villein.

Virgate: See yardland.

Viscount: OF: *visconte*. A deputy or lieutenant of a Norman count ranking between an 'earl' and a 'baron'. *Curzon* (Scarsdale).

Wad/manganite: OE: *wad* = woad. 1. MnO(OH). Water-bearing manganese oxide found with iron, cobalt and copper oxides Bakewell *2168*, Hartington *1380* and Youlgreave *2164*. *Uses*: Heated in a kiln, to make black paint for ships; after [1774] in steel. *Figure 11,* Metal Ore Extraction, refers. 2. Dialect: A sighting stick to facilitate ploughing straight furrows. Elton *2260*.

Wain: OE = a wagon or cart. Wainstones *0277*.

Wall/country rock: OE: *weall*. The rock surrounding an intrusion of igneous rock or ore vein. Corker Walls *2689* and Turner Walls *2489* are near Furnace Hill *2589*.

Walnut: *juglans regia*. OE: *walh-hnutu* Its introduction to the British Isles was either, 1. from the Himalayas, Iran or Lebanon [15th-16th centuries] or 2. By the 'Romans'. *Uses*: Wood: furniture, gun stocks; oil for soap. The age of walnut wood, which superseded oak, began with the Restoration of *Charles II* in [1660]. Stanton *2563*.

Walt: Dialect. To overturn a cart.

Wapentake: SC: *vapnatak*, OE: *waepentaec*. Under the Danes, a combination of villages for the administration of justice mentioned in records [962]. In Derbyshire each wapentake district comprised 12 'carucates' which were also known as 'hundreds'. Bradfield *2692 and* Walderhaigh *2696*, 'bierlows', were in Upper Strafforth, Langsett *2120* in Staincross *3120*. The greater part of the land west of the River Derwent was in Appletree wapentake and owned by *Henry de Ferrars*.

Warren: ME: *wareine*. 1. The right of warren permitted the keeping or hunting of animals and birds. The franchise being in perpetuity meant the holder could sell the land but retain the right. *Hathersage; Griffin*, son of *Wenunwyn* at Ashford *1969* [1251]. 'Cistercian' Abbots of Rufford *6464* enjoyed free warren in Brushfield 'manor' *1672*. 2. A piece of land enclosed for breeding game. Warren Lodge *2574*, Warren 'Carr', Wensley *2661*.

Well dressing: Dialect. Tap dressing. A custom, probably originally Celtic or Roman, said to be revived* in [1349] after being forbidden by the Church as water worship. *The [1758] revival at Tissington *1752* is more reliably attested. Biblical scenes are common.

Wergild: OE: *wer* = man + *geld* = tribute. The sum of money, under Anglo Saxon law, paid to the kin of a slain man. Tariff in ascending order of value, in thrymass: 'Ceorl's' wife 266, 'Thane' 2,000. 'Saxons', priest 2,000, king's high reeve 4,000, 'Hold' 4,000, 'Ealdorman' 8,000, a son of a king 15,000, archbishop 15,000, king 30,000. (1 thrymass = 5p) 'Currency'.

Wheal: Cornish: = a mine. A protective revetement [barrier] made from woven hurdles [to prevent mining waste slipping into Deep Dale]. Over and Nether Wheal *1569*.

Wheel: OE = a [circular] wheel High Wheeldon [wheel shaped hill] *1066*.

Wheelwright: A maker and repairer of wheels.

Whim/wim: A machine, usually for drawing ore, worked by horses. The Whim *1357, 1366*.

Whin: Dialect. Gorse or broom which could be crushed for winter feed. [1400].

Whinstone: Dialect Any dark, fine grained rock eg basalt or 'dolerite'. Whinstone 'Lee' 'Tor' *2087*. *Figure 12*, Rock Extraction, refers.

Whisket: Dialect. A round basket made of oak strips up to 1 metre in diameter.

White Peak: The dales and metal ore mining area comprising mainly pervious limestone bordered by millstone grit. The bare rock, when not covered by vegetation, is off-white.

Wic/wike: OE = a hamlet. A dwelling, hamlet, farm or manufacturig centre. Parwich *1854*, Wike Head *1301*.

Wick: OE: *weoce*. 1. A twisted bundle of fibres in a candle 'Manufacturing'. 2. A dwelling. Hardwick *3364*, Wickinford *9674*.

Wiggy/wiggen/wibben: Dialect Mountain ash *sorbus aucuparia*. Wibben Hill *1852*.

Willow/Withen: OE *welig* A name derived from flexible twigs usually of bolled or pollarded willows. 'Panniers'. In the Peak willow is probably *salix fragilis*. OE: *withthe*. **Uses** 'Medical' - the bark contains the glucoside salicine $C_{13}H_{16}O_7$ (CL: *salix*) which has analgesic properties - and tanning. Wicker – 'Batwell'. Wet Withens *2376*, Withensake *9864*, Withers, Bakewell *2168*, Wythen Lache *0277*.

Windlass: See 'Gin'.

Woodbank: OE: *wudu* + OD: *banke*. A bank of earth erected to delineate external, or internal boundaries, around, or inside, woodland.

Woodward: A forest official responsible for timber, undergrowth and venison.

Workhouse: Initially a house where work was provided for the unemployed, nick-named Bastile. Later it was an institution administered by 'parish' officers called Overseers of the Poor unil [1835]. Alstonefield *1355*, Fawfieldhead *0763*, Tissington [1753] *1752*, Warslow *08581*, Youlgreave *2168* [1746] spinning wheel and yarn bought.

Worth: OLG The suffix meaning either an open space or an enclosure. Chatsworth *2670*, Sugworth *2389*. Wentworth = a winter enclosure.

Wyzel: Dialect. The haulm of a potato plant.

Xanthasiderate: FeO(OH).nH$_2$) Greek: *xantha* = yellow + *sideros* = iron. A former name for yellow 'limonite'. *Figure 11*, Metal Ore Extraction, refers.

Yardland/virgate: = 2 'oxgangs' = 6-12 hectares = 15-30 acres.

Yeoman: An umbrella term. Originally 'freeholders', commoners, who either cultivated their own or leased land, acted as assistants to officials, such as 'sheriffs' or acted as trade middlemen. *Thomas Bateman*. In the [15th century] yeomen sent wool to the West Riding of Yorkshire and one year old cattle to Leicestershire for fattening. *Milnes, Lionel Tynley*, a Presbyterian, of Holmesfield *3277* lead merchant and mine investor. Lowly status *Garlick* 'Brenner', 'Edale chapel'.

Yew: *taxus baccata*. OE: *iw*. **Habitat**: church yards, uplands and low hills. **Properties**: Slow growth contributes to the elasticity and durability of the wood. **Symbolism**: It was planted in churchyards either as a symbol of sadness or eternity. Stanton *2563*. **Uses**: Bows, posts, striker part of a corn threshing flail.

Derwent Hall   Chatsworth House

Derwent Valley Residences

ADDITIONAL INFORMATION

Publications: *Local Titles*

Adams, M Derbyshire in Betjeman, J; 1958 editor Collins Guide to English Parish Churches

Andrews, C B; 1935 The Torrington Diaries -A Tour in the Midlands chapter. (London: Methuen).

Andrews, M; 1948 Long Ago in Peakland. (Nottingham: Milward).

Anonymous; 1879 Notes on the Heraldic Glass at Warkworth Castle, Banbury and now at Hassop Hall. Notes and Queries Series 5, 12; pp303, 333, 517.

Arnold-Bemrose, H H & E; 1910 The County Geograohy of Derbyshire (Cambridge University Press)

Baddeley, M J B; 1908 The Peak District. (Nelson).

Bagshawe, W H G; 1887 A Memoir of William Bagshawe "Apostle of the Peak".

Baker, E A 1903; Moors, Crags and Caves of the High Peak and the Neighbourhood.

Barnatt, J & Smith, K; 1997 Peak District. (English Heritage).

Bateman, Thomas; Vestiges of the Antiquities of Derbyshire.

Beresford, H de la P; 1977 The Book of Beresfords. (Chichester: Phillimore).

Beresford, W; 1981 Beresford of Beresford. (Morten).

Birchenall, J; 2002 Memorials of the late Mr John Lomas of Hollinsclough (Methodist Publishing).

Black's Tourists' Guide to Derbyshire; 1855 edited Jewitt, L F W.

Blundell, N; February 2002 Plague Legacy. Saga Magazine pp 45-47.

Bradbury, E; 1895 Over the Dore and Chinley Railway. (Derby: Richard Keene, All Saints).

Bramwell, D; 1973 Archaeology in the Peak District. (Moorland).

Bray, W; 1783 A Tour of Derbyshire and Yorkshire.

Brentnall, J M; 1970 William Bagshawe: the Apostle of the Peak.

Brighton, T; 1981 Royalists and Roundheads in Derbyshire (Bakewell Historical Society).

Brocklehurst, P L; 1998 Swythamley and Its Neighbourhood. (The Silk Press).

Buckley, D; 1966 Tissington and Its Parish Church.

Burt, R & Others; 1981 The Derbyshire Mineral Statistics. (Exeter University).

Byford, J S; 1981 Moorland Heritage. (Bamford: Byford).

Calladine, A & Fricker, J; East Cheshire Textile Mills.

Cameron, K; 1959 The Place Names of Derbyshire. (Cambridge University Press).

Chalmers, D T; Factors influencing the choice of building stone and masonry techniques in east Cheshire churches.

Chapman, Edwin; Hope Methodist Church 1835-1977.

Cheetham, F H; 1904 Haddon Hall. (London: Sherratt & Hughes).

Christian, Roy; 1975 The Peak District. (British Topographical Series).

Christian, Roy; 1996 Well dressing in Derbyshire. (Derby: Derbyshire Countryside).

Clark, J; 1919-20 Survivals of the Dialect and Customs of the Moorlands. Transactions of the North Staffordshire Field Club.

Clarke, J I & Others; 1957 Edale: A South Pennine Valley. (University of Durham: Geography).

Clifford, J; 1995 Eyam Plague 1665-66.

Cockin, T; 2000 The Staffordshire Encyclopaedia (Stoke on Trent: Malthouse Press).

Collier R & Wilkinson R; 1999 Dark Peak Air Crashes (Barnsley: Pen & Sword).

Cook, Eliza; [1812-89] prolific poetess 1837 Guide and Travelling Companion.

Cooke, G. A; ?1820 Topographical and Statistical Information of the County of Derby. (London: Sherwood, Neely & Jones).

Cope, F W; 1976 Geology Explained in the Peak District. (David & Charles).

Cotton, C; 1671 The Wonders of the Peak

Cox, J Charles; 1874 Notes on the Churches of Derbyshire Vol 2 High Peak and Wirksworth. (London: Bemrose).

Cox, J. Charles; 1907 Memorials of Old Derbyshire. (London: Bemrose).

Crane E & Walker P; August 1999 Early English Beekeeping The Local Historian 20.3 p146.

Cresswell, M; 1993 Walking Peakland Trackways. (Wilmslow: Sigma).

Crichton, P; 1970 Pictorial Derbyshire. (Derbyshire Countryside).

Crossley, D & Kiernan, D; 1992 The Lead Smelting Mills of Derbyshire. (Derbyshire Archaeological Journal 112 p6-47).

Croston, J; 1868 2nd edition On foot through the Peak. (Manchester: Heywood).

Dalton, R; 1998 Farm Sales Advertisements in Derbyshire 1792-1870. The Local Historian 28.1 p36 - 49.

Daniel, C; undated A Peakland Portfolio.

Daniel, C; undated Pinnacles of Peak History.

Davies, D P; 1811 View of Derbyshire. (Belper: Mason).

Derbyshire Guide to the Record Office 1994 (Derbyshire County Council).

Derbyshire Villages 1991 (Derbyshire Federation of Women's Institutes and Countryside).

Derbyshire Within Living Memory. 1996 Derbyshire Federation of Women's Institutes (Countryside).

Devonshire, Duchess of. 1990 The Chatsworth Estate. (Macmillan).

Dilworth-Harrison, T; 1952 Our Glorious Derbyshire Churches.

Dodd, A E & E M; 1980 Peakland Roads and Trackways. (Moorland Publishing).

Dodgson, J M; 1970 The Place Names of Cheshire. (Cambridge University Press).

Doe, V S; 1978 The Diary of James Clegg. (Derbyshire Record Society).

Earwaker, John Parsons; 1877 East Cheshire Past and Present: The Hundred of Macclesfield.

Erdeswick, Sampson; 1798 History of Staffordshire.

Evans, Seth; Methodism in Bradwell.

Evans, Seth; April 1902 A Pilgrimage in Peakland. The Methodist Recorder.

Farey, John. 1817 A View of the Agriculture and Minerals of Derbyshire, Volumes I and II.

Farley, J; 1989 Hathersage Methodist Church.

Fawcett, C B; 1917 Edale: A Study of a Pennine Dale. (Scottish Geographical Magazine).

Field, H E; The Monumental Brasses of Derbyshire, Volumes III and V Transactions of the Monumental Brass Society.

Firth, J B; 1920 Highways and Byways in Derbyshire.

Fitton, R S; 1989, The Arkwrights (Manchester: University Press).

Fletcher, J M J; 1915 Tideswell and Its Church. (Chapman).

Fletcher, J M J; 1927 Tideswell in the Days of Parson Brown. (Tideswell Women's Institute).

Ford, T D; October 1964 The Black Marble Mines of Ashford in the Water.

Ford, T D; 1977 editor Limestone and Caves of the Peak District. (Geological Abstracts).

Ford, T D & Rieuwerts, J H; 2000 Lead Mining in the Peak District. (Landmark).

Geological Surveys: Castleton Area 1971. HMSO

Gill, H; 1970 The Lost Villages of Derwent and Ashopton.

Glover, Stephen; 1829 editor Noble, T A History and Gazetteer of the County of Derby.

Glover, Stephen; 1839 editor Noble, T The Peak Guide.

Gomme, G L; 1899 Topographical History of Staffordshire and Suffolk. (London: Elliott Stock).

Grayson, P J; 1969 Derbyshire Minerals and Rocks.

Grayson, P & M; 1966 A Short History of Edensor.

Hackney, G; 1994 Pott Shrigley Cricket Club 75th Anniversary.

Hadfield, P; undated Youlgreave Parish Church and Records.

Hall C E; 1896 Hathersage: A Tale of North Derbyshire.

Hall, S C & Jewitt L; 1871 Haddon Hall. (Buxton: J C Bates)

Hall, T W; 1946 A Descriptive Catalogue of Early Land Charts in the County of Derby. (Sheffield: Northend).

Hallam, T & Skeat W W; 1894 editors, Pegee's Derbicisms. (English Dialect Society)

Hallam, V J; 1983 Silent Valleys. [Ashopton & Derwent].

Hammond J L & B; 1937 5th edition, The Rise of Modern Industry. (London: Methuen).

Hanks, P & Hodges, F; 1988 A Dictionary of Surnames. (Oxford University Press).

Harris, H; 1971 The Industrial Archaeology of the Peak District. (Newton Abbot: David & Charles).

Hayward, F M; 1905 Padley Chapel and Padley Martyrs. (London: Bemrose).

Heath, John; Illustrated History of Derbyshire. (Derby: Breedon).

Heathcoat, J P; 1926 Birchover: Its Pre-historic and Druidical Remains. (Winster: Marshall).

Heathcote, J P; 1950 Birchover Church.

Hey, D; 1980 Packmen, Carriers and Packhorse Roads, Trade and Communication, North Derbyshire and South Yorkshire. (Leicester University Press).

Hibbert, F A; 1908 Monasticism in Staffordshire. (Stafford: Mort).
Himsworth J B; 1929-30 Some Fragments of Stained Glass in South Yorkshire and Derbyshire – Bradfield. Journal of British Society of Glass Painters 3 pp66-73
Hine, Sheila; 2007 Around Longnor. (Leek: Churnet).
History and Topography of Derbyshire. [Author unknown] 1822 (Pinnock & Maunder).
Hobbes, Thomas; 1588-1679 & 'Cotton, Charles'; 1678 Wonders of the Peak.
Holland, R; 1884-86 Glossary of Words Used in Cheshire. (English Dialect Society).
Holland, W R; ? 1886 Alsop and Other Charters. (London: Bemrose).
Hooson, W; 1747 The Miners Dictionary. (Hooson & Payne) 1979 reprint for The Institution of Mining and Metallurgy London.
Hope, W H S; 1885 Royal Archaeological Institute of Great Britan and Ireland Notes for the Annual Meeting at Derby 1885. (London: Bemrose).
Hunter, A L; 1974 Wormhill Wakes.
Hunter, J; 1821 Hallamshire Glossary
Ingram, J H; 1948 2nd edition Companion into Cheshire. (London:Methuen).
Innes-Smith, R; 1982 editor The Derbyshire Guide. (Derbyshire Countryside).
James, N & Bristow, A; 1997 The Peak District. (Wilmslow: Sigma).
Jeayes, I H; 1906 Derbyshire Charters. (London: Bemrose).
Jewitt, Ll; 1828 editor Blacks Tourists' and Visitors' Guide to the Beauties of the Peak. (London: Gray).
Jewitt Ll; 1867 The Ballads and Songs of Derbyshire. (London: Bemrose & Lothian).
Kemsley, R M; 2000 Landowners and Communities in East Cheshire. PhD Thesis.
Kerr, C; 1900 The Painted Windows in the Chapel of St Nicholas, Haddon Hall. Derbyshire Archaeological Natural History Society 22 pp30-39.
Kerry, C & Calverley, C S; editors Undated Topography: Derbyshire and Cumberland.
Kiernan, ?; 1989 The Derbyshire Lead Industry in the sixteenth century. (Derbyshire Record Society).
Kirkham, N; 1949 Ecton Mines. (Dalesman).
Large, J; 2000 Stories of the Derbyshire Dales.
Leach, John; 1993 2nd edition, Methodism in the Moorlands. (Leek: Churnet Valley).
Leigh, E; 1877 A Glossary of Country Words Used in the Dialect of Cheshire.
Lemire B; 1991 Fashion's Favourite: The Cotton Trade and the Consumer in Britian 1660-1800, (Pasold. OUP)
Lewis, C & Kemsley, R M; Undated. Shrigley Hall and Its Owners.
Lowther, L C, 1950 The Parish Church of St John the Baptist, Tideswell 1350-1950. (Gloucester: British Publishing).
Lysons, Daniel and Samuel; 1806-22 Magna Britannia: A precise topographical account of several counties of Great Britain. Vol 2 Cheshire; Vol 5 Derbyshire. (London: Cadell & Davis).
Mander, J; 1824 The Derbyshire Miners' Glossary.
Manifold; 1952 The North Staffordshire Railway. (Ashbourne: Henstock).
Matthews, A G; 1924 The Congregational Churches of Staffordshire. (Congregational Union).
Mawe, John; 1802 The Mineralogy of Derbyshire.
Mehew, S; Packhorse Bridges in Derbyshire. (Derbyshire Miscellany.Local History Section of the Derbyshire Archaeological Society).
Middleton, T; 1933 Tideswell Grammar School.
Miller, Celia; 1980 Baslow Wesleyan Methodist Chapel.
Miller, Y R; 1995 The Old Chapel Great Hucklow 1696-1996.
Milward R; 1986 3rd edition A Glossary of Household, Farming and Trade Terms from Probate Inventories. (Derbyshire Record Society).
Mitchell, H M; 1930 The Woodlands Love Feast. [Alport Castles Farm *1391*]. (New Mills: Kinder).
Morrill, J S; 1974 Cheshire 1630-60. (Oxford University Press).
Morris, J; 1978 general editor Domesday Books: Cheshire, Derbyshire, Staffordshire, Yorkshire. (Chichester: Phillimore).
Murray's Hand-book: Derby, Notts, Leicester, Stafford 1874 2nd edition. (London: John Murray).
Naylor, P J; 1983 Ancient Wells and Springs of Derbyshire. (Cromford: Scarthin).
Naylor, P J; 1983 Celtic Derbyshire. (Derbyshire Heritage Series).
Nithsdale, W H; 1906 In the Highlands of Staffordshire. (Leek: Eaton).
Nixon, F; 1969 The Industrial Archaeology of Derbyshire. (David & Charles).

Nonconformist Chapels and Meeting Houses in Derbyshire. 1986. (HMSO).
Norman, J; 1968 Ashford in the Water and Its Church.
Oakden J P; 1984 The Place Names of Staffordshire. (English Place Names Society).
Ollershaw and Harrison; The History of Blue John.
Over Haddon and Lathkill Dale. Undated. (Over Haddon Women's Institute).
Palliser, D M; 1976 The Staffordshire Landscape. (Hodder & Stoughton).
Peace, D B; Staffordshire in Betjeman, J; 1958 Collins Guide to English Parish Churches.
Peak District National Park. 1960. HMSO.
Pendleton, J; 1886 A History Of Derbyshire. (London: Elliott Stock).
Pennington, Rooke; Notes on the Barrows and Bone Caves of Derbyshire.
Peters, R; 1991 Ancient Life and Place Names in Nottinghamshire, Derbyshire, Yorkshire, Lincolnshire, Staffordshire. (Sutton in Ashfield: North Trent).
Pilkington, James; 1789 State of Derbyshire. (Derby: Drewry).
Plot, R; 1686 Natural History of Staffordshire. (Oxford).
Poole, C H; 1880 An attempt towards a Glossary of Archaic and Provincial Words of Staffordshire.
Porter, L; 1984 The Peak District: Pictures from the Past. (Moorland).
Porter, L; 1994 4th edition, Visitors' Guide to the Peak District. (Wilmslow: MPC).
Porter, L & Robey, J; 2000 The Copper and Lead Mines Around the Manifold Valley and North Staffordshire. (Ashbourne: Landmark).
Pott Shrigley Township Pack 31 1992. (Cheshire Libraries, Arts & Archives).
Powicke, F J; 1907 A History of the Cheshire County Union of Congregational Churches. (Manchester: Griffiths).
Price, C; 1994 Mostly Downhill in the Peak District: White Peak. (Wilmslow: Sigma).
Price, C; 1994 Mostly Downhill in the Peak District: Dark Peak. (Wilmslow: Sigma).
Radcliffe, N; 1949 Cheshire's Only Coal Mine. (Cheshire Life 15.11).
Raistrick, A. & Jennings, B; 1968 A History of Lead Mining in the Pennines. (Longmans).
Rhodes, Ebenezer; 1818-23 Peak Scenery.
Rhodes, Ebenezer; 1837 The Derbyshire Tourists' Guide and Travelling Companion with an Excursion from Dove Dale to Ilam.
Rhodes, Ebenezer; 1837 Modern Chatsworth.
Rieuwerts, J H; 1980 The Earliest Lead Mine Soughs in Derbyshire. (Bulletin: Peak District Mines Historical Society 7 pp 241-314).
Rieuwerts, J H; 1998 Glossary of Derbyshire Lead Mining Terms. (Peak District Mines Historical Society).
Rieuwerts, J H; 1987 History and Gazetteer of the Lead Mine Soughs of Derbyshire.
Rieuwerts, J H; 2008 Lead Mining in Derbyshire (Landmark)
Riley, R B; 1994 Alcock's Lamp: A Historical Tour of Hartington.
Rintoul, M C; 1993 Dictionary of People and Places in Fiction. (Routledge).
Roberts, J; 1900 History of Wetton, Thor's Cave and Ecton Mines. (Ashbourne: Osborne).
Robinson, B; undated Memoirs of Tin Town: The Navvy Village of Birchinlee. (Sheffield: Northend).
Robinson, B; 1983 Birchinlee.
Robinson, B; 1994 The Seven Blunders of the Peak. (Cromford: Scarthin).
Rolfe, D; 1986 The Derbyshire Domesday. (Derbyshire Museum Service).
Sharpe, N T 1999 Peakland Pickings. (Leek: Churnet).
Shaw, Don; 2004 The Hike. [Derbyshire Peak].
Sheen; St Luke's Church.
Simpson, I M; 1982 The Peak District. (Unwin).
Skeat W W; 1874 Derbyshire Lead Mining Terms.
Slack, R; 2000 Lead Miner's Heyday.
Sleigh, J; 1865 An attempt at a Derbyshire Glossary.
Smith, A H; 1961 The Place Names of the West Riding of Yorkshire (Cambridge University Press)
Smith, B; undated Padley Manor House and Its Place in History. (Blackfriars).
Smith, Barbara M; 1990 Padley Chapel.
Smith, Barbara M; 1997 Two Recusant Families of South Yorkshire and North Derbyshire. (Blackfriars).
Smith, Barbara M; 2001 The Eyres of Hassop 1470-1640.
Smith, Barbara M; 2001 A History of the Catholic Chapel at Hathersage.

Smith, G L B; 1906 Haddon. (London: Paternoster).
Smith, R; 1987 The Peak National Park. (Webb & Bower).
Smith, R; 1988 Bog trotting and other delights in Hillaby, J. editor Walking in Britain. (Collins).
Smith, R; 1999 Towns and Villages of Derbyshire. (Sigma Leisure).
Staffordshire Historical Collections. Staffordshire Record Society.
Staffordshire Within Living Memory 1992. Staffordshire Federation of Women's Institutes. (Countryside).
Stamper, W P; 1902 Youlgreave. (Bakewell: Gratton).
Shaw, Stebbing; 1798-1801 The History and Antiquities of Staffordshire. (J Robson)
Steer, G; 1734 Compleat Mineral Laws of Derbyshire.
Sterndale, M 1824 Vignettes of Derbyshire. (London: Whittaker).
Stevenson, I P & Gaunt, G D; 1971 Geology of the Country around Chapel en le Frith. HMSO.
Stokes, A H; 1964 Lead and Lead Mining in Derbyshire. (Peak District Mines Society).
Stone, B; 1992 Derbyshire in the Civil War. (Cromford: Scarthin).
Stoney Middleton: A Working Village.
Stuckey, L C; 1917 Lead Mining in Derbyshire. Mining Magazine Volume XVI Number 1.
Sweeney, G; 1978 A Pilgrim's Guide to Padley.
Swinscoe, D & M; 1998 Swinscoe, Blore and the Bassets. (Leek: Churnet).
Sylvester, D; 1971 A History of Cheshire. (Henley on Thames: Darwen Finlayson).
Taylor, E K; Forgotten Shrines of the Peak.
Tebbutt M; December 2006 Manly Identity in Derbyshire's Dark Peak 1880s-1920s. The Historical Journal 49.4
Thirsk J; 1967 Agrarian History of England. (Cambridge University Press).
Thomas H M; 1993 Vassals, Heiresses, Crusaders and Thugs. (University of Pennsylvania).
Thornhill, R; 1958 About a Derbyshire Village. (Longstone Local History Group).
Thorold, H; 1972 Derbyshire. (Faber & Faber).
Thorold, H; 1978 Staffordshire. (Faber & Faber).
Tilley, Joseph. (J T); 1892 The Old Halls, Manors and Families of Derbyshire: High Peak Hundred. (London: Simpkin, Marshall, Hamilton, Kent).
Truelove, W; editor, No Flowers for Elizabeth: Reflections from Castleton, Edale and Hope. (Yorkshire Art Circus).
Turbutt, G; 1999 A History of Derbyshire. (Cardiff: Merton Priory).
Turner, Keith; 1980 The Leek and Manifold Light Railway.
Verney Lady F P; 1868 Stone Edge.
Victoria County History series; Cheshire, Derbyshire, Staffordshire, Yorkshire.
Wainwright, A; Green Close Methodist Church, Pott Shrigley 1861-1961.
Wakeford, R; Cheshire in Betjeman, J 1958. Collins Guide to English Parish Churches.
Walker, W; 1944 A History of Tideswell Congregational Church. (Tideswell: Warrington).
Walker, W; ?1951 A History of Tideswell.
Weston, R; 2000 Hartington: A Landscape History. (Derbyshire CC Libraries & Heritage).
Wilbraham, R; 1826 An Attempt at a Glossary of Some Words Used in Cheshire.
Williams A et al; 1991 Dark Age Britain. (London: Seaby).
Williams, T; undated Points of Interest in Tissington and the Church.
Willies, L; 1971 The Introduction of the Cupola for Smelting Down Lead. (Bulletin Peak District Mines Historical Society 4,5 pp384 - 394).
Willies, L; Technical Development in Derbyshire Lead Mining 1700-1880. (Bulletin Peak District Mines Historical Society).
Willies, L; 1990 Derbyshire Lead Smelting in the eighteenth and nineteenth centuries. (Bulletin Peak District Mines Historical Society).
Willies, L & Parker, H; 1999 Peak District Mining and Quarrying. (Tempus).
Wilson, D; 1974 Staffordshire Dialect Words. (Moorlands).
Wilson, N; 2000 The Tap Dressers [Youlgreave]. (County Books).
Winfield, J; Gunpowder Mills of Fernilee 1909-1920.
Wood, A; 1999 The Politics of Social Conflict: The Peak County 1520-1770. (Cambridge University Press).
Wood, W; 1862 Tales and Traditions of the High Peak. (London: Bell & Daldy).
Wood, W; 1865 The History of Antiquities of Eyam. (London: Bell & Daldy).
Wright, S M; 1983 The Derbyshire Gentry in the fifteenth century Vol 3. (Derbyshire Record Society).

Yeatman, J P and others; 1886 The Feudal History of the County of Derby. (London: Bemrose).
Youlgrave Women's Institute; 1931 Some Account of Youlgrave, Middleton and Alport.

Publications: *General Title excluding standard textbooks*
Adrosko, R J; 1971 Natural Dyes and Home Dyeing. (New York: Dover).
Albert, W; 1972 The Turnpike Road System 1663-1840. (Cambridge University Press).
Ames, H G; 1998 Country Words. (London: Christchurch Publishers).
Astill, G. & Grant, A; 1988 The Countryside of Medieval England. (Basil Blackwell).
Bailey, B; 1987 Churchyards of England and Wales. (London: Hale).
Barley, M W; 1961 The English Farmhouse. (London: Routledge & Kegan Paul).
Barnhart, C L; 1954 editor, The New Century Cyclopedia of Names. (New York: Appleton-Century-Crofts).
Batsford, H & Fry, C; 1938 The English Cottage. (Batsford).
Betjeman, J; 1958 editor, Collins Guide to English Parish Churches. (London: Collins).
Birrell, A; 1910 A Quaker Post Bag 1693-1742. (London: Longmans Green).
Blake, N; 1992 editor, The Cambridge History of the English Language Volume II. (Cambridge University Press).
Bolton, J L; The English Medieval Economy 1150-1500. (London: Dent).
Bozorgnia, S M H; 1998 The Role of Precious Metal in European Economic Development. (Greenwood Press).
Broughton, B B; 1986 Dictionary of Medieval Knighthood and Chivalry. (Greenwood).
Burgess, F; 1979 English Churchyard Memorials. (London:SPCK).
Burkes Peerage & Baronetage 1921. (Burke).
Calamy, Edmund; 1723 Presbyterian Preachers.
Cannon, J; 1997 editor Oxford Companion to British History. (Oxford University Press).
Chesterman, C W; 1995 Rocks and Minerals. (New York: Knopf).
Chown, J F; 1994 A History of Money. (Routledge).
Clemoes, P & Hughes, K; 1971 England Before the Norman Conquest. (Cambridge University Press).
Clifton-Taylor, A; 1965 The Pattern of English Building. (London: Batsford).
Clifton-Taylor A & Ireson A S; 1983 English Stone Building. (Victor Gollancz).
Collins English Dictionary 2000 5th edition. (HarperCollins).
Cottle, B; 1978 2nd edition Dictionary of Surnames. (Penguin).
Cowen, P; 1985 A Guide to Stained Glass in Britain. (Michael Joseph).
Cox, J C; 1905 Royal Forests of England. (Methuen).
Cox, J C & Harvey, M; 1908 2nd edition, English Church Furniture. (London: Methuen).
Craddock, P T; 1995 Early Metal Mining and production. (Edinburgh University Press).
Crossley, F H; 1921 English Church Monuments. (London: Batsford).
Crowley J E; 2001 The Invention of Comfort. (John Hopkins).
Culpeper, Nicholas; 1953 New Edition, The Complete Herbal. (Birmingham: Kynoch).
Curtler, W H R; 1920 The Enclosure and Redistribution of our Land. (Oxford: Clarendon Press).
Cutts, E L; 1849 Sepulchral Slabs and Crosses. (Oxford: John Henry Parker).
Davies, G; 1996 A History of Money. (Cardiff: University of Wales).
Debretts Landed Gentry.
Dictionary of National Biography 2004.
Drayton, Michael; 1613 Poly Olbion: A Chorographical Description of all the Tracts, Rivers, Mountains, Forests and Other parts of Great Britain.
Dugdale W; 1830 Monasticon Anglicanum. (Jospeg Harding; Harding & Lepard).
Duignan W H; 1902 Notes on Staffordshire Place Names.
Eagle D & Carnell H; 1977 editors, The Oxford Literary Guide to the British Isles. (Clarendon).
Ekwall, E; 1928 English River Names. (Oxford: Clarendon Press).
Ekwall, E; 1960 English Place Names. (Oxford: Clarendon Press).
Ewen, C L; 1968 A History of Surnames of the British Isles. (Baltimore: Genealogical Publishing).
Felkin's History of Machine Wrought Hosiery and Lace Manufacturers 1967. (David & Charles).
Field Archaeology 1963 4th edition OS Professional Papers No 13. HMSO.
Field. J; 1972 English Field Names. (Newton Abbot: David & Charles).
Finberg. H P R; 1972 Anglo Saxon England to 1042 in the Agrarian History of England and Wales. (Cambridge University Press).

Fontaine, L; 1996 History of Pedlars in Europe. (Cambridge: Polity).
Fryer. C F; 1925 Wooden Monumental Effigies of England and Wales. (London: Elliott Stock).
Gardner, A; 1940 Alabaster Tombs of the Pre-Reformation Period in England. (Cambridge University Press).
Garnier, R M; 1908 The History of the Land Interest. (Swan Sonnenschein).
Gelling, M; 1984 Place Names in the Landscape. (Dent).
Gibbs, V; editor, The Complete Peerage. (London St Catherine's Press).
Gilmour, J & Walters, M; 1969 4th edition, Wild Flowers. (Collins).
Gotch, J A; 1928 2nd edition, The Growth of the English Country House. (Batsford).
Grayson, A; Rock Solid. (Natural History Museum).
Gullick, T J & Timbs, J; 1876 Painting Popularly Explained. (London: Crosby Lockwood).
Hanks, P & Hodges, F; 1988 A Dictionary of English Surnames. (Oxford University Press).
Harris, J R; 1964 The Copper King. (Liverpool: University Press).
Hassall, W O; 1967 History through Surnames. (Pergamon).
Hatcher, J; 1993 The History of the British Coal Industry. (Oxford: Clarendon Press).
Hayes, P & Hodges, F; 1988 A Dictionary of English Surnames. (Oxford University Press).
Hey, D; 2001 Packmen, Carriers and Packhorse Roads. (Ashbourne: Landmark).
Higgs, J; 1964 The Land. (London: Studio Vista).
Houghton, Thomas; 1668 The Compleat Miner.
Howe, J A; 1910 The Geology of Building Stones. (Edward Arnold).
Hunter D; 1947 Papermaking. (London: Pleiades).
Hywel-Davies, J & Thom, V; 1986 Guide to Britain's Nature Reserves. (Macmillan).
Jones, A; 2000 A Thousand Years of the English Parish. (Gloucestershire: Windrush).
Jones, D K C; 1985 in Woodall, S R J editor The English Countryside. (Oxford University Press).
Jones, S R; 1936 English Village Houses. (London: Batsford).
Kain R J P; 1986 An Atlas and Index of Tithe Files in mid-nineteenth century England and Wales. (CUP).
Knowles, D; 1966 The Monastic Orders in England. (Cambridge University Press).
Knowles, D & Haddock, R; 1953 Medieval Religious Houses in England and Wales. (Longmans).
Lawrence, C H; 1989 Medieval Monasticism. (Longman).
Mander J; 1824 The Miners' Glossary.
Margary, I; 1973 Roman Roads in Britain. (London:John Bates).
Marsden, B M; 1999 The Early Barrow Diggers. (Tempus).
Matthew, H C G & Harrison, B; 2004 Oxford Dictionary of National Biography. (Oxford University Press).
McArthur, T; 1992 editor The Oxford Companion to the English Language. (Oxford University Press).
McKisack, M; 1959 The Fourteenth Century. (Oxford University Press).
Mehag A A; 2003 Science in Culture: The Arsenic Green. Nature 423, 688.
Middle English Dictionary 1980. (Ann Arbor: University of Michigan).
Miller, E & Hatcher, J; 1978 Medieval England. (Longman).
Mui, Hoh- Vheung; 1916 Shops and Shopkeeeping in 18th century England. (London: Routledge).
Muir, R; 1986 The Stones of Britain. (London: Michael Joseph).
Nef, J. U; 1960 The Rise of the British Coal Industry. (Cass).
Orton, H; 1978 Linguistic Atlas of England.
Pickford, D; 1993 Magic, Myth and Memories. (Sigma).
Postan, M M; 1972 The Medieval Economy and Society. (London: Weidenfeld & Nicholson).
Power, E; 1941 The Wool Trade. (Oxford University Press).
Rackham, Oliver ;1986 The History of the Countryside. (London, Dent).
Reaney, P H & Wilson, R M; 1976 A Dictionary of British Surnames. (London: Routledge & Kegan Paul).
Sanderson, S & Widdowson, J; undated Word Maps – A Dialect Atlas of England.
Searle, W G; 1899 Anglo Saxon Bishops, Kings and Nobles. (Cambridge University Press).
Sinkankas, J & Boegel, H; 1968 Minerals and Gemstones. (Thames & Hudson).
Skipp, V; 1967 Out of the Ancient World. (Penguin).
Sleigh J; 1856-6 An Attempt at a Derbyshire Glossary
Smith, A H; 1961 The Place Names of the West Riding of Yorkshire. (Cambridge University Press).
Strange, Richard le; 1972 British Monumental Brasses. (London: Thames and Hudson).

Tate W E; 1967 The English Village Community and Enclosure Movements. (London:Victor Gollancz).
Thirsk, J & Cooper, J P; 1972 editors Seventeenth Century Economic Documents. (Oxford: Clarendon Press).
Thompson, M W; 1995 The Medieval Hall. (Aldershot: Scolar Press).
Trapp J B; 1973 Medieval English Literature. (Oxford University Press).
Tymms, S; 1835 The Family Topographer. (London: Nichols).
Watson, J; 1911 British and Foreign Building Stones. (Cambridge University Press).
Watson, J; 1916 British and Foreign Marbles. (Cambridge University Press).
Watts, M R; 1978 The Dissenters. (Oxford: Clarendon Press).
Webster's Dictionary of the English Language 1977 (J G Ferguson Publishing Company)
White, G H & Lea, R S; 1959 The Complete Peerage. (London: St Catherines Press).
Whitten D G A & Brooks J R V; 1972 Dictionary of Geology. (Penguin).
Wilson, R; 1979 The Hedgerow Book. (R Wilson).
Wilson, W A; 1994 Word Origins in Science and Technology. (Lexitheque Sudsexe).
Worley, N & Ford, T D; Minerals and Mines.
Wright, E M; 1913 Rustic Speech and Folk-lore. (Humphrey Milford: Oxford University Press).
Wright, J; 1898 & 1970 editor, English Dialect Dictionary. (Oxford University Press).
Wyk, B-E van & Wink, M; 2004 Medicinal Plants of the World. (Briza).
Wyld H C; 1932 editor, The Universal Dictionary of the English Language. (Routledge).
Yeatman, J P 1887 The Red Book of the Exchequer. (London: Bemrose).

Associations, Institutions and Societies
Bakewell Historical Society.
Cheshire Record Offfice.
Derbyshire Archaeological Society.
Publications: Derbyshire Archaeological Journal Derbyshire Miscellany.
Derbyshire Federation of Women's Institutes.
Derbyshire Record Office.
Derbyshire Record Society.
English Place Names Society.
Longstone History Group.
National Archives formerly Public Records Office.
Over Haddon Women's Institute.
Peak District Mines Historical Society. Publication: Bulletin.
Sheffield Archives.
Staffordshire Federation of Women's Institutes.
Staffordshire Record Office.
Yorkshire Art Circus.
Youlgrave Women's Institute.

Museums in the Peak National Park
Bakewell, Birchover, Castleton, Eyam.

Maps
Ordnance Survey 1inch = 1 mile; 1:25,000; 1: 50,000
Saxton [1557], Speede [1610], Marden [1710], Bowen [1750], Ellis [1777].

Worldwide Web
Places in the Peak Park
Surnames Database